T0233979

Communications in Computer and Information Science   557

Commenced Publication in 2007
Founding and Former Series Editors:
Alfredo Cuzzocrea, Dominik Ślęzak, and Xiaokang Yang

More information about this series at http://www.springer.com/series/7899

Wenjia Niu · Gang Li
Jiqiang Liu · Jianlong Tan
Li Guo · Zhen Han
Lynn Batten (Eds.)

Applications and Techniques in Information Security

6th International Conference, ATIS 2015
Beijing, China, November 4–6, 2015
Proceedings

 Springer

Editors
Wenjia Niu
Chinese Academy of Sciences
Beijing
China

Gang Li
Deakin University
Burwood, VIC
Australia

Jiqiang Liu
Beijing Jiaotong University
Beijing
China

Jianlong Tan
Chinese Academy of Sciences
Beijing
China

Li Guo
Chinese Academy of Sciences
Beijing
China

Zhen Han
Beijing Jiaotong University
Beijing
China

Lynn Batten
Faculty of Science and Technology
Deakin University
Burwood, VIC
Australia

ISSN 1865-0929   ISSN 1865-0937 (electronic)
Communications in Computer and Information Science
ISBN 978-3-662-48682-5   ISBN 978-3-662-48683-2 (eBook)
DOI 10.1007/978-3-662-48683-2

Library of Congress Control Number: 2015952039

Springer Heidelberg New York Dordrecht London

Printed on acid-free paper

Springer-Verlag GmbH Berlin Heidelberg is part of Springer Science+Business Media
(www.springer.com)

Preface

The International Conference on Applications and Techniques in Information Security (ATIS) has been held every year since 2010. This year, the sixth in the series was held at Beijing Jiaotong University, Beijing, China, during November 4–6, 2015. ATIS 2015 focused on all aspects of techniques and applications in information security research, and provided a valuable connection between the theoretical and the implementation communities, attracting participants from industry, academia, and government organizations.

The selection process this year was competitive. We received 103 submissions, which reflects the recognition of and interest in this conference. Each submission was reviewed by three members of the Program Committee. Following this independent review, there were discussions among reviewers and chairs. A total of 25 papers were selected as full papers, and another ten papers were selected as short papers, yielding a combined acceptance rate of 34 %.

We would like to thank everyone who participated in the development of the ATIS 2015 program. In particular, we would like to give special thanks to the Program Committee, for their diligence and their concern for the quality of the program, and also for their detailed feedback to the authors. The general organization of the conference relied on the efforts of the ATIS 2015 Organizing Committee. We especially thank Wenjia Niu for the registration process and general administrative issues, and Shaowu Liu, who put a great deal of effort into the conference website.

Finally, but most importantly, we thank all the authors, who are the primary reason why ATIS 2015 was so exciting; they ensured it was a premier forum for presentation and discussion of innovative ideas, research results, applications, and experience from around the world, highlighting activities in the related areas. Because of your great work, ATIS 2015 was a great success.

November 2015

Lynn Batten
Wenjia Niu
Gang Li
Jiqiang Liu
Jianlong Tan
Li Guo
Zhen Han

Organization

ATIS 2015 was organized by the School of Computer and Information Technology, Beijing Jiaotong University, China

ATIS 2015 Organizing Committee

Steering Chair

Lynn Batten — Deakin University, Australia

Honorary Chairs

Li Guo — Institute of Information Engineering, Chinese Academy of Sciences, China

Zhen Han — Beijing Jiaotong University, China

Conference Co-chairs

Jiqiang Liu — Beijing Jiaotong University, China

Jianlong Tan — Institute of Information Engineering, Chinese Academy of Sciences, China

PC Co-chairs

Wenjia Niu — Institute of Information Engineering, Chinese Academy of Sciences, China

Gang Li — Deakin University, Australia

Local Chairs

Yongzhong He — Beijing Jiaotong University, China

Wei Wang — Beijing Jiaotong University, China

Publicity Co-chairs

Ping Xiong — Zhongnan University of Economics and Law, China

Tianqing Zhu — Deakin University, Australia

Secretary

Ziqi Yan — Beijing Jiaotong University, China

Web Master

Shaowu Liu — TULIP Lab, Australia

ATIS 2015 Program Committee

Lejla Batina	Radboud University, The Netherlands
Maumita Bhattacharya	Charles Sturt University, Australia
Guoyong Cai	Guilin University of Electronic Technology, China
Yanan Cao	Institute of Information Engineering, Chinese Academy of Science, China
Liang Chang	University of Manchester, UK
Morshed Chowdhury	Deakin University, Australia
Bernard Colbert	Deakin University, Australia
Jiaxin Han	Xi'An Shiyou University, China
Zahid Islam	Charles Sturt University, Australia
Rafiqul Islam	Charles Sturt University, Australia
Dawei Jin	Zhongnan University of Economics and Law, China
Syed Samsul Islam	University of Western Australia, Australia
Mohammad Kaosar	Charles Sturt University, Australia
Kwangjo Kim	KAIST, Korea
Jie Kong	Xi'An Shiyou University, China
Heejo Lee	CCS Lab, Korea University, Korea
Elisabeth de Leeuw	IdTopIQ, The Netherlands
Qingyun Liu	Institute of Information Engineering, Chinese Academy of Sciences, China
Quazi Mamun	Charles Sturt University, Australia
Vicky Mak	Deakin University, Australia
Md Anwar H. Masud	Charles Sturt University, Australia
Lei Pan	Deakin University, Australia
Udaya Parampalli	Melbourne University, Australia
Kui Ren	University at Buffalo, USA
Wei Ren	China University of Geosciences (Wuhan), China
Sumon Sahriar	Intelligent Sensing and Systems Laboratory, CSIRO ICT Centre, Australia
Jinqiao Shi	Institute of Information Engineering, Chinese Academy of Sciences, China
Zhongzhi Shi	Institute of Computing Technology, Chinese Academy of Sciences, China
Jianlong Tan	Institute of Information Engineering, Chinese Academy of Sciences, China
Steve Versteeg	CA Labs, Australia
Paul A. Watters	Massey University, New Zealand
Gang Xiong	Institute of Information Engineering, Chinese Academy of Sciences, China
Ping Xiong	Zhongnan University of Economics and Law, China
Rui Xue	Institute of Information Engineering, Chinese Academy of Sciences, China
John Yearwood	Deakin University, Australia

Fei Yan	Wuhan University, China
Xun Yi	RMIT University, Australia
Chengde Zhang	Southwest Jiaotong University, China
Yuan Zhang	Nanjing University, China
Sheng Zhong	Nanjing University, China
Yongbin Zhou	Institute of Information Engineering, Chinese Academy of Sciences, China
Liehuang Zhu	Beijing Institute of Technology, China
Tianqing Zhu	Deakin University, Australia
Tingshao Zhu	Institute of Psychology, Chinese Academy of Sciences, China

Sponsoring Institutions

Beijing Jiaotong University
Institute of Information Engineering, Chinese Academy of Sciences, China
Deakin University, Australia

Invited Speeches

Memory Scrapper Attacks - Threats and Mitigations

C. Pandu Rangan

Indian Institute of Technology Madras, Chennai, India
prangan55@gmail.com

Abstract. Memory scrappers are among the new but deadliest of all threats that may be posed by an attacker. VISA has categorised this as a threat that is causing most damage but much less studied. We begin our discussions with an in depth study of the threat posed by this kind of attack. We describe the real world scenario where this type of attacks are made by hackers. We show its power by showing attacks on existing secure schemes. Specifically, we show how even a CCA2 secure encryption scheme is easily cracked by this kind of attacks. We will discuss novel solutions that withstand this kind of attacks and suggest ways to counter these attacks in an hybrid environment.

Keywords: Memory Scrappers · Attack Threats · Mitigations · Hybrid Environment · Security

A Simple and Provable Secure (Authenticated) Key Exchange Based on LWE

Jintai Ding

Department of Mathematical Sciences
University of Cincinnati, Cincinnati, USA
jintai.ding@gmail.com

Abstract. We present practical and provably secure (authenticated) key exchange protocols over (ideal) lattices, which is conceptually simple and has similarities to the Diffie-Hellman and the related protocols such as HMQV. Our method does not involve other cryptographic primitives - in particular, it does not use signatures for the authenticated version - which simplifies the protocol and enables us to base the security directly on the hardness of the (ring) learning with errors problem. The security is proven in the Bellare-Rogaway model with weak perfect forward secrecy in the random oracle model for the authenticated version. Several concrete choices of parameters are provided, and a proof-of-concept implementation shows that our protocols are indeed practical.

Keywords: Key Exchange · LWE · Signatures · Protocols · Security

Contents

System Design and Implementations

Cryptograph

An Image Encryption Algorithm Based on Zigzag Transformation and 3-Dimension Chaotic Logistic Map

Yuzhen Li[1,2,3], Xiaodong Li[1,2], Xin Jin[1,2(✉)], Geng Zhao[1,2], Shiming Ge[4], Yulu Tian[1,2], Xiaokun Zhang[1,2], Kejun Zhang[1,2], and Ziyi Wang[1,2]

[1] Beijing Electronic Science and Technology Institute, Beijing 100070, China
jinxin@besti.edu.cn
[2] GOCPCCC Key Laboratory of Information Security, Beijing 100070, China
[3] Xidian University, Xi'an 710071, China
[4] Institute of Information Engineering, Chinese Academy of Sciences, Beijing 100093, China

Abstract. An image encryption algorithm based on Zigzag transformation and 3-Dimension Logistic chaotic map by making use of the permutation-diffusion encryption structure is proposed. The algorithm consists of two parts: firstly, Zigzag transformation is used to scramble pixel position of the color image through three channels; then, 3-Dimension Logistic chaotic map is utilized to diffuse pixel values through three channels. To solve the problem of large computation and space overhead of color image encryption algorithm, the iterative chaotic sequences are used several times in the diffusion process to improve encryption efficiency. The key space of the algorithm is large enough to resist brute-force attack and simulation results show that it also has high key sensitivity, high encryption speed and the strong ability to resist exhaustive attack and statistical attack.

Keywords: Zigzag transformation · 3-Dimension logistic chaotic map · Color image · Encryption algorithm

1 Introduction

With the rapid development of computer network and multimedia technology, security of digital images has caused serious concern. Digital image has large and direct information [1, 2], whose security problem and confidential means are entirely different from traditional text data. So it causes obvious limitation of traditional encryption algorithms. The chaotic system is a deterministic nonlinear system [3]. It possesses varied characteristics, such as high sensitivity to initial conditions, determinacy, pseudo-randomness and so on, which is very suitable for image encryption. In other words, chaotic system can improve the security of encryption system. Thus, the encryption algorithms based on chaotic system have become a hot topic in the field of image encryption in recent years. The extant cryptography algorithms based on chaotic maps can be classified into two kinds: permutation–diffusion [4, 5]. In the permutation

© Springer-Verlag Berlin Heidelberg 2015
W. Niu et al. (Eds.): ATIS 2015, CCIS 557, pp. 3–13, 2015.
DOI: 10.1007/978-3-662-48683-2_1

stage, the positions of pixels from the original image are changed without changing the pixel value by chaotic sequences or some matrix transformation, however, its security could be threatened by the statistical analysis. In the diffusion stage, the pixel values of the original image are changed by chaotic sequences, leading to higher security.

The image encryption algorithms based on low dimension chaotic system [6, 7] are rapid and easy to implement, but security provided by them is limited since they provide the limited key space and possess some weaknesses. Therefore, they cannot satisfy requirement of image security in practice. Recently, combinational encryption algorithms based on chaotic map [8–12] are proposed and performed well. Yet, they only exploit iterative amount to increase the complexity of the system. Since each iteration requiring a lot of computer resources and spending a lot of time, it is an unwise method to increase the complexity of the system by using the amount of iterations.

Color image has advantage in fidelity and color performance compared to monochrome image and is more widely used, thus color image encryption based on chaotic system is more valuable. In order to overcome the above shortcomings, an image encryption algorithm based on Zigzag transformation and 3-Dimension chaotic logistic map is presented in this paper. Simulation demonstrates that it enlarges key space, take full advantage of chaotic map iterative values and well resistance of exhaustive attack and statistical attack. The paper is organized as follows. In Sect. 2, we introduce basic theory of the proposed algorithm. The design of the algorithm in detail is described in the Sect. 3. Simulation results put in the Sect. 4. The security analysis is discussed in Sect. 5. Section 6 gives the conclusion.

2   Basic Theory of the Proposed Algorithm

2.1   Zigzag Transformation

Zigzag transformation [13] is a kind of scrambling method, which begins to scan and take a number with the left upper corner of a matrix, and then one by one takes other numbers by Zigzag path. And the numbers of the scanned sequentially are stored in a one-dimensional array, then it is converted into a two-dimensional matrix in a certain way. Thus these numbers in the old matrix achieve scrambling. The implementation of Zigzag transformation is easy, and time complexity is relatively low. Furthermore, it can effectively change original position of data and is popularly applied on the processing of digital images. Zigzag transformation has already had an extensive application in image encryption and data compression.

Standard Zigzag transformation processing target is square. For general matrix $m \times n(m \neq n)$, the standard Zigzag transformation can be simply extended. In this paper, the extended Zigzag transformation is used to scramble the position of image pixels. What's more, times $N(N \geq 1)$ of transformation can be more than once. So N can be regarded as key of the algorithm.

Combined with the corresponding block diagram, extended Zigzag scanning process is given that supposed the original matrix is a 5×6 one, as shown in Fig. 1. Accordingly, Zigzag inverse transformation is used to recover the original matrix.

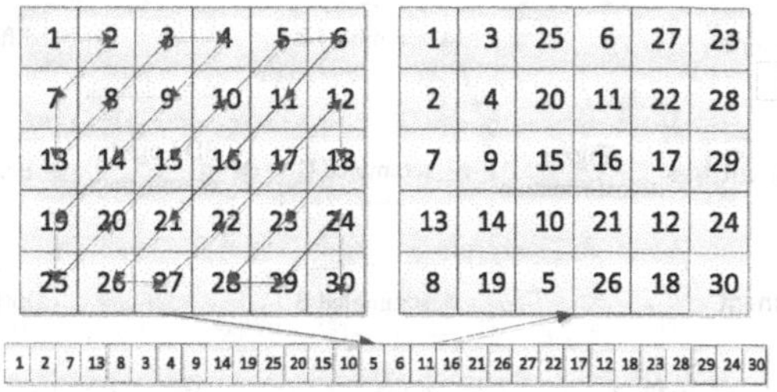

Fig. 1. Zigzag scanning process of 5×6 matrix

2.2 3-Dimension Logistic Chaotic Map

Many authors have proposed the image encryption algorithms based on low dimension chaotic functions. Security provided by them is limited since they possesses some weaknesses, for example, providing the limited key space, having low complexity, and cannot resist exhaustive attack, yet security is not good. This paper use 3-Dimensional (3D) [14] Logistic chaotic map to generate chaotic sequence for the color image encryption. Therefore, the system parameters and the number of variables have increased, and at the same time key space increases, obviously the anti-attack capability is improved.

The definition of 3D Logistic chaotic map is as follows. It is described as Eq. (1):

$$\begin{cases} X_{i+1} = \lambda X_i(1 - X_i) + \beta Y_i^2 X_i + \alpha Z_i^3 \\ Y_{i+1} = \lambda Y_i(1 - Y_i) + \beta Z_i^2 Y_i + \alpha X_i^3 \\ Z_{i+1} = \lambda Z_i(1 - Z_i) + \beta X_i^2 Z_i + \alpha Y_i^3 \end{cases} \tag{1}$$

Three quadratic coupling constant factors are presented to strengthen the difficulty and security of 3D Logistic map. Where, X, Y, Z is the system's trajectory, λ, β, α indicates the parameters of system. When $3.53 < \lambda < 3.81$, $0 < \beta < 0.022$, $0 < \alpha < 0.015$ and the range of the initials value is [0,1], the system is in a chaotic state and can generate three chaotic sequences in the region [0,1]. Thus, the parameters and the initial values can be seen as secret keys.

3 Algorithm Described

In this section, we will study the procedure of image encryption based on Zigzag transformation and 3D Logistic chaotic map in detail. The widely used "permutation–diffusion" architecture is adopted. The encryption algorithm includes two parts: firstly, using Zigzag transformation to scramble pixel positions through three channels of color image; secondly, using 3D Logistic chaotic map to generate three chaotic sequences for each scrambled channel to diffuse pixel values. Because of a strong correlation between the red, green, and blue channels, RGB color space is one of the most widely used method for the processing and storing image data. Here, the encryption algorithm is implemented on the RGB color space. The process of the proposed image encryption algorithm is shown in Fig. 2.

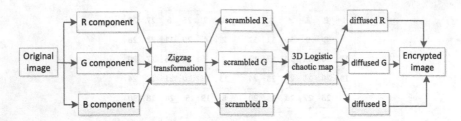

Fig. 2. Block diagram of image encryption algorithm

According to Fig. 2, for a given color image $I(m,n,3)$ that its size is $m \times n$, the proposed image encryption algorithm can be divided into the following steps:

Step 1: The color image $I(m,n,3)$ is decomposed into R channel, G channel, B channel, marked as $I_R(m,n)$, $I_G(m,n)$, $I_B(m,n)$ respectively, certainly, the size of each channel is $m \times n$;

Step 2: Make use of Zigzag transformation to scan $I_R(m,n)$, $I_G(m,n)$, $I_B(m,n)$ respectively for t times so as to scramble the pixel positions, generally, t taking 2 to 4 can able to meet the requirement, each scrambled channel is marked as $I_{ZR}(m,n)$, $I_{ZG}(m,n)$, $I_{ZB}(m,n)$, at present, the first part of the encryption algorithm has been completed;

Step 3: For 3D Logistic chaotic map which is given initial values x_1, y_1, z_1 and system parameters λ, β, α, it generates three chaotic sequences, as shown in Eqs. (2)–(4):

$$X = \{x_1, x_2, x_3, \ldots, x_i, \ldots, x_{m \times n-1}, x_{m \times n}\} \tag{2}$$

$$Y = \{y_1, y_2, y_3, \ldots, y_i, \ldots, y_{m \times n-1}, y_{m \times n}\} \tag{3}$$

$$Z = \{z_1, z_2, z_3, \ldots, z_i, \ldots, z_{m \times n-1}, z_{m \times n}\} \tag{4}$$

Step 4: The range of the chaotic sequences value above is [0,1], however, the range of the image pixel values is [0,255], therefore, there is need to process the above sequences. Taking into account the accuracy of the computer, each chaotic sequence values are taken 16 decimals, as shown in Eqs. (5)–(7):

$$x_i = 0.m_1 m_2 \cdots m_j \cdots m_{15} m_{16}(1 \leq j \leq 16) \tag{5}$$

$$y_i = 0.n_1 n_2 \cdots n_j \cdots n_{15} n_{16}(1 \leq j \leq 16) \tag{6}$$

$$z_i = 0.p_1 p_2 \cdots p_j \cdots p_{15} p_{16}(1 \leq j \leq 16) \tag{7}$$

The study concludes that select k bits digital in the 4th to the 14th decimal places, randomly divide into two groups, namely compose two new integers, and the integers result randomness well. It can take full advantage of fractional parts of 3D Logistic chaotic map iterations to achieve a good encryption effect. Since each iteration requiring a lot of computer resources and spending a lot of time, it is an unwise method

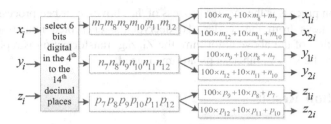

Fig. 3. Process of chaotic sequence values

to increase the complexity of the system by using the amount of iterations. In the paper, k takes 6, the specific process (eg. 7th to the 12th decimal places) as shown in Fig. 3.

After that, the obtaining integers mod 256. Finally, we get six sequences whose values are all in the region [0,255], denoted as X_1, Y_1, Z_1, X_2, Y_2, Z_2 respectively;

Step 5: The six sequences above are converted into the form of $m \times n$ matrix respectively, denoted as JX_1, JY_1, JZ_1, JX_2, JY_2, JZ_2; We can use these six matrix to diffuse twice continuously for the scrambled channels, reaching the effect of changing the pixel values. For an example of R channel, the diffusion process is described as the Eq. (8). As the other two channels are the same as R, we omit equations here. Now, the second part of the encryption algorithm has been completed.

$$bitxor(bitxor(I_{ZR}(m,n), JX_1), JX_2) \tag{8}$$

Fig. 4. The result of encryption and decryption: (a1)–(a6) the original images; (b1)–(b6) the encrypted images; (c1)–(c6) the decrypted images

Decryption process is the reverse process of the above-described process. Receivers obtain secret keys from the sender. To decrypt the encrypted image according to reverse operation of the above algorithm, the Zigzag transformation is replaced by the inverse one in the step 2, other steps are unchanged.

4 Simulation Result

In the Intel 2 Core, 2.70 GHz 2.19 GHz CPU, RAM 4.00 GHz Win7 32bit operating system and MATLAB R2014a environment, we use the color image Lena (512×512), Baby (720×960), Dog (1024×661), Rick (600×405), Black (300×300), White (256×256) as the original image to do encryption and decryption. And we set parameters $x_1 = 0.9761$, $y_1 = 0.6773$, $z_1 = 0.9732$, $\lambda = 3.6099$, $\beta = 0.0212$, $\alpha = 0.0134$, $t = 3$, take 7th to the 12th decimal places, moreover, 7th to 9th is one group and 10th to 12th is the other one, the same as Fig. 3. The simulation results are shown in Fig. 4. From the result of our simulation, we can see that it is difficult to recognize the original images from Fig. 4(b1)–(b6). Figure 4(c1)–(c6) is the same as Fig. 4(a1)–(a6) correspondently, namely decrypted correctly.

5 The Security Analysis

A good encryption algorithm should resist all kinds of known attacks, such as exhaustive attack, statistical attack, etc [15]. In this section, we will discuss the security analysis of the proposed encryption algorithm. Use the color image 512×512 Lena as the simulation image.

5.1 Resistance to Exhaustive Attack

5.1.1 Analysis of Key Space

The algorithm uses the initial values x_1, y_1, z_1 and system parameters λ, β, α of the 3D Logistic chaotic map and times $N(N \geq 1)$ of Zigzag transformation as the secret keys, besides the way of decimal places selecting and grouping can also be seemed as the secret keys. Thus, the key space is large enough to against exhaustive attack.

5.1.2 Keys' Sensitivity Analysis

The 3D Logistic chaotic map is sensitive to the system parameters and initial values. If they have a slight difference, the decryption fails. The secret key sensitivity tests are shown in Fig. 5. Using the correct secret keys in Sect. 4 to decrypt the encrypted image, we have obtained the original image shown in Fig. 4. However, the wrong keys cannot recover the original image. As shown in Fig. 5, changing only one value of the key obtains the following wrong images. Based on the above argument, our algorithm is sensitive to the secret keys, which demonstrates that it has ability to resist exhaustive attack.

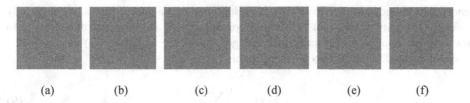

Fig. 5. Keys' sensitivity analysis: (a)–(c) the initial values x_1, y_1, z_1 change 10^{-15}, respectively; (d)–(f) the system parameters λ, β, α change 10^{-15} respectively

5.2 Resistance to Statistical Attack

5.2.1 The Grey Histogram Analysis

Grey histogram can be a direct reflection of the distribution of pixels. In Fig. 6, (a1), (b1), (c1) are the original Lena image histogram for each channel, (a2), (b2), (c2) are encrypted Lena image histogram for each channel. We can find that the original image pixels' distribution is concentrated, but the encrypted image pixels' distribution is very uniform, which is difficult for an attacker using statistical characteristic of pixel values to restore the original image. In addition, they are nearly as uniform as those of the RGB method [8]. So it can effectively resist the statistical analysis, meaning high safety.

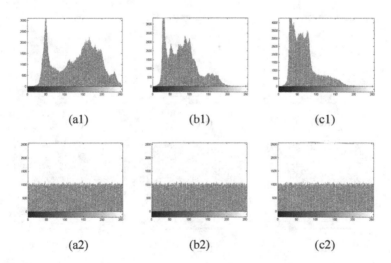

Fig. 6. Histogram analysis: (a1), (b1), (c1) the histograms of the original image on R, G, B respectively; (a2), (b2), (c2) the histograms of the encrypted image on R, G, B respectively

5.2.2 Correlation Coefficient Analysis

The essential characteristics of the image correlation determine that the correlation of adjacent pixels is very high. It makes the encrypted image vulnerable to statistical attack. A good encryption algorithm must reduce the correlation of adjacent pixels of encrypted image. In order to test the correlation of two adjacent pixels, we randomly select 3000 pairs of adjacent pixels (horizontal, vertical and diagonal direction) from the original image and the encrypted image. And using Eqs. (9)–(12) calculates the correlation coefficient of two adjacent pixels.

$$E(x) = \frac{1}{N} \sum_{i=1}^{N} x_i \qquad (9)$$

$$D(x) = \frac{1}{N} \sum_{i=1}^{N} [x_i - E(x)]^2 \qquad (10)$$

$$Conv(x, y) = \frac{1}{N} \sum_{i=1}^{N} [x_i - E(x)][y_i - E(y)] \qquad (11)$$

$$r_{xy} = \frac{Conv(x, y)}{\sqrt{D(x)}\sqrt{D(y)}} \qquad (12)$$

Where x and y are gray values of two adjacent pixels, $Conv(x, y)$ is the covariance, $D(x)$ is the variance, and $E(x)$ is the mean.

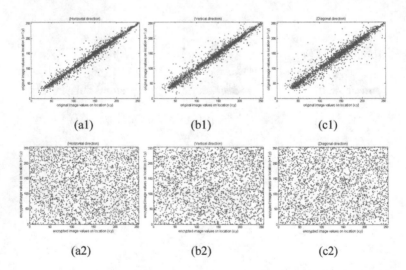

(a1)   (b1)   (c1)

(a2)   (b2)   (c2)

Fig. 7. Correlation coefficient analysis of R: (a1), (b1), (c1) Horizontal direction, vertical direction, diagonal direction of the original image R respectively; (a2), (b2), (c2) Horizontal direction, vertical direction, diagonal direction of the encrypted image R respectively;

Figure 7 (a1), (b1), (c1) show the correlation of the original image's R channel in the horizontal direction, diagonal direction, the vertical direction respectively. The corresponding directions of encrypted image's R channel are shown in Fig. 7 (a2), (b2), (c2).

As we can see, no matter from which direction, the original image of R channel has a strong correlation. The structure and characteristics of the encrypted image's R channel are disrupted, whose correlation are greatly reduced without doubt. What's more, the correlation coefficients of adjacent pixels on R, G, B channels in different directions are shown in the Table 1, which contain original image and encrypted image. From the Table 1, we can find that the correlation coefficients of adjacent pixels in encrypted image are very small, which are close to 0. Hence, the proposed algorithm has a strong ability to resist statistical attack.

Table 1. The correlation coefficients of two adjacent pixels on t three channels of original and encrypted in different directions

	The original image			The encrypted image		
	R	G	B	R	G	B
Horizontal	0.9879	0.9838	0.9392	0.0327	$6.2297\,e^{-04}$	0.0095
Vertical	0.9819	0.9772	0.9610	0.0219	0.0159	0.0121
Diagonal	0.9681	0.9688	0.9731	0.0180	0.0016	0.0212

5.3   Information Entropy Analysis

The information entropy can be used to express uncertainty of the image information. If the distribution of the pixel values is more uniform, the information entropy is greater. The information entropy is defined as the Eq. (13).

$$H(x) = - \sum_{i=1}^{2^N-1} P(x_i) \log_2 P(x_i) \tag{13}$$

Where x_i is the ith pixel value for 2^N level grey image, N is the number of bits of pixels, $P(x_i)$ is the emergence probability of x_i, so $\sum_{i=1}^{2^N-1} P(x_i)=1$. For a 256-level grayscale image, the pixel values have 2^8 types, and the ideal information entropy is 8. For this reason, an effective encryption algorithm should make the information entropy tend to 8. The information entropy of encrypted image on R, G, B channels is 7.9993, 7.9993, 7.9992 respectively, very close to 8, which indicates that the encryption algorithm is very effective, with high security.

5.4   Compare the Efficiency of Encryption and Decryption

In this paper, the chaotic sequences are processed twice in the diffusion part, making full use of computing resources, not only improving security, but also accelerating the encryption speed. The image encryption scheme is implemented in the above environment. From Fig. 8, we can find that the speed of our method has been greatly improved.

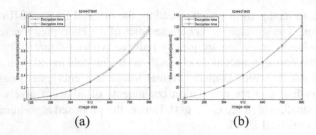

Fig. 8. The comparison of the speed test: (a) our method; (b) the RGB method [8]

6 Conclusion

In this paper, we proposed a new image encryption algorithm based on Zigzag transformation and 3-Dimensional Logistic chaotic map. The iterative chaotic sequences are used several times in the diffusion process to improve encryption efficiency. Simulation results show that the algorithm has a great secret key space, highly sensitivity to the secret key and can resist exhaustive attack and statistical attack, with a broad application prospect in security area of image.

Acknowledgements. This work is partially supported by the National Natural Science Foundation of China (No.61402021, No.61402023, No.61170037), the Fundamental Research Funds for the Central Universities (No.2014XSYJ01, No.2015XSYJ25), and the Science and Technology Project of the State Archives Administrator. (No.2015-B-10).

References

1. Jin, X., Liu, Y., Li, X.D., Zhao, G., Chen, Y.Y., Guo, K.: Privacy preserving face identication through sparse representation. In: To Appear in the Proceedings of the 10th Chinese Conference on Biometric Recognition (CCBR) (2015)
2. Guellier, A., Bidan, C., Prigent, N.: Homomorphic cryptography-based privacy-preserving network communications. In: Batten, L., Li, G., Niu, W., Warren, M. (eds.) ATIS 2014. CCIS, vol. 490, pp. 159–170. Springer, Heidelberg (2014)
3. Zhen, P., Zhao, G., Min, L., et al.: Chaos-based image encryption scheme combining DNA coding and entropy. Multimedia Tools Appl. (2015). doi:10.1007/s11042-015-2573-x
4. Patidar, V., Pareek, N.K., Purohit, G., et al.: A robust and secure chaotic standard map based pseudorandom permutation-substitution scheme for image encryption. Opt. Commun. **284** (19), 4331–4339 (2011)
5. Zhao, J., Guo, W., Ye, R.: A chaos-based image encryption scheme using permutation-substitution architecture. Int. J. Comput. Trends Technol. **15**(4), 174–185 (2014)
6. Mandal, M.K., Banik, G.D., Chattopadhyay, D., et al.: An image encryption process based on chaotic logistic map. Iete Technical Review **29**(5), 395–404 (2012)
7. Ye, G., Wong, K.W.: An efficient chaotic image encryption algorithm based on a generalized Arnold map. Nonlinear Dyn. **69**(4), 2079–2087 (2012)

8. Wang, Y., Ren, G., Jiang, J., et al.: Image encryption method based on chaotic map. In: ICIEA 2007, 2nd IEEE Conference on IEEE Industrial Electronics and Applications, pp. 2558–2560 (2007)
9. Huang, F., Zhang, G.: A new image permutation approach using combinational chaotic maps. Inf. Technol. J. **12**(4), 835–840 (2013)
10. Zhang, J., Xiao-Yang, Y.U.: Image encryption scheme based on cat map and lu chaotic map. Chin. J. Electron Devices **30**, 155–157 (2007). doi:10.3969/j.issn.1005-9490.2007.01.041
11. Sathishkumar, G.A., Bhoopathy Bagan, K., Sriraam, N.: Image encryption based on diffusion and multiple chaotic maps. Int. J. Netw. Secur. Appl. **3**(2), 181–194 (2011). doi:10.5121/ijnsa.2011.3214
12. Wang, Y., Wong, K.W., Liao, X., et al.: A new chaos-based fast image encryption algorithm. Appl. Soft Comput. **11**(1), 514–522 (2011)
13. Xu, X., Feng, J.: Research and Implementation of Image Encryption Algorithm Based on Zigzag Transformation and Inner Product Polarization Vector, 2013 IEEE International Conference on Granular Computing (GrC) pp. 556–561. IEEE (2010)
14. Khade, P.N., Narnaware, M.: 3D chaotic functions for image encryption. Int. J. Comput. Sci. Issues **9**(3), 323–328 (2012)
15. Çokal, C., Solak, E.: Cryptanalysis of a chaos-based image encryption algorithm. Physics Letters A **373**(15), 1357–1360 (2009)

An Improved Cloud-Based Revocable Identity-Based Proxy Re-encryption Scheme

Changji Wang[1,2]([⊠]), Jian Fang[2,3], and Yuan Li[2,3]

[1] School of Software, Yunnan University, Kunming 650500, China
wchangji@gmail.com
[2] Guangdong Key Laboratory of Information Security Technology,
Sun Yat-sen University, Guangzhou 510275, China
[3] School of Information Science and Technology, Sun Yat-sen University,
Guangzhou 510275, China

Abstract. Key revocation and ciphertext update are two prominent security requirements for identity-based encryption systems from a practical view. Several solutions to offer efficient key revocation or ciphertext update for identity-based encryption systems have been proposed in the literature. However, how to achieve both key revocation and ciphertext update functionalities simultaneously in identity-based encryption systems is still an open problem. Recently, Liang et al. introduce the notion of cloud-based revocable identity-based proxy re-encryption (CR-IB-PRE) scheme with the aim to achieve both ciphertext update and key revocation functionalities, and present a CR-IB-PRE scheme from bilinear pairings. In this paper, we first showed Liang et al.'s scheme has serious security pitfalls such as re-encryption key forgery and collusion attack, which lead to revoked users can decrypt any ciphertext regarding their identities at any time period. We then redefined the syntax and security model of CR-IB-PRE scheme and proposed an improved CR-IB-PRE scheme from bilinear pairings. The improved scheme not only achieves collusion resistance, but also takes lower decryption computation and achieves constant size re-encrypted ciphertext. Finally, we proved the improved CR-IB-PRE scheme is adaptively secure in the standard model under DBDH assumption.

Keywords: Identity-based encryption · Proxy re-encryption · Key revocation · Ciphertext update · Cloud computing

1 Introduction

The concept of identity-based public key cryptography (ID-PKC) was originally introduced by Shamir [1] to avoid cumbersome certificate management. In an identity-based crypto-system, users do not need to pre-compute public key and private key pairs and obtain certificates for their public keys. Instead, users' identifiers information such as email addresses, telephone numbers or social security numbers can be used as users' public keys, while private keys are derived at

© Springer-Verlag Berlin Heidelberg 2015
W. Niu et al. (Eds.): ATIS 2015, CCIS 557, pp. 14–26, 2015.
DOI: 10.1007/978-3-662-48683-2_2

any time by a trusted third party, called private key generator (PKG), upon request by the designated users. Since Boneh and Franklin [2] proposed the first practical and provable secure identity-based encryption (IBE) scheme in 2001, research on ID-PKC has become a hot topic in cryptography [3–6].

Revocation capability is indispensable to IBE systems from a practical point of view [2]. Suppose that a user Alice whose private key is compromised or stolen, or she has left the organization, the PKG should revoke Alice's private key in time to mitigate the damage that an adversary with Alice's compromised private key to access confidential data encrypted under her identity. Note that revocable IBE only assures that revoked users cannot decrypt ciphertexts generated after revocation, however, it cannot prevent a revoked user from accessing ciphertexts which were created before the revocation, since the old private key of the revoked user is enough to decrypt these ciphertexts. Thus, ciphertext update or re-encryption is necessary and crucial to IBE systems [7].

Several solutions to offer efficient revocation functionality or ciphertext update functionality for IBE systems have been proposed in the literatures [8–16]. However, how to achieve both key revocation and ciphertext update functionalities simultaneously in IBE systems is still an open problem. Recently, Liang et al. [17] introduce the notion of cloud-based revocable identity-based proxy re-encryption (CR-IB-PRE) scheme with the aim to achieve both ciphertext update and revocation functionalities for IBE systems. In a CR-IB-PRE scheme, ciphertexts are encrypted under a certain identity and time period and stored in the cloud. At the end of a given time period, the cloud service provider (CSP), acting as a semi-trust proxy, will re-encrypt all ciphertexts of the user under the current time period to the next time period, no matter a user is revoked or not. If a user Alice is revoked in the forthcoming time period, she cannot decrypt the ciphertexts by using her expired private key anymore.

In this paper, we first showed that Liang et al.'s scheme has serious security pitfalls such as re-encryption key forgery and collusion attack, which lead to revoked users can decrypt any ciphertext regarding their identities at any time period. Then, we refined the syntax definition and security model for CR-IB-PRE scheme. The refined syntax for CR-IB-PRE scheme is similar to that of self-updatable encryption scheme recently proposed by Lee [18], where the CSP can update stored ciphertexts without any interaction with data owners as long as the revocation event happens. In our refined security model for CR-IB-PRE scheme, an adversary can choose an original ciphertext or a re-encrypted ciphertext as the challenge ciphertext. In particular, we consider the decryption key exposure attack [10], which means an adversary can obtain long-term private keys and decryption keys corresponding to identities and some time periods of his choice. Next, we proposed an improved CR-IB-PRE scheme from bilinear pairings. The improved scheme not only achieves collusion resistance, but also takes lower decryption computation and achieves constant size re-encrypted ciphtertext. Finally, we proved the improved CR-IB-PRE scheme is adaptively secure in the standard model under DBDH assumption.

2   Preliminaries

We denote by $x \overset{\$}{\leftarrow} \mathbf{S}$ the operation of picking an element x uniformly at random from the set $\mathbf{S}$, by $\mathrm{Enc}(k, m)$ and $\mathrm{Dec}(k, c)$ the operation of encrypting and decrypting with respect to a semantically secure symmetric cipher Γ under the session key k, respectively.

A bilinear group generator $\mathcal{G}$ is an algorithm that takes as input a security parameter κ and outputs a bilinear group $(q, \mathbf{G}, \mathbf{G}_T, \hat{e}, g)$, where $\mathbf{G}$ and $\mathbf{G}_T$ are cyclic groups of prime order q, g is a generator of $\mathbf{G}$, and $\hat{e} \colon \mathbf{G} \times \mathbf{G} \to \mathbf{G}_T$ is a bilinear map with the following properties:

- Bilinearity: $\hat{e}(g_1^a, g_2^b) = \hat{e}(g_1, g_2)^{ab}$ for $g_1, g_2 \overset{\$}{\leftarrow} \mathbf{G}$ and $a, b \overset{\$}{\leftarrow} \mathbf{Z}_q^*$.
- Non-degeneracy: There exists $g_1, g_2 \in \mathbf{G}$ such that $\hat{e}(g_1, g_2) \neq 1$.
- Computability: There is an efficient algorithm to compute $\hat{e}(g_1, g_2)$ for all $g_1, g_2 \in \mathbf{G}$.

The Decisional Bilinear Diffie-Hellman (DBDH) assumption in a prime order bilinear group $(q, \mathbf{G}, \mathbf{G}_T, \hat{e}, g)$ states that, given $(g, g^a, g^b, g^c, \hat{e}(g, g)^z)$, it is computationally intractable to determine whether $\hat{e}(g, g)^z = \hat{e}(g, g)^{abc}$, where $a, b, c, z \overset{\$}{\leftarrow} \mathbf{Z}_q^*$.

To achieve efficient revocation for IBE schemes, Boldyreva et al. [8] introduced the **KUNode** algorithm, which is described in Algorithm 1. Denote by **root** the root node of the tree $\mathbb{T}$, by $\mathrm{Path}(\eta)$ the set of nodes on the path from η to **root** for a leaf node η, by ζ_L and ζ_R the left and right child of a non-leaf node ζ, respectively. The **KUNode** algorithm determines the smallest subset $\mathbf{Y}$ of nodes that contains an ancestor of all leaves corresponding to non-revoked users at each time period.

Algorithm 1. KUNode Algorithm

1: Input $(\mathbb{T}, \mathbf{RL}, \mathsf{T})$;
2: For $\forall (\eta_i, \mathsf{T}_i) \in \mathbf{RL}$, $\mathbf{X}, \mathbf{Y} \leftarrow \emptyset$;
3: **if** $\mathsf{T}_i \leq \mathsf{T}$ **then**
4:    Add $\mathrm{Path}(\eta_i)$ to $\mathbf{X}$;
5: **end if**
6: $\forall x \in \mathbf{X}$;
7: **if** $x_L \notin \mathbf{X}$ **then**
8:    Add x_L to $\mathbf{Y}$;
9: **end if**
10: **if** $x_R \notin \mathbf{X}$ **then**
11:    Add x_R to $\mathbf{Y}$;
12: **end if**
13: **if** $\mathbf{Y} = \emptyset$ **then**
14:    Add **root** to $\mathbf{Y}$;
15: **end if**
16: Output $\mathbf{Y}$;

Upon registration, the PKG assigns a leaf node η of a complete binary tree $\mathbb{T}$ to the user, and provides the user with a set of distinct private keys, wherein each private key is associated with a node on Path(η). At time period T, the PKG broadcasts key updates for a set $\mathbf{Y} \subset \mathbb{T}$ of nodes which contains no ancestors of revoked users and precisely one ancestor of any non-revoked user.

3   Security Analysis of Liang et al.'s CR-IB-PRE Scheme

Denote Waters' identity hash function $F_{\text{Wat}}(\text{id}) = u_0 \prod_{i=1}^{n} u_i^{\text{id}_i}$ [6], where $\text{id} = \{\text{id}_i\}_{i=1}^n \in \{0,1\}^n$, and $u_0, u_1, \cdots, u_n \in \mathbf{G}$. Denote Boneh and Boyen's hash function $F_{\text{BB}}(T) = v_1 v_2^T$ [19], where $v_1, v_2 \in \mathbf{G}$. Liang et al.'s CR-IB-PRE scheme [17] is described as follows.

- **Setup**($1^\kappa, N$): The PKG generates $(q, \mathbf{G}, \mathbf{G}_T, \hat{e}, g)$, chooses $\gamma, \alpha, \hat{\alpha}, \beta \xleftarrow{\$} \mathbf{Z}_q^*$, $g_2, g_3, v_1, v_2, u_0, u_1, \ldots, u_n \xleftarrow{\$} \mathbf{G}$, two target collision resistant (TCR) hash functions $\text{TCR}_1 : \mathbf{G} \to \mathbf{Z}_q^*$ and $\text{TCR}_2 : \mathbf{G}_T \to \{0,1\}^\kappa$. Then, the PKG sets $g_1 = g^\alpha$, $v_0 = g^\gamma$, $\mathbf{RL} = \emptyset$ and $\mathbf{ST} = \mathbf{DB}$. Finally, the PKG publishes system parameter $mpk = (g, g_1, g_2, g_3, v_0, v_1, v_2, u_0, u_1, \cdots, u_n, \text{TCR}_1, \text{TCR}_2, \Gamma)$, and keeps the master secret key $msk = (\gamma, \hat{\alpha}, g_2^\alpha, g_3^\beta)$ secret.

- **KeyGen**(msk, id): The PKG chooses $r_{\text{id}} \xleftarrow{\$} \mathbf{Z}_q^*$, computes $sk_{\text{id}_1} = g_3^\beta F_{\text{Wat}} (\text{id})^{r_{\text{id}}}$, $sk_{\text{id}_2} = g^{r_{\text{id}}}$ and $sk_{\text{id}_3} = g_2^\gamma$. Then, the PKG sets additional public parameters $g_z = g^{\hat{\alpha}^z}$, $g_{z+1} = g^{\hat{\alpha}^{z+1}}$, $g_{\lambda+1-z} = g^{\hat{\alpha}^{\lambda+1-z}}$, $g_{\lambda+1+z} = g^{\hat{\alpha}^{\lambda+1+z}}$ for user id, where z is the index for identity id and $\lambda = N + 1$. Finally, the PKG sets the partial private key $sk_{\text{id}} = (sk_{\text{id}_1}, sk_{\text{id}_2}, sk_{\text{id}_3})$.

- **TokenUp**($msk, \text{id}, T_i, \mathbf{RL}, \mathbf{ST}$): The PKG chooses $r_{T_i}, \hat{t} \xleftarrow{\$} \mathbf{Z}_q^*$, $K \xleftarrow{\$} \mathbf{G}_T$, sets $E_{T_i}^{(1)} = (T_1, T_2, T_3)$ and $E_{T_i}^{(2)} = \text{Enc}(k, \tau_{i,1} \| \tau_{i,2})$, where i is the index for the time period, id is a set of identities, and

$$T_1 = K \cdot \hat{e}(g_{\lambda+1}, g)^{\hat{t}}, \quad T_2 = g^{\hat{t}}, \quad T_3 = (v_0 \prod_{\omega \in \text{id}} g_{\lambda+1-\omega})^{\hat{t}},$$

$$\tau_{i,1} = (g_2^\alpha / g_3^\beta) F_{\text{BB}}(T_i)^{r_{T_i}}, \quad \tau_{i,2} = g^{r_{T_i}}, \quad k = \text{TCR}_2(K)$$

Finally, the PKG uploads the token $\tau_i = (E_{T_i}^{(1)}, E_{T_i}^{(2)})$ for a set id of identities to the CSP.

- **DeKeyGen**(sk_{id}, τ_i): A user id chooses $\tilde{r}, r_1, r_2 \xleftarrow{\$} \mathbf{Z}_q^*$, computes

$$K = T_1 / (\hat{e}(T_3, g_z) / \hat{e}(sk_{\text{id}_3} \prod_{\omega \in \text{id} \setminus \{z\}} g_{\lambda+1-\omega+z}, T_2)), \quad k = \text{TCR}_2(K)$$

$$\text{Dec}(k, E_{\tau_i}^{(2)}) = (\tau_{i,1}, \tau_{i,2}), \quad \tau_{i,1} \leftarrow \tau_{i,1} F_{\text{BB}}(T_i)^{\tilde{r}}, \quad \tau_{i,2} \leftarrow \tau_{i,2} g^{\tilde{r}}$$

$$dk_{\text{id}|i,1} = sk_{\text{id}_1} \tau_{i,1} F_{\text{Wat}}(\text{id})^{r_1} F_{\text{BB}}(T_i)^{r_2} = g_2^\alpha F_{\text{Wat}}(\text{id})^{\hat{r}_1} F_{\text{BB}}(T_i)^{\hat{r}_2},$$

$$dk_{\text{id}|i,2} = sk_{\text{id}_2} g^{r_1} = g^{\hat{r}_1}, \quad dk_{\text{id}|i,3} = \tau_{i,2} g^{r_2} = g^{\hat{r}_2},$$

where $\hat{r}_1 = r_{id} + r_1$ and $\hat{r}_2 = r_{T_i} + \tilde{r} + r_2$. Finally, the user sets the updated secret key $dk_{\mathsf{id}|i} = (dk_{\mathsf{id}|i,1}, dk_{\mathsf{id}|i,2}, dk_{\mathsf{id}|i,3})$ for identity id and time period T_i. Note that the user will share $r_1, r_2, \tilde{r}$ with the PKG such that the PKG can store $(\mathsf{id}|i, \hat{r}_1, \hat{r}_2)$ in a list $\mathbf{List}^{dk_{\mathsf{id}|i}}$ for further use.

- **ReKeyToken**$(msk, T_i, T_{i'})$: If a user with identity id is allowed to update his key to another time period $T_{i'}$, the PKG chooses $\xi \xleftarrow{\$} \mathbf{G}_T$, computes $\varphi^{(1)}_{i \to i'} = F_{\mathrm{BB}}(T_{i'})^{\mathrm{TCR}_1(\xi)} / F_{\mathrm{BB}}(T_i)^{\hat{r}_2}$, $\varphi^{(2)}_{i \to i'} = (\hat{C}_0, \hat{C}_1, \hat{C}_2, \hat{C}_3) \leftarrow \mathbf{IBEnc}(\mathsf{id}, T_{i'}, \xi)$, where $\hat{r}_2$ is recovered from $(\mathsf{id}|i', \hat{r}_1, \hat{r}_2)$ which is stored the $\mathbf{List}^{dk_{\mathsf{id}|i}}$. Finally, the PKG sets the re-encryption key token $\varphi_{i \to i'} = (\varphi^{(1)}_{i \to i'}, \varphi^{(2)}_{i \to i'})$.

- **ReKey**$(dk_{\mathsf{id}|i}, \varphi_{i \to i'})$: After receiving $\varphi_{i \to i'}$ from the PKG, a user with identity id chooses $\rho \xleftarrow{\$} \mathbf{Z}_q^*$, sets $rk_1 = dk_{\mathsf{id}|i,1} \varphi^{(1)}_{i \to i'} F_{\mathrm{Wat}}(\mathsf{id})^\rho$, $rk_2 = dk_{\mathsf{id}|i,2} g^\rho$, and $rk_3 = \varphi^{(2)}_{i \to i'}$. Finally, the user outputs the re-encryption key $rk_{\mathsf{id}|i \to i'} = (rk_1, rk_2, rk_3)$.

- **IBEnc**(id, T_i, m): Given an identity id, a time period T_i, and a message $m \in \mathbf{G}_T$, a sender chooses $t \xleftarrow{\$} \mathbf{Z}_q^*$, computes $C_0 = m \cdot \hat{e}(g_1, g_2)^t$, $C_1 = g^t$, $C_2 = F_{\mathrm{Wat}}(\mathsf{id})^t$ and $C_3 = F_{\mathrm{BB}}(T_i)^t$. The sender then sets the ciphertext $C_{\mathsf{id}\|T_i} = (C_0, C_1, C_2, C_3)$. We assume that the identity id and the time period T_i are implicitly included in the ciphertext.

- **ReEnc**$(rk_{\mathsf{id}|i \to i'}, C_{\mathsf{id}\|T_i})$: The CSP first parses $C_{\mathsf{id}\|T_i} = (C_0, C_1, C_2, C_3)$ and $rk_{\mathsf{id}|i \to i'} = (rk_1, rk_2, rk_3)$, then sets the re-encrypted ciphertext $C_{\mathsf{id}\|T_{i'}} = (C_0, C_1, C_4, rk_3)$, where

$$C_4 = \frac{\hat{e}(C_1, rk_1)}{\hat{e}(C_2, rk_2)} = \hat{e}(g^t, g_2^\alpha F_{\mathrm{BB}}(T_{i'})^{\mathrm{TCR}_1(\xi)}),$$

Note if $C_{\mathsf{id}\|T_{i'}}$ needs to be further re-encrypted to the time period $T_{i''}$ with a given re-encrypt key $rk_{\mathsf{id}|i' \to i''} = (rk_1', rk_2', rk_3')$, the CSP first parses rk_3 as $(\hat{C}_0, \hat{C}_1, \hat{C}_2, \hat{C}_3)$, then sets the ciphertext $C_{\mathsf{id}\|T_{i''}} = (C_0, C_1, C_4, \hat{C}_0, \hat{C}_1, \hat{C}_4, rk_3')$, where

$$C_4' = \frac{\hat{e}(\hat{C}_1, rk_1')}{\hat{e}(\hat{C}_2, rk_2')},$$

- **IBDec**$(dk_{\mathsf{id}|i}, C_{\mathsf{id}\|T_i})$: The decryptor responses as follows with respect to the following three cases:

  Case 1: For the original ciphertext $C_{\mathsf{id}\|T_i} = (C_0, C_1, C_2, C_3)$, the decryptor can recover message by computing

  $$\frac{\hat{e}(C_1, dk_{\mathsf{id}|i,1})}{\hat{e}(C_2, dk_{\mathsf{id}|i,2}) \hat{e}(C_3, dk_{\mathsf{id}|i,3})} = \hat{e}(g_1, g_2)^t \Rightarrow m = \frac{C_0}{\hat{e}(g_1, g_2)^t}$$

  Case 2: For the re-encrypted ciphertext $C_{\mathsf{id}\|T_i}$ and it is re-encrypted only once, i.e., $C_{\mathsf{id}\|T_i} = (C_0, C_1, C_4, rk_3 = (\hat{C}_0, \hat{C}_1, \hat{C}_2, \hat{C}_3))$, the decryptor recover message by computing

$$\hat{C}_0 \frac{\hat{e}(\hat{C}_2, dk_{\mathsf{id}|i,2}) \cdot \hat{e}(\hat{C}_3, dk_{\mathsf{id}|i,3})}{\hat{e}(C_1, dk_{\mathsf{id}|i,1})} = \xi \Rightarrow m = C_0 \frac{\hat{e}(C_1, F_{\mathrm{BB}}(T_i)^{\mathrm{TCR}_1(\xi)})}{C_4}.$$

Case 3: For the re-encrypted ciphertext $C_{\mathsf{id}\|T_i}$ and it is re-encrypted ℓ times from period T_1 to $T_{\ell+1}$. Denote by $C^{(\ell+1)} = (C_0^{(1)}, C_1^{(1)}, C_4^{(1)}, \cdots, C_0^{(\ell)}, C_1^{(\ell)}, C_4^{(\ell)}, rk^{(\ell+1)})$ the re-encrypted ciphertext, where $C_0^{(1)}$ and $C_1^{(1)}$ are the components of original ciphertext under (id, T_1). For $1 \le i \le \ell$, $r_3^{(i+1)} = (C_0^{(i+1)}, C_1^{(i+1)}, C_2^{(i+1)}, C_3^{(i+1)})$ is the ciphertext under (id, T_{i+1}). The decryptor first sets

$$C_0^{(\ell+1)} \frac{\hat{e}(C_2^{(\ell+1)}, dk_{\mathsf{id}|\ell+1,2}) \hat{e}(C_3^{(\ell+1)}, dk_{\mathsf{id}|\ell+1,3})}{\hat{e}(C_1^{(\ell+1)}, dk_{\mathsf{id}|\ell+1,1})} = \tilde{m}^{(\ell)}.$$

Then the decryptor sets

$$C_0^{(i)} \frac{\hat{e}(C_1^{(1)}, F_{\mathrm{BB}}(T_{i+1})^{\mathrm{TCR}_1(\tilde{m}^{(i)})})}{C_4^{(i)}} = \tilde{m}^{(i-1)}, \text{ for } i = \ell, \ell-1, \cdots, 2$$

Finally, the decryptor recovers the message by computing

$$m = C_0^{(1)} \frac{\hat{e}(C_1^{(1)}, F_{\mathrm{BB}}(T_2)^{\mathrm{TCR}_1(\tilde{m}^{(1)})})}{C_4^{(1)}}.$$

- **Revoke**$(\mathsf{id}, T_i, \mathbf{RL}, \mathbf{ST})$: The PKG updates the revocation list by $\mathbf{RL} \leftarrow \mathbf{RL} \cup \{\mathsf{id}, T_i\}$ and returns the updated revocation list.

Theorem 1. *A revoked user Alice can decrypt any ciphertext regarding her identity at any time period in Liang et al.'s CR-IB-PRE scheme.*

Proof. A revoked user Alice with identity id can decrypt any ciphertext regarding her identity at any time period as follows.

- *Re-encryption key forgery attack:* Suppose Alice was not revoked at the time period T_i, but she is revoked at the current time period $T_{i'}$. We denote Alice's decryption key at the time period T_i by

$$dk_{\mathsf{id}|i} = (dk_{\mathsf{id}|i,1}, dk_{\mathsf{id}|i,2}, dk_{\mathsf{id}|i,3}) = (g_2^\alpha F_{\mathrm{Wat}}(\mathsf{id})^{\hat{r}_1} F_{\mathrm{BB}}(T_i)^{\hat{r}_2}, g^{\hat{r}_1}, g^{\hat{r}_2})$$

Assume that there is an original ciphertext $C = (C_0, C_1, C_2, C_3)$, which is encrypted under (id, T_i). Alice chooses ϵ_R at random from the plaintext space, and sends the re-encryption key $rk_{\mathsf{id}|i \to i'}$ from T_i to $T_{i'}$ to the CSP, where

$$rk_{\mathsf{id}|i \to i'} = (rk_1, rk_2, rk_3), \ rk_1 = dk_{\mathsf{id}|i,1} = g_2^\alpha F_{\mathrm{Wat}}(\mathsf{id})^{\hat{r}_1} F_{\mathrm{BB}}(T_i)^{\hat{r}_2},$$
$$rk_2 = dk_{\mathsf{id}|i,2} = g^{\hat{r}_1}, \ rk_3 = \mathbf{IBEnc}(\mathsf{id}, T_{i'}, \epsilon_R)$$

Upon receiving the re-encryption key from Alice, the CSP re-encrypts the original ciphertext C and obtains $C' = (C_0, C_1, C_4, rk_3)$, where

$$C_4 = \frac{\hat{e}(C_1, rk_1)}{\hat{e}(C_2, rk_2)} = \frac{\hat{e}(g^t, g_2^\alpha F_{\text{Wat}}(\text{id})^{\hat{r}_1} F_{\text{BB}}(T_i)^{\hat{r}_2})}{\hat{e}(F_{\text{Wat}}(\text{id})^t, g^{\hat{r}_1})} = \hat{e}(g_1, g_2)^t \cdot \hat{e}(g^t, F_{\text{BB}}(T_i)^{\hat{r}_2})$$

Note that Alice knows $C_3 = F_{\text{BB}}(T_i)^t$ and $dk_{\text{id}|i,3} = g^{\hat{r}_2}$. Thus, Alice can recover m by computing

$$\frac{C_4}{\hat{e}(C_3, dk_{\text{id}|i,3})} = \frac{\hat{e}(g_1, g_2)^t \cdot \hat{e}(g^t, F_{\text{BB}}(T_i)^{\hat{r}_2})}{\hat{e}(F_{\text{BB}}(T_i)^t, g^{\hat{r}_2})} = \hat{e}(g_1, g_2)^t, \quad m = \frac{C_0}{\hat{e}(g_1, g_2)^t}.$$

The re-encryption key forgery attack holds because the CSP cannot verify re-encryption key submitted by the user. A legal re-encryption key generated by Alice can be described as $rk_1 = g_2^\alpha F_{\text{Wat}}(\text{id})^{\hat{r}_1 + \rho} F_{\text{BB}}(T_{i'})^{\text{TCR}_1(\epsilon)}$, $rk_2 = g^{\hat{r}_1 + \rho}$, $rk_3 = \textbf{IBEnc}(\text{id}, T_{i'}, \epsilon)$, while a malicious re-encryption key generated by Alice can be described as $rk_1 = g_2^\alpha F_{\text{Wat}}(\text{id})^{\hat{r}_1} F_{\text{BB}}(T_i)^{\hat{r}_2}$, $sk_2 = g^{\hat{r}_1}$, $rk_3 = \textbf{IBEnc}(\text{id}, T_{i'}, \epsilon_R)$ where ϵ_R is independent of ϵ. The CSP can not distinguish $\textbf{IBEnc}(\text{id}, T_{i'}, \epsilon_R)$ from $\textbf{IBEnc}(\text{id}, T_{i'}, \epsilon)$ because the underlying SE-RIBE scheme [10] is proved to be IND-CPA secure in the standard model.

- *Collusion attack:* Suppose Alice is a revoked user and Bob is a non-revoked user at the current time period T_i. The PKG generates and broadcasts the update token $\tau_i = (E_{\tau_i}^{(1)}, E_{\tau_i}^{(2)})$ corresponding to a set of identities **id** and time period T_i. Bob can perform the **DeKeyGen** algorithm and obtain $(\tau_{i,1}, \tau_{i,2})$ corresponding to T_i. If Bob colludes with Alice, he sends $(\tau_{i,1}, \tau_{i,2})$ to Alice. Then Alice performs the **DeKeyGen** algorithm as Bob does. Finally, Alice obtains her valid decryption key in the time period T_i. Thus, Alice can decrypt any ciphertext regarding her identity at any time period by using her valid decryption key. The collusion attack holds because the update token $\tau_i = (E_{\tau_i}^{(1)}, E_{\tau_i}^{(2)})$ corresponding to a set of identities **id** and time period T_i consists of two independent components, where $E_{\tau_i}^{(1)}$ only depends on **id** and $E_{\tau_i}^{(2)}$ only depends on T_i.

This ends the proof.

4 Syntax and Security Definition for CR-IB-PRE Scheme

Let **ID**, **T**, **M** and **C** be identity space, time space, plaintext space and ciphertext space, respectively. A CR-IB-PRE scheme Π can be defined by the following eight polynomial-time algorithms:

- **Setup:** The probabilistic setup algorithm is run by the PKG. It inputs a security parameter κ and a maximal number of users N. It outputs the public system parameters mpk, the master key msk, an empty revocation list **RL** and initial state **ST**.

- **IBKeyGen:** The probabilistic identity-based private key generation algorithm is run by the PKG. It inputs the public parameters mpk, the master key msk, an identity id $\in$ **ID**. It outputs the corresponding identity-based initial private key sk_{id} and an update state **ST**.
- **TokenUp:** The probabilistic token update algorithm is run by the PKG. It inputs the public parameters mpk, the master key msk, the key update time period $T_i \in$ **T**, the current revocation list **RL** and state **ST**. It outputs the key update token τ_i corresponding to the key update time period T_i.
- **DeKeyGen:** The probabilistic decryption key generation algorithm is run by a user. It inputs the public parameters mpk, the user's initial private key sk_{id}, and the key update token τ_i. It outputs decryption key $dk_{id|i}$ for the user with identity id under time period T_i.
- **IBEnc:** The probabilistic identity-based encryption algorithm is run by a sender. It inputs the public parameters mpk, the receiver's identity id $\in$ **ID**, the time period $T_i \in$ **T** and a message $m \in$ **M**. It outputs an original ciphertext $C_{id|i}$ under (id, T_i) which can be further re-encrypted.
- **ReEnc:** The probabilistic re-encryption algorithm is run by the CSP. It inputs the public parameters mpk, the receiver's identity id $\in$ **ID**, an original ciphertext $C_{id|i} \in$ **C** or a re-encrypted ciphertext $C_{id|i \rightarrow k} \in$ **C** that is re-encrypted from the original ciphertext $C_{id|i}$, and a time period T_j. It outputs a re-encrypted ciphertext $C_{id|i \rightarrow j}$.
- **IBDec:** The deterministic identity-based decryption algorithm is run by a receiver. It inputs the public parameters mpk, an original ciphertext $C_{id|i}$ or a re-encrypted ciphertext $C_{id|i \rightarrow j}$, the receiver's decryption key $dk_{id|i}$ for time period T_i or the receiver's decryption keys for time period T_i and T_j, i.e., $dk_{id|i}$ and $dk_{id|j}$. It outputs the message m if decryption keys are valid. Otherwise, it outputs a reject symbol $\perp$.
- **Revoke:** The deterministic revocation algorithm is run by the PKG. It inputs the public parameters mpk, a set id of identity to be revoked, the revocation time period T, the current revocation lists **RL** and state **ST**. It outputs the updated revocation lists **RL**$'$.

We define indistinguishability against adaptive chosen identity and plaintext attack (IND-ID-CPA) experiment for CR-IB-PRE scheme as follows.

$\text{Exp}_{\Pi,\mathcal{A}}^{\text{IND-ID-CPA}}(1^\kappa, N)$.

    $(mpk, msk, \mathbf{RL}, \mathbf{ST}) \leftarrow \mathbf{Setup}(1^\kappa, N)$.

    $(m_0, m_1, \text{id}^*, \boldsymbol{T}^*, \mathbf{ST}) \leftarrow \mathcal{A}^{\mathcal{O}}(\text{Find}, mpk)$ such that $|m_0| = |m_1|$,

    where $\boldsymbol{T}^*$ is a time period vector of (T_{i^*}) or (T_{i^*}, T_{j^*}) with $T_{j^*} > T_{i^*}$.

    $b \xleftarrow{\$} \{0, 1\}$.

    If $\boldsymbol{T}^* = (T_{i^*})$, then $C^* \leftarrow \mathbf{IBEnc}(mpk, \text{id}^*, T_{i^*}, m_b)$;

    If $\boldsymbol{T}^* = (T_{i^*}, T_{j^*})$, then $C^* \leftarrow \mathbf{ReEnc}(mpk, \text{id}^*, T_{j^*},$

            $\mathbf{IBEnc}(mpk, \text{id}^*, T_{i^*}, m_b))$,

    $b' \leftarrow \mathcal{A}^{\mathcal{O}}(\text{Guess}, C^*, \mathbf{ST})$.

    Return 1 if $b' = b$ and 0 otherwise.

In the above experiment, $\mathcal{O}$ is a set of oracles defined as follows.

- *IBKeyGen Oracle:* For id $\in$ **I**, it returns sk_{id} and update state **ST** by running **IBKeyGen**$(mpk, msk, id, \mathbf{ST}) \rightarrow (sk_{id}, \mathbf{ST})$.
- *TokenUp Oracle:* For $T_i \in$ **T**, it returns update token τ_i by running **TokenUp**$(mpk, msk, T_i, \mathbf{RL}, \mathbf{ST}) \rightarrow \tau_i$.
- *DKeyGen Oracle:* For id $\in$ **I** and $T_i \in$ **T**, it returns decryption key $dk_{id|i}$ under (id, T_i) by running **DeKeyGen**$(mpk, sk_{id}, \tau_i, \mathbf{ST}) \rightarrow dk_{id|i}$.
- *ReEnc Oracle:* For an original ciphertext $C_{id|i} \in$ **C**, id $\in$ **I** and $T_j \in$ **T** with $T_j > T_i$, it returns a re-encrypted ciphertext $C_{id|i \rightarrow j}$ of $C_{id|i}$ by running **ReEnc**$(mpk, id, T_j, C_{id|i})$. For a re-encrypted ciphertext $C_{id|i \rightarrow k} \in$ **C**, id $\in$ **I** and $T_j \in$ **T** with $T_j > T_k > T_i$, it returns a re-encrypted ciphertext $C_{id|i \rightarrow j}$ of $C_{id|i \rightarrow k}$ by running **ReEnc**$(mpk, id, T_j, C_{id|i \rightarrow k})$.
- *Revoke Oracle:* For id $\in$ **I** and $T_i \in$ **T**, it returns an updated revocation list **RL**$'$ by running **Revoke**$(mpk, id, T_i, \mathbf{RL}, \mathbf{ST}) \rightarrow \mathbf{RL}'$.

The above oracles can be queried by $\mathcal{A}$ with the following restrictions:

- $\mathcal{A}$ is only allowed to query *TokenUp Oracle* and *Revoke Oracle* in non-decreasing order of time.
- $\mathcal{A}$ is not allowed to query *Revoke Oracle* on time T_i if *TokenUp Oracle* was queried on T_i.
- $\mathcal{A}$ is not allowed to query *DeKeyGen Oracle* on time T_i before *TokenUp Oracle* was queried on T_i.
- For $\mathcal{A}$'s queries corresponding to vector of challenge time period $\boldsymbol{T}^* = (T_{i^*})$ or $\boldsymbol{T}^* = (T_{i^*}, T_{j^*})$, **DeKeyGen**$(id^*, T_{i^*})$ cannot be queried; If **IBKeyGen**(id^*) was queried, then **Revoke**(id^*, T_i) must be queried for $T_i \leq T_{i^*}$.

A CR-IB-PRE scheme is said to be IND-ID-CPA if for any PPT adversary $\mathcal{A}$, the following advantage is negligible in the security parameter κ.

$$\mathrm{Adv}_{\Pi, \mathcal{A}}^{\mathrm{IND\text{-}ID\text{-}CPA}}(1^\kappa, N) = \left| \Pr[\mathrm{Exp}_{\Pi, \mathcal{A}}^{\mathrm{IND\text{-}ID\text{-}CPA}}(1^\kappa, N) = 1] - \frac{1}{2} \right|.$$

5 Our Improved CR-IB-PRE Scheme

Our improved CR-IB-PRE scheme is described as follows.

- **Setup**$(1^\kappa, N)$: The PKG generates $(q, \mathbf{G}, \mathbf{G}_T, \hat{e}, g)$, chooses $\alpha \xleftarrow{\$} \mathbb{Z}_q^*$ and $g_2, u_0, u_1, \cdots, u_n, v_0, v \xleftarrow{\$} \mathbf{G}$, sets $g_1 = g^\alpha$, $\mathbf{RL} = \emptyset$ and $\mathbf{ST} = \mathbb{T}$, where $\mathbb{T}$ is a binary tree. Finally, the PKG publishes $mpk = \{g, g_1, g_2, u_0, u_1, \cdots, u_n, v_0, v\}$, while keeps $msk = \{g_2^\alpha\}$ secret.
- **IBKeyGen**$(mpk, msk, id, \mathbf{ST})$: The PKG chooses an unassigned leaf node η from $\mathbb{T}$, stores id in the node η. For each node $\theta \in$ Path(η), the PKG performs as follows.
  1. Recall g_θ if it is defined. Otherwise, $g_\theta \xleftarrow{\$} \mathbf{G}$ and store $(g_\theta, \tilde{g}_\theta = g_2/g_\theta)$ in node θ.

2. Choose $r_\theta \xleftarrow{\$} \mathbf{Z}_q^*$.
3. Compute $(D_{\theta,0}, D_{\theta,1}) = (g_\theta^\alpha F_{\text{Wat}}(\text{id})^{r_\theta}, g^{r_\theta})$.

Finally, the PKG sends $sk_{\text{id}} = \{(\theta, D_{\theta,0}, D_{\theta,1})\}_{\theta \in \text{Path}(\eta)}$ back to the user.

- **TokenUp**$(mpk, msk, T_i, \mathbf{RL}, \mathbf{ST})$ The PKG parses $\mathbf{ST} = \mathbb{T}$. For each node $\theta \in \mathbf{KUNode}(\mathbb{T}, \mathbf{RL}, T_i)$, the PKG performs as follows.
  1. Retrieve $\tilde{g}_\theta$. Note that $\tilde{g}_\theta$ is always pre-defined in the **IBKeyGen** algorithm.
  2. Choose $s_\theta \xleftarrow{\$} \mathbf{Z}_q^*$.
  3. Compute $(\tilde{D}_{\theta,0}, \tilde{D}_{\theta,1}) = (\tilde{g}_\theta^\alpha F_{\text{BB}}(T_i)^{s_\theta}, g^{s_\theta})$.

Finally, the PKG returns $\tau_i = \{(\theta, \tilde{D}_{\theta,0}, \tilde{D}_{\theta,1})\}_{\theta \in \mathbf{KUNode}(\mathbb{BT}, \mathbf{RL}, T_i)}$.

- **DeKeyGen**$(mpk, sk_{\text{id}}, \tau_i)$: The user first parses $sk_{\text{id}} = \{(\theta, D_{\theta,0}, D_{\theta,1})\}_{\theta \in \mathbf{I}}$ and $\tau_i = \{(\theta, \tilde{D}_{\theta,0}, \tilde{D}_{\theta,1})\}_{\theta \in \mathbf{J}}$. If $\mathbf{I} \cap \mathbf{J} = \emptyset$, then returns $\bot$. Otherwise, the user chooses $\theta \in \mathbf{I} \cap \mathbf{J}$, $r, s \xleftarrow{\$} \mathbf{Z}_q$ and computes $dk_{\text{id}|i,1} = D_{\theta,0} \cdot \tilde{D}_{\theta,0} \cdot F_{\text{Wat}}(\text{id})^r \cdot F_{\text{BB}}(T_i)^s = g_2^\alpha \cdot F_{\text{Wat}}(\text{id})^{\hat{r}} \cdot F_{\text{BB}}(T_i)^{\hat{s}}$, $dk_{\text{id}|i,2} = D_{\theta,1} \cdot g^r = g^{\hat{r}}$ and $dk_{\text{id}|i,3} = \tilde{D}_{\theta,1} \cdot g^s = g^{\hat{s}}$, where $\hat{r} = r_\theta + r, \hat{s} = s_\theta + s$. Finally, the user sets $dk_{\text{id}|i} = (dk_{\text{id}|i,1}, dk_{\text{id}|i,2}, dk_{\text{id}|i,3})$.

- **IBEnc**(mpk, id, T_i, m): The sender chooses $t \xleftarrow{\$} \mathbf{Z}_q^*$, computes

$$C_0 = m \cdot \hat{e}(g_1, g_2)^t, \quad C_1 = g^t, \quad C_2 = F_{\text{Wat}}(\text{id})^t, \quad C_3 = F_{\text{BB}}(T_i)^t.$$

Finally, the sender sets the original ciphertext $C_{\text{id}|i} = (C_0, C_1, C_2, C_3)$.

- **ReEnc**(mpk, id, C, T_j): There are two cases according to C. If C is an original ciphertext, i.e., $C = C_{\text{id}|i} = (C_0, C_1, C_2, C_3) = (C_{(0,0)}, C_{(0,1)}, C_{(0,2)}, C_{(0,3)})$, then the CSP chooses $t_1 \xleftarrow{\$} \mathbf{Z}_q^*$, and computes $C_{(1,0)} = C_{(0,0)} \cdot \hat{e}(g_1, g_2)^{t_1}$, $C_{(1,1)} = g^{t_1}$, $C_{(1,2)} = F_{\text{Wat}}(\text{id})^{t_1}$ and $C_{(1,3)} = F_{\text{BB}}(T_j)^{t_1}$. Finally, the CSP sets the one time re-encrypted ciphertext $C_{\text{id}|i \to j}$ associated with time period T_i and T_j as

$$C_{\text{id}|i \to j} = (C_{(1,0)}, C_{(0,1)}, C_{(0,2)}, C_{(0,3)}, C_{(1,1)}, C_{(1,2)}, C_{(1,3)}).$$

If C is an $\ell - 1$ times re-encrypted ciphertext, i.e.,

$$C = C_{\text{id}|i \to k} = (C_{(\ell-1,0)}, C_{(0,1)}, C_{(0,2)}, C_{(0,3)}, C_{(\ell-1,1)}, C_{(\ell-1,2)}, C_{(\ell-1,3)}),$$

then the CSP chooses $t_\ell \xleftarrow{\$} \mathbf{Z}_q^*$, and computes $C_{(\ell,0)} = C_{(\ell-1,0)} \cdot \hat{e}(g_1, g_2)^{t_\ell - t_{\ell-1}}$, $C_{(\ell,1)} = g^{t_\ell}$, $C_{(\ell,2)} = F_{\text{Wat}}(\text{id})^{t_\ell}$ and $C_{(\ell,3)} = F_{\text{BB}}(T_j)^{t_\ell}$, where $\ell \geq 2$, $T_i < T_k < T_j$, and $t_{\ell-1}$ was chosen by the CSP at the time period T_k. Finally, the CSP returns the new re-encrypted ciphertext $C_{\text{id}|i \to j}$ associated with time period T_i and T_j, where $= (C_{(\ell,0)}, C_{(0,1)}, C_{(0,2)}, C_{(0,3)}, C_{(\ell,1)}, C_{(\ell,2)}, C_{(\ell,3)})$.

- **IBDec**$(mpk, C, dk_{\text{id}|i}, dk_{\text{id}|j})$: Note that the current time period is T_j where $T_i \leq T_j$. $dk_{\text{id}|i}$ and $dk_{\text{id}|j}$ are the decryption keys of T_i and T_j, respectively. There are two cases according to C.
  1. If $C = C_{\text{id}|i} = (C_0, C_1, C_2, C_3)$ is an original ciphertext, i.e., $T_i = T_j$ and $dk_{\text{id}|i} = dk_{\text{id}|j}$, the decryptor can recover the plaintext m by computing

$$C_0 \cdot \frac{\hat{e}(C_2, dk_{\text{id}|i,2})\hat{e}(C_3, dk_{\text{id}|i,3})}{\hat{e}(C_1, dk_{\text{id}|i,1})} = m \cdot \hat{e}(g_1, g_2)^t \cdot \frac{1}{\hat{e}(g_1, g_2)^t} = m.$$

2. If $C = C_{\text{id}|i \rightarrow j} = (C_{(\ell,0)}, C_{(0,1)}, C_{(0,2)}, C_{(0,3)}, C_{(\ell,1)}, C_{(\ell,2)}, C_{(\ell,3)})$ is re-encrypted ℓ times, i.e., $T_i < T_j$ and $\ell \geq 1$, the decryptor can recover the plaintext m by computing

$$C_{(\ell,0)} \cdot \frac{\hat{e}(C_{(\ell,2)}, dk_{\text{id}|j,2})\hat{e}(C_{(\ell,3)}, dk_{\text{id}|j,3})}{\hat{e}(C_{(\ell,1)}, dk_{\text{id}|j,1})} \cdot \frac{\hat{e}(C_{(0,2)}, dk_{\text{id}|i,2})\hat{e}(C_{(0,3)}, dk_{\text{id}|i,3})}{\hat{e}(C_{(0,1)}, dk_{\text{id}|i,1})}$$

$$= m \cdot \hat{e}(g_1, g_2)^{t + t_\ell} \cdot \frac{1}{\hat{e}(g_1, g_2)^{t_\ell} \cdot \hat{e}(g_1, g_2)^t} = m.$$

– **Revoke**(mpk, id, T_i, **RL**, **ST**): The PKG updates the revocation list by **RL** $\leftarrow$ **RL** $\cup \{(\text{id}, T_i)\}$ and return the updated revocation list.

Table 1. Computation cost comparison

Schemes	Decryption cost	Storage cost	Update cost	RE-CT size
[17]	$O(\ell)t_{\hat{e}} + O(1)t_{\mathbf{G}_T}$	$O(p(|\mathbf{Z}_q^*|))$	$O(1)t_{\mathbf{G}} + O(1)t_{\mathbf{G}_T} + O(1)t_{\hat{e}}$	$(2\ell + 1)|\mathbf{G}_T| + (\ell + 3)|\mathbf{G}|$
Ours	$O(1)t_{\hat{e}} + O(1)t_{\mathbf{G}_T}$	$O(p(|\mathbf{T}|))$	$O(1)t_{\mathbf{G}} + O(1)t_{\mathbf{G}_T}$	$|\mathbf{G}_T| + 6|\mathbf{G}|$

6   Security and Efficiency Analysis

Theorem 2. *If there exists an adversary $\mathcal{A}$ attacking IND-ID-CPA security of the improved CR-IB-PRE scheme, then there exists another adversary $\mathcal{B}$ breaking IND-RID-CPA security of the SE-RIBE scheme.*

Proof. We will give the security proof in the extended version.

We compare our improved CR-IB-PRE scheme with Liang et al.'s CR-IB-PRE scheme in terms of the computation cost of re-encryption algorithm and decryption algorithm, and the size of re-encrypted ciphertext. The results are illustrated in Table 1, where ciphertext is re-encrypted ℓ times. We use big O notation and denote by $p(\cdot)$ some polynomial, $|\mathbf{T}|$ the bit-length of an element in time space $\mathbf{T}$, $|\mathbf{G}|$ the bit-length of an element in group $\mathbf{G}$, $|\mathbf{Z}_q^*|$ the bit-length of an element in $\mathbf{Z}_q^*$, and $|\mathbf{G}_T|$ the bit-length of an element in group $\mathbf{G}_T$, respectively. We denote by $t_{\hat{e}}$, $t_{\mathbf{G}}$ and $t_{\mathbf{G}_T}$ the computation cost of a bilinear pairing $\hat{e}(\mathbf{G}, \mathbf{G}) \rightarrow \mathbf{G}_T$, an exponentiation in group $\mathbf{G}$ and in group $\mathbf{G}_T$, respectively.

7   Conclusion

In this paper, we first showed that there are several security pitfalls in Liang et al.'s cloud-based revocable identity-based proxy re-encryption scheme. Then, we refined the syntax and security model for cloud-based revocable identity-based proxy re-encryption scheme. Finally, we proposed an improved cloud-based revocable identity-based proxy re-encryption scheme, which not only achieves collusion resistance, but also achieves constant size re-encrypted ciphtertext. It is interesting to construct a cloud-based revocable hierarchical identity-based proxy re-encryption scheme.

References

1. Shamir, A.: Identity-based cryptosystems and signature schemes. In: Blakely, G.R., Chaum, D. (eds.) CRYPTO 1984. LNCS, vol. 196, pp. 47–53. Springer, Heidelberg (1985)
2. Boneh, D., Franklin, M.: Identity-based encryption from the weil pairing. In: Kilian, J. (ed.) CRYPTO 2001. LNCS, vol. 2139, pp. 213–229. Springer, Heidelberg (2001)
3. Baek, J., Newmarch, J., Safavi-naini, R., et al.: A survey of identity-based cryptography. In: Proceedings of Australian Unix Users Group Annual Conference, pp. 95–102 (2004)
4. Boneh, D., Canetti, R., Halevi, S., et al.: Chosen ciphertext security from identity-based encryption. SIAM J. Comput. **36**, 915–942 (2006)
5. Kang, L., Tang, X.H., Liu, J.F.: Tight chosen ciphertext attack (CCA)-secure hybrid encryption scheme with full public verifiability. Sci. China Inf. Sci. **57**, 112112(14) (2014)
6. Waters, B.: Efficient identity-based encryption without random oracles. In: Cramer, R. (ed.) EUROCRYPT 2005. LNCS, vol. 3494, pp. 114–127. Springer, Heidelberg (2005)
7. Green, M., Ateniese, G.: Identity-based proxy re-encryption. In: Katz, J., Yung, M. (eds.) ACNS 2007. LNCS, vol. 4521, pp. 288–306. Springer, Heidelberg (2007)
8. Boldyreva, A., Goyal, V., Kumar, V.: Identity-based encryption with efficient revocation. In: Proceedings of the 15th ACM Conference on Computer and Communications Security, pp. 417–426. ACM, New York (2008)
9. Libert, B., Vergnaud, D.: Adaptive-ID secure revocable identity-based encryption. In: Fischlin, M. (ed.) CT-RSA 2009. LNCS, vol. 5473, pp. 1–15. Springer, Heidelberg (2009)
10. Seo, J.H., Emura, K.: Revocable identity-based encryption revisited: security model and construction. In: Kurosawa, K., Hanaoka, G. (eds.) PKC 2013. LNCS, vol. 7778, pp. 216–234. Springer, Heidelberg (2013)
11. Wang, C.J., Li, Y., Xia, X.N., et al.: An efficient and provable secure revocable identity-based encryption scheme. PLoS ONE **9**(9), e106925 (2014). doi:10.1371/journal.pone.0106925
12. Chu, C.-K., Tzeng, W.-G.: Identity-based proxy re-encryption without random oracles. In: Garay, J.A., Lenstra, A.K., Mambo, M., Peralta, R. (eds.) ISC 2007. LNCS, vol. 4779, pp. 189–202. Springer, Heidelberg (2007)
13. Wang, L., Wang, L., Mambo, M., Okamoto, E.: New identity-based proxy re-encryption schemes to prevent collusion attacks. In: Joye, M., Miyaji, A., Otsuka, A. (eds.) Pairing 2010. LNCS, vol. 6487, pp. 327–346. Springer, Heidelberg (2010)
14. Shao, J., Cao, Z.F.: Multi-use unidirectional identity-based proxy re-encryption from hierarchical identity-based encryption. Inf. Sci. **206**, 83–95 (2012)
15. Tang, Q., Hartel, P., Jonker, W.: Inter-domain identity-based proxy re-encryption. In: Yung, M., Liu, P., Lin, D. (eds.) Inscrypt 2008. LNCS, vol. 5487, pp. 332–347. Springer, Heidelberg (2009)
16. Luo, S., Shen, Q., Chen, Z.: Fully secure unidirectional identity-based proxy re-encryption. In: Kim, H. (ed.) ICISC 2011. LNCS, vol. 7259, pp. 109–126. Springer, Heidelberg (2012)
17. Liang, K., Liu, J.K., Wong, D.S., Susilo, W.: An efficient cloud-based revocable identity-based proxy re-encryption scheme for public clouds data sharing. In: Kutyłowski, M., Vaidya, J. (eds.) ICAIS 2014, Part I. LNCS, vol. 8712, pp. 257–272. Springer, Heidelberg (2014)

18. Lee, K., Choi, S.G., Lee, D.H., Park, J.H., Yung, M.: Self-updatable encryption: time constrained access control with hidden attributes and better efficiency. In: Sako, K., Sarkar, P. (eds.) ASIACRYPT 2013, Part I. LNCS, vol. 8269, pp. 235–254. Springer, Heidelberg (2013)
19. Boneh, D., Boyen, X.: Efficient selective-ID secure identity-based encryption without random oracles. In: Cachin, C., Camenisch, J.L. (eds.) EUROCRYPT 2004. LNCS, vol. 3027, pp. 223–238. Springer, Heidelberg (2004)

Cryptographic Public Key Length Prediction

M. Amain[✉] and L.M. Batten

School of Information Technology, Deakin University, Geelong, Australia
{mkamain, lmbatten}@deakin.edu.au

Abstract. In the late 1900s, suitable key lengths were determined by cryptographers who considered four main features based on implementation, expected lifespan and associated security. By 2010, recommendations are aimed at governmental and commercial institutions, which take into consideration practical implementations that provide data security. By aggregating the key length predictive data since 1985, we notice that while the figures proposed between 1990 and 2010 increase linearly, those proposed for 2010 to 2050 do not. This motivates us to re-think the factors used as a basis for key length predictions and we initiate this re-evaluation in this paper. Focusing first on implementation, we clarify the meaning of Moore's Law by going back to his original papers and commentary. We then focus on the period 2010-2015, when non-linearity appears, and test Moore's Law based on three different hardware platforms. Our conclusion is that current assumptions about Moore's law are still reasonable and that non-linearity is likely to be caused by other factors which we will investigate in future work.

Keywords: Public key length · RSA cryptosystem · Moore's Law

1 Introduction

An important component of the security of cryptographic schemes in practical implementations is the choice of the key size used for encryption and decryption. For symmetric systems, selection of a security-providing key size is fairly straightforward; while for public key schemes, it is more complex. To quote Chapter 5, page 13 of [1], "If the cryptosystem as such can be assumed to be secure for the lifetime of protected data, the only attack means is usually a brute force key search/guessing attack whose time/success ratio only depends on the maximum amount of computing power P, (number of computers, special purpose hardware, etc.), the foreseen attacker(s) have at their disposal. Thus, we select an n-bit key so that $2^n/P$ is somewhat larger than the life-time of the protected data." The earlier ECRYPT publication [2], pages 10-11 states "When security is to be maintained for longer periods than a few months, we must also take into consideration that the attacker may upgrade his/her resources according to developments in state-of-the-art. The sometimes debated, but commonly accepted way to handle this point is to assume Moore's law. Moore's formula is considered very inaccurate at describing CPU clock-speed, but for the probably more relevant measure of PC performance in terms of MIPS capacity, it seems to apply" the authors of this 2008 report go on to say that "Industry experts seem to agree that it is

© Springer-Verlag Berlin Heidelberg 2015
W. Niu et al. (Eds.): ATIS 2015, CCIS 557, pp. 27–35, 2015.
DOI: 10.1007/978-3-662-48683-2_3

likely that Moore's law will continue to apply for at least a decade or more. Therefore, we have chosen to adopt this assumption here". We discuss Moore's law in more detail in Sect. 3 and it is the motivation for our experimental Sect. 4.

According to Chapter 6 of both [1, 2], prediction of appropriate public key sizes is difficult because if keys are 'too large', this decreases performance; in addition, some unexpected developments have occurred in attacks on public key schemes, and also special purpose hardware has been developed for these schemes. Thus, a straightforward application of Moore's law is not possible in this case. In their approach (Subsection 6.2.1), they estimate 'equivalent' key sizes for DES and various public key schemes in terms of expected levels of security. This equivalence forms the basis of their Chapter 7 predictions for all public key scheme sizes.

In this paper, we review the literature since 2000 on predicting key sizes for cryptographic public keys until 2050. This review, in Sect. 2, includes three sources of key size prediction along with four sources of key size recommendation.

The main contributions of our paper include:

- A review of aggregated data on predicted cryptographic public key sizes up to the year 2050 from several sources,
- A discussion of the impact of Moore's Law on key size prediction,
- An experiment confirming that Moore's Law is still on target at the present time.

Section 2 deals with key length prediction since the 1980s, including a table providing a general overview from 1985 up to 2050. Section 3 presents Moore's Law and we discuss its impact on key size prediction; in Sect. 4, we test Moore's Law as it relates to the discrepancies in prediction beyond 2015 noted in Sect. 2. In Sect. 5, we conclude and give some suggestions for extending this work.

2   Key Length Prediction

Since the introduction of public key cryptography in the 1970's the determination of the appropriate key length to use for encryption and decryption has been a major source of interest and discussion. Adding to the complexity of the decision is the fact that during the late 1990's, many cryptosystems appeared and their uses varied.

'Getting the key length right' is important from two points of view. In practical terms, any cryptosystem must be efficient and fast. The size of the key plays a major role in both of these requirements. Secondly, the key length is a major factor in specifying the level of security of the information to be protected. Unfortunately, efficiency and security are opposing requirements in terms of key size, 'small' being good for efficiency and 'large' being good for security. So a suitable balance must be found.

Usually, the developers of a cryptosystem recommended an appropriate key size at the time the new system was publicized; but computing environments change and attackers implement new attacks, and so key sizes must be adjusted over time. By the late 1990s work had begun on comparing cryptosystems based on current and future key sizes as functions of what were then thought to be the major contributing factors. Lenstra and Verheul, in [3] state that these are:

1. Life span: the expected time the information needs to be protected.
2. Security margin: an acceptable degree of infeasibility of a successful attack.
3. Computing environment: the expected change in computational resources available to attackers.
4. Cryptanalysis: the expected developments in cryptanalysis.

We analyse seven major contributions to the literature attempting to predict or recommend suitable key sizes for various symmetric and public key cryptosystems and in the seven subsections below, we give a brief description of each of these contributions. The first three predict key lengths up to 2050 while the last four focus on recommendations for use of key lengths at the time written and for the near future.

2.1 Lenstra and Verheul Equations

Lenstra and Verheul [3] estimate key sizes of cryptographic systems using a mathematical equation-based approach as functions of some parameters. One of the parameters is a security margin (item 2 in the list in the previous section) which is related to user trust in DES. The other three principal features are as listed in the previous section. Predictions on cryptographic key lengths are given from 1982 to 2050.

2.2 Lenstra Update Equations

In an updated version of the work mentioned in Subsection 2.1, Lenstra [4] considers key length from a slightly different perspective in this 2004 publication. He again emphasizes that he defines 'adequate protection' as the security offered in 1982 by the DES, and that 'this is synonymous with security level 56 (bits) in 1982'. However, he spends some time examining the assumptions on computing capacity as predicted by Moore's Law [5] which is often quoted as stating that 'the computing power per chip doubles every 18 months' and which clearly has an impact on the success of attacks on any cryptosystem. In particular, for systems whose security is based on the difficulty of factoring, such as RSA, the general view is that the cost of factoring any fixed modulus drops by a factor of 2 every 9 months' Both 'optimistic' and 'conservative' bitlength predictions on RSA modulus lengths are given from 2010 to 2050.

2.3 The Network Working Group RFC3766

The report established by this working group [6] defines mathematical formulas determining the minimal security key length of public key schemes depending on the level of security wanted. They recommend that the attack resistance be determined "by estimating the minimum number of computer operations that the attacker will be forced to do in order to compromise the security of the system and then take the logarithm base two of that number." They go on to suggest that 90 bits were sufficient in 1996 and that this figure should be increased by about 2/3 of a bit every year, leading to 96 bits in 2005.

2.4   ECRYPT and ECRYPT II

These ECRYPT [1, 2] reports estimate key length by specifying the period of key use for protection over short, medium and finally long terms. The reports cover a spectrum of symmetric and asymmetric cryptosystems as well as message authentication schemes and hash functions. Security estimates for RSA are based on the equivalent security of DES, short term being 80 bits, medium-term 112 bits and long term 128 bits for DES keys. The earlier report states that there appears to be no reason to use anything larger than 1024 bit RSA keys until 2010, whereas, the later report recommends the values appearing in our Table 1 past that time.

2.5   Nist

NIST [7] is a non-regulatory Federal agency within the Office of Technology Administration in the U.S. Department of Commerce. The agency provides recommendations for key length for multiple types of key uses in signing, authentication, and cryptography and provides an associated 'crypto period', which is the time span the key size is predicted to last. Their current recommended key size for RSA is 2048 bits for all of its applications.

2.6   Anssi

ANSSI [8], the Agence nationale de la sécurité des systèmes d'information (National agency of security of system information), is a French agency operating under the auspices of the Office of the Prime Minister of France. It advises the French government and other organizations on the use of cryptographic and data security mechanisms.

An ANSSI report [8] dated 2010 states that although to that date, no RSA modulus of 1024 bits is known to have been broken, a modulus of this size constitutes undue risk and that moduli of 2048 bits should be used up to the year 2030 after which RSA systems should convert to 4096 bit moduli.

2.7   BSI

BSI [9], the German Federal Network Agency for Electricity, Gas, and Telecommunications, makes recommendations on cryptographic key sizes on behalf of the German federal office for information security. The 2006-8 document recommends a 1024 bit RSA key for the near future and a move to 2048 bits from about 2014, while the 2014 document recommends RSA key size of 2048 bits for the present and the next few years.

We have aggregated the cryptographic public key predictions and recommendations from these seven sources into a single table, Table 1, for easy analysis. While some of the sources, in particular, those from [3, 4, 6] give values for each year, some group into time periods, so in the table, we have adjusted the results to five-yearly intervals over the 65 year period from 1985 to 2050. The BlueKrypt website [10] gives

Table 1. Predicted cryptographic public key length in bits

Techniques	Year	Predicted cryptographic key length in bits													
		1985	1990	1995	2000	2005	2010	2015	2020	2025	2030	2035	2040	2045	2050
Predictive	[3]	88	622	777	952	1149	1369	1613	1881	2174	2493	2840	3214	3616	4047
	[4]	27	539	667	811	973	1112	1245	1387	1538	1698	1869	2049	2239	2440
	[6]	326	1423	1525	1667	1778	1894	2056	2182	2313	2495	2637	2783	2986	3144
In actual use from 2010	[2,1]	-	-	-	-	-	-	1248	1776	2432	2432	3248	3248	15424	15424
	[7]	-	-	-	-	-	1024	2048	2048	2048	2048	3072	3072	7680	7680
	[8]	-	-	-	-	-	-	2048	2048	2048	3072	3072	3072	3072	3072
	[9]	-	-	-	-	-	-	1976	1976	1976	-	-	-	-	-

many of the values appearing in the seven sources and we used it to complete any otherwise missing information from the papers themselves.

Discussion of Table 1

The predictive techniques of [3, 4, 6] depend, for their estimation of key length, on mathematical formulas and on the three points mentioned in Sect. 2, including assumptions about Moore's Law (which we discuss in the next section). Values are provided from 1985 until 2050. From 1990 to 2010, the key length increases almost linearly for [3, 4, 6] (as is easy to see by graphing). However, from 2010 onwards linearity seems to disappear, which raises for us the question of whether the four major factors identified at the beginning of Sect. 2 are still relevant. In fact, the astonishing increase in suggested key size for 2045-2050 in the ECRYPT publications [1, 2] is to deal with the anticipated impact of quantum computing.

The three sites [7–9] give recommendations for key length beginning from about 2010; since these recommendations are aimed at governmental and commercial institutions, they take into consideration practical implementations that provide data security. This, along with possible future disruptive technologies appears to us to be motivation to re-think the factors used as a basis for the predictions of [3, 4, 6].

3   Moore's Law

Lenstra and Verheul [3, 4] state that "the number of components (transistors) on a microchip will double every 18 months". However, in his 1965 article [11], Moore states "The complexity for minimum component costs has increased at a rate of roughly a factor of two per year ... over the short term this rate can be expected to continue, if not to increase. Over the longer term, the rate of increase is a bit more uncertain, although there is no reason to believe it will not remain nearly constant for at least 10 years."

Ten years later, as part of a 1975 interview with Intel Corp., ('Excerpts from A Conversation with Gordon Moore: Moore's Law' (2005). Copyright Intel Corporation.

PDF file available from upenn.edu via Google Scholar), Moore says "I changed it to looking forward, we'd only be doubling every couple of years, and that was really the two predictions I made. Now the one that gets quoted is doubling every 18 months." "Initially, just an observation an attempt to predict this was a way to cheap electronics but the industry made it a self-fulfilling prophesy now, the industry road maps are based on that continued rate of improvement, various technology nodes come along on a regular basis to keep us on that curve, so all the participants in the business recognize that if they don't move that fast they fall behind technology, so essentially from being just a measure of what has happened, it's become a driver of what is going to happen."

That Moore's Law has indeed become a driver is supported by Bohr in his 2011 article [5] where he states: "Traditional transistor scaling methods served our industry well for more than three decades until the early 1990s when leakage current and active power constraints threatened to end the continued improvements provided by Moore's Law. The end of the traditional scaling era ushered in the beginning of the innovation era.... Microprocessor design and architecture innovations such as multi-core designs combined with power gates were significant contributors to improved performance and improved power efficiency." Bohr concludes that "The time has passed when traditional scaling techniques were adequate to meet the needs of new microprocessor products, but that has not meant the end of Moore's Law or the end of improvements in microprocessor performance and power. In the new era of device scaling, innovations in materials and device structure are just as important as dimensional scaling. The past trend of using smaller transistors to build larger microprocessor cores operating at higher frequency and consuming more power is also at an end. The new era of microprocessor scaling is a system-on-chip approach that combines a diverse set of components using adaptive circuits, sophisticated power management techniques and increased parallelism to build products that are many-core, multi-core, and multi-function."

None-the-less, Bohr sees the necessity for an adaptation of Moore's Law over the coming years as visualized in Fig. 1, taken from [5] with permission of the author.

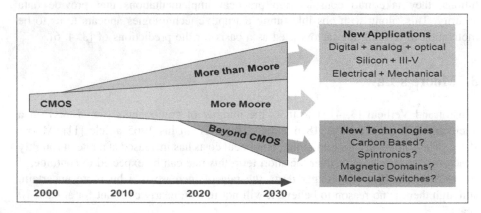

Fig. 1. [5] Future technology directions including scaled CMOS combined with "More than Moore" devices and "Beyond CMOS" devices.

4 Experiments and Environment

As already mentioned, one of the most important factors in predicting appropriate key length of a cryptographic system is the computing environment. The hardware platform used influences its behavior when implementing it from the points of view of speed (time for generating the key, time for encryption and decryption) and memory used. As a small test of Moore's Law for the period 2010-2015, identified above as the start of non-linearity in well-established predictions, we looked for research papers published in this time period which had used older versions of computing environments than available today and which had presented results on public key generation. Our objective was to determine if perhaps Moore's Law was beginning to fail and that might be a motivation for additional work along these lines.

Unfortunately, we were able to identify only two papers, [12, 13], published in this time period, which had timed key generation, encryption and decryption for the public key scheme RSA, and so we added our current platform to the mix to generate similar data. Because the relevant key sizes in Table 1 for this 5-year time period vary from 1024 to 2048 bits, we used these values and chose message sizes 512, 1024 and 2048 bits.

The computing platform used by the authors of [12] was P-IV CPU 2 GHZ with 1.256 GB RAM, and by the authors of [13] was Dual Core CPU 2.2 GHZ with 1 GB RAM, while we chose Intel (R) Core (TM) i7-4500 CPU 2.4 GHZ with 8 GB RAM. Table 2 shows a comparison between our key generation and decryption times with those of the authors of [12, 13] based on key sizes of 1024 and 2048 bits for message sizes as mentioned above. The papers are listed in increasing order of hardware capability. As recommended in [14], in all cases decryption key size is that of the modulus. We do not present encryption key sizes as these are, in practice chosen as special values and encryption times are therefore not comparable across the papers.

Table 2. A comparison of key generation and decryption times (in ms) on different computing platforms.

Modulus (bits)	Message size (bits)	P-IV CPU 2 GHZ RAM: 1.256 GB [12]	Dual Core CPU 2.2 GHZ RAM: 1 GB	Intel (R) Core (TM) i7-4500 CPU 2.4 GHZ RAM: 8 GB
1024	512			
	Key Gen	844	469	121
	Decryption	640	375	89
1024	1024			
	Key Gen	844		121
	Decryption	312	xxxx	93
2048	512			
	Key Gen	2688	2453	1072
	Decryption	4547	2750	623

(Continued)

Table 2. (*Continued*)

Modulus (bits)	Message size (bits)	P-IV CPU 2 GHZ RAM: 1.256 GB [12]	Dual Core CPU 2.2 GHZ RAM: 1 GB	Intel (R) Core (TM) i7-4500 CPU 2.4 GHZ RAM: 8 GB
2048	1024			
	Key Gen	2688	2453	1072
	Decryption	2297	1375	656
2048	2048			
	Key Gen	2688	xxxx	1072
	Decryption	1140	xxxx	722

We do not have the exact details of the computing platforms in [12] and [13], so cannot be precise about a comparison. However, from sales websites, we were able to determine the following features of the three platforms: P-IV CPU with 2 GHZ has a single core, a 32 bit bus and 42 million transistors; CPU 2.2 GHZ has a double core, a 64 bit bus and 167 million transistors; Intel (R) Core (TM) i7-4500 CPU 2.4 GHZ has a Quad core, a 64 bit bus and 781 million transistors. Since 781 million is four and a half times 167 million which in turn is roughly four times 42 million, these differences, along with the improvement in times shown in Table 2, are fairly representative of Moore's Law.

5 Summary and Conclusions

We have discussed the importance of choosing correct key sizes for public key cryptographic algorithms and have analyzed the work done on this from the late 1990s to the present time. The key size predictions were summarized in Table 1, from which we see that the figures proposed between 2010 and 2050 for actual use do not increase linearly. This motivated us to re-think the factors used as a basis for the predictions of [3, 4, 6]. One of the major underlying hypotheses on which much of the original work [3, 4] in this area was done is based on Moore's Law. Thus, we examined in detail the thrust of this law in Sect. 3, explaining that the new era of microprocessor scaling combines a diverse set of components to build products that are multi-function. This is encapsulated in Bohr's Fig. 1, taken from [5], which indicates that some adaptations are needed for this law into the future.

We set up an experiment to compare computing platforms generating RSA public keys over the period 2010-2015 in order to determine if indeed, an assumption of Moore's Law might not be usable for future key length predictions. On the contrary, our experiment confirms Moore's Law. None-the-less, in order to obtain accurate predictions for cryptographic key sizes moving into the future, we suggest that developments affecting and affected by Moore's Law should be followed carefully. This in turn affects the capability of attackers to mount as yet unseen attacks on cryptographic systems which must also be precisely monitored.

References

1. Smart, N. (ed.).: ECRYPT II yearly report on algorithms and keysizes. In: European Network of Excellence in Cryptology, ICT-2007-216676 (2011–2012)
2. Naslund, M. (ed.): ECRYPT yearly report on algorithms and keysizes. In: European Network of Excellence in Cryptology, IST-2002-507932 (2007–2008)
3. Lenstra, A.K., Verheul, E.R.: Selecting cryptographic key sizes. In: Imai, H., Zheng, Y. (eds.) PKC 2000. LNCS, vol. 1751, pp. 446–465. Springer, Heidelberg (2000)
4. Lenstra, A.K.: Key Lengths. The Handbook of Information Security (2004). Thirty-two pages
5. Bohr, M.: Moore's Law in the Innovation Era. In: SPIE Advanced Lithography on International Society for Optics and Photonics, p. 797402 (8 pages) (2011)
6. Orman, H., Hoffman, P.: Determining strengths for public keys used for exchanging symmetric keys. RFC 3766, April 2004. https://tools.ietf.org/html/rfc3766#page-11(Accessed 13 July 2015)
7. NIST.: Cryptographic algorithms and key sizes for personal identity verification. 800–78-4, May 2015. http://dx.doi.org/10.6028/NIST.SP.800-78-4
8. ANSSI 2010, Mécanismes cryptographiques - Règles et recommandations, Rev. 1.20, ANSSI, January 2010 and Rev. 2.03, ANSSI, February 2014
9. BSI 2009 and 2014, Bundesnetzagentur für Elektrizität, Gas, Telekommunikation, Post und Eisenbahnen, Algorithms for Qualified Electronic Signatures, BNetzA, BSI, January 2014. Version 1.4 (2009) and version 13.1.2014 (2014)
10. Damien, G., Quisquater, J.-J.: BlueKrypt Cryptographic Key Length Recommendation, v.28.6, February 2015. http://www.keylength.com/en/8/
11. Moore, G.E.: Cramming more components onto integrated circuits. Reprinted from Electronics, 38(8), pp. 114, 19 April 1965. Reprinted in IEEE Solid-State Circuits Newsletter 3(20), pp. 33–35 (2006)
12. Purohit, I., Somani, R.K.: Hybrid Cryptography Algorithm based on prime factorization. Int. J. Recent Dev. Eng. Technol. 2(2), 90–96 (2014). www.ijrdet.com. (ISSN 2347–6435)
13. Dhakar, R.S., Gupta, A.K., Sharma, P.: Modified RSA Encryption Algorithm (MREA). In: 2nd IEEE International Conference on Advanced Computing & Communication Technologies (ACCT), pp. 426–429. IEEE (2012)
14. Menezes, A.J., Van Oorschot, P.C., Vanstone, S.A.: Handbook of applied cryptography. CRC press (1996)

An Image Encryption Algorithm Based on Chua's Chaos and Baker's Transformation

Chupei Chen[✉], Jing Li, and Hongmin Deng

School of Electronics and Information Engineering,
Sichuan University, Chengdu, Sichuan 610065, China
chen@stu.scu.edu.cn

Abstract. This paper presents a new image encryption algorithm based on Chua's chaos with the combination of baker transformation. First, we divide the original image into blocks with size 8×8 and transform each block into three-dimensional image of binary number with size 8×8×8. Then, preprocess the real chaotic sequences output by Chua's system and revise grey level of the pixel in three-dimensional image according to sequences value. Finally, use baker's transformation to scramble image blocks and an encryption image will be obtained by this algorithm. The experimental results show that this algorithm has good encryption performance and high security.

Keywords: Chua's chaos · Three-dimensional · Baker's transformation · Image encryption

1 Introduction

In recent years, the digital multimedia technology has a rapid development and multimedia data security is also gotten more and more attention due to the wide spread of various communication networks. In order to solve the image safety during transmission, many image encryption methods were proposed [1]. Traditional encryption algorithms mainly include: the DES algorithm, the IDEA algorithm and RSA algorithm, etc., they haven't consider image having a large capacity of data, high redundancy and other characteristics, therefore, it is insufficient to use them in image encryption.

The scrambling transformation is a common method of image encryption. There are many image scrambling transformation methods [2,3], for example, Arnold transformation, magic square transformation and the knight tour transformation. As for the traditional image scrambling algorithms, they have many advantages including lots of scrambling methods, fast time and convenient inverse transform. However, they need multi-steps to achieve good encryption effect. Also, this type of encryption technology only changes the pixel position, but

---

C. Chen – This research is partly supported by the Natural Science Foundation of China under Grant No. 61174025.

© Springer-Verlag Berlin Heidelberg 2015
W. Niu et al. (Eds.): ATIS 2015, CCIS 557, pp. 36–43, 2015.
DOI: 10.1007/978-3-662-48683-2_4

doesn't change the pixel value, and the histogram is the same as after scrambling. Though this technology is simple and accessible, it's also been attacked easily. For the information security and the limitations of the traditional encryption technology, the chaos theory has been widely used in image information security. The application of image encryption algorithm based on chaotic sequences is commonly used in image encryption [4–9], the sensitivity of chaos to initial values makes it difficult for attackers to decipher image information. Low dimensional chaotic systems such as logistic mapping and Henon mapping, etc., their confidentiality remains to be improved because of the less parameters and small secret key space compared with multidimensional chaotic systems. The algorithm based on Chua's chaos and baker's transformation proposed by our research increases the key space and preventes the attack from deciphers effectively. The correlation between pixels can be reduced by processing the image with three-dimensional technology and scrambling the blocks, so as to enhance the image security.

2 Chaos Theory

As one of the three science revolution in the 20th century, chaos theory is as famous as quantum mechanics and theory of relativity, and has three vital characters: sensitive to original values, fractal and singular attractors. The American scientist L.O.Chua first advanced the theory of Chua's circuit in 1983 [10], which playing an important role during the development of chaotic and making it possible for us to design and control chaotic initiatively rather than passive imagination. Chua's circuit is the most representative among the numerous chaotic circuits at present. It's the simplest third-order autonomous circuit which can generate the chaotic behavior, and Fig. 1 is its circuit diagram.

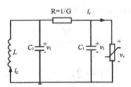

Fig. 1. Chua's circuit

According to Fig. 1, we can get the third-order equation of Chua's circuit as follows:

$$
\begin{cases}
C_1 \dfrac{dv_1}{dt} = G(v_2 - v_1) - f(v_1) \\[2mm]
C_2 \dfrac{dv_2}{dt} = G(v_1 - v_2) + i_L \\[2mm]
L \dfrac{di_L}{dt} = -v_2
\end{cases}
\tag{1}
$$

By rescaling the variables, the non-dimensional normalized equation of Eq. (1) is:

$$\begin{cases} \dfrac{\mathrm{d}x}{\mathrm{d}\tau} = \alpha(y - x - f(x)) \\[2mm] \dfrac{\mathrm{d}y}{\mathrm{d}\tau} = x - y + z \\[2mm] \dfrac{\mathrm{d}z}{\mathrm{d}\tau} = -\beta y \end{cases} \tag{2}$$

where f(x) = bx+$\frac{1}{2}(a - b)(|x + 1| - |x - 1|)$, $\alpha = \frac{C_2}{C_1}$, $\beta = \frac{C_2}{G^2 L}$.Through exper-
imental analysis, we know that Chua's circuit would be in a state of chaotic
and exist double scroll chaotic attractor if we set $\alpha = 10$, $\beta = 15$, a = -0.2 and
b = 0.4. The fourth-order Runge-Kutta method was adopted to control these
parameters:$(\alpha, \beta, a, b) = (10, 15, -0.2, 0.4)$, integration step is 0.001, and then
we will obtain the 3D chaotic sequence of real numbers$(X_i, Y_i, Z_i), i = 1, 2, 3...n$,
where n is iteration epochs.

3   Baker's Transformation

Baker's transformation is a conversion technology which stretches and folds a
continuous planar area repeatedly [11,12]. We can use a matrix $A_{M \times N}$ to indicate a 2D digital image, the matrix element a(i, j) shows grey level value of
line i and column j in this image (i = 1,2...M; j = 1,2...N). Essentially, scram-
bling location space is a matrix convertion $(P : A_{M \times N} \rightarrow A'_{M \times N})$ from original
image matrix to encrypted image matrix, here $A'_{M \times N}$ is the image after scrambling. Scrambling will not change grey level value of the original image, that
is to say, encrypted image $A'_{M \times N}$ has the same grey level histogram as original
image $A_{M \times N}$. However, encrypted image changes the position of adjacent pixels,
which makes vision system can't acquire the information of original image from
the disconnected image, thus to achieve the purpose of encryption. Equation (3)
shows the discrete baker's transformation:

$$a(i, j) = \begin{cases} (2i, 2j - 1), 1 \leq i \leq \dfrac{M}{2}, 1 \leq j \leq \dfrac{N}{2} \\[2mm] (2i - 1, 2N - 2j + 2), 1 \leq i \leq \dfrac{M}{2}, \dfrac{N}{2} < j \leq N \\[2mm] (2i - M, 2j), \dfrac{M}{2} < i \leq M, 1 \leq j \leq \dfrac{N}{2} \\[2mm] (2i - M - 1, 2N - 2j + 1), \dfrac{M}{2} < i \leq M, \dfrac{N}{2} < j \leq N \end{cases} \tag{3}$$

Figure 2 presents the original image and encrypted image after four iterations,
we can see that there is no change in histogram.

4   Encryption Methodology

Suppose there is an M×M image and 64 can be exactly divisible by M×M, so we
can divide an image into $l = \frac{M \times M}{8 \times 8}$ blocks and identifier them to be $L_1, L_2, ...L_l$.

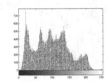 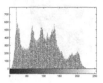

(a) Original image (b) Grey level value (c) Encrypted image (d) Grey level value
histogram of original after four iterations histogram of image
image after four iterations

Fig. 2. Images and histograms before and after baker's transformation

For each block L_i, we set its size to be 8×8, first, transfer this 2D image into 8 bit binary number with three dimensions. Figure 3 demonstrates the transformation form planar 4×4 matrix to 8 bit binary with three dimensions.

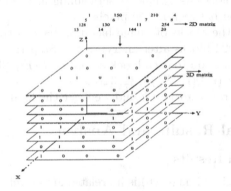

Fig. 3. Three-dimension matrix of 8×4×4

Step 1. Change of pixels' values in blocks based on Chua's chaos
a. Use equation (2) to obtain the 3D chaotic sequence of real numbers (X_i, Y_i, Z_i), and then process its values. Since pixel values of the image are $(0,255)$, the range of the 3D sequences X_i, Y_i, Z_i after processing are integers from 0 to 255. In order to ensure good randomness, we eliminate the values of previous t times and pick up 64 values belonging to $(0,255)$ from X_i, Y_i, Z_i at the $(t+1)^{th}$ time separately. Then, convert the decimal number into 8 bit binary number $X_{bi}, Y_{bi}, Z_{bi}...i = 1,2,3...64$;
b. Divide an image of 256×256 into 1024 pieces of 8×8. Get 64 columns of 8 bit binary values paralleling to X-, Y- and Z-axes separately after converting the 2D matrix into 3D 8 bit binary matrix for each piece L_i and label them in sequence $X'_{bi}, Y'_{bi}, Z'_{bi}...i = 1,2,3...64$;
c. Do binary exclusive-OR to X_{bi}, Y_{bi}, Z_{bi} obtained from Chua's chaos with $X'_{bi}, Y'_{bi}, Z'_{bi}$ separately, where $X"_{bi}, Y"_{bi}, Z"_{bi}$ are 3D binary values of the new image;

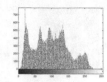 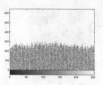

(a) Original image   (b) Grey level value (c) Encrypted image (d) Grey level val-
                        histogram of original   ue histogram of en-
                        image   crypted image

Fig. 4. Images and their related grey level value histogram

d. Transfer the new generated 3D binary values into 2D matrix of 8×8, that is encrypted L'_i;

e. Encrypt every block L_i...i = 1,2,...1024 as mentioned above and achieve the new image L'_i...,i = 1,2,...1024. The order among the 1024 blocks didn't change. Scramble these 1024 blocks using baker's scrambling method to enhance security and reduce correlation between image pixels.

   Step 2. Scramble the blocks of image based on baker's transformation

a.Obtain 32×32 = 1024 blocks after encryption in Step 1;

b.Do baker's transformation to each block according to Eq. (3), (i,j) presents the location of each block ($i \in [1, 32]; j \in [1, 32]$) ;

c.Repeat b, preset iterations to be k and we'll get the final encrypted image.

5   Experimental Results and Analysis

5.1   Experimental Results

Figure 4 (a) is the original image, (b) is its related grey level value histogram; (c) is the encrypted image according to our research and (d) is its grey level value histogram

5.2   Experimental Analysis

5.2.1   Histogram Analysis

Grey level value histogram is used to describe distribution of the image pixels and attackers could achieve image information through it. Therefore, histogram equalization can prevent attack effectively. Comparing Fig. 4 (b) with Fig. 4 (d), we would acknowledge that the histogram is equalized after encryption using the proposed algorithm in our research. Consequently, its valid for our algorithm to cover original image information and resist attack from outside.

5.2.2   Information Entropy Analysis

Information entropy can reveal the information uncertainty. Its definition is as follow: suppose $X = \{X_i \mid i = 1, 2, ..., n\}$ is a random variable, the probability of occurrence of X_i is P(X_i) and $\sum_{i=1}^{n} p(X_i) = 1$, so the information entropy of X is:

$$H(X) = -\sum_{i=1}^{n} p(X_i) \log_2 p(X_i) \tag{4}$$

If the probability of occurrence of each variable is the same, that is to say, $p(X_1) = p(X_2) = ...p(X_n) = \frac{1}{n}$, information entropy would get the maximum value; Otherwise, if $p(X_1) = 1, p(X_2) = ...p(X_n) = 0$, it would get the minimum value. A good encryption algorithm should make the image information entropy value close to 8 because of the maximum information entropy value of 256 grey level image is 8. The image information entropy value is calculated to be 7.987 according to Equation (4).

5.2.3   Key Space and Sensitivity Analysis

The key space for a good encryption should be large enough to make brute-force attack impossible. In the proposed algorithm, the keys are the Chua's circuit initial values x_1, y_1, z_1, it can increase the secret key space compared with the one dimensional and two dimensional chaotic map. Using initial value as the key can guarantee the key space is large enough because of the initial value sensitivity of chaotic sequence. So the algorithm can resist the brute-force attack in such a large enough key space.

An ideal image encryption procedure should be sensitive to cipher key. Figure 5(a) is the decrypted image with the correct key, while Fig. 5(b) is the decrypted image with a tiny difference of 10^{-7}. From Fig. 5, we know that attacker can't decrypt the plain image correctly even with a tiny difference of the initial value.

5.2.4   Correlation Coefficient Analysis

There is a strong correlation among the data of digital image. We can view the digital image as a matrix, the elements in it are pixel grey level values. Through the analysis, there are many neighbored pixels in grey level image with the same grey level or small difference. Therefore, scrambling image is a effective method to reduce image correlation. The following equation is to compute the correlation coefficient of interfacing pixels:

(a) Decrypted image with   (b) Decrypted image with a
the correct key   tiny difference of 10^{-7}

Fig. 5. Decrypted image with the different keys

Table 1. Correlation coefficients of adjacent pixels

Image	Horizontal	Vertical	Diagonal
Original image	0.9594	0.9481	0.9394
Encrypted image by our algorithm	0.0067	0.0051	0.0295
Encrypted image by baker's transformation	0.5751	0.5081	0.4419

$$\begin{cases} E_x = \dfrac{1}{N} \sum_{i=1}^{N} x_i \\[2mm] COV(x,y) = \dfrac{1}{N} \sum_{i=1}^{N} (x_i - E_x)(y_i - E_y) \\[2mm] D_x = \dfrac{1}{N} \sum_{i=1}^{N} (x_i - E_x)^2 \\[2mm] R_{xy} = \dfrac{COV(x,y)}{\sqrt{D_x D_y}} \end{cases} \tag{5}$$

where x, y is the grey level value of interfacing pixels, E_x is the mean value of x, D_x, D_y is variance of x and y separately and $COV(x,y)$ is covariance of x and y. Calculate the correlation coefficient of interfacing pixels in the horizontal, vertical and diagonal direction using equation (5) and compare them with the results of baker's transformation. The results can be seen in Table 1.

As it can be seen from Table 1, the correlation coefficients of adjacent pixels obtained by the proposed algorithm in our study are close to zero, which demonstrates that the proposed algorithm reduced correlation greatly and achieved relatively good encryption effect.

6   Conclusion

The proposed encryption algorithm is based on Chua's chaos and baker's transformation. Using the feature that chaotic system is sensitive to initial value can generate multiple different keys. We firstly use the algorithm to encrypt the 3D image, attacker can't restore the original image even with a tiny difference as long as the initial values are unknown. Furthermore, scrambling the blocks of image by baker's transformation can reduce the correlation of pixels effectively. Experiment results and analysis show that the proposed method of our study has an effective encryption effect.

References

1. Zhao, L., et al.: On the security analysis of an image scrambling encryption of pixel bit and its improved scheme based on self-correlation encryption. Commun. Nonlinear Sci. Numer. Simul. **17**(8), 3303–3327 (2012)

2. Cheng-Mao, W.: An improved discrete arnold transform and its application in image scrambling and encryption (2014)
3. Wu, L., et al.: Arnold transformation algorithm and anti-Arnold transformation algorithm. In: 1st International Conference on Information Science and Engineering (ICISE). IEEE (2009)
4. Guan, Z.-H., Huang, F., Guan, W.: Chaos-based image encryption algorithm. Phys. Lett. A **346**(1), 153–157 (2005)
5. Liu, L., Zhang, Q., Wei, X.: A RGB image encryption algorithm based on DNA encoding and chaos map. Comput. Electr. Eng. **38**(5), 1240–1248 (2012)
6. Ma, X., et al.: A novel chaos-based image encryption scheme with an improved permutation process. Int. J. Advancements Comput. Technol. **3**(5), 223–233 (2011)
7. Pareek, N.K., Patidar, V., Sud, K.K.: Image encryption using chaotic logistic map. Image Vis. Comput. **24**(9), 926–934 (2006)
8. Wang, X., Luan, D.: A novel image encryption algorithm using chaos and reversible cellular automata. Commun. Nonlinear Sci. Numer. Simul. **18**(11), 3075–3085 (2013)
9. Wen, C.-C., et al.: Self-adaptive encryption algorithm for image based on affine and composed chaos. J. Commun. **11**, 016 (2012)
10. Chua, L.O., Komuro, M., Matsumoto, T.: The double scroll family. IEEE Trans. Circuits Syst. **33**(11), 1072–1118 (1986)
11. Lelandais, S., et al.: A new color invariant for image retrieval using the Baker's transformation. In: International Conference on Imaging Technology and Applications for the 21th century (2005)
12. Zhao, X.: Digital image scrambling based on Baker's transformation. J. Northwest Normal Univ. (Nat. Sci.) **39**(2), 26–29 (2003)

Quantum Differential Cryptanalysis
to the Block Ciphers

Hongwei Li[1,2,3,4] and Li Yang[1,3]([✉])

[1] State Key Laboratory of Information Security,
Institute of Information Engineering, Chinese Academy of Sciences,
Beijing 100093, China
{lihongwei,yangli}@iie.ac.cn
[2] School of Mathematics and Statistics, Henan Institute of Education,
Zhengzhou 450046, Henan, China
[3] Data Assurance and Communication Security Research Center,
Chinese Academy of Sciences, Beijing 100093, China
[4] University of Chinese Academy of Sciences, Beijing 100049, China

Abstract. Differential cryptanalysis is one of the most popular methods in attacking block ciphers. However, there are still some limitations in traditional differential cryptanalysis. On the other hand, researches of quantum algorithms have made great progress nowadays. This paper proposes two methods to apply quantum algorithms in differential cryptanalysis, and analysis their efficiencies and success probabilities. One method is using quantum algorithm in the high probability differential finding period for every S-Box. The second method is taking the encryption as a whole, using quantum algorithm in this process.

Keywords: Differential cryptanalysis · Quantum algorithm · Bernstein–Vazirani algorithm

1 Introduction

Differential cryptanalysis plays a central role in attacking modern crypto systems, especially in block ciphers [1]. Now, this method has been developed to various forms, such as truncated differential attack [2] and impossible differential attack [3]. However, current ciphers (such as AES) were designed along the wide trail strategy to resist differential cryptanalysis. On the other hand, quantum computation based on quantum mechanics has been built up, and has shown great speedups over classical computation in some areas. It is thus conceivable to use quantum algorithms in differential cryptanalysis.

Deutsch and Jozsa [4] presented a quantum algorithm to distinguish a balanced Boolean function from a constant function efficiently without error, which first show exponential speedup over classical algorithm. Using the same network as the above algorithm, Bernstein and Vazirani [5] gave a quantum algorithm to identity linear functions. Later, Simon [6] suggested a quantum algorithm for finding the period of a Boolean function. Inspired by Simon's algorithm, Shor [7]

© Springer-Verlag Berlin Heidelberg 2015
W. Niu et al. (Eds.): ATIS 2015, CCIS 557, pp. 44–51, 2015.
DOI: 10.1007/978-3-662-48683-2_5

discovered polynomial-time algorithms for factoring integers and solving discrete logarithms. Different from the above algorithms which rely on some promises of the problems, Grover's algorithm [8] searches a target element in an unsorted database and shows a quadratic speedup over the classical one.

In recent years, researches of quantum algorithm mainly focus on developments of the above mentioned algorithms. For example, there are quantum tests for whether a function has some properties or ϵ-far from it [9–11], and there are also quantum algorithms for learning of Boolean functions [9,12], but still with a promise that the Boolean functions belong to a small special set. Meanwhile, there are quantum polynomial algorithms to approximate some problems [13–15]. Amongst these algorithms, [15] gave an efficient algorithm to find some high probability differentials of a Boolean function. In [16], the authors gave quantum related-key attacks based on Simon's algorithm.

Our Contributions. Inspired by [15,16], using the result in [15], and combining with the classical differential cryptanalysis approach, we investigated the differential cryptanalysis based on quantum algorithm and gave quantum algorithms to implement the differential cryptanalysis.

In Contrast to Previous Works. In [17], the authors gave properties of an S-box and proposed a classical automatic approach to find (related-key) differential characteristics. Regarding the quantum differential cryptanalysis methods, one must mention [18], which presented a quantum differential cryptanalysis based on the quantum counting and searching algorithms, and obtained a quadratic speedup over classical one. Their quantum algorithm is used after the time that the differential characteristics has been found. Contrary to the above works, our quantum algorithms are to find the differential characteristics.

2   Preliminaries

In this section, we give some preliminaries and notations, which will be used in the following sections.

Let $F : \{0, 1\}^m \to \{0, 1\}^n$ be a multi-output Boolean function with input $x = (x_1, x_2, \cdots x_m)$ and output $y = (y_1, y_2, \cdots y_n)$, where m, n are both positive integers. Let $F(x') = y'$ and $F(x'') = y''$, then $\triangle x = x' \oplus x''$ and $\triangle y = y' \oplus y''$ are called the input difference and output difference, respectively, where $\oplus$ is the bit-wise exclusive-OR. Hence,

$$\triangle x = (\triangle x_1, \triangle x_2, \cdots \triangle x_m),$$

and

$$\triangle y = (\triangle y_1, \triangle y_2, \cdots \triangle y_n),$$

where $\triangle x_i = x_i' \oplus x_i''$ and $\triangle y_i = y_i' \oplus y_i''$. The pair $(\triangle x, \triangle y)$ is called a *differential*.

A *differential characteristic* is composed of input and output differences, where the input difference to one round is determined by the output difference of the last round.

2.1 Classical Differential Cryptanalysis

Differential cryptanalysis is a chosen-plaintext attack. It is usually used to attack various block ciphers. Roughly speaking, differential cryptanalysis is composed by two procedures:

1. Find some high probability differential characteristics.
2. According to the differential characteristics which have been found, test possible candidate subkey, then recover the key of the cryptosystem.

In this paper, our quantum algorithm is used at the first process. While in [18], their quantum algorithm was at the second stage.

2.2 The Bernstein–Vazirani Algorithm

Before showing the Bernstein–Vazirani algorithm, we first give the following definition:

Definition 1. *For a Boolean function* $f : \{0,1\}^m \to \{0,1\}$, *the Walsh transform of* f *is*

$$S_f(w) = \frac{1}{2^m} \sum_{x \in F_2^m} (-1)^{f(x)+w \cdot x} \tag{1}$$

for all $w \in F_2^m$.

Definition 2. *For a Boolean function* $f : \{0,1\}^m \to \{0,1\}$, *define the transform*

$$U_f|x\rangle|y\rangle = |x\rangle|y+f(x)\rangle. \tag{2}$$

note that U_f is unitary.

Now let us illustrate the Bernstein–Vazirani algorithm.

1. Input the initial state $|\psi_0\rangle = |0\rangle^{\otimes m}|1\rangle$, then do the Hadamard transform $H^{\otimes(m+1)}$, the result is

$$|\psi_1\rangle = \sum_{x \in F_2^m} \frac{|x\rangle}{\sqrt{2^m}} \cdot \frac{|0\rangle - |1\rangle}{\sqrt{2}}. \tag{3}$$

2. Evaluate f by using U_f, giving

$$|\psi_2\rangle = \sum_{x \in F_2^m} \frac{(-1)^{f(x)}|x\rangle}{\sqrt{2^m}} \cdot \frac{|0\rangle - |1\rangle}{\sqrt{2}}. \tag{4}$$

3. Execute the Hadamard transform $H^{\otimes(m)}$ on the first qubit of $|\psi_2\rangle$, we have

$$|\psi_3\rangle = \sum_{y \in F_2^m} \frac{1}{2^m} \sum_{x \in F_2^n} (-1)^{f(x)+y \cdot x}|y\rangle \cdot \frac{|0\rangle - |1\rangle}{\sqrt{2}}$$

$$= \sum_{y \in F_2^m} S_f(y)|y\rangle \cdot \frac{|0\rangle - |1\rangle}{\sqrt{2}}. \tag{5}$$

If we measure the first m qubit in the computational basis, we will obtain y with probability $S_f^2(y)$.

2.3 Results After Running the Bernstein–Vazirani Algorithm

In this section, we show that we will get some high probability differentials after running the Bernstein–Vazirani algorithm several times.

Theorem 1. *[15] For a Boolean function $f : \{0, 1\}^m \to \{0, 1\}$, let $p = p(m)$ be a polynomial of m. Assuming one has run the Bernstein–Vazirani algorithm p times, and has obtained a set S. Solving the linear systems of equations $S \cdot X = 0$ and $S \cdot X = 1$ respectively gives two sets A^0 and A^1. Then $\forall a \in A^i (i = 0, 1)$, $\forall \epsilon$, $0 < \epsilon < 1$,*

$$Pr \left(1 - \frac{|\{x \in F_2^m | f(x \oplus a) + f(x) = i\}|}{2^m} < \epsilon \right) > 1 - e^{-2p\epsilon^2}, \tag{6}$$

where $Pr(E)$ denotes the probability of the event E happens.

3 Quantum Algorithm to Execute Differential Cryptanalysis

Assume the plaintexts and the ciphertexts of the block cipher we would attack are of length $k = lm$, and every S-box is a map F from $\{0, 1\}^m$ to $\{0, 1\}^n$, where m, n, l are all positive integers. In the following we give two technics to implement quantum differential cryptanalysis.

3.1 The First Method

For every S-Box F, let $F = (f_1, \dots, f_n)$, where each $f_j (j = 1, \dots, n)$ is a Boolean function $\{0, 1\}^m$ to $\{0, 1\}$. For every f_j, run the Bernstein–Vazirani algorithm $p = p(m)$ times, and later solve a linear system of equations to get A_j^0 and A_j^1. If there exists $a \in A_1^{i_1} \cap A_2^{i_2} \cap \dots \cap A_n^{i_n}$, where $i_j \in \{0, 1\}$, $j = 1, 2, \dots, n$, then $(a, i_1 i_2 \dots i_n)$ is a high probability differential.

Algorithm 1.
Input: An S-Box $F = (f_1, \dots, f_n)$.
Output: Some high probability differentials of each $f_j (j = 1, 2, \dots, n)$.
1 Let $\mathcal{H} := \emptyset$, $\mathcal{A} := \emptyset$, where $\emptyset$ is the empty set.
2 for $j = 1, 2, \dots, n$ do
3   for $p = 1, 2, \dots, p(m)$ do
4   Run the Bernstein–Vazirani algorithm, and get an n-bit output w;
5   Let $\mathcal{H} := \mathcal{H} \cup \{w\}$
     end
6   Solve the equations $\mathcal{H}X = 0$ and $\mathcal{H}X = 1$ to get A_j^0 and A_j^1, respectively.
7   Output A_j^0 and A_j^1.
    end

After running the Algorithm 1, we obtain A_j^i ($j = 1, 2, \ldots, n$; $i = 0, 1$). In the following, we will analyse these sets to get some high probability differentials of a S-Box F.

We may choose first the $p(m) = cm$ (where c is a constant and $c \geq 2$) in Algorithm 1, since this can make every vector a in A_j^i ($j = 1, 2, \ldots, n$; $i = 0, 1$) satisfy

$$\frac{|\{x \in F_2^m | f_j(x \oplus a) + f_j(x) = i\}|}{2^m} > \frac{1}{2}$$

with high probability according to [15].

In other words, for any vector a in A_j^i ($j = 1, 2, \ldots, n$; $i = 0, 1$), (a, i) is a differential of f_j with the probability more than uniform distribution.

If most of the A_j^i ($j = 1, 2, \ldots, n$; $i = 0, 1$) have a great deal of vectors (for example, a half of the whole), then we will choose $p(m)$ to be more large (for example, $p(m) = m^2$). The purpose of doing this is to prevent $|A_j^i|$ (where $|A|$ denotes the cardinality of a set A) from being too large.

Otherwise we execute the following algorithm to find some high probability differentials of F.

Algorithm 2.
Input: A_j^i ($j = 1, 2, \ldots, n$; $i = 0, 1$).
Output: Some high probability differentials of F.
1 **for** each $a \in A_1^{i_1}$ ($i_1 = 0, 1$) **do**
2   **for** $j = 2, \ldots, n$ **do**
3   **for** $i_j = 0, 1$ **do**
4   **if** $a \in A_j^{i_j}$ **then**
                $(x_a, y_a) := (a, i_1 \ldots i_j)$
            end
        end
5   **else if** $a \notin A_j^0$ and $a \notin A_j^1$ **then**
            $(x_a, y_a) := (0, 0)$
            goto 6
    end
6   Output (x_a, y_a)
  end

The outputs of Algorithm 2 will be some vectors like $(a, i_1 \ldots i_n)$ or $(0, 0)$. Those non-zero vectors are the high probability differentials that we are looking for, which will be used to construct differential characteristics. For convenience, let $\mathcal{A}$ be the set of these non-zero vectors.

Next, complete the remaining works just as the classical differential cryptanalysis do.

Analysis of the First Method. Now, let us see the efficiency of the first method.

In Algorithm 1, the time of running the Bernstein–Vazirani algorithm (in order to evaluate the function F) is $np(m)$, and the time needed to solve the system of linear equations is $nq(m)$ (where $q(m)$ is another polynomial of m). So the total time of Algorithm 1 is $np(m) + nq(m)$.

The maximum time of running the Algorithm 2 is $O(2^n)$. In fact, this upper bound may be a little rough, because for some $a \in A_1^{i_1}$ ($i_1 = 0, 1$), they may be not in A_j^0 and A_j^1, where the j is much less than n.

Next, let us consider the success probability of the first method.

The vectors $(a, i_1 \ldots i_n) \in \mathcal{A}$ obtained by Algorithm 2 all satisfy the inequality (6) for every i_j and corresponding f_j ($j = 1, 2, \ldots, n$). The number of x satisfying

$$\frac{|\{x \in F_2^m | f_j(x \oplus a) + f_j(x) = i_j\}|}{2^m} = 1 - \epsilon \tag{7}$$

for two different $j = j_1$ and $j = j_2$ is at least $2(1 - \epsilon) - 1 = 1 - 2\epsilon$. From (6) and (7), we can know that

$$\Pr\left(\frac{|\{x \in F_2^m | F(x \oplus a) + F(x) = i_1 \ldots i_n\}|}{2^m} > 1 - n\epsilon \right) > (1 - e^{-2p\epsilon^2})^n. \tag{8}$$

From the above inequality (8), we see that if $\epsilon = \frac{1}{c_1 n}$ (where $c_1 \geq 2$ is a constant), $p = \frac{c_2}{\epsilon^2} = c_2 c_1^2 n^2$ (where $c_2 \geq 1 + \frac{\ln n}{2}$ is also a constant), then

$$(1 - e^{-2p\epsilon^2})^n \geq (1 - e^{-2c_2})^n \geq 1 - ne^{-2c_2} \geq 1 - \frac{1}{e^2} \tag{9}$$

In summary, let $p = \max\{p(m), c_2 c_1^2 n^2\}$, after a total time of $np + nq(m) + O(2^n)$, we will get a set $\mathcal{A}$ constituted by vectors like $(a, i_1 \ldots i_n)$, which satisfy

$$\Pr\left(\frac{|\{x \in F_2^m | F(x \oplus a) + F(x) = i_1 \ldots i_n\}|}{2^m} > 1 - \frac{1}{c_1} \right) > 1 - \frac{1}{e^2}. \tag{10}$$

As compared to the above quantum algorithm, the classical algorithm need 2^{m+n} times computation to give the difference distribution table, from which one can easily know some high probability differentials. Generally speaking, the S-Box used in a block cipher is not large, i.e., m and n are both small, so 2^{m+n} is very small too. In other words, evaluation of the difference distribution table is very efficient, our quantum algorithm does not show much speedup over the classical algorithm. However, that provide a new approach to the problem, and may throw light on some other questions.

The above method only focuses on each S-Box. In the following, we will give another method. The difference is it will focus on the entire process of the encryption.

3.2 The Second Method

Recall that the difficulty in the differential cryptanalysis is to construct high probability differential characteristics. And in the classical differential cryptanalysis, high probability differential characteristics are unambiguously given, from which S-Box to which S-Box. In fact, the purpose of doing that is to find which input differences will probably lead to which output differences. In the following, we will give a quantum algorithm to complete this.

Assume $G : \{0, 1\}^k \rightarrow \{0, 1\}^k$ is a function which maps the plaintext x to the input y of the last round under a secret key K. Certainly, G can be written as $G = (g_1, g_2, \ldots, g_k)$. Assume also there is a polynomial-size quantum circuit to evaluate G.

The Method 2 will be composed of the following procedures.

At first, run an algorithm similar to Algorithm 1. Nevertheless, the input to the algorithm is G instead of F, the outputs are some high probability differentials B_j^0 and B_j^1 of each g_j $(j = 1, 2, \ldots, k)$.

Secondly, operate an algorithm similar to Algorithm 2. The differences are the inputs, the procedures and the outputs. The inputs are B_j^0 and B_j^1 $(j = 1, 2, \ldots, k)$. The procedures do not include line 5. The outputs will be some high probability differentials $\mathcal{B} = \{(b, i_{j_1} \cdots i_{j_t})\}$, where $j_1, \cdots, j_t \in \{1, 2, \ldots, k\}$ and $j_1 < \cdots < j_t$.

The reason why we delete line 5 is that the purpose of Algorithm 2 is to find out some shared differentials of all f_j $(j = 1, 2, \ldots, n)$. If $a \notin A_j^0$ and $a \notin A_j^1$ for a j, then a must not their shared differential. At this time, breaking out of the loop is for saving time. What we do in the second method is to find some differentials of part g_j $(j = 1, 2, \ldots, k)$ sharing.

Thirdly, determine the subkey in the last round according to the differentials obtained.

Analysis of the Second Method. Let us consider the time complexity. In the first and second procedures, the running time are all polynomial of k. The time of the last procedure is determined by the high probability differentials we have obtained. If the probabilities of the differentials are very high, this method would probably succeed by using much less time. The superiority of this approach is that it avoid finding concrete high differential characteristics.

4   Discussions and Conclusions

Because high probability differential characteristics are independent of the subkey of every round, we can construct an efficient quantum circuit to find some of them. This paper proposes two methods for applying quantum algorithms to differential cryptanalysis. Although the first method does not show much speedup over classical method because the total number of the differences of an S-Box is not very large in practice, and the analysis of the second method is not very elaborate, these two methods give us a new clue to resolute the problem. Maybe they can be used in some ciphers and show much more speedups over classical approaches.

Acknowledgments. This work was supported by the National Natural Science Foundation of China under Grant No. 61173157.

References

1. Biham, E., Shamir, A.: Differential cryptanalysis of DES-like cryptosystems. J. Cryptology **4**(1), 3–72 (1991)
2. Knudsen, L.R.: Truncated and higher order differentials. In: Preneel, B. (ed.) FSE 1994. LNCS, vol. 1008, pp. 196–211. Springer, Heidelberg (1995)
3. Biryukov, A.: Impossible differential attack. In: van Tilborg, H.C.A., Jajodia, S. (eds.) Encyclopedia of Cryptography and Security, p. 597. Springer, New York (2011)
4. Deutsch, D., Jozsa, R.: Rapid solution of problems by quantum computation. In: Proceedings of the Royal Society of London, Volume A, vol. 439, pp. 553–558 (1992)
5. Bernstein, E., Vazirani, U.: Quantum complexity theory. In: Proceedings of the 25th Annual ACM Symposium on Theory of Computing, pp. 11–20. ACM Press, New York (1993)
6. Simon, D.R.: On the power of quantum computation. SIAM J. Comput. **26**, 1474–1483 (1997)
7. Shor, P.W.: Polynomial-time algorithm for prime factorization and discrete logarithms on quantum computer. SIAM J. Comput. **26**, 1484–1509 (1997). A primary version appeared in FOCS, 124–134 (1994)
8. Grover, L.K.: Quantum mechanics helps in searching for a needle in a haystack. Phys. Rev. Lett. **79**(2), 325–328 (1997)
9. Atici, A., Servedio, R.: Quantum algorithms for learning and testing juntas. Quantum Inf. Process. **6**(5), 323–348 (2007)
10. Chakraborty, S., Fischer, E., Matsliah, A., de Wolf., R.: New results on quantum property testing. In: FSTTCS, pp. 145–156 (2010)
11. Hillery, M., Anderson, E.: Quantum tests for the linearity and permutation invariance of Boolean functions. Phys. Rev. A **84**, 062326 (2011)
12. Floess, D., Andersson, E., Hillery, M.: Quantum algorithms for testing and learning Boolean functions. Math. Struct. Comp. Sci. **23**, 386–398 (2013)
13. Aharonov, D., Jones, V., Landau, Z.: A polynomial quantum algorithm for approximating the Jones polynomial. Algorithmica **55**, 395–421 (2009). Preliminary version in Proceedings of the 38th Annual ACM Symposium on Theory of Computing STOC, pp. 427–436 (2006)
14. Nakajima, Y., Kawano, Y., Sekigawa, H.: Efficient quantum circuits for approximating the Jones polynomial. Quantum Inf. Comput. **8**(5), 489–500 (2008)
15. Li, H.W., Yang, L.: A quantum algorithm to approximate the linear structures of Boolean functions. arXiv:1404.0611v2 [quant-ph], 20 Jan 2015
16. Roetteler, M., Steinwandt, R.: A note on quantum related-key attacks. Inf. Process. Lett. **115**, 40–44 (2015)
17. Sun, S., Hu, L., Wang, P., Qiao, K., Ma, X., Song, L.: Automatic security evaluation and (related-key) differential characteristic search: application to SIMON, PRESENT, LBlock, DES(L) and other bit-oriented block ciphers. In: Sarkar, P., Iwata, T. (eds.) ASIACRYPT 2014. LNCS, vol. 8873, pp. 158–178. Springer, Heidelberg (2014)
18. Zhou, Q., Lu, S.F., Zhang, Z.G., Sun, J.: Quantum differential cryptanalysis. Quantum Inf. Process. **14**(6), 2101–2109 (2015)

An Enhanced Authentication Scheme for Virtual Private Network Access Based on Platform Attributes of Multi-level Classification

Xun Chen[✉], Jiqiang Liu, Yanfeng Shi, and Zhen Han

Beijing Jiaotong University, Beijing China
{chenxun,jqliu,09112060,zhan}@bjtu.edu.cn

Abstract. Simple username and password are used as the only credential for virtual private network (VPN) access in most authentication schemes. The absence of strong security measures in user's platform invites attacks on integrity and confidentiality of data in private networks and consequently posts threats to other users who use the same VPN service. An authentication scheme based on verifying platform attributes is presented in this paper, which contains a notion of multi-level classification to satisfy different VPN systems. The implementation of the attribute expression and the authentication framework under an example of access policy is provided. Two cryptographic methods are introduced to achieve privacy protection in the network communication, including hash value conversion and attribute based encryption. Trusted computing is also included to guarantee the authenticity of platform attributes. This authentication scheme is distinctive that combines platform attributes with traditional credentials for VPN access attestation.

Keywords: Authentication · Classification · Platform attributes · VPN · ABE

1 Introduction

Virtual private network (VPN) has been used to access resources in private network through public area of internet for decades. The compromised platform environment is the major threat to the privacy of the information in private network. Sensitive data could possibly be stolen sneakily by malware and also could be tampered with once the compromised VPN client connects to private network. Most of credentials required to be authenticated are only simple username and password in nowadays commodity system, which is not sufficient to guarantee the trust of the platform. In this article, we study another security credential needed for authentication phase in VPN access, which is motivated by attacks on sensitive data through remote private network. With the existence of extended credential that verifies the platform integrity, while the correct traditional credential ensure the user's identity, the reliability of the existing authentication system can be enhanced.

There are lots of contributions about remote attestation that are related to our work. George and Maunier utilize the identification and integrity measurement mechanism of trusted platform module (TPM) to combine user and platform trust properties to enhance

© Springer-Verlag Berlin Heidelberg 2015
W. Niu et al. (Eds.): ATIS 2015, CCIS 557, pp. 52–64, 2015.
DOI: 10.1007/978-3-662-48683-2_6

VPN client authentication [1]. Liu's authentication scheme can authenticate the integrity of VPN using platform configuration mechanism of the TPM [2]. VIMS is based on virtualization technology and measures the integrity of the client virtual machine for remote attestation through the channel between an additional virtual machine and the hypervisor [3]. The remote attestation scheme using trusted network connect techniques is proposed by Bente et al. as in [4]. A third-party certification body which authenticates the identity and attribute certificates of the trusted platform is included in Liang's attestation scheme [5]. All the attributes mentioned in these solutions come from either the platform configuration registers of TPM or the integrity measurement results of loaded binaries. They can not authenticate other customized platform attributes. Yang indicates to use CP-ABE algorithm for dynamic remote attestation but the attributes Yang refers to are user related instead of platform attributes [6].

We aim to provide an additional methodology as an enhanced extension subsystem for VPN authentication system in order to make registration, management and utilization more convenient and efficient. Platform security status can be considered as one kind of credential that is related to the possibility of security impact on private network. In particular, we focus on what data needs to be collected and verified to guarantee the privacy and integrity of data in private network. Besides, to protect users' privacy, the collected security data should be converted into attribute data that can exactly report the security status of the VPN terminal and meanwhile the platform detailed information would not be exposed.

The next section describes some background knowledge involved in this paper. Then we define the problem as well as the threat model and assumptions in Sect. 3, and explain the design details in Sect. 4. Section 5 shows the implementation in detail, and Sect. 6 discusses the security and performance analysis. Finally, we make conclusion in Sect. 7.

2 Preliminaries

2.1 VPN

Virtual Private Network (VPN) allows a computer send or receive data across shared or public networks as if it is directly connected to the private network [7]. Remote access is achieved by VPN gateway through encrypting data package and transforming package address. By using this technology, data can be transferred securely and reliably even across the insecure network.

Other kinds of encrypted internet protocol are used for some websites instead of VPN, such as Secure Hypertext Transfer Protocol (HTTPS). Data are also transferred in cyphertext mode. The authentication scheme provided by this article can be utilized in these protocols as well.

The Internet Key Exchange (IKE) protocol can be used to ensure the security of VPN negotiation [8]. It was defined in IKEv2 that the shared key used to encrypt data before transmitting in VPN channel is computed from shared secret generated by the client and the sever. The shared secret to be sent to the opposite side will be encrypted using ABE (Attribute Based Encryption) method, which will be further discussed in the rest part of this paper.

2.2 Platform Security Attributes

Platform security attributes are extracted information that reflects how secure the platform is. Here are some examples. For PC, platform security attributes may contain antivirus software information, firewall status, background malicious software status, etc. For mobile phone, privileged control ability (jailbreak or root access status) may be one of the concerns. These attribute data are collected to form a list of values to represent the security status of the platform.

2.3 Attribute Based Encryption

Attribute based encryption (ABE), which was first proposed by Sahai and Waters in 2005 [9], is designed to encrypt a data blob that is allowed to decrypt by a group of users with particular attributes. It's a kind of fuzzy identity based encryption. The sender uses a combination of attributes as the public key for encryption. The private key is generated by authorized agency according to receiver's attributes and then is assigned to the receiver so as to do the decryption. ABE is used to encrypt the message happened in authentication, which will be discussed in detail later in this paper.

3   Problem Definition

3.1   Our Goals

There are lots of approaches proposed to make the authentication secure and stable [10–12]. But most of them are aiming at the user's identification. However, the valid identification doesn't stand for harmlessness to the private network. A compromised remote computer will be a threat and might spread malwares into the private network [13]. Therefore, in this article, we mainly focus on the security status of the platform. Specifically, we collect platform security attributes which will be used as the extended credential for VPN connection along with the user's identification.

3.2   Threat Model and Assumptions

In our threat model, we consider the malicious software residing in the VPN terminal and the insiders as the adversary. The malware or the insiders may access any sensitive data transferred from remote system after the establishment of VPN connection. They can also attack the target system through the VPN connection as they do in the same network [14]. As a result, both the privacy and the integrity of the target system will be at risk because of the unsafe VPN connection establishment.

We assume the malware can not subvert the underlying data transferred through network interface. Since the platform security attributes data are sent to VPN server for authentication along with the user password, some kernel level malware may manipulate the attributes data to meet the security requirements so that the compromised VPN terminal can still pass the verification. In addition, some proposed white list based startup mechanism can be applied to forbid the malware from running [15].

4   Design

4.1   Authentication Scheme Overview

In our scheme the platform attributes collected by VPN terminal are verified by VPN authentication server along with the user token. The user token reflects the VPN user is the identified person while the platform attributes illustrate the computing environment meets the security requirements. Security requirements are different from various application scenarios. For example, the firewall must be launched for a player who wants to join a video game competition while the digital rights management (DRM) software must be installed for an audience who wants to watch some local television series using VPN. Therefore, the classification of the security requirements is necessary, which will be discussed in Sect. 4.3 in details. After validating the platform attributes according to the appropriate policy generated from security requirements classification, the VPN server returns the authentication result to the VPN terminal and then the terminal determines whether VPN access is allowed. In our scheme, only the trusted terminal can successfully pass the authentication. The data transmission in this trusted VPN channel could be considered as more secure.

4.2   Platform Attributes Extraction

The authentication result depends on the collected platform attributes. The variety could be vast and different in many application scenarios. The VPN service provider could define its own specification of extracting platform attributes to meet the security requirements. In this section an example based on our previous work [16] is provided. Platform attributes could consist of contents as follows:

Operating System. The operating system that users use to access the VPN should be widely considered secure enough. Older version of commodity operating system has more vulnerabilities. The Microsoft Windows operating system has an enormously large number of users of desktop or laptop computer. Windows 7, which has mature mechanism for isolating applications, sessions and services, is considered as more secure than any other older windows operating system. Thus the attribute here is that the version of windows operating system should be windows 7 or above.

Operating System Updates. No system is born as perfect. New system updates are produced constantly whenever new vulnerabilities are discovered. Hence, the VPN terminal must provide the full list of installed operating system updates to the server so as to determine the platform's security level.

Commodity Secure Software. Commodity secure software may include anti-virus software, firewall, and any other software that helps to make the computer more secure. The existence (e.g., the anti-virus software is installed) and status (e.g., the database of anti-virus is up to date) could be part of the platform attributes.

Trusted Processes. The VPN server must ensure that there is no malware running on the platform before the user access the confidential information in the private network. This could be achieved by various proposed approaches [17, 18]. For example, we use the white list based process verification. The server verifies the client's currently running applications services, and even kernel modules.

Other kinds of status could also be regarded as platform attributes, such as isolation situation, virtualization state, and other desired conditions that is related to the specific business system.

4.3 Security Requirements Classification

It's not necessary for every VPN terminal to meet all the security requirements. The VPN access could be authorized as long as they reach the minimum requirements. For example, a user wants to join the video game competition that is only for local players. He decides to use VPN to become a valid player. It's not necessary for him to meet the highest secure level, such as installing all the OS updates. Classification method is adopted in this article to classify the requirements into different security levels. From the lowest to the highest, IT managers can choose the appropriate level that contains only the most necessary platform attributes for the VPN access requirements.

The security level among thousands of VPN systems should be different. Here we put forward an example of detailed classification upon platform attributes given in Sect. 4.2. In this example, there are 4 levels that have more secure requirements one after another, which are demonstrated in Table 1.

Table 1. An example of security requirements classification

Application scenarios	Anti-virus software	Firewall	OS version	OS updates	Trusted processes
Individual	✓				
Academic organizations	✓	✓			
Enterprises	✓	✓		Important level and above	
Government offices	✓	✓	Windows 7 or above	Business related	✓

Individual. Checking the anti-virus software might be sufficient for personal usage.

Academic Organizations. The anti-virus software with latest virus database and the firewall installed are required for members in school or research institute. Some DRM software or auto-encrypting system could also be necessary for further protection against manually propagating secret data.

Enterprises. People such as staffs who are on business trip need to achieve the requirements in the Table 1 so as to prevent leaks of enterprise's confidential data.

Government Offices. If it is allowed to remotely access government resource through the internet for a part of government staffs, the VPN terminal must be at the top security level to protect the classified data.

All the platform attributes mentioned above could be alternative for authentication before the VPN access in different scenarios. Other requirements can be chosen as platform attributes as well, which could be further refined in more levels of security requirements.

5 Implementation

In this section, we mainly talk about how we use the platform attributes for VPN authentication along with the traditional user tokens, the username and the password. Based on the classification example mentioned in Sect. 4.3, we choose the top secure level that includes all the requirements mentioned in Table 1 for implementation.

5.1 Platform Attributes Expression

The platform attributes details need to be converted before reporting to the server to protect user's privacy. Instead of reporting the detailed information, hash value is one of the appropriate options because of its irreversible calculation. The operating system version can be hashed directly since the server has stored some hash values of all valid OS versions. The anti-virus and the firewall status information can be combined into a 16-bit or 32-bit value and then can also be converted into a hash value.

For OS updates, a collection of hash values of each OS updates ID are calculated and reported to the VPN server. The server will check whether every required hash value exists in the collection.

For currently launched process information, the corresponding file binary data is converted into a hash value. To match precisely, we combine the file name, the hash value of the binary data and the file size together and do the hash calculation one more time to form a final hash value.

After extracting the entire platform attributes information, a group of hash values are reported to the VPN server. It is difficult for side channel attackers to obtain the detailed information of the VPN client.

5.2 Remote Authentication Framework

The prototype of the VPN client we present consists of the platform scanning module and the chrome plugin, as shown in Fig. 1. The platform scanning module is in charge of extracting the platform security attributes information. When a user tries to sign in the VPN system in the browser, the chrome plugin will retrieve the attributes data from the platform scanning module and send to the VPN attestation server together with the username and the password. After validating all the presented information, the VPN client will finally setup the VPN connection. If the client doesn't meet the security requirements, the chrome plugin will prompt the verification result and suggest which attributes need to be improved.

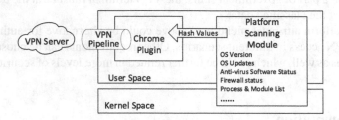

Fig. 1. The remote authentication framework

5.3 ABE Based Authentication

Under some certain circumstances, a user doesn't want the service provider to know about his detailed attribute information. Similarly, an administrator perhaps doesn't want anyone knows which particular attributes are included in server's authentication policy. Even though the attribute information is transformed into hash values before the report, the malicious server may figure out the particular attributes because a list of attribute mapping must have existed in the server. Malicious clients might successfully guess the entire authentication policy by means of repeated attempts. Besides, some side channel attackers might record the required attributes and perform replay attacks to pass through the authentication. Hence, we introduce the attribute based encryption method for further enhancement of authentication.

The shared session secrets from which VPN cryptographic keys are derived is encrypted using ABE during the key exchange phase of VPN connection establishment. The server encrypts one of the shared session secrets according to the policy that contains the required attributes. Only the client that owns all the attribute values has the ability to decrypt the secret. An example of the attributes is illustrated in Table 2.

The method to use these attributes in ABE are different, which is discussed as below. For OS version, the client's corresponding attribute must be one of the string. After scanning the running status of third party security software, the flag of anti_virus_up2date and firewall_on can be provided. If the client were able to decrypt the secret, the client's list of installed OS updates must contain all the items defined in the encryption policy. Note that the set of the client's installed OS updates U_C and the set of the OS updates in the encryption policy defined by the server U_S satisfy $U_S \subseteq U_C$.

We can see that the relation is just opposite for the attribute of trusted processes, which makes the authentication more complicated. The set of the client's processes waiting for validated is called P_C while the list of trusted processes in the encryption policy defined by the server is called P_S. If the client meets the requirement that all the programs the client runs are trusted processes, P_C and P_S satisfy $P_C \subseteq P_S$. This can be achieved by using reverse authentication. The client encrypts the other shared session secret using another ABE policy, which contains P_C, and sends it to the server. We can say P_C and P_S satisfy $P_C \subseteq P_S$ if the server who has the attributes of P_S were able to decrypt the shared session.

Table 2. An example of attributes used in CPABE toolkit

Attributes	Content	Expression
OS version	Windows 7 6.10.7600	Windows_7_6.10.7600
	Windows Server 2008 R2 6.10.7600	Windows_Server_2008_R2_6.10.7600
	Windows Server 2008 SP2 6.00.6002	Windows_Server_2008_SP2_6.00.6002
Security software	anti_virus_up2date	anti_virus_up2date
	firewall_on	firewall_on
Trusted processes	demo_file.exe	PROCESS_E222E4FD9DB41 06BA359A71593AAE62E
	demo_file.dll	PROCESS_70AE71F9C80267 C8C02A0BE2D8DE1DDD
	…	…
OS updates	MS11-022 (KB2920812)	MS11_034
	MS15-035 (KB3046306)	MS15_035
	…	…

After correctly decrypting the two session secrets, both of the client and the server can calculate the cryptographic key needed for the VPN channel. The final VPN cryptographic keys will be different from each other as long as any of the client's attributes is incorrect, which will lead to the failure of the VPN connection establishment. The entire authentication protocol using ABE is illustrated in Figs. 2 and 3. Note that the public key and the master key in Fig. 2 are encrypted using a symmetric key K, which will be discussed in Sect. 5.4.

5.4 Trusted Computing Based Attributes

The truth that the client actually own the required attributes can be guaranteed by utilizing the trusted computing techniques. A trusted computing chip, such as TPM, can veritably report the platform's status information. In our implementation, the symmetric key which is issued by the VPN service provider at the service registration step is well protected by the TPM and will be used for decrypting both of the public key and the

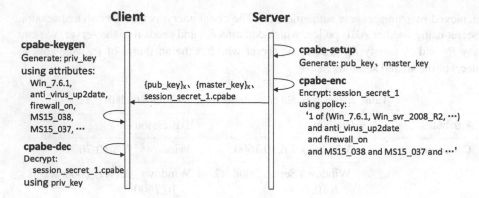

Fig. 2. The ABE protocol for authenticating the most of the attributes

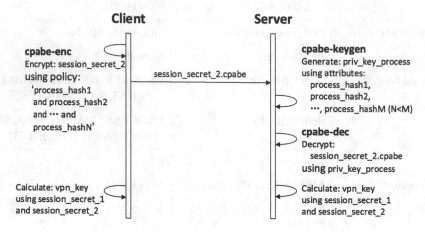

Fig. 3. The ABE protocol for authenticating the attribute of trusted processes

master key sent from the authentication server. Thus, side channel attackers can not obtain the master key in plaintext for later private key generating. At the same time, only the valid client that meets the requirements of the TPM is able to decrypt the symmetric key.

The symmetric key is protected by TPM in the method described as follows. When the user signs up for the VPN service, the registration server generates a symmetric key and issues to the client. The symmetric key is safely sealed by TPM using the TPM command TPM_Seal, which encrypts the symmetric key inside of TPM and binds to the PCRs in right state. The right state is defined in our implementation that only the client with the control system installed and the control system is the first process to start after the OS kernel is loaded. Only under this circumstance can the symmetric key be obtained to correctly decrypt both of the public key and the master key so as to exactly generate the private key for ABE based authentication. Therefore, the validity of the platform's attributes can be guaranteed with the support of trusted computing.

6 Analysis

We analyze the practicability of the authentication scheme from the security and the performance aspect.

6.1 Security Analysis

The platform scanning module consists of 2 parts which run both in kernel space and user space. Specifically the kernel module runs as a windows driver which is launched with the windows kernel so that every driver that the OS kernel loads will be logged. The same happens in the user space. Therefore, every program and its binary data will be recorded from the moment OS starts. The entire list of process hash values demonstrates the trust of the VPN client and will affect the attestation result. The VPN server will reject the access as long as any untrusted process is ever launched.

A VPN terminal may be considered as trusted if all the platform attributes meet the security requirements for a period of time. But some time later when its virus knowledge database is out of date or when some new operating system updates are released, the VPN attestation will fail to avoid the impact of new discovered malware. In another case of some zero-day attack, the VPN server has a list of trusted processes which doesn't contain the hash value of the unknown malware.

As discussed in Sect. 5.3, directly transferring hash values might not defend from some side channel attacks. The attacker might pass the platform attributes based authentication by providing the same hash values sniffed from other authorized terminal. Nevertheless, this kind of exploitation can be fixed by cooperating with some other techniques, such as adding salt values. On the other hand, ABE based authentication defends against side channel attacks effectively as the result of ABE's design that nothing else transferred except the encrypted session secrets, which vary from every authentication. Hence, replay attack methods won't work. Besides, malicious clients are unable to guess what the server's attribute policy includes from the data they have received. Even if the malicious client once passed the authentication, it will fail in the next attempt if it tries to forge the same attributes it doesn't own because of the support of trusted computing based techniques.

In order to generate the correct ABE private key, both public key and master key are needed. These keys are sent from server and encrypted using the symmetric key, which is safely sealed in client's TPM. The sealed key can only be decrypted by this particular TPM when it is in a correct environment. When the control system starts as the first process after the OS kernel is loaded, the specific PCR value of the TPM is correctly extended to ensure the integrity of the control system. Thus, the control system can unseal the symmetric key under this correct state. After that, the PCR value will change and other application will no longer decrypt the key. As a result, the control system will guarantee the use of real attributes in authentication phase.

6.2 Performance Analysis

Compared with the traditional VPN authentication scheme, the addition calculation in our scheme contains the extraction and the transmission of the platform attributes data.

During the windows starting procedure, the attributes extraction has already started. The OS version, the installed OS updates and the security software status can be obtained by some windows management mechanism such as WMI query, register query. The hash calculation of launched processes takes place whenever the process loads. The time cost by these actions is short and doesn't greatly affect the OS start procedure. Instead, the extra delay happening in VPN login procedure is the major concern.

The data for transmission contain a list of hash values. The information of OS version and the security software status is the small amount of data, which is only 2 hash values. Most of the data needed to be transmitted are the installed OS updates and the launched processes. According to [19], the total number of all the product updates bulletined by the Microsoft is no more than 1300 since 1998 to April 2015. In the worst situation, if the VPN client has installed all the updates, the size of the hash value data is around 20 KB. We assume that the VPN client has launched 100 processes and each of them loads 20 different modules. The number of hash values is around 2000 and the size of the data is around 32 KB. Therefore, the size of all the data reported to the VPN server will not be big.

Another concern about the additional time spent in authentication is the duration of server verification. We experimented with a query example on a workstation with Intel(R) Core(TM) i5 CPU M520 @2.40 GHz, 4 GB main memory, running Windows 7 Professional. In the query example, the sample list containing 2000 hash values was checked whether all the hash values exist in the white list library that contains 600,000 items of hash value. Without utilizing any optimized algorithm, which is not discussed in this paper, the hash values were compared one by one and the number of comparing times was 1.2 billion. The whole process cost 947 ms in average. So we can conclude under this scheme the additional authentication work will not cost much time.

However, the performance of ABE based authentication is worse than hash values transferring based scheme. We used the cpabe toolkit mentioned in [20] for reference in our implementation and gave some performance measurements. In the ABE based authentication protocol, running cpabe-keygen, cpabe-enc and cpabe-dec costs most of the time. We assumed the attributes of client contained 240 OS updates and 2000 hash values of different programs. The attribute policy of server contained 230 OS updates and 35000 hash values of different programs. Using the same workstation mentioned above, the average time cost by cpabe-enc, cpabe-keygen and cpabe-dec in Fig. 2 were 3.6 s, 3.6 s and 2.0 s. The average time cost by cpabe-enc, cpabe-keygen and cpabe-dec in Fig. 3 were 37.2 s, 638.9 s and 31.9 s. Considering the phase cpabe-keygen in Fig. 3 can be executed in the initial work of server, which generates the private key according to the process white list, the time cost in this phase is not included in authentication. So the total time cost by ABE based authentication was 78.3 s. This authentication overhead is intolerable for most authentication systems but might be endurable for some special application scenarios in which people don't hope any leakage of platform attributes, e.g., classified network. So the ABE based authentication is safe but not efficient enough for most cases.

7   Conclusion

We have proposed an enhanced platform attribute based authentication scheme in which the security requirements could be classified in multi-level. The appropriate level of requirements could be chosen for different application scenario according to its access policy. This authentication scheme could be adapted for VPN access or referenced in other attestation system. To protect user's privacy and make the whole authentication process more effective, platform attribute data are transformed into a collection of hash values before reporting to VPN server for verifying. To further protect the privacy of both side, the attribute based encryption method is introduced to achieve secure authentication while hiding attribute information in the communication channel. By using trusted computing related technology, attributes can never be forged to meet the access requirements. The security can be guaranteed for both hash values transferring based authentication and ABE based scheme. The ABE based scheme is better from the result of security analysis. However, the performance analysis illustrates that the hash values transferring based scheme is more efficient in most cases. After comparing with others' related works, our solution could be considered as the distinctive authentication scheme using platform attributes along with traditional credentials.

Acknowledgements. We gratefully thank the anonymous reviews for their valuable feedback. This research was supported by the National Natural Science Foundation of China (NSFC) under grants No. 61502030. Any opinions, findings, and conclusions expressed in this material are those of the authors and do not necessarily reflect the views of the NSFC.

References

1. George, P., Maunier, G.: Combining user and platform trust properties to enhance VPN client authentication. Secur. Manage. **5**, 297–303 (2005)
2. Liu, H.-w., Wei, G.-b.: Application of trusted computing compliance in VPN. J. Comput. Appl. **12**, 2935–2937 (2006)
3. Baiardi, F., Cilea, D., Sgandurra, D., Ceccarelli, F.: Measuring semantic integrity for remote attestation. In: Chen, L., Mitchell, C.J., Martin, A. (eds.) Trust 2009. LNCS, vol. 5471, pp. 81–100. Springer, Heidelberg (2009)
4. Bente, I., Hellmann, B., Vieweg, J., von Helden, J., Welzel, A.: Interoperable remote attestation for VPN environments. In: Chen, L., Yung, M. (eds.) INTRUST 2010. LNCS, vol. 6802, pp. 302–315. Springer, Heidelberg (2011)
5. Liang, Y., Guo, K., Li, J.: The remote attestation design based on the identity and attribute certificates. In: 11th International Computer Conference on Wavelet Active Media Technology and Information Processing, pp. 325–330. IEEE (2014)
6. Yang, S. Y.: Dynamic remote attestation on CP-ABE algorithm. In: Applied Mechanics and Materials, pp. 259–265. Trans Tech Publications (2015)
7. Mason, A.: CCSP Self-Study: Cisco Secure Virtual Private Networks. Pearson Higher Education (2004)
8. Internet key exchange (IKEv2) protocol. RFC 4306 (Proposed Standard). https://tools.ietf.org/html/rfc4306
9. Sahai, A., Waters, B.: Fuzzy identity-based encryption. In: Cramer, R. (ed.) EUROCRYPT 2005. LNCS, vol. 3494, pp. 457–473. Springer, Heidelberg (2005)
10. Thanh, P.N., Kim, K.: A methodology for implementation and integration two-factor authentication into VPN. In: IEEE 31st International Performance Computing and Communications Conference, pp. 195–196. IEEE (2012)

11. Pan, T., Xu, C., Hu, D., Li, Y., Wang, Y.: A proxy type identity authentication scheme based on SSL VPN. In: Proceedings of the 2013 Fifth International Conference on Multimedia Information Networking and Security, pp. 9–12. IEEE Computer Society (2013)

12. Jeong, J., Chung, M.Y., Choo, H.: Integrated OTP-based user authentication scheme using smart cards in home networks. In: Proceedings of the 41st Annual Hawaii International Conference on System Sciences, pp. 294–294. IEEE (2008)

13. Schiller, E.I., Luminita, D.C.C.: SSL VPN security issues. Global J. Technol. **2**, 120–126 (2012)

14. Insider threat control: using a SIEM signature to detect potential precursors to IT sabotage. http://www.cert.org/archive/pdf/SIEM-Control.pdf

15. Li, X.-Y., Zuo, X.-D., Shen, C.-X.: System behavior based trustworthiness attestation for computing platform. Acta Electronica Sinica **35**, 1234 (2007)

16. Chen, X., Han, Z., Liu, J.-Q.: Data protection technology in classified networks. J. Univ. Electron. Sci. Technol. Chin. **42**, 144–149 (2013)

17. Zhao, B., Zhang, H., Guo, H., Qi, Y.: White list security management mechanism based on trusted computing technology. System **1**, 6 (2015)

18. Simpson, A.K., Schear, N., Moyer, T.: Runtime integrity measurement and enforcement with automated whitelist generation. IEEE Trans. **8**, 1230–1242 (2013)

19. Microsoft security bulletin. https://technet.microsoft.com/en-us/security/bulletin/

20. Bethencourt, J., Sahai, A., Waters, B.: Ciphertext-policy attribute-based encryption. In: IEEE Symposium on Security and Privacy, pp. 321–334. IEEE (2007)

Public Key Timed-Release Attribute-Based Encryption

Ke Yuan[1], Nan Shen[2], Yonghang Yan[1(✉)], Zheli Liu[2], and Chufu Jia[2]

[1] School of Computer and Information Engineering,
Henan University, Kaifeng 475004, China
yanyonghang@henu.edu.cn
[2] College of Computer and Control Engineering,
Nankai University, Tianjin 300071, China

Abstract. This paper introduces and explores a new concept of public key timed-release attribute-based encryption (PKTRABE) which can be used to solve the time-dependent ABE problem. In our PKTRABE model, the sender encrypts a message so that only the intended receivers who own some specified attributes can decrypt it after a specified time in the future. We begin by explaining what is PKTRABE. Then, we formalize the notion of basic PKTRABE and its security game model. Finally, we give two concrete schemes which are secure under the BDH and DBDH assumption in the random oracle model. Conclusions and future work are also summarized.

Keywords: Timed-release · Attribute-based encryption · Time trapdoor · Bilinear map

1 Introduction

Attribute-based encryption (ABE) is a new type of identity-based encryption (IBE) where identity is viewed as a set of descriptive attributes. In ABE, a user's public key and ciphertexts are labeled with sets of descriptive attributes and a particular private key can decrypt a particular ciphertext only if there is a match between the attributes of the ciphertext and the target user's public key. Further more, the target receiving entity of ABE cryptosystem is a user group whose each member's exact identity needn't to be known by the sender, rather than a single user. Along with the development of research, the ABE scheme can provide more and more powerful methods to achieve both multi-receiver data security and fine-grained access control. Time has always played an important role in time-sensitive practical applications, but the research work of time-relevant ABE has not been carried out so far. The property of time here means to encrypt a message such that the receiver cannot decrypt the ciphertext until a specific time in the future. This is called timed-release encryption (TRE). For solving the problem of time-relevant ABE, we propose a new concept of public key timed-release attribute-based encryption which is abbreviated as PKTRABE. PKTRABE is

© Springer-Verlag Berlin Heidelberg 2015
W. Niu et al. (Eds.): ATIS 2015, CCIS 557, pp. 65–73, 2015.
DOI: 10.1007/978-3-662-48683-2_7

a combination of TRE and ABE. In our PKTRABE cryptosystem, the sender uses a user group's attributes set to encrypt a message with a release time so that only the intended member can decrypt the target ciphertext after a pre-set release time in the future.

1.1 Our Contributions

The contribution of this paper is to solve the time-dependent ABE problem by combining the existing cryptographic mechanism TRE and basic ABE. Firstly, we formalizes the notion of PKTRABE and its security game model. Secondly, we proposes two provably secure constructions of PKTRABE which are secure under the BDH and DBDH assumption in the random oracle model. The former focuses on the single time server scenarios while the latter pays attention to the multiple time servers scenarios.

1.2 Related Work

We give a brief overview of the TRE and the ABE as follows:

TRE allows a sender to encrypt a message so that only the intended receiver can decrypt it only after a pre-set time. The problem of TRE was first advocated by May [11] in 1993 and demonstrated in detail by Rivest et al. [12] in 1996. And since then, extraordinary progress has been made in its theory and practice. In theoretical aspect, some new concepts of TRE was proposed in succession. The first attempt at scalable, server-passive, user-anonymous TRE was due to Chan and Blake [4] and the first try at TRE with pre-open capability was due to Hwang et al. [8] in 2005. Afterwards, Cheon et al. [6] formalize the concept of a secure public key TRE in 2008. More recently, Unruh [14] proposed revocable quantum TRE in 2014. In practical aspect, TRE has been utilized in oblivious transfer [10] and searchable encryption [15].

ABE allows users to encrypt and decrypt messages based on user attributes. The cryptology mechanism of ABE was first proposed by Sahai and Waters [13] in 2005. This original ABE is less efficient and cannot provide fine-grained access control. To solve these problems, many revisions and extensions have been given. Baek et al. [1] gives two more efficient ABE schemes in 2007. Goyal et al. [7] proposed key-policy ABE in 2006. Bethencourt et al. [2] proposed ciphertext-policy ABE and Chase [5] proposed multi-authority ABE in 2007. More recently, Li et al. [9] introduced secure outsourcing techniques into ABE in 2013.

1.3 Organization

We begin by explaining what is PKTRABE. In Sect. 2 we review our security assumptions. In Sect. 3 We formalize the notion of PKTRABE and its security game model. In Sects. 4 and 5 we provide two concrete construction schemes for PKTRABE respectively. Finally, we conclude in Sect. 6.

2   Preliminaries

Below, we briefly review the definitions of bilinear map and discuss the complexity assumption on which the security of our schemes are based.

2.1   Bilinear Maps

Let $\mathcal{G}_1$ and $\mathcal{G}_2$ be two multiplicative cyclic groups of order p for some large prime p. A bilinear map is a map $e : \mathcal{G}_1 \times \mathcal{G}_1 \to \mathcal{G}_2$ satisfies the following properties:

- Computable: There is an efficient algorithm to compute $e(g, h) \in \mathcal{G}_2$ for any $g, h \in \mathcal{G}_1$.
- Bilinear: For any integers $a, b \in \mathbb{Z}_p^*$ we have $e(g^a, h^b) = e(g, h)^{ab}$.
- Non-degenerate: If g is a generator of $\mathcal{G}_1$ then $e(g, g)$ is a generator of $\mathcal{G}_2$.

2.2   Complexity Assumptions

The BDH problem [3] in $\mathcal{G}_1$ is as follows: given a tuple $g, g^a, g^b, g^c \in \mathcal{G}_1$ as input, output $e(g, g)^{abc} \in \mathcal{G}_2$. An attacker $\mathcal{A}$ has advantage ϵ in solving BDH in $\mathcal{G}_1$ if

$$\Pr[\mathcal{A}(g, g^a, g^b, g^c) = e(g, g)^{abc}] \geq \epsilon$$

where the probability is over the random choice of generator $g \in \mathcal{G}_1^*$, the random choice of $a, b, c \in \mathbb{Z}_p^*$, and the random bits used by $\mathcal{A}$.

Similarly, we say that an challenger $\mathcal{B}$ that has advantage ϵ in solving the Decisional BDH (DBDH) problem in $\mathcal{G}_1$ if

$$|\Pr[\mathcal{B}(g, g^a, g^b, g^{c,e}(g, g)^{abc}) = 0]$$
$$-\Pr[\mathcal{B}(g, g^a, g^b, g^c, \mathcal{T}) = 0]| \geq \epsilon$$

where the probability is over the random choice of generator $g \in \mathcal{G}_1^*$, the random choice of $a, b, c \in \mathbb{Z}_p^*$, the random choice of $\mathcal{T} \in \mathcal{G}_1$, and the random bits consumed by $\mathcal{B}$.

Definition 1. *We say that (Decisional) (t, ϵ)-BDH assumption holds in $\mathcal{G}_1$ if no t-time algorithm has advantage at least ϵ in solving the (Decisional) BDH problem in $\mathcal{G}_1$.*

Occasionally we drop the t and ϵ and refer to the BDH and DBDH assumptions in $\mathcal{G}_1$.

3   PKTRABE: Definitions

Suppose Bob as a professor needs to arrangement an online exam in next Monday for all students of the Computer Science Department of Computer College of Henan University, but unfortunately, he has to go to an important meeting from next Monday to next Wednesday. In such case, Bob can adopt PKTRABE mechanism to solve his problem. Bob sends the following message in advance:

$$[Enc(ID', ts_{pub}, r, M, T), T)$$

where $ID' = ($ *"Computer Science Department"*, *"Computer College"*, *"Henan University"*$)$ is the target user group's common identity attributes set, ts_{pub} is the public key of the time server, r is a random fresh factor, M is the test questions, T is the release time. All the intended students can get the ciphertext in advance and decrypt it after the pre-set release time in the future. We call such a system non-interactive PKTRABE.

Definition 2. *A non-interactive basic PKTRABE scheme with single time server consists of the following polynomial time randomized algorithms:*

Setup. Takes a security parameter, and generates master key mk and public parameters *params* which contains an error tolerance parameter d.

TRSetup. Generates public/private key (ts_{pub}, ts_{priv}) of the time server.

KeyGen. Given the master key mk and an identity ID as input, generates a private key associated with ID, denoted by D_{ID}.

Enc. For public key ID', ts_{pub}, a release time T and a plaintext M, produces a ciphertext (C, T).

RtTrd. Given the time server's private key ts_{priv} and a release time T, produces a time trapdoor S_T.

Dec. Given the private key D_{ID}, the time trapdoors S_T and the ciphertext (C, T) encrypted with an identity ID' such that $ID \bigcap ID' \geq d$, generates the plaintext M or a "Reject" message.

Formally, we define security against an active attacker using the simulation game between a challenger $\mathcal{B}$ and the attacker $\mathcal{A}$ as follows:

Initialization. The adversary $\mathcal{A}$ outputs an identity ID^* and a release time T^* where it wishes to be challenged.

Setup. The challenger $\mathcal{B}$ generates the public parameters *params* and ts_{pub}, sends them to $\mathcal{A}$.

Phase 1. The adversary $\mathcal{A}$ issues queries $q_1, q_2, \ldots, q_m$ where query q_i is one of:

1. Private key query (ID_i) where $ID_i \bigcap ID^* < d$. $\mathcal{B}$ responds by running algorithm *KeyGen* to generate the private key D_{ID_i} corresponding to the identity ID_i. $\mathcal{B}$ sends D_{ID_i} to $\mathcal{A}$.
2. Time trapdoor query (T_i) where $T_i \neq T^*$. $\mathcal{B}$ responds by running algorithm *RtTrd* to generate the time trapdoor S_{T_i} corresponding to the release time T_i. $\mathcal{B}$ sends S_{T_i} to $\mathcal{A}$.

3. Decryption query (C_i, T_i) for identity ID^* and release time T^*. $\mathcal{B}$ runs algorithm Dec to decrypt the ciphertext (C_i, T_i) using the private key D_{ID_i} and time trapdoor S_{T_i}. $\mathcal{B}$ sends the plaintext M to $\mathcal{A}$.

These queries may be asked adaptively; that is, each query q_i may depend on the replies to $q_1, q_2, \ldots, q_{i-1}$.

Challenge: $\mathcal{A}$ outputs two equal length plaintexts $M_0, M_1 \in \mathcal{G}_2$ on which it wishes to be challenged. $\mathcal{B}$ picks a random bit $b \in \{0, 1\}$ and sets the challenge ciphertext to $(C^*, T^*) = Enc(ID^*, ts_{pub}, r, M, T^*)$. $\mathcal{B}$ sends (C^*, T^*) as the challenge to $\mathcal{A}$.

Phase 2: $\mathcal{A}$ issues additional queries $q_{m+1}, \ldots, q_{num}$ and $\mathcal{B}$ responds as in Phase 1.

Guess: Finally, the adversary outputs a guess $b' \in \{0, 1\}$. $\mathcal{A}$ wins if $b = b'$.

We refer to such an adversary $\mathcal{A}$ as an IND-sID-T-CCA adversary. We define the advantage of the adversary $\mathcal{A}$ in attacking the scheme $\mathcal{E}$ as

$$Adv_{\mathcal{E}, \mathcal{A}}^{CCA} = |P_r[b = b'] - \frac{1}{2}|$$

The probability is over the random bits used by the challenger $\mathcal{B}$ and the adversary $\mathcal{A}$.

Definition 3. *We say that a PKTRABE scheme $\mathcal{E}$ is $(t, q_{ID}, q_T, q_C, \epsilon)$-selective identity and release time, adaptive chosen ciphertext secure if for any t-time IND-sID-T-CCA adversary $\mathcal{A}$ that makes at most q_{ID} chosen private key queries, q_T chosen release time queries and q_C chosen decryption queries we have that $Adv_{\mathcal{E}, \mathcal{A}}^{CCA} < \epsilon$. As shorthand, we say that $\mathcal{E}$ is $(t, q_{ID}, q_T, q_C, \epsilon)$ IND-sID-T-CCA secure.*

Semantic Security. As usual, we define selective identity and release time, chosen plaintext security for a PKTRABE system as in the preceding game, except that the adversary is not allowed to issue any decryption queries.

Definition 4. *We say that a PKTRABE scheme $\mathcal{E}$ is $(t, q_{ID}, q_T, \epsilon)$-selective identity and release time, adaptive chosen plaintext secure if $\mathcal{E}$ is $(t, q_{ID}, q_T, 0, \epsilon)$-selective identity and release time, chosen ciphertext secure. As shorthand, we say that $\mathcal{E}$ is $(t, q_{ID}, q_T, \epsilon)$ IND-sID-T-CPA secure.*

Similarly, we can formolize the notion of PKTRABE with multiple time servers and its security model.

4   Construction 1: Single Time Server

In this subsection, we propose our concrete single time server PKTRABE scheme and give the security assertion of our scheme.

4.1   Description of the Scheme

We build a non-interactive PKTRABE scheme from such a bilinear map defined above. The construction is based on [1]. Our PKTRABE scheme with random oracle works as follows:

Setup. Given security parameter $k \in \mathbb{Z}^+$, the following steps are taken.

1. Take k and generate a prime p. Let $(\mathcal{G}_1, \mathcal{G}_2)$ be a multiplicative group with prime order p, $e : \mathcal{G}_1 \times \mathcal{G}_1 \to \mathcal{G}_2$ be an admissible bilinear map and $g \in \mathcal{G}_1$ be a arbitrary generator.
2. Choose $g_1 \in_R \mathcal{G}_1$. Pick $y \in_R \mathbb{Z}_p^*$ and compute $g_2 = g^y$.
3. The following cryptographic hash function is chosen: $H : \{0,1\}^* \to \mathcal{G}_1$.
4. Select a tolerance parameter d.
5. Define the Lagrange coefficient $\triangle_{a,S(x)}$ for $a \in \mathbb{Z}_p^*$ and a set S of elements in $\mathbb{Z}_p^*$:

$$\triangle_{a,S(x)} = \prod_{a \in S, a \neq b} \frac{x-b}{a-b}$$

6. Output a public parameter $params = (p, \mathcal{G}_1, \mathcal{G}_2, g, g_1, g_2, e, d, H)$ and a private master key $mk = y$.

TRSetup. Choose $s \in_R \mathbb{Z}_p^*$ as the private key ts_{priv} and set g^s as the public key ts_{pub} of the time server.

KeyGen. To generate a private key for identity $ID = (\mu_1, \mu_2, \ldots, \mu_n)$ where $\mu_i \in \mathbb{Z}_p^*$ the following steps are taken.

1. Pick a random lagrange interpolation polynomial $f(\cdot)$ of degree $d-1$ over $\mathbb{Z}_p$ such that $f(0) = y$.
2. Compute $D_{\mu_i} = (\gamma_{\mu_i}, \delta_{\mu_i}) = ((H(\mu_i)^{f(\mu_i)}, g^{f(\mu_i)})$ for $i = 1, 2, \ldots, n$.
3. Output a private key $D_{ID} = (D_{\mu_1}, D_{\mu_2}, \ldots, D_{\mu_n})$.

Enc. To encrypt a message $M \in \mathcal{G}_2$ under identity $ID' = (\mu_1', \mu_2', \ldots, \mu_n')$, pick $r \in_R \mathbb{Z}_p^*$ and output the ciphertext $(C, T) = (c_1, c_2, c_{31}, c_{32}, \ldots, c_{3n}, c_4, T)$ where $c_1 = ID'$, $c_2 = g^r$, $c_{3i} = (g_1 H(\mu_i'))^r (i = 1, 2, \ldots, n)$, $c_4 = e(g_1, g_2)^r C_T$ and $C_T = e(ts_{pub}, H(T)^r) M$.

RtTrd. Output the time trapdoor $S_T = H(T)^s \in \mathcal{G}_1$.

Dec. To decrypt a ciphertext (C, T) using an arbitrary $S \subseteq ID \bigcap ID'$ such that $|S| = d$ and compute

$$C_T = \frac{e(\prod_{\mu_i \in S} \gamma_{\mu_i}^{\triangle_{\mu_i, S(0)}}, c_2)}{\prod_{\mu_i \in S} e(c_{3i}, \delta_{\mu_i}^{\triangle_{\mu_i, S(0)}})} \cdot c_4$$

$$M = \frac{C_T}{e(c_2, S_T)}$$

4.2 Security of the Scheme

The single time server scheme above is a non-interactive PKTRABE scheme semantically secure against a chosen plaintext attack in the random oracle model.

Theorem 1. *If an adversary $\mathcal{A}$ has advantage ϵ in breaking the PKTRABE scheme above, then a challenger $\mathcal{B}$ can be constructed to solve the BDH problem with probability at least $\epsilon' = \epsilon^2/e$ where e is the base of the natural logarithm.*

We will give the rigorous proof in the full version of this paper.

5 Construction 2: Multiple Time Servers

In this subsection, we propose our concrete multiple time servers PKTRABE scheme and give the security assertion of our scheme.

5.1 Description of the Scheme

We build a non-interactive PKTRABE scheme from such a bilinear map defined above. The construction is based on [1]. Our PKTRABE scheme with random oracle works as follows:

Setup. Given security parameter $k \in \mathbb{Z}^+$, the following steps are taken.

1. Take k and generate a prime p. Let $(\mathcal{G}_1, \mathcal{G}_2)$ be a multiplicative group with prime order p, $e : \mathcal{G}_1 \times \mathcal{G}_1 \to \mathcal{G}_2$ be an admissible bilinear map and $g \in \mathcal{G}_1$ be a arbitrary generator.
2. Choose $g_1 \in_R \mathcal{G}_1$. Pick $y \in_R \mathbb{Z}_p^*$ and compute $g_2 = g^y$.
3. The following cryptographic hash function is chosen: $H : \{0,1\}^* \to \mathcal{G}_1$.
4. Select a tolerance parameter d.
5. Define the Lagrange coefficient $\triangle_{a,S(x)}$ for $a \in \mathbb{Z}_p^*$ and a set S of elements in $\mathbb{Z}_p^*$:

$$\triangle_{a,S(x)} = \prod_{a \in S, a \neq b} \frac{x - b}{a - b}$$

6. Output a public parameter $params = (p, \mathcal{G}_1, \mathcal{G}_2, g, g_1, g_2, e, d, H)$ and a private master key $mk = y$.

TRSetup. Choose $s_i \in_R \mathbb{Z}_p^*$ as the private key ts_{priv}^i and set g^{s_i} as the public key ts_{pub}^i of the ith time server where $i = 1, 2, \ldots, n$.

KeyGen. To generate a private key for identity $ID = (\mu_1, \mu_2, \ldots, \mu_n)$ where $\mu_i \in \mathbb{Z}_p^*$ the following steps are taken.

1. Pick a random lagrange interpolation polynomial $f(\cdot)$ of degree $d-1$ over $\mathbb{Z}_p$ such that $f(0) = y$.

2. Compute $D_{\mu_i} = (\gamma_{\mu_i}, \delta_{\mu_i}) = ((H(\mu_i)^{f(\mu_i)}, g^{f(\mu_i)})$ for $i = 1, 2, \ldots, n$.

3. Output a private key $D_{ID} = (D_{\mu_1}, D_{\mu_2}, \ldots, D_{\mu_n})$.

Enc. To encrypt a message $M \in \mathcal{G}_2$ under identity $ID' = (\mu_1', \mu_2', \ldots, \mu_n')$, pick $r \in_R \mathbb{Z}_p^*$ and output the ciphertext $(C, T) = (c_1, c_2, c_{31}, c_{32}, \ldots, c_{3n}, c_4, T)$ where $c_1 = ID'$, $c_2 = g^r$, $c_{3i} = e(ts_{pub}^i, H(T)^r) \cdot c_{3i}'(i = 1, 2, \ldots, n)$, $c_4 = e(g_1, g_2)^r M$ and $c_{3i}' = (g_1 H(\mu_i'))^r$.

RtTrd. Output the time trapdoor $S_T^i = H(T)^{s_i} \in \mathcal{G}_1$ where $i = 1, 2, \ldots, n$.

Dec. To decrypt a ciphertext (C, T) using an arbitrary $S \subseteq ID \bigcap ID'$ such that $|S| = d$ and compute

$$c_{3i}' = \frac{c_{3i}}{e(c_2, S_T^i)}$$

$$M = \frac{e(\prod_{\mu_i \in S} \gamma_{\mu_i}^{\Delta_{\mu_i, S(0)}}, c_2)}{\prod_{\mu_i \in S} e(c_{3i}', \delta_{\mu_i}^{\Delta_{\mu_i, S(0)}})} \cdot c_4$$

5.2 Security of the Scheme

The multiple time servers scheme above is a non-interactive PKTRABE scheme semantically secure against a chosen plaintext attack in the random oracle model.

Theorem 2. *If an adversary $\mathcal{A}$ has advantage ϵ in breaking the PKTRABE scheme above, then an challenger $\mathcal{B}$ can be constructed to solve the BDH problem with probability at least $\epsilon' = \epsilon^{d+1}/e^d$ where e is the base of the natural logarithm.*

We will give the rigorous proof in the full version of this paper.

6   Conclusions and Future Work

We propose a new concept of PKTRABE which can be used to solve the time-dependent ABE problem. In our PKTRABE model, the sender encrypt a message so that it cannot be decrypted by anyone, including the designated receivers who have some attributes specified by the sender, until a future release time chosen by the sender. We formalize the notion of PKTRABE and its security model and propose two construction schemes of PKTRABE with single time server and multiple time servers respectively.

PKTRABE would have many practical applications. In this paper, we only research the basic PKTRABE. We will study such PKTRABE that can provide fine-grained access policy in our future work.

References

1. Baek, J., Susilo, W., Zhou, J.: New constructions of fuzzy identity-based encryption. In: Proceedings of the 2nd ACM Symposium on Information, Computer and Communications Security, pp. 368–370. ACM (2007)

2. Bethencourt, J., Sahai, A., Waters, B.: Ciphertext-policy attribute-based encryption. In: IEEE Symposium on Security and Privacy. SP 2007, pp. 321–334. IEEE (2007)
3. Boneh, D., Franklin, M.: Identity-based encryption from the weil pairing. In: Kilian, J. (ed.) CRYPTO 2001. LNCS, vol. 2139, pp. 213–229. Springer, Heidelberg (2001)
4. Chan, A.F., Blake, I.F.: Scalable, server-passive, user-anonymous timed release cryptography. In: Proceedings. 25th IEEE International Conference on Distributed Computing Systems. ICDCS 2005, pp. 504–513. IEEE (2005)
5. Chase, M.: Multi-authority attribute based encryption. In: Vadhan, S.P. (ed.) TCC 2007. LNCS, vol. 4392, pp. 515–534. Springer, Heidelberg (2007)
6. Cheon, J.H., Hopper, N., Kim, Y., Osipkov, I.: Provably secure timed-release public key encryption. ACM Trans. Inf. Syst. Secur. 11(2), 1–44 (2008)
7. Goyal, V., Pandey, O., Sahai, A., Waters, B.: Attribute-based encryption for fine-grained access control of encrypted data. In: Proceedings of the 13th ACM Conference on Computer and Communications Security, pp. 89–98. ACM (2006)
8. Hwang, Y.-H., Yum, D.H., Lee, P.J.: Timed-release encryption with pre-open capability and its application to certified e-mail system. In: Zhou, J., López, J., Deng, R.H., Bao, F. (eds.) ISC 2005. LNCS, vol. 3650, pp. 344–358. Springer, Heidelberg (2005)
9. Li, J., Chen, X., Li, J., Jia, C., Ma, J., Lou, W.: Fine-grained access control system based on outsourced attribute-based encryption. In: Crampton, J., Jajodia, S., Mayes, K. (eds.) ESORICS 2013. LNCS, vol. 8134, pp. 592–609. Springer, Heidelberg (2013)
10. Ma, X., Xu, L., Zhang, F.: Oblivious transfer with timed-release receivers privacy. J. Syst. Softw. 84(3), 460–464 (2011)
11. May, T.: Timed-release crypto (Unpublished manuscript) (1993)
12. Rivest, R.L., Shamir, A., Wagner, D.A.: Time-lock puzzles and timed-release crypto. Technical report MIT/LCS/TR-684, MIT LCS Tech, Cambridge, MA (1996)
13. Sahai, A., Waters, B.: Fuzzy identity-based encryption. In: Cramer, R. (ed.) EURO-CRYPT 2005. LNCS, vol. 3494, pp. 457–473. Springer, Heidelberg (2005)
14. Unruh, D.: Revocable quantum timed-release encryption. In: Nguyen, P.Q., Oswald, E. (eds.) EUROCRYPT 2014. LNCS, vol. 8441, pp. 129–146. Springer, Heidelberg (2014)
15. Yuan, K., Liu, Z., Jia, C., Yang, J., Lv, S.: Public key timed-release searchable encryption in one-to-many scenarios. Acta Electronica Sinica 43(4), 760–768 (2015)

Color Image Encryption in CIE L*a*b* Space

Xin Jin[1,2(✉)], Yingya Chen[1,2], Shiming Ge[3], Kejun Zhang[1,2],
Xiaodong Li[1,2(✉)], Yuzhen Li[1,2,4], Yan Liu[1,2,4], Kui Guo[1,2], Yulu Tian[1,2],
Geng Zhao[1,2], Xiaokun Zhang[1,2], and Ziyi Wang[1,2]

[1] Beijing Electronic Science and Technology Institute, Beijing 100070, China
{jinxin,lxd}@besti.edu.cn
[2] GOCPCCC Key Laboratory of Information Security, Beijing 100070, China
[3] Institute of Information Engineering,
Chinese Academy of Sciences, Beijing 100093, China
[4] Xidian University, Xi'an 710071, China

Abstract. To protect the contents of images in the mobile internet era during image storage and transmission, image encryption has achieved a tremendous success during the last decades. Currently, little attention has been paid to non-RGB color spaces such as HSV, YUV and L*a*b* color spaces in the color image encryption community. In this paper we use *high level* encryption schemes in more informative channels and *low level* encryption schemes in less informative channels. This paper is the first time to encrypt color image in CIE L*a*b* color space. First we convert RGB to L*a*b* color space. The 2D Arnold's cat map followed by the 3D Lu chaotic map are conducted in the L* channel. The less complicated DNA coding and 1D logistic map based encryption scheme is leveraged in the a* and b* channels, which contain less information than that in the L* channel. The experimental results reveal that our method achieves similar results with the method that conducts the same scheme in each channel of the RGB color space, while consuming less time. In addition, our method can resistant several attacks such as brute-force attack, statistic attack, correlation attack.

Keywords: Color image encryption · L*a*b* · Chaotic map · Selective encryption

1 Introduction

Cameras and smart phones are now used in everyday life. Tremendous images are transmitted to thousands of people by social network software and cloud storages. On August 31, 2014, a collection of almost 500 private pictures of various celebrities, mostly women, and with many containing nudity, were posted on the image board 4chan, and later disseminated by other users on websites and social networks such as Imgur, Reddit and Tumblr. The images were believed to have been obtained via a breach of Apple's cloud services suite iCloud. This event alerts that the privacy of us in the cloud is being threatened. Besides, once

© Springer-Verlag Berlin Heidelberg 2015
W. Niu et al. (Eds.): ATIS 2015, CCIS 557, pp. 74–85, 2015.
DOI: 10.1007/978-3-662-48683-2_8

the government or military images are leaked, the state security are violated. Thus image encryption technologies are required in order to accomplish a high level of security, integrity, confidentiality and to prevent unauthorized access of sensitive information during image storage or transmission over an insecure channels [1,3,4].

Current image encryption technologies mainly concentrate on gray image encryption [2,5]. The use of RGB color space dominate the color image encryption methods. Little attention has been paid to non-RGB color spaces such as HSV, YUV or L*a*b* color spaces. RGB color space is one of best widely used for handling and storing the data of image due to high connection between the red, green and blue components. Actually, RGB color space mixes the chrominance and luminance components so it can't use in color analysis and segmentation methods based on color criteria [1].

As shown in Fig. 1, most of the non-RGB color spaces share a property that one or two channel(s) contain(s) more visual recognition information than those in (the) other channel(s). This property enables us to use *high level* encryption schemes in more informative channels and *low level* encryption schemes in less informative channels.

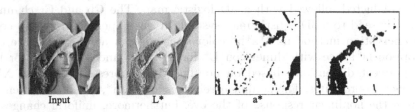

Fig. 1. Converting RGB to L*a*b*. The L*a*b* color space is a color-opponent space with dimension L* for lightness and a* and b* for the color-opponent dimensions, based on non-linearly compressed (e.g. CIE XYZ color space) coordinates. The L* channel is more independent to color component and more close to human perception on lightness than RGB color space [6]. One can easily recognize Lena from the L* channel, but can almost find nothing from the a* and b* channel.

In this paper, it is the first time for the color image encryption to be operated in CIE L*a*b* color space. First, we convert RGB to L*a*b* color space. The 2D Arnold's cat map followed by the 3D Lu chaotic map are conducted in the L* channel. The less complicated DNA coding and 1D logistic map based encryption scheme is leveraged in the a* and b* channels, which contain less information than that in the L* channel. Our method in this study has been tested on some images and showed good results. The experimental results reveal our method achieves similar results with the method that conducts the same scheme in each channel of the RGB color space, while consuming less time. In addition, our method can resistant several attacks such as brute-force attack, statistic attack and correlation attack.

2   Previous Work

The particular properties of chaos, such as sensitivity to initial conditions and system parameters, pseudo-randomness, ergodicity and so on, have granted chaotic dynamics as a promising alternative for the conventional cryptographic algorithms. The inherent properties connect it directly with cryptographic characteristics of confusion and diffusion, which is presented in Shannon's works. High-dimensional chaotic system is more reliable to design secure image encryption scheme because of its high complexity. Some cryptosystems, which are based on a low-dimensional chaotic map, have obvious drawbacks, such as short period and small key space [2,9].

Zhang et al. [5] propose a gray image encryption method by using DNA encoding and 1D logistic map. However, in 2014, Hermassi et al. [10] points out that the method of [5] is not reversible, namely, it can only encrypt the plain image, and had no method on the cipher image in the case of known the secret key. We add a random matrix to the DNA addition and make the encryption reversible.

The most similar work to ours is Mahdi et al. [1]. They propose a color image encryption method in the YCbCr color space. In the Y channel, the Arnold cat map is conducted followed with a 3D logistic map. The Cb and Cr channels are directly send to a 3D logistic map system. In this paper we propose a color image encryption method in L*a*b* color space. The L*a*b* color space is a color-opponent space with dimension L* for lightness and a* and b* for the color-opponent dimensions, based on non-linearly compressed (e.g. CIE XYZ color space) coordinates. The nonlinear relations for L*, a*, and b* are intended to mimic the nonlinear response of the eye. Furthermore, uniform changes of components in the L*a*b* color space aim to correspond to uniform changes in perceived color, so the relative perceptual differences between any two colors in L*a*b* can be approximated by treating each color as a point in a three-dimensional space (with three components: L*, a*, b*) and taking the Euclidean distance between them [6].

3   Preliminaries

We adopt a low dimensional chaotic map: 1D logistic map and two high dimensional chaotic maps: the 2D Arnold's cat map and the 3D Lu map.

3.1   1D Logistic Map

The simple but efficient 1D logistic map is defined as follows:

$$
\begin{aligned}
&x_{n+1} = \mu x_n (1 - x_n) \\
&3.569945672\ldots < \mu \leq 4, 0 \leq x_n \leq 1 \\
&n = 0, 1, 2, \ldots
\end{aligned}
\tag{1}
$$

3.2 2D Arnold's Cat Map

In mathematics, Arnold's cat map is a chaotic map from the torus into itself, named after Vladimir Arnold, who demonstrated its effects in the 1960s using an image of a cat, hence the name [7]. Arnolds Cat Map transformation use for shuffling the pixels of color image and to perform extra security of cipher system. The 2D Arnolds cat transform does not alter the value of the image pixels. It only shuffles the data of image and it given in Eq. 2 for image encryption and Eq. 3 for image decryption [1].

$$\begin{bmatrix} X' \\ Y' \end{bmatrix} = \begin{bmatrix} 1 & p \\ q & p*q+1 \end{bmatrix} * \begin{bmatrix} X \\ Y \end{bmatrix} \mod 256 \tag{2}$$

$$\begin{bmatrix} X \\ Y \end{bmatrix} = \begin{bmatrix} 1 & p \\ q & p*q+1 \end{bmatrix}^{-1} * \begin{bmatrix} X' \\ Y' \end{bmatrix} \mod 256, \tag{3}$$

where p and q represent the positive secret keys. X, Y is the original position of the image pixel before shuffling. X', Y' is the new position of the image pixel after shuffling.

3.3 3D Lu Map

The Lu map is a 3D chaotic map. It is described by Eq. 4

$$\begin{cases} \dot{x} = a(y - x) \\ \dot{y} = -xz + cy , \\ \dot{z} = xy - bz \end{cases} \tag{4}$$

where (x, y, z) are the system trace. (a, b, c) are the system parameters. When $a = 36, b = 3, c = 20$, the system contain a strange attractor and being in chaotic state. Giving the initial value x_0, y_0, z_0 of the Lu map, let the system iterate $N \times N$ times, produce three sequence values each time. Then these sequences have the same characteristics of chaos signals namely the characteristics of randomness, ergodic, and the sensibility to initial value, so they can be used on image encryption [8].

4 Color Image Encryption in L*a*b*

In this section, we describe the proposed color image encryption method in CIE L*a*b* color space. As shown in Fig. 2, first we convert we convert the plan image from RGB color space to L*a*b* space. Then the informative L* channel encrypted by 2 high dimensional chaotic map. The less informative a* and b* channels are encrypted by a low dimensional chaotic map for efficient computation.

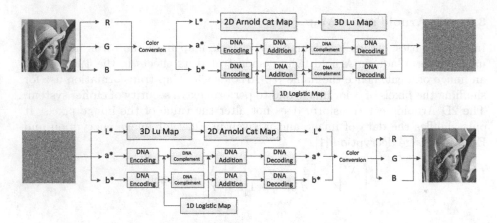

Fig. 2. Our proposed method for color image encryption in L*a*b* space. First we convert the plan image from RGB color space to L*a*b* space. Then the L* channel is shuffled by the 2D Arnold cat map followed by the diffusion via the 3D Lu map. The a* and b* channel are encrypted by DNA encoding and 1D Logistic map. The decryption method is the inverse version of the encryption method.

4.1 Color Conversion

The L* coordinate ranges from 0 to 100. The possible range of a* and b* coordinates is independent of the color space that one is converting from, since the conversion below uses X and Y, which come from RGB. The a* and b* channels range from −128 to 127. For the encryption using chaotic map and DNA encoding we convert all the 3 channels of L*, a* and b* to the range of 0 to 255 (8 bits).

4.2 The L* Channel

In the L* channel we adopt a 2D and a 3D chaotic maps. The 2D Arnold cat map is used for confusion of image pixels. The 3D Lu map is used for diffusion of image pixels.

Image Confusion. The different iteration times make the different confusion results. For a gray image with the resolution 256 ∗ 256, above 6 iterations can make good shuffling result. However, after 64 iterations the result image is the same as the original plan image because of the periodicity of the Arnold cat map. The different image sizes have different periods. The periodicity of the Arnold cat map make the confusion become less safety. Thus, in the next step we leverage the 3D Lu map for the diffusion of the confusion result, so as to enhance the safety.

Image Diffusion. We use the 3D Lu map for the diffusion of the confusion result. The step that through the Lu map to change each pixel value are as follows [9]:

- Giving the initial value x_0, y_0, z_0 of the Lu map, let the system iterate $N \times N$ times, produce three sequence values each time.
- Take the decimal fraction of three values, and put fourths of three fractions together, constitute a new integer A.
- The remainder of $A(\mathrm{mod}\,256)$ is converted binary. The gray value of the image is between 0–255, therefore, the result of $A(\mathrm{mod}\,256)$ must be in this scope.
- Convert the value which is encrypted by the cat map to binary, and let two binary values exclusive or processing, total $N \times N$ times.
- The result of the above step is converted decimal again. It returns the 2D image, and completes the second encryption.

4.3   The A* and B* Channel

The a* or b* channel is firstly encoded by DNA encoding [5]. Then, we use 1D logistic map to generate a random matrix with the same size of a* or b* and use DNA addition to add it to the encoded result. After that, another random matrix with the same size of a* or b* is generated by 1D logistic map and convert it to a binary matrix with the threshold 0.5. The DNA addition result is then converted to the DNA complement result when the corresponding value in the second random matrix is 1. The last step is DNA decoding to obtain the 8-bit encryption result.

5   Simulation Results

We use plenty of plan images to test our method, as shown in Fig. 3, with the secret key

$$\left\{ \begin{array}{l} \text{1D logistic: } \mu^{a*} = 3.9, x_0^{a*} = 0.62, \mu^{b*} = 3.99999, x_0^{b*} = 0.26 \\ \text{2D Arnold: } N_{iteration} = 20, p = 1, q = 1 \\ \text{3D Lu:} a = 36, b = 3, c = 20, x_0 = -6.045, y_0 = 2.668, z_0 = 16.363 \end{array} \right. \qquad (5)$$

The images with various contents are tested. All the encryption results can be correctly decrypted to the original plan images with the correct secret keys. We can see that the simulation results are quite satisfactory.

6   Security and Performance Analysis

A well designed image encryption scheme should be robust against different kinds of attacks, such as brute-force attack and statistical attack [2]. In this section, we analyse the security of the proposed encryption method in an example image named *Baby & Car* with size 851 × 851. We also compare our method (referred

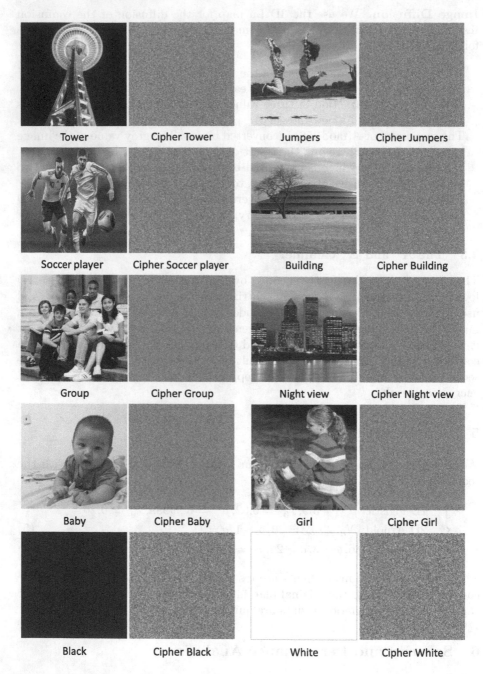

Fig. 3. The simulation results. we test our method on images with various contents including portraits, landscape, architecture, and a pure black image and a pure white image.

Fig. 4. The example image *Baby & Car*. From the left to the right: the Original plan image, the cipher image using the YCbCr, the RGB and the L*a*b*(our) method, and the decrypted image.

as L*a*b* method in the following) with the method of [1] (referred as YUV method in the following) and an encryption method in the RGB color space (referred as RGB method in the following): in each channel of R, G and B, the same encryption scheme to the one used in the L* channel of our proposed method is adopted [9], as shown in Fig. 4.

6.1 Resistance to the Brute-Force Attack

Key Space. The key space of the image encryption scheme should be large enough to resist the brute-force attack, otherwise it will be broken by exhaustive search to get the secret key in a limited amount of time. In our encryption method, we have the key space as follow:

$$\begin{cases} \text{1D logistic: } 3.569945672\ldots < \mu \le 4, x_0 \in [0,1] \\ \text{2D Arnold: } N_{iteration} > 15, p, q \text{ are positive integers} \\ \text{3D Lu:} a = 36, b = 3, c = 20, -40 < x_0 < 50, -100 < y_0 < 80, 0 < z_0 < 140 \end{cases} \quad (6)$$

The precision of 64-bit double data is 10^{-15}, thus the key space is about $(10^{15})^8 = 10^{120} \approx 2^{399}$, which is much lager than the max key space (2^{256}) of practical symmetric encryption of the AES. Our key space is large enough to resist brute-force attack.

Sensitivity of Secret Key. The chaotic systems are extremely sensitive to the system parameter and initial value. A light difference can lead to the decryption failure. To test the secret key sensitivity of the image encryption scheme, we change the secret key as follow:

$$\begin{cases} x_0 \text{ from } -6.045 \text{ to} & -6.04500000000001 \\ x_0^{a*} \text{ from } 0.62 \text{ to} & 0.62000000000001 \\ x_0^{b*} \text{ from } 0.26 \text{ to} & 0.26000000000001 \end{cases} \quad (7)$$

We use the changed key to decrypt the *Lena* cipher image in Fig. 5, while the other secret keys remain the same. The decryption result and its corresponding

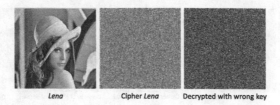

Lena   Cipher Lena   Decrypted with wrong key

Fig. 5. Decrypted with wrong key. We slightly change the key and get the wrong decrypted result.

histogram are shown in Fig. 5. We can see that the decrypted image is completely different from the original *Lena* image. The test results of the other secret key are similar. The experiments show that the image encryption scheme is quite sensitive to the secret key, which also indicates the strong ability to resist exhaustive attack.

6.2   Resistance to the Statistic Attack

The Histogram Analysis. The histogram is used to show the distribution of pixel values of a gray image. The histogram of cipher image should be flat enough, otherwise some information can be leaked to cause the statistical attack. This makes cipher-only attack possible through analysing the statistic property of the cipher image. Figure 6 shows the histograms of the *Baby & Car* image and its corresponding cipher image, respectively. Comparing the two histograms we can see that the pixel values of the original *Baby & Car* image are concentrated on some values, but the histograms of its cipher image are very uniform, which makes statistical attacks impossible.

We also test the YCbCr method [1] and the RGB method [9] and show the histogram in each channel of their method in Fig. 6. The histograms of our method are nearly as flat as those of the RGB method, which are both better than those of the YCbCr method.

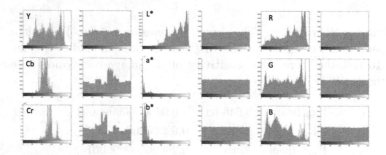

Fig. 6. The histogram of each channel of YCbCr, L*a*b* and RGB before and after encryption.

The Information Entropy. The information entropy [2] is used to express randomness and can measure the distribution of gray values in the image. The more uniform the distribution of pixel gray values, the greater the information entropy is. It is defined as follows:

$$H(m) = -\sum_{l=0}^{L} P(m_i) \log_2(m_i) \tag{8}$$

where m_i is the i-th gray value for an L level gray image, $L = 255$. $P(m_i)$ is the probability of m_i in the image and $\sum_{i=0}^{L} P(m_i) = 1$. The information entropy of an ideal random image is 8, which shows that the information is completely random. The information entropy of the cipher image should be close to 8 after encryption. The closer it is to 8, the smaller possibility for the scheme leaks information. The information entropy of *Baby & Car* cipher image using our method, the RGB [9], and the YCbCr method [1] can be summarized as follow:

$$\begin{cases} H(L*) = 7.9994, H(a*) = 7.9998, H(b*) = 7.9997 \\ H(R) = 7.9997, H(G) = 7.9998, H(B) = 7.9996 \\ H(Y) = 7.9940, H(Cb) = 7.9350, H(Cr) = 7.9196 \end{cases} \tag{9}$$

The results show that our method performs as well as the RGB method [9] (the entropy is very close to 8), and both outperform the YCbCr method [1].

The Correlation Analysis. Correlation indicates the linear relationship between two random variables. In image processing, it is usually employed to investigate the relationship between two adjacent pixels. Usually, the correlation of between adjacent pixels in the plain image is very high. A good encryption scheme should reduce the correlation between adjacent pixels, i.e., the less correlation of two adjacent pixels have, the safer the cipher image is. In order to test the correlation of two adjacent pixels, we test 3 directions (horizontal, vertical and diagonal) of adjacent pixels from the original *Baby & Car* image and its corresponding cipher image.

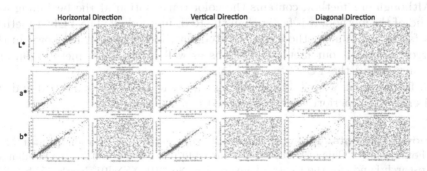

Fig. 7. The correlation of each channel of L*a*b* before and after encryption in 3 directions (horizontal, vertical and diagonal).

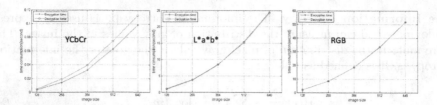

Fig. 8. The comparison of the speed of the encryption and decryption progress using the YCbCr method [1], our method and the RGB method [9] in several image resolutions: 128*128, 256*256, 384*384, 512*512, 640*640.

6.3   The Speed of the Encryption and Decryption

The image encryption scheme is implemented by Matlab on personal computer with AMD Athlon(tm) X4 750 Quad Core Processor 3.4 GHz and 4.00G RAM. The encryption and decryption consumption time is recorded for the images of different size. The larger size of the image, the more time it needs for encryption and decryption.

As show in Fig. 8, we test the speed of the encryption and decryption using the YCbCr method [1], our method and the RGB method [9] with various image sizes. The comparison show that although our method contains the color conversation at the beginning and the end of the method, it is faster than the RGB method [9]. The YCbCr method [1] is faster than both our method and the RGB method. However, as shown in the other experiments, our method performs as well as the RGB method [9], and both outperform the YCbCr method [1].

7   Conclusion and Discussion

In this paper, we are the first to encrypt color images in the CIE L*a*b* color space. In the informative L* channel, 2 high dimensional chaotic maps are adopted. While in the less informative a* and b* channel, we use the 1D logistic map with DNA encoding. Thus, we obtain good encryption results and high efficiency of color image encryption and decryption.

Although our method contains the color conversation at the beginning and the end of the method, it is faster than the RGB method [9]. The YCbCr method [1] is faster than our method and the RGB method. However, as shown in the other experiments, our method performs as well as the RGB method [9], and both outperform the YCbCr method [1].

In future work, we will utilize the fast speed of the YCbCr method and the good encryption performance of proposed L*a*b* method.

Acknowledgements. This work is partially supported by the National Natural Science Foundation of China (No. 61402021, No. 61402023, No. 61170037), the Fundamental Research Funds for the Central Universities (No. 2014XSYJ01, No. 2015XSYJ25), and the Science and Technology Project of the State Archives Administrator (No. 2015-B-10).

References

1. Mahdi, A., Alzubaiti, N.: Selective image encryption with 3D chaotic map. Eur. Acad. Res. **2**(4), 4757–4773 (2014)
2. Zhen, P., Zhao, G., Min, L.Q., Jin, X.: Chaos-based image encryption scheme combining DNA coding and entropy. Multimedia Tools and Applications (MTA), 10 April 2015
3. Jin, X., Liu, Y., Li, X.D., Zhao, G. Chen, Y.Y., Guo, K.: Privacy preserving face identification through sparse representation. In: Proceedings of the 10th Chinese Conference on Biometric Recognition (CCBR) (To Appear) (2015)
4. Guellier, A., Bidan, C., Prigent, N.: Homomorphic cryptography-based privacy-preserving network communications. In: Proceedings of 5th International Conference on Applications and Techniques in Information Security (ATIS), pp. 159–170. Melbourne, VIC, Australia, 26–28 November 2014
5. Zhang, Q., Guo, L., Wei, X.: Image encryption using DNA addition combining with chaotic maps. Math. Comput. Model. **52**(11), 2028–2035 (2010)
6. Lab color space. https://en.wikipedia.org/wiki/Lab_color_space
7. Arnold's cat map. https://en.wikipedia.org/wiki/Arnold's_cat_map#cite_note-Arnold-1
8. Ling, B., Liu, L.C.: Image encryption algorithm based on chaotic map and S-DES. Int. Conf. Adv. Comput. Control (ICACC) **5**, 41–44 (2010)
9. Wang, Y.Z., Ren, G.Y., Jiang, J.L., Zhang, J., Sun, L.J.: Image encryption method based on chaotic map. In: 2nd IEEE Conference on Industrial Electronics and Applications (ICIEA), pp. 2558–2560 (2007)
10. Hermassi, H., Belazi, A., Rhouma, R., Belghith, S.M.: Security analysis of an image encryption algorithm based on a DNA addition combining with chaotic maps. Multimedia Tools Appl. (MTA) **72**(3), 2211–2224 (2014)

Evaluation, Standards and Protocols

Discover Abnormal Behaviors Using HTTP Header Fields Measurement

Quan Bai, Gang Xiong[✉], Yong Zhao, and Zhenzhen Li

Institute of Information Engineering,
Chinese Academy of Sciences, Beijing, China
{baiquan,xionggang,zhaoyong,lizhenzhen}@iie.ac.cn

Abstract. In recent years, in order to be secure, more and more Intrusion Detection Systems (IDS) and firewalls have been used to detect and block malicious applications or even unknown protocols. As a result, some malicious applications begin to shape themselves as common application protocols to get rid of detection. Being an important protocol for many Internet services, HTTP is responsible more than half of the total traffic volume. As a result, many applications choose HTTP protocol as their shaping object, leading to many abnormal behaviors. In the paper, we study the problem of discovering these abnormal behaviors in HTTP protocol. A method based on HTTP header fields' measurement is proposed. We measure HTTP header fields' information from HTTP traffic from normal application such as IE-8, find some characteristics and we use them to find abnormal behaviors of shaping HTTP protocol.

Keywords: HTTP header fields · Measurement · Abnormal behaviors · Protocol format

1 Introduction

With the development of the Internet, more and more Intrusion Detection Systems (IDS) and firewalls have been used to detect and block malicious applications or even unknown protocols. As a result, some malicious applications begin to shape themselves as normal application protocols to get rid of detection.

However, a malicious application can do protocol confusion, but its web traffic may have abnormal protocol format. Houmansadr et al. [1] shows that, "unobservability by imitation" is a fundamentally flawed approach. The web traffic produced by malicious application has abnormal protocol format. So we can find those abnormal behaviors based on the discovery of abnormal protocol format.

Being an important protocol for many Internet services, HTTP is responsible more than half of the total traffic volume. Our measurement on HTTP traffic shows that, there are nearly 12000 types of HTTP header field in HTTP request traffic and nearly 32000 types in HTTP response traffic. The diversity of HTTP header fields of HTTP message brings a difficult problem for web applications based intrusion detection [2]. As a result, many applications choose HTTP protocol as their shaping object, which leads to many abnormal behaviors.

© Springer-Verlag Berlin Heidelberg 2015
W. Niu et al. (Eds.): ATIS 2015, CCIS 557, pp. 89–100, 2015.
DOI: 10.1007/978-3-662-48683-2_9

Take FTE (Format-Transforming Encryption) proxy as an example. FTE works by transforming encrypted data in words of a specific language based on a regular expression. It is now integrated in Tor and is mainly transformed into HTTP traffic. The principle of Format-Transforming Encryption is shown in Fig. 1.

The FTE client transforms original traffic into HTTP-like traffic using a regular expression shown in Fig. 2. The shaped data is detected as HTTP traffic by the firewall and get through the firewall. Then the proxy will reverse the data into original traffic. In this way, FTE sends its data through the firewall by shaping as HTTP [3].

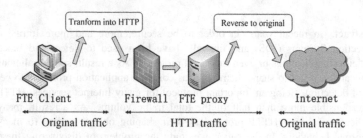

Fig. 1. FTE proxy principle

```
'^HTTP/1\\.1\\ 200 OK\\r \\nContent-Type:\\ ([a-zA-Z0-9]+)\\r\\n\\r\\n\\C*$'.
'^GET\\ \\ /([a-zA-Z0-9\\.\\/]*) HTTP/1\\.1\\r\\n\\r\\n$'.
```

Fig. 2. Example of regular expression used by FTE proxy

These shaping applications hazard the Internet security seriously and they create many abnormal behaviors in the web. So it is necessary to find a method to detect abnormal behavior of web traffic. In the paper, we study the problem of discovering these abnormal behaviors in HTTP protocol. A method based on HTTP header fields' measurement is proposed. We measure HTTP header fields' information from HTTP traffic from normal application, find some characteristics and we use them to find abnormal behaviors of shaped HTTP protocol.

The rest of the paper is organized as follows. Section 2 reviews the related work. Section 3 shows our approach to find abnormal behaviors. A method base on measurement is proposed. In Sect. 4 we take HTTP protocol as an example to show that method based on measurement and statistics is useful to find behaviors of network evasion and protocol obfuscation. Finally, Sect. 5 concludes our work.

2 Related Work

2.1 Discovery of Abnormal Behaviors

There are many researches on discovery of abnormal behaviors, and many feasible methods are proposed. These methods have something in common, that is they are all done in the application layer. These methods can be used to find abnormal behaviors such as network evasion and protocol obfuscation.

Roelker [4] reviews HTTP IDS (Intrusion Detection System) evasions approaches such as invalid protocol parsing and invalid protocol field decoding. And the work divides the detection methods into two classes: protocol analysis and pattern matching.

Hernacki et al. [5] overviews the existing network evasion methods based on abnormal protocol format. The work summarizes them into five classes: Tunneling, Flooding, Desynchronization, Encoding variations and Segmentation & reordering. They also show that network attack based on network evasion technology may affect the network security seriously.

Hjelmvik et al. [6] proposes a traffic classification method based on statistical analysis. This work divides traffic classification methods into four classes: payload examination, social host behavior, statistical flow fingerprints and obfuscated traffic. Besides this paper give some examples of protocol obfuscation behaviors. For example, Skype obfuscates VoIP protocol, BitTorrent has its Message Stream Encryption (MSE) protocol, which is also called Protocol Header Encryption, (PHE) and eDonkey obfuscates UDP protocol or TCP protocol. Using these protocol obfuscation behaviors, these P2P (Peer to Peer) applications get through the Intrusion Detection Systems and realized network evasion behaviors. At last, this paper proposes that one can improve the obfuscation behaviors' obfuscation performance by randomizing data stream structure, randomizing packet header, obfuscating the direction of packet and so on.

Mahoney et al. [7] proposes a method based on payload keyword to detect abnormal web behaviors. This work detects the application layer attack using specific keywords of the data packet payload and they also construct union attribute pairs (pairs of keyword and destination port) to find attack behaviors.

Wang and Stolfo [8] proposes a method based on statistical distributions of character of payload. They discover and detect application layer network attack using statistical distributions of character of payload.

Hjelmvik and John [6] also proposes a frame for protocol identification called SPID, which is short for Statistical Protocol Identification. The frame analyzes the payload by attribute classification and successfully identifies application protocol of obfuscated traffic based on the traffic characteristics of the session.

Shen [9] proposes a algorithm to detect web anomaly behaviors using the characteristic of length of HTTP request, characters distribution, structure of attribute fields, enumeration of attribute fields and so on.

2.2 Automatic Discovery of Protocol Format

There are also researches on distinguishing unwanted crawlers and valid ones.

Reverse engineering is the traditional method of protocol format analysis. Reverse engineering, also called back engineering, is the process of extracting knowledge or design information from anything man-made and re-producing it or reproducing anything based on the extracted information.

Traditional reverse engineering is done by artificial manual analysis, which is a Boring process and is easy to make errors. As a result, Analysis of automation discovery is becoming a new Research point. Luo et al. [10] summarizes the methods of analysis of Unknown protocol into three classes.

Program Analysis. These methods are based on the protocol information in the application by using dynamic stain spread and binary tracking to track process of the protocol. Caballero et al. [11] proposes the system Polyglot to mine the packet format is based on dynamic stain technology. If the length of a field is controlled by certain parameters, then this filed can be recognized as fixed-length fields. Unfixed-length fields are usually recognized by the length of the field and the separators. This system can not only extract the information format, but also discover protocol keywords by tracking stain data and comparing them with constant character strings.

Research on Protocol Similarity. These methods are all doing clustering with network data packets and using sequence pairs alignment, similar matrix, evolutionary tree and other algorithms to extract the protocol [12].

Data Mining. These methods extract protocol format by searching the common characteristics of the protocols.

The first class of method is Suitable for both text protocol and binary protocol. While the last two classes can get good results when dealing with text protocol but their accuracy is not ideal with dealing with binary protocol.

Above all we can find that there will be further works on discovering the protocol format automatically. At the same time, accuracy of the analysis results will become much higher. Realizing the automatic analysis with much higher accuracy will become hot research point on protocol structure. We can also see that, the existed works are mainly to get the abnormal format of protocol through snifferring certain applications. And what we do is to discover abnormal protocol format in the real network environment, and further more to find abnormal behaviors based on traffic measurement.

3 Methodology

The purpose of protocol confusion is to implement the features of "unobservability". Intuitively, unobservability means that a censor can neither recognize the traffic generated by the circumvention system, nor identify the endpoints engaged in circumvention. However, to implement unobservability, the malicious applications need to mimic the protocol in its entirety (include Correct, IntraDepend, InterDepend), mimic reaction to errors and network conditions (include Errors, Network), mimicking typical traffic (include Content, Patterns, geographic location), and mimic implementation-specific artifacts (include Soft, operating system). Houmansadr et al. [1] shows that, it is impossible to satisfy all these requests.

So we can see that although a malicious application may shape itself as a common protocol, it cannot get all the characteristics of the common protocol, especially the general characteristics of message structure in statistics.

Once again we take FTE as an example: although it can shape itself as HTTP protocol using a regular expression, it cannot get all the characteristics of fields of normal HTTP request message. We find a regular expression in its configuration file of Tor Browser, an application which FTE is integrated in. It format is like below:

"^GET\\ \\/([a-zA-Z0-9\\.\\/]*) HTTP/1\\.1\\r\\n\\r\\n$"

Figure 3 shows the HTTP request message created by Tor Browser using this regular expression. We can see that the shaped HTTP request message only has key words like "GET" and "HTTP" and even no HTTP Header Fields.

```
GET //
Hffe9ctIaZK/.W3VC.OM3yNms1Zn9QXks6TTmikswoQioh6Ext4qHQNVTV35zS3rROt1zet8Zz
vCOBSLjJrZZSKipCcck5IpoBcTeBQPu.qRSdOCGCN9TALQpfNLPAmp.mBgPNfTwNq54T5fjKKW
8zEpve2cPNkkG2V/HZy3K4LwNns.uwkaPY44cJqjAbTzbwJhRWPt8x4F15kCpRH HTTP/1.1

Um....0.*.=.id......43..t.Q.@0........uL.~...........0..a.x..r41... [pOY.m
<.........1.i.N.............C...A..,..w.....<..e.|...y.R...E.m.v..|......
{.B.$m..n....i0.D.....w.....]J.)[..&1.:....!..k.$..e..,...;fy.).....G..
I.Z.......L.cd.b....W.4t..8........T....!.=4.`........x........K.4`..)....
H.?dd^,.W2.w;..L2........B.f..&
```

Fig. 3. HTTP request message created by FTE proxy

Figure 4 shows the HTTP request message created by normal web Browser (IE Browser). We can see that the normal HTTP request message not only has key words like "GET" and "HTTP" but also and has HTTP Header Fields like "Host", "Connection", "Accept", "User-Agent" and so on, and they are placed in a specific order.

```
Follow TCP Stream
Stream Content
GET / HTTP/1.1
Host: www.baidu.com
Connection: keep-alive
Accept: text/html,application/xhtml+xml,application/xml;q=0.9,*/*;q=0.8
User-Agent: Mozilla/5.0 (Windows NT 6.1) AppleWebKit/537.36 (KHTML, like Gecko)
Chrome/28.0.1500.95 Safari/537.36 SE 2.X MetaSr 1.0
Accept-Encoding: gzip,deflate,sdch
Accept-Language: zh-CN,zh;q=0.8
```

Fig. 4. HTTP request message created by normal web Browser

So we can see, for a specific HTTP application like IE Browser, its HTTP header fields is usually constant, some other applications may shape their data or declare themselves by User-Agent as traffic of IE Browser, but their HTTP header fields information will still be abnormal in fields' details and orders. We can firstly measure the traffic of a certain normal application protocol in real network; and secondly we do statistics on HTTP header fields to summarize general characteristics; finally we use these characteristics to do match and those shaped traffic may be classified as abnormal ones.

4 Experiments and Results

4.1 Environment

We take *IE-8 Browser* as an example. We know that HTTP request message from normal *IE-8 Browser* has string like "*Mozilla/4.0 (compatible; MSIE 8.0;....*" [13]. According to our idea, we began with matching this User-Agent to do statistics with massive of *IE-8 Browser* traffic in the real network CSTNET, one of Chinese ISPs. We focus on how much HTTP header fields the traffic will have on average and the general order of them. We got some statistical characteristics of HTTP header fields to use them to discover abnormal behaviors of web flow. We did measurement for a full week.

4.2 The Basic Statistical Analysis of HTTP Header Field

We measured the count of HTTP header fields the traffic will have on average and the frequency of them. To get a more accurate result, we did this in two directions: C2S (which is short of Client to Server) and (S2C which is short for Server to Client).

There are 11248 kinds of HTTP header field keywords in the 208360203 measured HTTP flows in the direction of C2S. There are 9.80534 header fields on average, as is shown in Table 1.

Table 1. The basic statistical analysis in the direction of C2S

Ranking	HTTP request field	Count	Frequency
1	Host	137121850	65.81 %
2	Connection	125776314	60.99 %
3	User-Agent	121032201	58.57 %
4	Accept-Encoding	102451704	50.25 %
5	Accept	95398172	46.70 %
......			

There are 31330 kinds of HTTP header field keywords in the 237540382 measured HTTP flows in the direction of S2C. There are 6.64656 header fields on average, as is shown in Table 2.

Table 2. The basic statistical analysis in the direction of S2C

Ranking	HTTP response field	Count	Frequency
1	Date	232314493	97.80 %
2	Server	231734078	97.56 %
3	Connection	214881782	90.46 %
4	Content-Type	194919502	82.06 %
5	Content-Length	175658286	73.95 %
......			
22	Age	6546036	3.47 %

The results of the measurement can be used as a characteristic to discover Abnormal HTTP traffic, which we will use in Section C. And with these results, we can future mining the order of the Top 20 field keywords in the two directions.

4.3   The Mining Analysis of HTTP Header Field Order

Scheme I, Mining the header keyword based on position: Firstly, We the count of each HTTP header field of each position and sort them. And then we deal with each sorted position synthetically and get the most frequent HTTP header field of each position. For example, firstly we divide the data set into 20 files based on the position of each HTTP header field. As is shown in Fig. 5, "File 1" stands for HTTP header field keyword appeared in the first position in the whole data set. At last we summarize "File 1" to "File 20" to get the final file, which is the most common field keyword of the 20 positions.

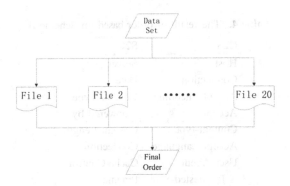

Fig. 5. Mining the header keyword based on position

Table 3 shows the result of order based on Scheme I.

The advantage of Scheme I is that its model is simple to understand, and the disadvantage is that it is sensitive to difference. If adding a new field at the beginning, all the fields' value will change.

Table 3. The result of order based on Scheme I

C2S	S2C
Host	Data
Connection	Server
Accept-Encoding	Content-Length
User-Agent	Connection
Content-Type	X-Rowered-By
Accept	Cache-Control
Referer	Accept-Ranges
From	Set-Cookie
......	......

Scheme II, Mining the header keyword based on the weighted order: To overcome the sensibility to difference in Scheme I, We mining the data set again in another dimension. Scheme II is based on order rather than position. We scored each HTTP header field keywords based on their coming order. Keyword with higher score means it will coming earlier in the position.

We traversed each HTTP protocol request or response packet, the keyword coming first weight higher (N), and the keyword coming later weight lower, the weight value diminishes according to the order. The weight formula is shown below:

$$score[F] = \sum_j (N - order[F][j])$$

Score[F] stands for order score of HTTP header F, and order[F][j] means the order of F in the jth HTTP flow of the data set. N is set 20 because we only checked the top 20 header fields. Table 4 shows the result of order based on **Scheme II**.

Table 4. The result of order based on Scheme II

C2S	S2C
Host	Server
Connection	Date
Accept-Encoding	Content-Type
Accept	x-powered-by
Content-type	Content-Length
Accept-Language	Connection
User-Agent	Cache-Control
X-Requested-With	Pragma
......	......

The advantage of Scheme II is that it is based on order rather than position, so that it can recover the sensibility in Scheme I. And the disadvantage is that it will ignore special header field. As it is just addition simply, the field appears more will get more changes to addition which will lead to a higher score in position order.

Scheme III, Mining the header keyword based on the average weighted order: To recover the problem of field appears more will score higher in Scheme II, we modified the formula on the basis of Scheme II: we added a variable count[F] to record the coming count of field keyword, and averaged the value at last, The weight formula is shown below:

$$score[F] = \frac{\sum_j (N - order[F][j])}{count[F]}$$

Variable count[F] stands for count of HTTP request messages that contain HTTP header F. Table 5 shows the result of order based on Scheme III.

Table 5. The result of order based on Scheme III

C2S	S2C
Host	Date
Connection	Server
Accept-Encoding	Connection
Accept	Content-Length
User-Agent	Content-Type
Accept-Language	X-Powered-By
Content-Type	Cache-Control
X-Requested-With	Last-Modified
......	......

The advantage of Scheme III is that it is based on order rather than position, and it can recover the disadvantage in Scheme II. But the disadvantage is that this scheme is strongly statistical. However, in the real network, it is reasonable for HTTP protocol header field keywords to have a variety of orders. This is similar to the overfitting in machine learning.

We compared the different results of 3 schemes and took C2S direction as an example, the result is shown in Fig. 6.

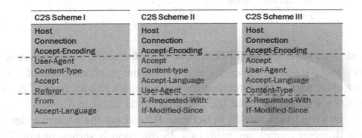

Fig. 6. Comparison of different results of these three schemes

Firstly, Scheme II and Scheme III are in the dimension of order, Scheme III is an improvement of Scheme II, while Scheme I is in the dimension of position. As a result, the results of Scheme II and III are relatively more similar than Scheme I.

Secondly, although the results of these three schemes are different in detail, they still have some similarities. For example, the first three header field keywords of three schemes are the same, they are "Host", "Connection" and "Accept-Encoding". As for the 4th to 7th keywords, although the orders of them from three schemes have some differences, they are just simply different in position; they are still the same in the view of a set.

So we can see, in the view of set, the header field keywords order are the same in block from three schemes. We can use keywords block instead of keywords position: the 1st block includes keywords like "Host", "Connection" and "Accept-Encoding"; the 2nd block includes "Accept", "Content-Type", "Accept-Language", "User-Agent"...

and so on. In the view of keywords block, we can also solve the problem of overfitting in Scheme III.

4.4 Recognize Abnormal HTTP Flow

We analyzed the data we got and found some statistical characteristics of HTTP header fields. Table 1 shows the main header fields of IE-8 Browser traffic and their percentage of appearance.

Table 6. Statistical characteristics of HTTP header fields

HTTP header name C2S	HTTP header name S2C
Host	Date
Connection	Server
Accept-Encoding	Connection
Accept	Content-Length
User-Agent	Content-Type
Accept-Language	X-Powered-By
Content-Type	Cache-Control
X-Requested-With	Last-Modified
If-Modified-Since	Accept-Ranges
From	Pragma

Firstly, we used the count of HTTP header fields the traffic have on average and the frequency of them we got in Tables 1 and 2. As for the result may do not cover all the cases, for example, some HTTP request message contain header field of cookie while others do not. So we only checked the common fields listed in Table 6.

And then we sorted the score[F] in **Scheme III** and got the general order of header fields of IE-8 Browser traffic, the result of C2S direction is shown in Fig. 7.

We reviewed the data by matching the header fields and the general order of them by formula below. N stands for the set of header fields listed in Table 1, and F stands for the set of fields of HTTP request message being tested. Card (N) is the number of elements of set N. Inverse (F) means the inverse number compared with the common order of F. When the value_x(F) is less than the threshold value we set, this HTTP request message will be recognized as an abnormal one.

$$value\_x(F) = a\frac{card(F \cap N)}{card(N)} - b*Inverse\ (F)$$

We found that most of the request messages passed the test, while some are recognized as abnormal ones. We checked those data and found them indeed different from the common ones. They do not even have GET fields, which mean they do not for the purpose of requesting.

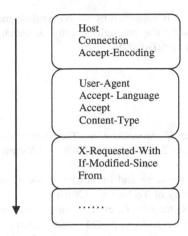

Fig. 7. General order of HTTP header fields of IE-8

There are also abnormal behaviors of IE-8 traffic with other request method. An example is shown in Fig. 8.

```
CONNECT api.foxitcloud.com:443 HTTP/1.0
User-Agent: Mozilla/4.0 (compatible; MSIE 8.0; Windows NT
    6.1; Trident/4.0; SLCC2; .NET CLR 2.0.50727; .NET CLR
    3.5.30729; .NET CLR 3.0.30729; Media Center PC 6.0;
    .NET4.0C; .NET4.0E)
Host: api.foxitcloud.com:443
Content-Length: 0
Proxy-Connection: Keep-Alive
Pragma: no-cache
```

Fig. 8. An abnormal HTTP flow of IE-8

This packet is started with request method **CONNECT** and it is not pass the formula test. The method name **CONNECT** is used for a proxy that can dynamically switch to being a tunnel, and we can see that this packet is used for Foxit cloud to switch to a SSL tunnel.

5 Conclusions

In the paper, we study the problem of discovering these abnormal behaviors in HTTP protocol. A method based on HTTP header fields' measurement is proposed. We measure header fields' information from HTTP traffic from normal application, find some characteristics in statistics such as count of header field in each packet on average, the frequency of each field and the order block of them. Using them we found some abnormal behaviors of shaped HTTP protocol. The result shows that it is possible to discover abnormal web behaviors using HTTP header fields' measurement.

Acknowledgements. This work is supported by the National Science and Technology Support Program (No. 2012BAH46B02); the Strategic Priority Research Program of the Chinese Academy of Sciences (No. XDA06030200).

References

1. Houmansadr, A., Brubaker, C., Shmatikov, V.: The parrot is dead: observing unobservable network communications. In: 2013 IEEE Symposium on Security and Privacy (SP), pp. 65–79. IEEE (2013)
2. Hjelmvik, E., John, W.: Breaking and improving protocol obfuscation. Technical report 123751, Chalmers University of Technology (2010)
3. Dyer, K.P., Coull, S.E., Ristenpart, T., et al.: Format-transforming encryption: more than meets the DPI. The IACR Cryptology, p. 494. ePrint Archive (2012)
4. Roelker, D.J.: HTTP IDS evasions revisited. Sourcefire Inc. (2003)
5. Hernacki, B., Bennett, J., Hoagland, J.: An overview of network evasion methods. Inf. Secur. Tech. Report **10**(3), 140–149 (2005)
6. Hjelmvik, E., John, W.: Breaking and improving protocol obfuscation. Technical report 123751, Chalmers University of Technology (2010)
7. Mahoney, M.V., Chan, P.K.: Learning nonstationary models of normal network traffic for detecting novel attacks. In: Proceedings of the Eighth ACM SIGKDD International Conference on Knowledge Discovery and Data Mining, pp. 376–385. ACM (2002)
8. Wang, K., Stolfo, S.J.: Anomalous payload-based network intrusion detection. In: Jonsson, E., Valdes, A., Almgren, M. (eds.) RAID 2004. LNCS, vol. 3224, pp. 203–222. Springer, Heidelberg (2004)
9. Shen, X.: A implementation of intrusion detection system based on web anomaly detection. Shanghai Jiaotong University (2010)
10. Luo, C., Zhang, Y., Wang, Q., et al.: Automatic network protocol analysis and vulnerability discovery based on symbolic expression. J. Grad. Univ. Chin. Acad. Sci. **30**(2), 278–284 (2013)
11. Caballero, J., Yin, H., Liang, Z., et al.: Polyglot: automatic extraction of protocol message format using dynamic binary analysis. In: Proceedings of the 14th ACM Conference on Computer and Communications Security, pp. 317–329. ACM (2007)
12. Li, W.M., Zhang, A.F., Liu, J.C., et al.: An automatic network protocol fuzz testing and vulnerability discovering method. Jisuanji Xuebao (Chinese Journal of Computers) **34**(2), 242–255 (2011)
13. Microsoft Developer Network (MSDN): Understanding user-agent strings. https://msdn.microsoft.com/zh-cn/library/ms537503(en-us).aspx

Reconstruction of Potential Attack Scenarios of the OpenID Protocol Towards Network Forensics Analysis

Dongyao Ji[✉], Junliang Liu, and Gang Yao

Institute of Information Engineering, Chinese Academy of Sciences,
Beijing 100093, China
jidongyao@iie.ac.cn

Abstract. We present a way to model web-based security protocols using TLA+, and describe a fully automatic analysis that supports reconstruction of the potential attack scenarios of web-based security protocols. Which could provide conclusive descriptions and non refutable proofs regarding the source of the attack, details of steps involved in the occurred attack scenario, exploited vulnerabilities, and generated system damages. This is of important significance for network forensic analysis. As a case study, we successfully find a new attack scenario of OpenID protocol and the modified protocol is introduced as well.

Keywords: Security protocols analysis · Attack scenarios reconstruction · Model checking · Temporal logic of actions

1 Introduction

Exploiting and attacking a vulnerable network protocol can cause devastating effects to networks and service providers. Forensic analysis can help maintain the security of protocol systems by identifying the root cause of a protocol system compromise or failure [1]. We propose a model for examining protocol features misused and validating the attack. This model has been built with specific reference to security attacks on OpenID protocol [2]. Even though OpenID is rapidly being adopted [3], its security has yet to be demonstrated. Besides the risks documented in the OpenID specification itself (e.g., phishing, Identity provider (IdP) masquerade, replay, denial-of-service attacks), several security issues have been reported in the literature. Tsyrklevich and Tsyrklevich demonstrate how to insidiously log a user into her Relying party (RP) via a cross-site request forgery (we refer to this attack as a "Single Sign-On Cross-site request forgery (CSRF)")[4], and how a fast network attacker could sniff an authentication response and reset the users TCP connection to masquerade as that user (an "impersonation" attack). Barth et al. showed that the OpenID protocol is vulnerable to session swapping, which forces the users browser to initialize a session authenticated as the attacker [5]. Sovis et al. examined the OpenID extension framework and

© Springer-Verlag Berlin Heidelberg 2015
W. Niu et al. (Eds.): ATIS 2015, CCIS 557, pp. 101–113, 2015.
DOI: 10.1007/978-3-662-48683-2_10

found that the extension parameters could be forged when the communication channel is not SSL-protected (a "parameter forgery" attack)[6]. In this paper, we use TLA+ [7], a model checking tool of a state-based logic that allows the description of states and state transitions, to generate executable attack scenarios showing with details how the attack scenario was conducted and how the system behaved accordingly. Through the analysis of OpenID protocols towards network forensic analysis, we will explore the deeper causes of those vulnerabilities found in the OpenID protocol. One main merit of TLA+ is that it can provide the power to express the details of the analysis.

Contribution. To the best of our knowledge, we are the first to apply TLA+ to examine the general vulnerabilities of web-based security protocols. Our main contribution consists in providing formal models of the web-based security protocols in the specification language of the TLA+. We show that the main emerging web single sign-on protocol, namely OpenID, suffer from an authentication flaw that allows a attacker to impersonate a user on any application. We also describe solutions that can be used to mitigate and even solve the problem.

Outline. In the next section, we give an overview of OpenID protocol. In Sect. 3, we illustrate our modeling approach. In Sect. 4, we describe the experimental results and discuss the verification results. In Sect. 5, we present our Defense measures. We conclude with a discussion about our contribution in Sect. 6. For shortage of space, the full versions of the models that can be used to reproduce our results are not included. They are available on demand.

2   Overview of the OpenID Protocol

The OpenID protocol concerns four players: User(U), Browser(B), Identity Provider (IdP) and Relying party (RP). Our formal model combines user U and browser B into one single entity, denoted as UB. OpenID authentication provides a way to prove that an end user controls a OpenID Identifier i. It does this without the RP needing access to end user credentials such as a password or to other sensitive information such as an email address. An end user can freely choose which IdP to use, and can preserve their OpenID Identifier i if they switch IdP. This means an end user can prove their Identity to a RP without having to leave their current Web page. The shared knowledge between each entity is defined as the follows: (1) IdP and UB share a secret key k_{UI} and a OpenID identifier i, (2) RP shares a secret key k_{RI} and a session handle h with IdP, and (3) RP does not have a prior knowledge of UB and OpenID identifier i. We assume that the RP knows the endpoint URL of the IdP based on a given OpenID identifier i. By using the shared knowledge defined above, an Alice-Bob formalization is as follows. We use "$A \rightarrow B : M$" to denote that A sends the message M to B. We write $x.y$ to denote the concatenation of the bit strings x and y. We write $E(x, k)$ to denote the encryption of x with the symmetric key k. We write $H(x)$ to denote Hash function on x. We write $HMAC(x, k)$ to denote HMAC on x with key k. In step 1, UB sends i to RP as a "Login Request". In step 2, RP sends i,h to UB as an "Authentication Request". Steps 3 to 5 use the challenge and response mechanism to authenticate UB to IdP. The first two messages serve to establish k_1, shared between UB and IdP, and the last one serves as a proof that A has the new key, k_1, and IdP can authenticate UB using n_b. Among which, n_a and n_b are the nonce chose by UB and IdP respectively. In step 6, IdP generate nonce n and compute signature s, then sends $i.h.n.s$ to UB as an "authentication response". In step 7, UB redirects the authentication response to RP, RP perform local validation on s.

(1). UB→RP: i,   Login Request (1.1).
(2). RP→UB: $IdP.i.h.RP$,   Auth Request (3.1).
(3). UB→IdP: $IdP.i.h.RP.\mathrm{E}(n_a, k_{UI})$,   UB-to-IdP auth (3.2).
(4). IdP→UB: $\mathrm{E}(n_b, k_{UI})$, $k_1 = H(n_a, n_b)$ (3.3 & 3.4).
(5). UB→IdP: $\mathrm{E}(n_b, k_1)$,   IdP auth UB on n_b (3.5).
(6). IdP→UB: $IdP.i.h.RP.n.s$, $s = HMAC(IdP.i.h.RP.n, k_{RI})$ auth resp (4.1).
(7). UB→RP: $IdP.i.h.RP.n.s$,   assertion validation (4.2 & 4.3).

3 Modeling Protocols in TLA+

3.1 General Flow

In TLA+, a network protocol, as any other concurrent reactive system, can be specified as a state transition system:

$$Protocol \triangleq Init \wedge \Box[Next]_{<x,y>} \wedge Fair$$

where x and y are tuples of variables, $Init$ is the initial state predicate, and the one temporal operator $\Box$, which means "forever". $Next$ is an action, and $Fair$ is a conjunction of fairness conditions on actions. If a protocol is specified as a combination of multiple principals, such as a User, IdP and RP, its TLA+ specification can be done accordingly as:

$$Protocol \triangleq User \wedge IdP \wedge RP$$

where User, IdP and RP are specified as systems with their own initial conditions and state transition actions. The communication between these components are done by shared variables. In order to check for vulnerability, we need to model hostile attackers.

Adversary Model. The attacker model proposed by Dolev and Yao [8] is widely adopted by the security protocols community. In which the attacker has the ability to read, alter, encrypt, decrypt, compose and deconstruct messages. Despite its flexibility, the Dolev-Yao model, is not ideal for the web environment due to the two reasons: Firstly. web protocols typically recommend or mandate usage of secure SSL/TLS communication. This assumption can result in substantial simplification of analysis. Secondly, Dolev-Yao can not model certain types of browser-based attacks. The adversary model we use for analyzing web protocols can be considered a variation of Dolev-Yao model in which the attacker does not have access to all messages, but at the same time has the ability to exploit browser-based communication to forge requests, manipulate redirection endpoints etc.

Property. We also need to formally state what are the requested properties of the protocol. Assume the requested property is specified in TLA+ as *Property*, the robustness of protocol under attack is stated as:

$$Protocol \land Attacker \Rightarrow Property$$

The general flow of our approach is to first specify the protocol, the attacker, and the property, and then to use TLC [9] to automatically prove the above formula.

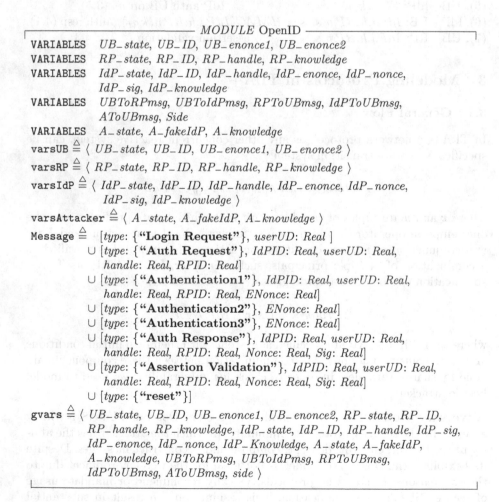

Fig. 1. Declarations.

The benefit of such an approach is that the checking is totally automatic and if there is any violation, a trace will be produced by the TLC.

3.2 Protocol Specification

We choose some representative parts of the specification to illustrate how the specification works. We first use declarations to explain the meaning of variables.

Declarations. To specify the protocol clearly, we declare *variables* respectively for each entity. As for UB, UB_state describes the UB's state, UB_ID describes the UB's identifier, $UB\_enonce1$ describes the nonce encrypted by shared key (K_{UI}) in step 3, $UB\_enonce2$ describes the nonce encrypted by new key (K_1) in step 5. The part of the RP and IdP follows in a similar manner. In order to represent the messages sent in the protocol, we declare a record type namely *Message*. A record is a function whose domain is a finite set of strings. For example, variable $UBToRPmsg$ is such a record with *type* and *userID* fields, and the domain of *type* is the set $\{$ *"Login Request"* $\}$, the domain of *userID* is the

---

──────── *MODULE* RP ────────

VARIABLES   *state, ID, handle, knowledge*

Init $\stackrel{\triangle}{=}$ $\wedge$ *state* ="**RP_start**" $\wedge$ *ID* $= 2 \wedge$ *handle* $= 1$
  $\wedge$ *knowledge* $= [type \mapsto$ **"RP"**, $U\_ID \mapsto 0, IdP\_ID \mapsto 3]$

Trans0 $\stackrel{\triangle}{=}$ $\wedge$ *state* ="**RP_start**" $\wedge$ *Side* $= 2 \wedge UBToRPmsg \neq \langle\rangle$
  $\wedge UBToRPmsg.type=$"**Login Request**"
  $\wedge$ *knowledge'* $= [knowledge$ **EXCEPT** !. $U\_ID=UBToRPmsg.userID]$
  $\wedge$ *RPToUBmsg'* $=[type \mapsto$ **"Auth Request"**, $IdP\_ID\mapsto$
                $knowledge.IdP\_ID, userID \mapsto UBToRPmsg.userID,$
                $handle \mapsto handle, RPID \mapsto ID]$
  $\wedge$ *Side'* $=4$, *state'* ="**RP_wait_sig**"
  $\wedge$ UNCHANGED$\langle$ *ID, handle, UBToRPmsg, UBToIdPmsg,*
                IdPToUBmsg, AToUBmsg $\rangle$

Trans1 $\stackrel{\triangle}{=}$ $\wedge$ *state* ="**RP_wait_sig**" $\wedge$ *Side* $= 2 \wedge UBToRPmsg \neq \langle\rangle$
  $\wedge UBToRPmsg.type=$"**Assertion Validation**" $\wedge$ $UBToRPmsg.Sig=1$
  $\wedge$ *state'* ="**RP_finish**"
  $\wedge$ UNCHANGED$\langle$ *ID, Side, handle, knowledge, UBToRPmsg, UBToIdPmsg,*
                RPToUBmsg, IdPToUBmsg, AToUBmsg $\rangle$

Trans2 $\stackrel{\triangle}{=}$ $\wedge$ *state* ="**RP_finish**" $\wedge$ *Side*$=2$
  $\wedge$ *knowledge'* $= [type \mapsto$ **"RP"**, $U\_ID \mapsto 0, IdP\_ID \mapsto 3]$
  $\wedge$ *RPToUBmsg'* $= \langle\rangle$, $\wedge$ *Side'*$=1 \wedge$ *state'* $=$ **"RP_start"**
  $\wedge$ UNCHANGED$\langle$ *ID, handle, UBToRPmsg, UBToIdPmsg,*
                IdPToUBmsg, AToUBmsg $\rangle$

Next $\stackrel{\triangle}{=}$ $\wedge$ $\vee$ Trans0 $\vee$ Trans1 $\vee$ Trans2
  $\wedge$ UNCHANGED$\langle$ *varsUB, varsIdP, varsAttacker* $\rangle$

Fig. 2. Modeling relying party.

set *Real*. According to the protocol, we declare five *variables* to represent the messages sent between different entities, for example, variables $UBToRPmsg$ represent the message that UB sends to RP. Consider that there is an attacker, we declare three *variables* to represent the *state* of attacker, the *identifier* of fake IdP and the *knowledge* grasped by attacker respectively. In order to use the variables conveniently, we put variables that belong to the same entity together and put all the variables in *gvars* for global use. As shown in the Fig. 1.

RelyingParty. The submodule RP specifies the actions of RP. The RP submodule begins with the declaration, then the initial state and the next-state relation are defined. As shown in the Fig. 2. There are four variables in the RP submodule, which represent respectively the *state* of RP, the *identifier* of RP, the shared *handle*, and the *knowledge* of RP . We first define the initial state of

---

——— MODULE IdP ———

VARIABLES $state, ID, handle, enonce, nonce, sig, knowledge$

$Init \triangleq \wedge\ state =$**"IdP_start"** $\wedge\ ID = 3 \wedge\ handle = 1$
$\qquad\ \wedge\ enonce=2, \wedge\ nonce=4, \wedge\ sig=0$
$\qquad\ \wedge\ knowledge = [type \mapsto$ **"IdP"**$,\ U\_ID \mapsto 0,\ RP\_ID \mapsto 0,\ uenonce \mapsto 0\ ]$

$Trans0 \triangleq \wedge\ state =$**"IdP_start"** $\wedge\ Side = 3 \wedge\ UBToIdPmsg \neq \langle\rangle$
$\qquad \wedge UBToIdPmsg.type=$**"Authentication1"**
$\qquad \wedge\ knowledge' = [knowledge$ **EXCEPT** $!.\ U\_ID=UBToIdPmsg.userID,$
$\qquad\qquad\qquad\qquad\qquad\qquad !.RP\_ID=UBToIdPmsg.RPID,$
$\qquad\qquad\qquad\qquad\qquad\qquad !.uenonce=UBToIdPmsg.ENonce]$
$\qquad \wedge\ IdPToUBmsg' =[type \mapsto$ **"Authentication2"**$, ENonce \mapsto enonce]$
$\qquad \wedge\ Side'=4 \wedge\ state'=$**"IdP_wait_nb"**
$\qquad \wedge$ UNCHANGED$\langle\ ID, handle, enonce, nonce, sig$
$\qquad\qquad\qquad\qquad\quad UBToRPmsg, UBToIdPmsg, RPToUBmsg, AToUBmsg\rangle$

$Trans1 \triangleq \wedge\ state =$**"IdP_wait_nb"** $\wedge\ Side = 3 \wedge\ UBToIdPmsg \neq \langle\rangle$
$\qquad \wedge UBToIdPmsg.type=$**"Authentication3"** $\wedge\ UBToIdPmsg.ENonce=3$
$\qquad \wedge\ sig'=1,\ Side'=4,\ state'=$ **"IdP_finish"**
$\qquad \wedge\ IdPToUBmsg' =[type \mapsto$ **"Auth Responce"**$, IdPID \mapsto ID,$
$\qquad\qquad\qquad\qquad\quad userID \mapsto knowledge.U\_ID, Handle \mapsto handle,$
$\qquad\qquad\qquad\qquad\quad RPID \mapsto knowledge.RP\_ID,$
$\qquad\qquad\qquad\qquad\quad Nonce \mapsto nonce, sig \mapsto 1]$
$\qquad \wedge$ UNCHANGED$\langle\ ID, handle, enonce, nonce, knowledge,$
$\qquad\qquad\qquad\qquad\qquad UBToRPmsg, UBToIdPmsg, RPToUBmsg, AToUBmsg\ \rangle$

$Trans2 \triangleq \wedge\ state =$**"IdP_finish"** $\wedge\ Side=3 \wedge\ sig'=0$
$\qquad \wedge\ knowledge' = [type \mapsto$ **"IdP"**$,\ U\_ID \mapsto 0,\ RP\_ID \mapsto 0,\ uenonce \mapsto 0]$
$\qquad \wedge\ IdPToUBmsg' = \langle\rangle, \wedge\ Side'=4 \wedge\ state' =$ **"IdP_start"**
$\qquad \wedge$ UNCHANGED$\langle\ ID, handle, enonce, nonce, UBToRPmsg,$
$\qquad\qquad\qquad\qquad\qquad UBToIdPmsg, RPToUBmsg, AToUBmsg\ \rangle$

$Next \triangleq \wedge\ \vee\ Trans0 \vee Trans1 \vee Trans2$
$\qquad \wedge$ UNCHANGED$\langle\ varsUB, varsRP, varsAttacker\ \rangle$

Fig. 3. Modeling identity provider.

```
┌─────────────────────── MODULE Attack ───────────────────────┐
  VARIABLES   state, ID, fakeIdP, knowledge
├──────────────────────────────────────────────────────────────┤
```

Init $\stackrel{\Delta}{=} \wedge$ state $=$"**Attacker_eavesdrop**" $\wedge$ fakeIdP $= 2$
  $\wedge$ knowledge$= =[type \mapsto$ "**Attacker**", $A\_ID \mapsto 2$, $U\_ID \mapsto 0$,
       $RP\_ID \mapsto 1$, $IdP\_ID \mapsto 0$, $Handle \mapsto 0$,
       $U\_enonce1 \mapsto 0$, $I\_enonce \mapsto 0$, $U\_enonce2 \mapsto 0$,
       $I\_nonce \mapsto 0$, $sig \mapsto 0$]

Trans0 $\stackrel{\Delta}{=} \wedge$ state $=$"**Attacker_eavesdrop**" $\wedge$ Side $= 4 \wedge$ UBToRPmsg $\neq \langle\rangle$
  $\wedge$ UBToRPmsg.type$=$"**Login Request**" $\wedge$ knowledge.$U\_ID=0$,
  $\wedge$ knowledge$' = [$knowledge **EXCEPT** !. $U\_ID=UBToRPmsg.userID]$
  $\wedge$ Side$'=2\wedge$ state$'=$"**Attacker_intercept**"
  $\wedge$ **UNCHANGED**$\langle$ fakeIdP, UBToRPmsg, UBToIdPmsg, RPToUBmsg,
       IdPToUBmsg, AToUBmsg$\rangle$

Trans1 $\stackrel{\Delta}{=} \wedge$ state $=$"**Attacker_intercept**" $\wedge$ Side $= 4 \wedge$ RPToUBmsg $\neq \langle\rangle$
  $\wedge$ RPToUBmsg.type$=$"**Auth Request**" $\wedge$ knowledge.$IdP\_ID=0$
  $\wedge$ knowledge$' = [$knowledge **EXCEPT** !. $IdP\_ID=RPToUBmsg.IdPID$,
           !.$Handle=RPToUBmsg.Handle]$
  $\wedge$ RPToUBmsg$' = \langle\rangle \wedge$ state$' = $"**Attacker_replay**"
  $\wedge$ **UNCHANGED**$\langle$ fakeIdP , Side, UBToRPmsg, UBToIdPmsg,
       IdPToUBmsg, AToUBmsg$\rangle$

Trans2 $\stackrel{\Delta}{=} \wedge$ state $=$"**Attacker_replay**" $\wedge$ Side $= 4$
  $\wedge$ RPToUBmsg$'=[type \mapsto$ "**Auth Request**", $IdPID \mapsto fakeID$,
         userID $\mapsto$ knowledge.U_ID, Handle $\mapsto$ knowledge.Handle,
         RPID $\mapsto$ knowledge.$RP\_ID]$
  $\wedge$ state$' = $"**Attacker_impersonate**" $\wedge$ Side$' =1$
  $\wedge$ **UNCHANGED**$\langle$ fakeIdP, knowledge, UBToRPmsg,
       UBToIdPmsg, IdPToUBmsg, AToUBmsg $\rangle$

Trans3 $\stackrel{\Delta}{=} \wedge$ state $=$"**Attacker_impersonate**" $\wedge$ Side $= 4 \wedge$ UBToIdPmsg $\neq \langle\rangle$
  $\wedge$ UBToIdPmsg.type$=$"**Authentication1**"
  $\wedge$ UBToIdPmsg.$IdPID=fakeIdP \wedge$ knowledge.$U\_enonce1=0$
  $\wedge$ knowledge$' = [$knowledge **EXCEPT** !.$U\_enonce1=UBToRPmsg.ENonce]$
  $\wedge$ UBToIdPmsg$' = [UBToIdPmsg$ **EXCEPT** !. $IdPID=knowledge.IdP\_ID]$
 $\cdots\cdots\cdots\cdots\cdots\cdots\cdots\cdots\cdots\cdots\cdots\cdots\cdots\cdots\cdots\cdots\cdots\cdots\cdots\cdots\cdots\cdots\cdots$

```
└──────────────────────────────────────────────────────────────┘
```

Fig. 4. Modeling attacker.

the RP. In the initial state, the *knowledge* means that RP knows the *identifier* of IdP, but does not know the *identifier* of user. Then we describe three actions which may be executed by RP. The *Trans0* represents that the RP receive a *"Login Request"* message and return an *"Auth Request"* message to UB. We use *Trans1* to describe that the RP receives and checks the assertion. At last, we reset the RP to *initial* state for the next execution.

Identity Provider. According to the protocol, the main task of IdP is to authenticate the user. In our specification, we use three actions to describe the authentication process. As shown in the Fig. 3. The *Trans0* represents that the

$$\text{—————— } MODULE \text{ OpenID ——————}$$

UserBrowser $\triangleq$ *INSTANCE UB WITH state←UB_state, ID←UB_ID,*
    enonce1←UB_enonce1, enonce2←UB_enonce2

RelayParty $\triangleq$ *INSTANCE RP WITH state←RP_state, ID←RP_ID*
    handle←RP_handle, knowledge←RP_knowledge

IdentyProvider $\triangleq$ *INSTANCE IdP WITH state←IdP_state, ID←IdP_ID*
    handle←IdP_handle, enonce←IdP_enonce
    nonce←IdP_nonce, sig←IdP_sig
    knowledge←IdP_knowledge

Attacker $\triangleq$ *INSTANCE Attack WITH state←A_state, fakeIdP←A_fakeIdP,*
    knowledge←A_knowledge

Init $\triangleq$ ∧ *UBToRPmsg* = ⟨⟩ ∧ *UBToIdPmsg* = ⟨⟩ ∧ *RPToUBmsg* = ⟨⟩
    ∧ *IdPToUBmsg* = ⟨⟩ ∧ *AToUBmsg* = ⟨⟩ ∧ *Side*=1 ∧ *UserBrowser!Init*
    ∧ *ReplyingParty!Init* ∧ *IdentityProvider!Init* ∧ *Attacker!Init*

Next $\triangleq$ □ [*UserBrowser!Next*∨ *ReplyingParty!Next*
    ∨ *IdentityProvider!Next* ∨ *Attacker!Next*]_*gvars*

Spec $\triangleq$ Init ∧ Next

Target $\triangleq$ □ (*A_knowledge.sig=0*)

Fig. 5. Specify the properties we want to check.

IdP chooses a nonce and encrypted it by the shared key, then sends it to the user ; The *Trans*1 represents that the IdP checks whether the received nonce is correct. Note that we use *integer* to denote the session token *Sig*, if the value of *Sig* equals to 0, that means the session token is unavailable. At last, we use action *Trans*2 to reset the IdP to *initial* state.

Attacker. As mentioned before, we assume that the user-to-IdP communication is protected with SSL, and an attacker can sniff and alter traffic between the browser and the RP. According to these assumptions, we specify the actions of attacker as follows: Firstly, an attacker can eavesdrop the message from UB to RP. Secondly, an attacker can intercept the message from UB to RP. Thirdly, an attacker can modify the message from UB to RP. Besides, if an attacker gets enough knowledge of some message, then he can send a counterfeit message. For example, if an attacker gets the *identifier* of user, the shared *session handle*, the *identifier* of IdP, and the *nonce* encrypted by K_{UI}, then he can pretend to be the user and send authentication message to the IdP. Note that, if the attacker intercepts some message, it might cause the user's state to be needed to reset, so we use an action to reset the UB to *initial* state, as shown in the Fig. 4.

Security Property. In our example of OpenID protocol, one of the goals is to find the attack trace. In order to achieve this goal, we firstly combine the submodule. As mentioned before, the specification consists of four submodule, that is UB, RP, IdP and Attacker. As shown in the Fig. 5. We use *INSTANCE* statement instantiates copies of the submodule with the global variables substitute for the local variables in submodule. The Initial predicate $Init$ contains the conjunction $UserBrowser!Init$, which asserts that the $UserBrowser$ has the same initial values as in $Init$. Besides, the Next-state relation predicate $Next$ contains the disjunction $UserBrowser!Next \lor RelayingParty!Next$, which asserts that the next state can be one of state in any submodule. So, our specification can be written as $Init \land Next$. In our specification, if the attacker pretending to be the user and login successfully, then the attacker must has known the Sig. Therefore, we use the following temporal logic formula as the target property: $\Box(A\_knowledge.Sig = 0)$. Which means that the attacker can not get the authentication from IdP.

4 Experimental Results and Discussion

The model checker TLC can be used to check whether the protocol satisfies the security properties. Firstly, the MaxReal value was set to be 5. Then, TLC is used to check the security property $Target$. TLC generates the result in Fig. 6 in less than 2 s on an Intel Core i5 3.2 GHz, 4 GB system. There are 36139 states be found, 6445 distinct states, 1 branch, a depth of 51. According to the error trace, the value of key variables in every state is analyzed in detail. From the change of the values of these variables in every state, we obtain an attack path of the OpenID protocol, as shown in the Fig. 6. Due to its strictness and exactness, we can conclude that the scheme can not resist those protocol attacks such as eavesdrop attacks, replay attacks and impersonation attacks under the test of TLA+ using the model checker TLC. This is very useful to the network forensic analysis. The Potential attack scenarios graph is described by Fig. 6. Event description $(A_1 - A_{13})$ is illustrated in Table 1. An attacker starts by eavesdropping the user. Starting from state s_2 the attacker executes action A_2 to get the ID of user and move the system to state s_3. After that the RP return the redirect information by executing action A_3, the attacker intercept the message at state s_5. Then, the attacker modifies the message to induce the user connect with a fake IdP sever, which is controlled by the attacker. Starting from state s_6, the user sends encrypted nonce n_a by executed action A_6 and the attacker replay the message by A_7. After the real IdP return the encrypted nonce n_b, the attacker replay it to the user by executing action A_9. Starting from the state s_{10}, the user sends the encrypted nonce n_b to the attacker. With the encrypted nonce n_b, the attacker execute action A_{11} pretending to be the user. After checking the encrypted nonce, the IdP sends the signature sig to the attacker, then the attacker can use the users identifier to login by executing action A_{13}. This correspond to the following attack on the OpenID protocol.

Attack on OpenID. An attacker controls a fake RP and induces the victim to login. The victim has an account (say v) at the valid RP site and the attacker get the victims identity v. Instead of returning the right redirect message to the victim, the attacker constructs a message lead the victim redirect to a fake IdP controlled by the attacker. After that, the victim sends his credentials to the

Table 1. Event description

Actions	Description
A_1	User sends login request to RP
A_2	Attacker eavesdrops the message and gets the identifier of user
A_3	RP returns the redirect information to user
A_4	Attacker intercepts the redirect message and gets the identifier of IdP and handle
A_5	Attacker uses fake IdPID to reconstruct the redirect information and sends it to user
A_6	User sends a nonce n_a (encrypted with k) to start authentication
A_7	Attacker gets the n_a message and replays it to the real IdP
A_8	IdP sends a nonce n_b (encrypted with k) as a response
A_9	Attacker replays the n_b message and replays it to user
A_{10}	User computes the new key k' and sends n_b (encrypted with k') to a fake IdP
A_{11}	Attacker replays the received message to the real IdP
A_{12}	IdP sends session token to attacker
A_{13}	Attacker replays the session token to RP

fake IdP and the attacker can easily get it. With the identity v and the user credentials, an attacker impersonates a legal user to utilize the user's privileges and services.

5   Defense Mechanisms

The lack of security guarantee in the OpenID protocol means that RP websites need to employ additional countermeasures. Our web attacker defense mechanism is stateless, and all required cryptographic functions (i.e., HMAC) and data (i.e., Auth Request and session cookie) are readily accessible to the RP. The mitigation approach uses an HMAC function to bind the session identifier to the protocol messages in order to provide contextual binding and ensure the integrity and authenticity of the authentication request. Using an HMAC code as a validation token avoids the exposure of the session identifier, and prevents an attacker who learned the token from inferring with the user's session identifier. To eliminate the uncovered weaknesses, we revised the formal model in which (1) the Auth Request is signed by RP and the user's session identifier is included in the signature, and (2) the Login Request is signed by UB. Following protocol illustrates the revised version in A-B notation with boldfaced elements showing the changes. The revised model was encoded in TLA+, and verified to be secured by TLC. Based on the check results above, we propose the following defense mechanism based on the revised model:

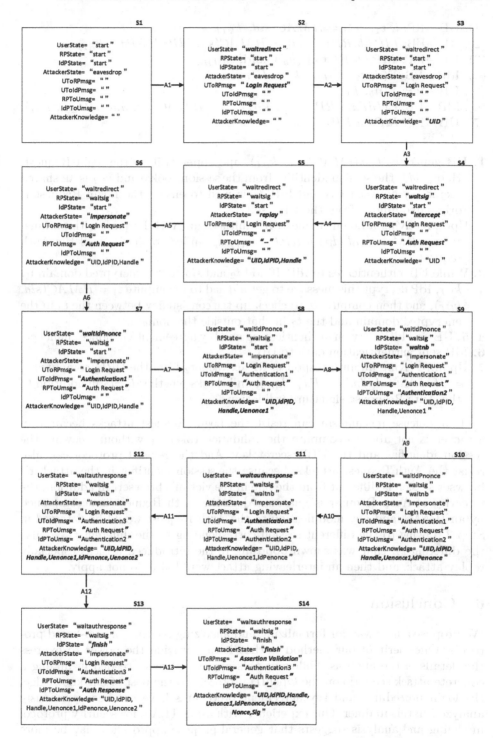

Fig. 6. Potential attack scenarios

(1). UB→RP: $i.\,\mathbf{t}_1$, $t_1 = HMAC(sid,\ k_{UI})$.
(2). RP→UB: $IdP.i.h.RP.\mathbf{t}_2$, $t_2 = HMAC(sid.IdP.i.h.RP.t_1,\ k_{RI})$.
(3). UB→IdP: $IdP.i.h.RP.\mathbf{t}_2.\mathrm{E}(n_a.\mathbf{t}_2.\mathbf{sid},\ k_{UI})$.
(4). IdP→UB: $\mathrm{E}(n_b.t_2,\ k_{UI})$, $k_1 = H(n_a, n_b)$.
(5). UB→IdP: $\mathrm{E}(n_b,\ k_1)$.
(6). IdP→UB: $\mathbf{E}(IdP.i.h.RP.t_2.n.s,\ k_{UI})$, $s = HMAC(IdP.i.h.RP.t_2.n,\ k_{RI})$.
(7). UB→RP: $IdP.i.h.RP.t_2.n.s$.

1. UB generates $t_1{=}HMAC(sid,\ k_{UI})$, and appends it to the login Request. Here, sid is the session identifier from the session cookie and k_{UI} is an shared secret key between UB and IdP. t_1 is used to ensure the Login Request is originated unique from the UB itself.

2. Upon receiving a Login Request, RP initiates an Auth Request with parameter $t_2{=}HMAC(sid.idp.i.h.RP.t_1,\ k_{RI})$ appended to the URL of the Auth request.

3. While UB authenticates to IdP, It add t_2 and sid to the encrypted domain by k_{UI}, IdP decrypt this message to get sid and to recompute $t_1 = HMAC(sid, k_{UI})$, and then compute t_2 to check up the consistency between the t_2 in the encrypted domain and the t_2 in that outside the domain.

4–5. UB and IdP carry on authenticating and key agreement via nonce challenge.

6. IdP sent authentication data to UB.

7. Upon receiving an auth response, RP extracts t_2 from the URL, computes $t_2' = HMAC(sid.idp.i.h.RP.t_1,\ k_{RI})$, and checks whether $t_2'{=}t_2$ in addition to the Auth Response signature validation.

Our defense mechanism can resist the Login Request attacks because an attacker is not able to compute the validation token t_1 without knowing the session identifier and the UB's secret key. And the revised protocol can also resist the Auth Request attacks, because the session identifier in the attacker's browser session is different from the one in the victim's browser. In addition, the integrity of Auth Request is guaranteed as the Auth Request is accompanied by an HMAC, and any modification to the Auth Request would be detected in Step 3. Owing to the different session corresponding to the different t_1, so also the different t_2, that was shown opposing to the introduced attacks especially replay attack, and then an interleaving attack would also do not apply.

6   Conclusion

We propose a new way for formalizing and analyzing security of web-based protocols. One merit of our method is that it can provide the power to express the details of the analysis. Following this approach, we succeeded in finding a concrete attack scenario on the OpenID protocol. To the best of our knowledge, the login procedures and key agreement procedures have not been previously analyzed in this manner. Our experience with using TLA+ for security protocol modeling and analysis suggests that general purpose approaches may be more suitable to reconstruct the concrete attack scenarios.

References

1. Rekhis, S., Boudriga, N.: Logic-based approach for digital forensic investigation in communication networks. Comput. Secur. **30**, 376–396 (2011)
2. Recordon, D., Fitzpatrick., B.: OpenID authentication 2.0, December 2007. http://openid.net/specs/openid-authentication-2_0.html
3. Khan, R.H., Ylitalo, J, Ahmed, A.S.: OpenID authentication as a service in openstack. In: 2011 7th International Conference on Information Assurance and Security (IAS), pp. 372–377, December 2011
4. Tsyrklevich, E., Tsyrklevich, V.: Single sign-on for the internet: a security story. In: Proceedings of the BlackHat07, July 2007
5. Barth, A., Jackson, C., Mitchell, J.: Robust defenses for cross-site request forgery. In: Proceedings of the 15th ACM Conference on Computer and Communications Security (CCS08), pp. 75–78. ACM, New York (2008)
6. Feld, S., Pohlmann, N.: Security analysis of OpenID. In: Pohlmann, N., Reimer, H., Schneider, W. (eds.) Proceedings of the Securing Electronic Business Processes-Highlights of the Information Security Solutions Europe 2010 Conference, pp. 13–25. Springer, Heidelberg (2010)
7. Lamport, L.: Specifying Systems: The TLA+ Language and Tools for Hardware and Software Engineers. Addison-Wesley Publishing Company, Boston (2002)
8. Dolev, D., Yao, A.: On the security of public key protocols. IEEE Trans. Inf. Theor. **29**(2), 198–208 (1983)
9. Lamport, L., Yu, Y.: TLC-The TLA+ Model Checker (2015). http://research.microsoft.com/en-us/um/people/lamport/tla/tlc.html

A Lightweight Code-Based Authentication Protocol for RFID Systems

Zhuohua Liu[1,2], Wei Zhang[1,2], and Chuankun Wu[1](✉)

[1] State Key Laboratory of Information Security Institute of Information Engineering
Chinese Academy of Sciences, Bejing 100093, China
{liuzhuohua,zhangwei,ckwu}@iie.ac.cn
[2] University of Chinese Academy of Sciences, Bejing 100190, China

Abstract. RFID is consider to be a common and useful tool in many applications, such as supply chain management, logistics, manufacturing, inventory control and so on. With the widespread adoption of RFID, the security and privacy issues of RFID systems are drawing more and more attention. In this paper, we propose a lightweight mutual authentication protocol based on error correction code for RFID systems with constant authentication time. Further analysis of the protocol shows that it also satisfies the essential requirements of RFID systems, including tag anonymity, location privacy, forward security, resistance to replay attack and de-synchronization attack, and immunity to tag compromise attack. We also compare our protocol with previous works in terms of security and performance.

Keywords: RFID protocol · Error correction code · Authentication · Privacy · Security

1 Introduction

Radio Frequency Identification (RFID) technology enables objects to be identified by radio waves, without the need for physical access or line of sight. It has been very popular in many applications, such as supply chain management, logistics, manufacturing and inventory control, and new applications are still arising, such as waste management, pets tracking, theft detection, environmental sensing and so on.

An RFID system basically consists of three components: a number of RFID tags, some readers and one or more backend databases. The RFID tag, which contains an unique identifier, is a radio transponder attached to physical objects. Generally, RFID tags can be divided into three categories: active tags, semiactive tags and passive tags. Passive tags contain no battery compared with active and semiactive tags. The RFID reader can obtain the unique identifier from the tag through a short-range wireless radio channel. And the backend database associates records with tag data collected by readers. An RFID reader can access the backend server via a secure network channel and then acquire the information

© Springer-Verlag Berlin Heidelberg 2015
W. Niu et al. (Eds.): ATIS 2015, CCIS 557, pp. 114–128, 2015.
DOI: 10.1007/978-3-662-48683-2_11

related to the tags. Hence, backend server and the reader are usually treated as a whole entity.

With the widespread adoption of RFID technology, security and privacy issues are drawing more and more attention. For example, an RFID tag can be continuously scanned by an attacker within a 10 m radius, thus the tag carrier can be easily traced without awareness. In addition, RFID tags may store some sensitive information about the carrier and these information should not be revealed to unauthorized one. In this case, tags should authenticate the reader before sending private data. Meanwhile, the reader should also authenticate tags to avoid counterfeit tags. This motivates a variety of RFID protocols to be proposed, which are designed to achieve mutual authentication, untraceability, and other security requirements.

Based on the computational cost and the operations supported on tags, the RFID authentication protocols can be classified into four classes [1]. The first class called "full-fledged" refers to those protocols that demand the support of conventional cryptographic functions like symmetric encryption, public key algorithms and cryptographic one-way functions [2–5]. The second class called "simple" is for those protocols that should support random number generator and one-way hash function on tags [6–9]. The third class called "lightweight" refers to those protocols that require a random number generator and simple functions like Cyclic Redundancy Code (CRC) checksum but not hash function [10–12]. The fourth class called "ultralightweight" refers to protocols that only involve simple bitwise operations (like XOR, AND, OR, etc.) on tags [1,13,14]. Since low-cost tags with limited resources will dominate the most of the RFID market, it is imperative to design lightweight and ultralightweight RFID authentication protocols for these low-cost tags. In this paper, we propose a lightweight mutual authentication protocol for low-cost RFID systems adopting error correction code, which can also resistant replay attack, compromise attack, deny of service (DoS) attack, and so on.

The rest of this paper is organized as follows: in the next Section, we review related works, then in Sect. 3, we give a brief introduction of the error correction codes used in this paper. Our proposed mutual authentication protocol is presented in Sect. 4. In Sects. 5 and 6, we give security and performance analysis. Finally, we conclude the paper in Sect. 7.

2   Related Work

With the rapid growth of RFID applications, more and more researches focus on the RFID with its security. A variety of RFID security authentication protocols have been proposed. Sarma et al. proposed a hash-lock protocol for RFID systems [15], which basically provides the privacy protection and access control, and can be implemented on low-cost tags since the tag needs only hash operation. However, the tag is vulnerable to location tracking attack as the response in each turn of the challenge remains unchanged. Moreover, the ID of the tag is sent in plain text, which will be vulnerable to replay and forgery attack. Then

Weis et al. proposed a randomized hash-locking protocol (RHL) in [16]. In order to prevent location tracking, the RHL use random numbers to variate the messages sent by the reader and tags. The RHL protocol can achieve strong privacy during the authentication, but the authentication efficiency is low, which has computation complexity of $O(N)$. Hence the RHL is not suitable for large scale RFID systems. A hash chain based protocol proposed by Ohkubo et al. [6] is also a challenge-response protocol with indistinguishability and forward security. The protocol achieves one-way authentication and is vulnerable to replay attack and tag impersonation. In addition, each authentication requires a larger amount of computation and comparison, and is not suitable for a large scale RFID system too. Alomair et al. proposed a symmetric-key privacy-preserving authentication protocol for RFID systems with constant-time identification [9]. In this protocol, the existence of a large device in RFID systems, the database, is utilized for improving the time efficiency of tag identification. Hence, it is a tradeoff between the tag's privacy and system complexity. Besides, the tag can be tracked before the pseudonym updated.

For the purpose of higher authentication efficiency for RFID systems, a lot of tree-based protocols are proposed, which can run in $O(log_k N)$ time to authenticate a tag [7, 8, 17–19], where N is the number of tags in the system and k is the balancing factor. However, as different tags may share a same group key in the system, tree-based protocols are vulnerable to tag compromise attack, although they are considered to be scalable. Lu et al. proposed a dynamic key updating protocol in 2007, called SPA [7]. Since keys in the system are dynamically updated, the number of tags sharing the compromised keys becomes less and less, which makes SPA to have a higher security than conventional tree-based protocols. However, it is still vulnerable to tag compromise attack because valid tags still share some group keys with compromised tags. Lu et al. proposed a new RFID protocol based on a sparse tree in [8], which is designed to reduce the dependence between group keys. In that protocol, each tag is assigned a path navigator that helps to speed up authentication. As shown in [20], the number of navigators is too small to thwart brute force attacks. This motivates Yao et al. to put forward a randomized RFID protocol [19], where different tags will not share any keys. However, a randomized hash function needs to be implemented in the tag, which may not be suitable for low-cost tags.

In order to further improve the authentication efficiency and meet the security requirements for RFID systems, a number of protocols based on public key cryptography are proposed. In 2008, Chen et al. designed a mutual authentication scheme based on quadratic residues [2]. This scheme uses direct indexing for each tag's authentication, so it can avoid server's brute search. Because of small key size and computational efficiency, Elliptic Curves Cryptography based algorithm is considered to be a good choice for RFID systems and some protocols based on Elliptic Curves Cryptography algorithm are proposed [3, 4, 21]. Due to the characteristic of the public key cryptography that the encryption key and decryption key are not the same, these protocols can improve the computational complexity of key searching to $O(1)$ [4, 21], hence they are scalable for RFID systems. However, even though RFID tags with full-fledged capacity are available, tags should be low-cost to attain great market penetration, which limits the utilization of these public key cryptography based schemes.

Table 1. Definition of notations

Symbols	Definition
N	The number of tags in the system
N_r, N_t	Random numbers generated by the reader and the tag respectively
ID_t	The identity of a tag
$Hw(x)$	The function to return the hamming weight of x
l	The security parameter
$L(x)$	The leftmost l bits of x
$R(x)$	The rightmost l bits of x
ECC	The abbreviated form of error correction code

3   Error Correction Code (ECC)

Error correction code (ECC) is a technique that enables the communication parties to correct the transmission errors which are incurred by the channel noise. A (binary) linear $[n, k]$ error-correcting code $\mathcal{C}$ is a subspace of F_2^n of dimension k. Such a code is specified by either a generator matrix $G \in F_2^{k \times n}$ such that $\mathcal{C} = \{uG \in F_2^n | u \in F_2^k\}$, or else by a parity-check matrix $H \in F_2^{r \times n}$ such that $\mathcal{C} = \{v \in F_2^n | vH^T = 0^r\}$ where $r = n - k$.

Definition 1 *Syndrome Decoding Problem (SDP). Given an $r \times n$ matrix H over F_q, a target vector $s \in F_q^r$ and an integer $\omega > 0$, is there a vector $x \in F_q^n$ with $Hw(x) \leq \omega$, such that $Hx^T = s^T$?*

The syndrome decoding problem (SDP) was proven to be NP-complete in [22]. Then McEliece proposed a new public-key cryptosystem based on the SDP [23]. McEliece cryptosystem is an efficient public-key cryptosystem for resource-constrained devices. It has a simple design in hardware and requires mostly binary operations that are commonly found in communication systems.

Let $[n, k, d]$ be a linear code with length n, dimension k and minimum distance d. Let G be the k-by-n generator matrix of an efficient code for which an efficient decoding algorithm exists. Select a random invertible k-by-k matrix S and a random permutation n-by-n matrix P. The public key is computed as the matrix as $F = SGP$ and $[n, k, d]$. To encrypt a message $m \in F_2^k$, first pick a random error vector $e \in F_2^n$ with $Hw(e) = \frac{d-1}{2}$, where $Hw(x)$ is the hamming weight of x. Then compute $y = mF \oplus e$ and output $y \in F_2^n$, where y is the cipher text of m. To decrypt the cipher text y, first calculate $yP^{-1} = mSG \oplus eP^{-1}$.

Since P^{-1} is a permutation matrix, eP^{-1} has the same weight as e. Then yP^{-1} can be decoded to obtain mS and remove S by applying S^{-1} to recover the message m.

Although the encryption of McEliece cryptosystem is very efficient, the key size is quite large. For example, when a $[450, 225, 56]$ linear code is selected for a McEliece cryptosystem, the public key will be a 450×225 matrix, almost $100k$ bits. Obviously, it is not suitable for low-cost tags. Gaborit and Girault choose double circulant matrices rather than purely random ones to decrease the key size [24]. In this case, the matrix is simply described from the first row which can be randomly chosen. With a small key size, the code-based cryptosystem is practical for low-cost device.

Chien et al. propose a lightweight authentication protocol for low-cost RFID adopting McEliece cryptosystem [10]. Instead of storing the whole generator matrix G, each tag only keeps some distinct rows of G. Hence, their scheme achieves a small key size and relatively high authentication efficiency. However, the number of tags in the system is very limited in this scheme. Specifically, assume that a secret linear code $C(n, k, d)$ over $GF(2)$ is chosen and l row vectors are assigned to each tag, then the number of tags in the system is $\lfloor \frac{k}{l} \rfloor$ at most. A novel lightweight authentication scheme combining rabin cryptosystem and error correction codes is proposed by Chien in [5]. The main idea of this scheme is that the sender randomly adds a noise e with $Hw(e) = \frac{d-1}{2}$ to its pre-assigned codeword c to have $m = c + e$, and then applies encryption of rabin scheme to have $y = m^2 mod N$. This scheme owns excelent performance in terms of security and scalability, but the tag needs to implement rabin encryption, which is not suitable for low-cost tags. Then Chen et al. [12] propose a secure RFID authentication protocol based on error correction code. Since each tag needs to keep the parity check matrix H, the storage consumption is too high for low-cost tags.

A recent proposal by Misoczki et al. [25] showed that quasi-cyclic moderate density parity-check (QC-MDPC) codes can be used in McEliece encryption reducing the public key to just 0.6 kByte to achieve a 80-bit security level. Then Maurich et al. [26] focus on lightweight implementations of code-based cryptography and demonstrate that McEliece encryption using QC-MDPC codes can be implemented with a significantly smaller resource footprint and still achieving reasonable performance sufficient. More precisely, their design requires only 68 slices for the encryption and is able to encrypt an input block in 2.2 ms on the Virtex-6 FPGA, which are also acceptable for low-cost tags. With small key size and lightweight implementation, the QC-MDPC McEliece is an attractive tool to be utilized to achieve security and privacy requirements of RFID systems. In this paper, we design a lightweight mutual authentication protocol for RFID systems adopting QC-MDPC McEliece.

4   Our Proposed Protocol

This section describes our new scheme, a lightweight mutual authentication protocol for RFID systems based on QC-MDPC McEliece cryptosystem. In this paper, we consider the RFID system which consists of N tags and a reader, the reader and the back-end server can securely communicate, thus the server and the reader can be treated as a whole entity. Let N_t and N_r represent nonces randomly selected by a tag and the reader, respectively. A pseudorandom number generator $g(\cdot)$ is implemented in each tag and the reader. Table 1 contains the definitions of the notations used in this paper.

4.1 QC-MDPC McEliece Encryption

A linear code $C(n, k, d)$ is quasi-cyclic (QC), if there exists some integer n_0 such that every cyclic shift of a codeword by n_0 positions yields again a codeword. If $n = n_0 p$ for some integer p, both generator and parity-check matrix are composed of $p \times p$ circulant blocks. Then the first row of each circulant block is sufficient to describe the matrices.

A (n, r, ω)-MDPC code is a binary linear (n, k) code with a parity-check matrix that has constant row weight ω, here $r = n - k$. A (n, r, ω)-QC-MDPC is a (n, r, ω)-MDPC code which is quasi-cyclic with $n = n_0 r$. In order to generate a (n, r, ω)-QC-MDPC code with $n = n_0 r$, the first rows $h_0, h_1, ..., h_{n_0-1}$ of the parity-check matrix blocks $H_0, H_1, ..., H_{n_0-1}$ with weight $\sum_{i=0}^{n_0-1} Hw(h_i) \leq \omega$ is selected at random. Then the following rows of the parity-check matrix blocks can be obtained by $r - 1$ quasi-cyclic shifts of $h_0, h_1, ..., h_{n_0-1}$, and the parity-check matrix is obtained by $H = [H_0|H_1|...|H_{n_0-1}]$. The generator matrix $G = [I|Q]$ can be obtained from H by concatenating the identity matrix I and matrix Q.

$$Q = \begin{pmatrix} (H_{n_0-1}^{-1} \cdot H_0)^T \\ (H_{n_0-1}^{-1} \cdot H_1)^T \\ \cdots \\ (H_{n_0-1}^{-1} \cdot H_{n_0-2})^T \end{pmatrix}$$

Given a (n, r, ω)-QC-MDPC code with t-error correcting, the McEliece operates key generation, encryption and decryption as follows.

Key-Generation: The system selects the first row h of H with at most ω set bits at random and computes the corresponding generator matrix G in row reduced echelon form, if H_{n_0-1} is not invertible, it generates a new random first row h and repeats. Instead of the full matrices, it suffices to store the first rows g and h to completely describe the public key G and private key H.

Encryption: A message $m \in F_2^k$ is encrypted into ciphertext $y \in F_2^n$ by $y = mG \oplus e$, where $e \in F_2^n$ is an error vector with at most t set bits at random.

Decryption: Let $\psi_H(y)$ be the decoder of the t-error correcting QC-MDPC equipped with the knowledge of the private H. To decrypt $y \in F_2^n$ into $m \in F_2^k$:

– Compute $mG \leftarrow \psi_H(mG \oplus e)$.
– Extract m from the first k positions of mG.

When selecting $n_0 = 2, n = 9600, r = 4800, \omega = 90$ and $t = 84$, the QC-MDPC McEliece is of 80-bit security level, the authors of [25] suggest parameters as given in Table 2.

Table 2. Parameters for different security levels for McEliece with QC-MDPC codes given by [25]

Security level	n_0	n	r	ω	t	Public key size
80 bit	2	9600	4800	90	84	4800 bit
80 bit	3	10752	3584	153	53	7168 bit
80 bit	4	12288	3072	220	42	9216 bit
128 bit	2	19712	9856	142	134	9856 bit
128 bit	3	22272	7424	243	85	14848 bit
128 bit	4	27200	6800	340	68	20400 bit
256 bit	2	65536	32768	274	264	32768 bit
256 bit	3	67584	22528	465	167	45056 bit
256 bit	4	81920	20480	644	137	61440 bit

In this paper, we assume that QC-MDPC McEliece is computational security which holds the following properties:

- Given an input $m \in F_2^k$, the time to calculate the ciphertext $y \in F_2^n$ is polynomially bounded.
- Given a ciphertext $y \in F_2^n$, it is computational infeasible to find the corresponding plaintext $m \in F_2^k$ without the private key.
- Any probabilistic polynomial time adversary can distinguish an output of the QC-MDPC McEliece from a random value with negligible probability of success.

4.2 Initialization

Initially, the server generates a pseudo-random number generator $g(\cdot)$ and a (n, r, ω)-QC-MDPC code with generator matrix G and parity-check matrix H. Each tag, denoted as $T_i, i = 0, 1, ..., N-1$, where N is the number of tags, has its unique identifier ID_t with l-bit length, where $l \leq \frac{n-r}{2}$. Then the reader writes the (ID_t, G) into each tag. It should be noted that each tag only needs to store the first row of G. Meanwhile, the server stores the identity of each tag as well as the corresponding information of the tag.

4.3 Authentication

Our protocol is to establish a mutual authentication relationship between a reader $\mathcal{R}$ and a specific tag $\mathcal{T}$ through three rounds of interactions as Fig. 1 shows.

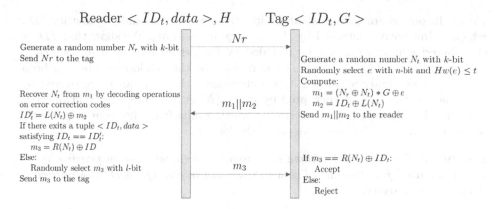

Fig. 1. The proposed protocol

(1) To launch a protocol instance, $\mathcal{R}$ randomly generates a nonce N_r with k-bit length and sends N_r to the tag.

(2) Upon receiving N_r, the tag firstly generates a random number N_t with k bit length and randomly selects a error vector e while $Hw(e) \leq t$. Then it computes m_1, m_2 as follows and sends $m_1 \| m_2$ to the reader.
$$m_1 = (N_r \oplus N_t) * G \oplus e$$
$$m_2 = ID_t \oplus L(N_t)$$

(3) After receiving $m_1 \| m_2$, the reader $\mathcal{R}$ decrypts m_1 to recover N_t. Then $\mathcal{R}$ obtains ID_t by $ID_t = L(N_t) \oplus m_2$ and checks if ID_t exists in the database. If it does, $\mathcal{R}$ computes $m_3 = R(N_t) \oplus ID_t$ and sends m_3 to the tag. Otherwise, $\mathcal{R}$ randomly selects a l-bit value and sends it to the tag.

(4) At the last, if the tag receives the message m_3 from the reader and the equation $m_3 == R(N_t) \oplus ID_t$ is established, the tag authenticates the reader successfully. Contrarily, if the tag does not receive the response message m_3 or the equation $m_3 == R(N_t) \oplus ID_t$ does not hold, the tag fails to authenticate the reader.

5 Security Analysis

In this section, we will present the security analysis of our scheme. In order to demonstrate that our scheme possesses the privacy properties, achieves mutual authentication and forward security, resists replay attack and DoS attack, five lemmas will be presented. The comparisons of various security attributes among our scheme and other related schemes are listed in Table 3.

Lemma 1. *The proposed scheme can provide tag anonymity, if the adopted PRNG function acts like a random oracle and QC-MDPC McEliece is computational security.*

Proof. In our scheme, the tag can be identified only by its unique identity ID_t, which is implicitly contained by the message m_2 and m_3. We show that ID_t is enciphered well and can not be revealed by any adversary. From $m_2 = ID_t \oplus L(N_t)$ and $m_3 = ID_t \oplus R(N_t)$, ID_t is masked by the random number N_t both in m_2 and m_3. Only when the N_t is determined, the ID_t can be recovered by an attacker. Since N_t is encrypted by $m_1 = (N_r \oplus N_t) * G \oplus e$, the attacker is computationally infeasible to attain N_t, which results from the security property of the QC-MDPC McEliece. We prove the lemma.

Lemma 2. *The proposed scheme can provide individual location privacy, if the adopted PRNG function acts like a random oracle and QC-MDPC McEliece is computational security.*

Proof. To prove this claim, we will show that the transcript (N_r, m_1, m_2, m_3) of a conversation can be produced by any tag with the reader. Thus we can argue that no conversation can be linked to a certain tag, which means the inability to distinguish between two tags by observing the transcripts with a probability better than random guessing. Firstly, for N_r is a random number, it obviously can not be linked to any particular tag. Next, we will demonstrate that the values of (m_1, m_2, m_3) can be produced by any tag. Since m_1 is computed from N_t by QC-MDPC McEliece, it can be considered as a random number due to the security property of QC-MDPC McEliece. The values of m_2 and m_3 are equal to $ID_t \oplus L(N_t)$ and $ID_t \oplus R(N_t)$, where N_t is a random number and unknown to any adversary. It is obvious that for fixed values m_1 and m_2, there can be two different tags ID_{t1} and ID_{t2} with the corresponding random numbers N_{t1} and N_{t2} such that $ID_{t1} \oplus L(N_{t1}) = ID_{t2} \oplus L(N_{t2})$ and $ID_{t1} \oplus R(N_{t1}) = ID_{t2} \oplus R(N_{t2})$. Therefore, we prove the lemma.

Lemma 3. *The proposed scheme achieves mutual authentication between tags and the reader, if the adopted PRNG function acts like a random oracle and QC-MDPC McEliece is computational security.*

Proof. The security of the mutual authentication is based on the challenge-response technique, using the PRNG function and QC-MDPC McEliece algorithm.

Given a reader $\mathcal{R}$ and a tag $\mathcal{T}$, and the attacker is noted as $\mathcal{A}$. In the learning phase, let $\mathcal{A}$ observe the protocol runs between $\mathcal{R}$ and $\mathcal{T}$ for n_1 times, interact with $\mathcal{R}$ for n_2 times and interact with $\mathcal{T}$ for n_3 times, where n_1, n_2, n_3 are polynomial bounded in l, which is the security parameter.

In the challenge phase, $\mathcal{A}$ can impersonate the target tag $\mathcal{T}$ n_4 times, and in each session i, $\mathcal{A}$ can generate a tuple (m_1, m_2), where $i \in \{1, ..., n_4\}$ and n_4 is polynomial bounded in l. Besides, $\mathcal{A}$ can impersonate the reader $\mathcal{R}$ n_5 times, and in each session i, $\mathcal{A}$ can generate a tuple (N_r, m_3), where $i \in \{1, ..., n_5\}$ and n_5 is polynomial bounded in l.

Assume that $\mathcal{A}$ can impersonate the target tag $\mathcal{T}$ successfully, which means that $\mathcal{A}$ sends a legal tuple (m_1, m_2) to $\mathcal{R}$ in any one of n_4 sessions during the challenge phase without knowing ID_t. As m_1 is enciphered by QC-MDPC

McEliece and m_2 is computed by $ID_t \oplus L(N_t)$, $\mathcal{A}$ wins only when she guesses the ID_t successfully or a N_r is repeated during the challenge phase. The probability to guess a correct ID_t is $\frac{n_4}{2^l}$, which is negligible, and the N_r will be repeated with probability of $1 - (1 - \frac{n_1+n_2}{2^k})^{n_4} \leq 1 - (1 - \frac{n_1+n_2}{2^{2l}})^{n_4}$, which is also negligible.

Assume that $\mathcal{A}$ can impersonate the reader $\mathcal{R}$ successfully, which means that $\mathcal{A}$ sends a legal message m_3 to $\mathcal{T}$ after receiving the response from $\mathcal{T}$ during the challenge phase without knowing the private key matrix H. Since QC-MDPC McEliece is computational security, it is infeasible to recover the N_t from the ciphertext $m_1 = (N_r \oplus N_t)*G \oplus e$ without private key. Hence $\mathcal{A}$ needs to construct a valid $m_3 = ID_t \oplus R(N_t)$ using the $ID_t \oplus L(N_t)$, which can take place only when a repeated N_t is selected by $\mathcal{T}$. The probability for $\mathcal{T}$ to choose a repeated N_t is $1 - (1 - \frac{n_1+n_3}{2^k})^{n_5} \leq 1 - (1 - \frac{n_1+n_3}{2^{2l}})^{n_5}$, which is negligible.

Therefore, the lemma is proved.

Lemma 4. *The proposed scheme can provide forward security, if the adopted PRNG function acts like a random oracle and QC-MDPC McEliece is computational security.*

Proof. Tags are simple devices and might be compromised by attackers. If a tag is compromised, the attacker could derive the secret inside the tag and try to trace responses from the same tag. Assume that the target tag is $\mathcal{T}$. Let the current resident data of $\mathcal{T}$ be $(ID_t, G, N_t^{(0)})$, and the last conversation be $(N_r^{(-1)}, m_1^{(-1)}, m_2^{(-1)}, m_3^{(-1)})$. Since $N_r^{(-1)}$ is a random number, it is independent of the triple $(ID_t, G, N_t^{(0)})$. In addition, as $m_1^{(-1)}$ is enciphered by QC-MDPC McEliece, which is computational security, it is infeasible to reveal the $N_t^{(-1)}$ from $m_1^{(-1)}$ without private key. Hence, the random number $N_t^{(-1)}$ is unknown to the adversary. Obviously, for fixed values $m_1^{(-1)}$ and $m_2^{(-1)}$, there can be two different tags ID_{t1} and ID_{t2} with the corresponding random numbers $N_{t1}^{(-1)}$ and $N_{t2}^{(-1)}$ such that $ID_{t1} \oplus L(N_{t1}^{(-1)}) = ID_{t2} \oplus L(N_{t2}^{(-1)})$ and $ID_{t1} \oplus R(N_{t1}^{(-1)}) = ID_{t2} \oplus R(N_{t2}^{(-1)})$. We prove the lemma.

Lemma 5. *The proposed scheme can resist replay attack, if the adopted PRNG function acts like a random oracle and QC-MDPC McEliece is computational security.*

Proof. Having eavesdropped previous communications, an adversary can replay the same message of the reader or the tag to forge the verification. Then the adversary may masquerade as the reader or the tag to launch a replay attack.

We first consider the reader impersonation against our scheme. In this case, the adversary $\mathcal{A}$ chooses a random number N_r which has been used by a legal reader before. After receiving the message (m_1, m_2) from the tag, $\mathcal{A}$ has to generates a message $m_3 = ID_t \oplus R(N_t)$ as a response. The success of $\mathcal{A}$ results from a repeated N_t generated by the tag or the revelation of ID_t and N_t using m_1 and m_2. Since the N_t is a random number generated by the tag in each session, it will be repeated with at most negligible probability. In addition, the revelation of ID_t and N_t contradicts the security property of QC-MDPC McEliece.

Then we consider the case of tag masquerade attack. Assume that $\mathcal{A}$ observes the protocol runs between the reader and tag n_1 times and interacts with the tag n_2 times, where n_1 and n_2 are polynomial bounded in l. Then $\mathcal{A}$ will obtain $n_1 + n_2$ tuples of (N_r, m_1, m_2). The replay message $(m_1 \| m_2)$ can pass the verification by the reader only when the random number N_r sent by the reader in current conversation is a repeated one, that is, N_r appears in $n_1 + n_2$ tuples of (N_r, m_1, m_2). Hence, $\mathcal{A}$ can impersonate the tag at most with probability of $\frac{n_1+n_2}{2^l}$, which is negligible. Hence, we prove the lemma.

Moreover, since the reader and tags do not need to update any internal state, our scheme is immune to desynchronization attack and it can be used to the distribution computing environment. In addition, each tag in our scheme only stores the unique identity ID_t and the public key G, which means that none of private data will be shared by tags, our scheme can resist tag compromise attack.

In the following, we show the comparisons between our protocol and other related protocols in terms of the security requirements. We take Chien's SASI protocol [1], Chien-Laih's ECC-based protocol [10], Juels-Weis' HB^+ protocol [13], and Chen's code-based protocol [12] into comparison. The comparison results are shown in Table 3.

Table 3. Comparison of security properties

	Our protocol	SASI [1]	Chien-Laih's [10]	HB^+ [13]	Chen's [12]
Tag anonymity	√	√	√	√	√
Location privacy	√	×	×	√	×
Mutual authentication	√	√	√	×	√
Forward secrecy	√	√	√	×	√
resistance to replaying	√	√	√	√	√
resistance to compromising	√	√	√	√	√
resistance to desynchronizing	√	×	√	√	√

SASI is a ultralightweight authentication protocol which requires only PRNG and simple bitwise operations in tags. But studies [27,28] show that SASI is vulnerable to desynchronizing and tracing attacks. Chien-Laih's ECC-based lightweight authentication protocol cannot defend the tracing attacks [29] and Juels-Weis' HB^+ multiround lightweight mutual authentication protocol is vulnerable to a man-in-the-middle attack [30]. A lightweight protocol using error correction codes has been proposed by Chen et al. in 2014 [12], and the authors claim that it is a realizable scheme with fulfilling security and privacy requirements. However, study [31] shows that this schemes is vulnerable to tracing attack.

6   Performance Analysis

In this section, we only compare the performance of the schemes with secure reader-server channel assumption. It is noted that only the reader (or the server) are required to be equipped with the decoding algorithms. The functions required on the tag are pseudo-random number generator, simple bit-wise operations like XOR and some additions. Compared to previous schemes, the computations on tags are very simple and efficient.

The following will present one possible implementation of the proposed scheme on low-cost tags. Assume that the identity of each tag is 128-bit length and the QC-MDPC code is selected as $n_0 = 2, n = 9600, r = 4800, \omega = 90$ and $t = 84$, which is of 80-bit security level. Then the public key size is 4800 bits, i.e. the first row of matrix Q is 4800 bits, and the total memory needed for a tag is $4800 + 128 = 4928$ bits, which is acceptable.

From the perspective of the computational cost of tags, apart from the pseudo-random number generation, the tag has to calculate $N_r \oplus N_t$ by 4800 XORs, compute $(N_r \oplus N_t) * G$ by approximately 400K XORs ($O(nlogn)$) and add e to the resultant by 9600 XORs. Besides, 256 XORs needed to compute $ID_t \oplus L(N_t)$ and $ID_t \oplus R(N_t)$. Obviously, the main computation is the matrix multiplication, which is also efficiently because the generator matrix G is quasi-cyclic.

Table 4. Comparison of performance

	Key size in database	Memory in tag	Computation in reader	Computation in tag	Communication (bits)	Scalable
Our protocol	$O(n)$	$O(n)$	$p, d, \oplus$	$p, \oplus, +, r$	$O(n)$	YES
SASI [1]	$O(N)$	$O(l)$	$p, \oplus, \wedge, \vee, +, r$	$p, \oplus, \wedge, \vee, +, r$	$O(l)$	YES
Chien-Laih's [10]	$O(nk)$	$O(n)$	$p, d, \oplus$	$p, \oplus, +$	$O(n)$	NO
HB^+ [13]	$O(N)$	$O(l)$	$p, \oplus, \cdot$	$p, \oplus, \cdot$	$O(Q)$	NO
Chen's [12]	$O(n^2)$	$O(n^2)$	$p, d, h, \oplus$	$p, d, h, \oplus$	$O(n)$	YES

p: PRNG; h: hash; d: decode; $\oplus$: XOR; $+$: addition; r: rotate; $\wedge$: and; $\vee$: or; $\cdot$: dot product.

When considering the communication, only three rounds of interactions are needed in each authentication. After receiving the authentication request from the reader, a message with constant length will be sent by the tag. Hence the communication complexity is $O(1)$. In particular, the message that need to be transported by the tag is 9728 bits, while the message transported by the reader is 4928 bits.

In the following, we compare our proposal with Chien's SASI protocol [1], Chien-Laih's ECC-based protocol [10], Juels-Weis' HB^+ protocol [13], and Chen's code-based protocol [12] as shown in Table 4, where assume that a C (n, k, d) error correction code is selected and N is the number of tags, Q is the number of interaction rounds between the reader and tags and l is the length of random numbers. Since the server has to brute search when identify a single tag, Juels-Weis' HB^+ scheme is not suitable for large scale systems. And Chien-Laih's scheme is also not scalable because the system can hold at most n tags, where n is the length of codeword. In Chen's proposal, the tag has to store a $n * (n - k)$ matrix, which is unsuitable for low-cost tags.

7   Conclusion

In this paper, we present a lightweight mutual authentication RFID protocol, which runs in $O(1)$ and can be applied into large scale RFID systems. The protocol is designed with encoding operations on error correction codes, pseudorandom number generating and other simple bitwise operations. These operations are proved lightweight enough to be implemented on low-cost RFID tags. Further analysis of the protocol shows that it also satisfies the essential requirements of RFID systems, including tag anonymity, location privacy, forward security, resistance to replay attack and de-synchronization attack, and immunity to tag compromise attack. Hence, we also anticipate that the results of this work can be applied to other authentication applications similar to RFID environment.

Acknowledgments. This work was supported by National 863 project (Grant No. 2013AA014002) and Strategic Priority Research Program of the Chinese Academy of Sciences (Grant No. XDA06010701).

References

1. Chien, H.Y.: Sasi: a new ultralightweight rfid authentication protocol providing strong authentication and strong integrity. IEEE Trans. Dependable Secure Comput. **4**(4), 337–340 (2007)
2. Chen, Y., Chou, J.S., Sun, H.M.: A novel mutual authentication scheme based on quadratic residues for rfid systems. Comput. Netw. **52**(12), 2373–2380 (2008)
3. Lee, Y.K. , Batina, L., Verbauwhede, I.: Ec-rac (ecdlp based randomized access control): provably secure rfid authentication protocol. In: 2008 IEEE International Conference on RFID, pp. 97–104. IEEE (2008)
4. Zhang, X., Li, L., Wu, Y., Zhang, Q.: An ecdlp-based randomized key rfid authentication protocol. In: 2011 International Conference on Network Computing and Information Security (NCIS), vol. 2, pp. 146–149. IEEE (2011)

5. Chien, H.Y.: Combining rabin cryptosystem and error correction codes to facilitate anonymous authentication with un-traceability for low-end devices. Comput. Netw. **57**(14), 2705–2717 (2013)
6. Ohkubo, M., Suzuki, K., Kinoshita, S.: Hash-chain based forward-secure privacy protection scheme for low-cost rfid. Proc. SCIS **2004**, 719–724 (2004)
7. Lu, L., Han, J., Hu, L., Liu, Y., Ni, L.M.: Dynamic key-updating: privacy-preserving authentication for rfid systems. In: Fifth Annual IEEE International Conference on Pervasive Computing and Communications, PerCom 2007, pp. 13–22. IEEE (2007)
8. Lu, L., Han, J., Xiao, R., Liu, Y.: Action: breaking the privacy barrier for rfid systems. In: IEEE INFOCOM 2009, pp. 1953–1961. IEEE (2009)
9. Alomair, B., Clark, A., Cuellar, J., Poovendran, R.: Scalable rfid systems: a privacy-preserving protocol with constant-time identification. IEEE Trans. Parallel Distrib. Syst. **23**(8), 1536–1550 (2012)
10. Chien, H.Y., Laih, C.S.: Ecc-based lightweight authentication protocol with untraceability for low-cost rfid. J. Parallel Distrib. Comput. **69**(10), 848–853 (2009)
11. Liu, A.X., Bailey, L.A., Krishnamurthy, A.H.: Rfidguard: a lightweight privacy and authentication protocol for passive rfid tags. Secur. Commun. Netw. **3**(5), 384–393 (2010)
12. Chen, C.M., Chen, S.M., Zheng, X., Chen, P.Y., Sun, H.M.: A secure rfid authentication protocol adopting error correction code. Sci. World J. **2014**, 12 (2014)
13. Juels, A., Weis, S.A.: Authenticating pervasive devices with human protocols. In: Shoup, V. (ed.) CRYPTO 2005. LNCS, vol. 3621, pp. 293–308. Springer, Heidelberg (2005)
14. Li, T., Deng, R.H., Wang, G.: The security and improvement of an ultra-lightweight rfid authentication protocol. Secur. Commun. Netw. **1**(2), 135–146 (2008)
15. Sarma, S.E., Weis, S.A., Engels, D.: Radio-frequency-identification security risks and challenges. Cryptobytes **6**(1), 2–9 (2003)
16. Weis, S.A., Sarma, S.E., Rivest, R.L., Engels, D.W.: Security and privacy aspects of low-cost radio frequency identification systems. In: Hutter, D., Müller, G., Stephan, W., Ullmann, M. (eds.) Security in Pervasive Computing. LNCS, vol. 2802, pp. 201–212. Springer, Heidelberg (2004)
17. Molnar, D., Wagner, D.: Privacy and security in library rfid: issues, practices, and architectures. In: Proceedings of the 11th ACM Conference on Computer and Communications Security, pp. 210–219. ACM (2004)
18. Dimitriou, T.: A secure and efficient rfid protocol that could make big brother (partially) obsolete. In: Fourth Annual IEEE International Conference on Pervasive Computing and Communications, PerCom 2006, pp. 269–275. IEEE (2006)
19. Yao, Q., Qi, Y., Han, J., Zhao, J., Li, X., Liu, Y.: Randomizing rfid private authentication. In: IEEE International Conference on Pervasive Computing and Communications, PerCom 2009, pp. 1–10. IEEE (2009)
20. Li, T., Luo, W., Mo, Z., Chen, S.: Privacy-preserving rfid authentication based on cryptographical encoding. In: INFOCOM, 2012 Proceedings IEEE, pp. 2174–2182. IEEE (2012)
21. Liao, Y.P., Hsiao, C.M.: A secure ecc-based rfid authentication scheme integrated with id-verifier transfer protocol. Ad Hoc Networks (2013)
22. Berlekamp, E.R., McEliece, R.J., Henk, C.A., Van, T.: On the inherent intractability of certain coding problems. IEEE Trans. Inf. Theor. **24**(3), 384–386 (1978)
23. McEliece, R.J.: A public-key cryptosystem based on algebraic coding theory. DSN Prog. Rep. **42**(44), 114–116 (1978)

24. Gaborit, P., Girault, M.: Lightweight code-based identification and signature. In: IEEE International Symposium on Information Theory, ISIT 2007, pp. 191–195. IEEE (2007)
25. Misoczki, R., Tillich, J.P., Sendrier, N., Barreto, P.S.: Mdpc-mceliece: new mceliece variants from moderate density parity-check codes. In: 2013 IEEE International Symposium on Information Theory Proceedings (ISIT), pp. 2069–2073. IEEE (2013)
26. von Maurich, I., Güneysu, T.: Lightweight code-based cryptography: qc-mdpc mceliece encryption on reconfigurable devices. In: Proceedings of the conference on Design, Automation & Test in Europe, p. 38. European Design and Automation Association (2014)
27. Sun, H.M., Ting, W.C., Wang, K.H.: On the security of chien's ultralightweight rfid authentication protocol. IEEE Trans. Dependable Secure Comput. **2**, 315–317 (2009)
28. Phan, R.W.: Cryptanalysis of a new ultralightweight rfid authentication protocol-sasi. IEEE Trans. Dependable Secure Comput. **6**(4), 316–320 (2009)
29. Chen, C.M., Chen, S.M., Zheng, X.Y., Yan, L., Wang, H., Sun, H.M.: Pitfalls in an ecc-based lightweight authentication protocol for low-cost rfid. J. Inf. Hiding Multimed. Signal Process. 5(4) (2014)
30. Gilbert, H., Robshaw, M., Sibert, H.: Active attack against hb+: a provably secure lightweight authentication protocol. Electronic. Lett. **41**(21), 1169–1170 (2005)
31. Erguler, I.: A key recovery attack on error correcting code based a lightweight security protocol

An Overview of Ad Hoc Network Security

Fan Yang[✉], Yulan Zheng, and Ping Xiong

School of Information and Security Engineering,
Zhongnan University of Economics and Law,
Wuhan, China
sally01_yang@163.com

Abstract. An ad hoc network is formed in haphazard manner. It has many different features from the conventional networks. So the security services applied to the traditional networks are not suitable for the ad hoc networks. In this paper, we will analyze some classical proposals for ad hoc network security and make a comparison on them. From which, we can have a brief idea of the existing circumstances. On the basis of that, we provided two models. Each of those models improves some performance compared to the original.

Keywords: Ad hoc networks · Threshold cryptography · Identity-based cryptography · Key management

1 Introduction

Ad hoc network is a kind of self-organized networks. That is, it doesn't rely on any fixed infrastructure; instead, all networking functions are performed by themselves. Thus it has many characteristics that are different to the traditional networks. Those features bring several security threats to the networks [1].

Firstly, all the communications between nodes are through wireless channels. This make the network susceptible to the link attacks, including passive (e.g., eavesdropping) and active (e.g., message replay, message distortion) attacks. Secondly, malicious attacks are supposed not only from outside but also from inside. Thirdly, because of the membership and the topology of the network are frequently changed, fixed security parameters are not suitable in this case. Finally, in an ad hoc network large number of nodes work in cooperation to complete task. The adversaries can compromise the security of the network by destroy the collaboration.

But the threats are also challenges. There are many solutions proposed to solve the problem. That is the issue this paper focuses on. In Sect. 2, different proposals are provided. In Sect. 3, we make a contrast between those proposals. In Sect. 4, we make some further study and put forward an outline of two new models. In the last section, some conclusions are made.

This work is sponsored by the fundamental research funds for the Central Universities projects.

© Springer-Verlag Berlin Heidelberg 2015
W. Niu et al. (Eds.): ATIS 2015, CCIS 557, pp. 129–137, 2015.
DOI: 10.1007/978-3-662-48683-2_12

2 Existing Typical Schemes

2.1 Threshold Mechanism Schemes

In an ad hoc network, a single trusted node is not existed. Therefore an ad hoc network should have a distributed architecture with no central entities (i.e., CA). We can do this by using threshold cryptography [2].

Zhou proposed a partial distributed key management scheme in [3]. The system has a public/private key pair. All nodes know the system public key. The system private key is divided into n shares held by n nodes (called as servers). With the configuration of (n, t + 1), any nodes get (t + 1) partial certificates signed by servers can reconstruct the correct certificate. To ensure safety, Zhou provides a scheme to refresh the secret shares computed from the old ones by the servers in cooperation. Based on the different features of the nodes in system, Yi proposed another distributed key management scheme MOCA in [4, 5]. MOCA differs from Zhou's by choosing MOCA nodes (i.e. servers) according to their characteristics such as physical security, computational capability, and so on. Yi also provides anonymous certification services with the routing layer support. In the schemes above, when in large network it may be difficult to find enough servers to finish certificating.

In [6] Yang proposes a scheme that use the routing protocol based on linking-status. In this scheme, all the server nodes make up a server-group. During the certificates issuing, the joining node only need contacts with one server, which will gather all the other servers' partial certificates. Kong in [7] proposes a full distributed key management framework. In the system, each node is a server and holds one share of the private key. Moreover, the scheme is able to detect malicious nodes and revoke their certificates. The drawback is that it is easy for the adversary to gather enough shares to restore the private key.

2.2 Self-organized Mechanism Schemes

In [8, 9] Hubaux proposes a fully self-organized public-key management system. In this system, like in PGP [10], users' public and private keys are created by themselves. Shown as Fig. 1, the certificates are presented as a graph in the system (the red edges represent the certificates that K_v stores, while the blue ones represent the certificates that K_u stores). The vertices represent public keys and the edges represent certificates. When K_u wants to authenticate K_v, they merge the certificates they stored, and try to find a certificate chain from K_u to K_v. If found, the authentication is successful, otherwise it fails. Hubaux obeys the manner of the ad hoc network, but the redundancy of certificates is non-ignorable.

Similar to Hubaux, Gokhale provided a novel in [11]. In the trust model, the trust is represented by a group membership, called troups. When two nodes in the network decide to establish a trust membership, a troup is created. Each node in a group has an identity within a group. The group membership is verified using zero-knowledge protocol of modular exponentiation [12]. For the network shown in Fig. 2, Node 1 can verify node 3 and 4 by transitive node 2. This model is not centrally controlled, but

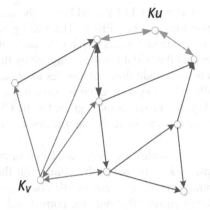

Fig. 1. The certificate graph (Color figure online)   **Fig. 2.** A trust model based on troups

every troup has a controller to generate a RSA accumulator. Though with a small storage cost, this scheme cannot resist active attacks.

2.3 Id-Based Mechanism Schemes

In 1984, Shamir put forward that an arbitrary string can be the public key, and some algorithm could be used to compute the corresponding private key [13]. From which, several id based schemes has been for proposed [14–16]. But none of them are satisfactory until Boneh proposes a fully functional identity-based encryption scheme in [17]. In the system, there is a trusted "Private Key Generation Service" (PKG). The PKG generate the master public/private key pairs and the private keys corresponding to the identities. The security of this system is based on a natural analogue of the computational Diffie-Hellman assumption on elliptic curves.

On the basis of Boneh, Khalili proposes an approach [18] which combines the idea of id-based and threshold cryptography. This method can solve the spoofing problem effectively. And in [19], Lv gives the polynome algorithm for nodes that in the network to compute the system private key.

2.4 Cluster-Based Mechanism Schemes

In [20] Venkatraman and Agrawal present an end-to-end data authentication scheme. The network is based on the hierarchical structure. All nodes in the network are divided into two types: cluster heads (CH) and ordinary nodes. A cluster head is elected for each cluster to maintain the cluster membership information and act as the CA within a cluster. When any two nodes want to communicate, they authenticate each other and negotiate session key through CHs. Venkatraman didn't give the authentication between two nodes that belong to different clusters.

Based on the above schemes, Li [21, 22], Liu [23] and Lu [24] make some improvements. They take advantages of the threshold cryptography and the id-based cryptography. The secret key is distributed to the CH nodes. In Li's and Liu's schemes, there is a trusted off-line Private Key Generation Service (i.e., PKG). The PKG generate the system public key and private key. Every node that wants to joins the network must register to the PKG and gain its private key and the initial certificate signed by the system private key. The scheme that Liu presents has an addition that handles the cases where the nodes leave the cluster/network. While in Lu's system, there is also a trusted third party, which doesn't generate the private key, but provides the register for the CH nodes only. The CHs will perform the authentication and issue the certificates to the nodes that want to join the cluster.

All proposals above are id-based. In [25], Xu provides a cluster-based key management and restoration framework. This framework uses two hash chains with the assumption that every node has a pair of public/private key to ensure the communication between the nodes and the CHs. The scheme ensures that only the correct nodes can reconstruct the session key but the adversity cannot. If certain nodes can't receive the session keys on time because of the lag, they can restore the session keys with the help of other nodes. CHs need to maintain a collection of legal users, but the author didn't give the algorithm to guarantee the collection.

3   The Comparisons of Those Schemes

We have listed a lot of schemes above; here we make a table to exhibit the strengths and weaknesses of all the schemes. The table as follows Table 1.

Among the above proposals, in Zhou's system, the server nodes have to maintain the public keys of every node in the network. That brings a lot of capacity cost. Moreover, the scheme doesn't have revocation mechanism, which is an important part of the security in ad hoc networks since every node in the network is possible to be compromised. Yang maybe improves the efficiency but this method has no good to the safety of the system, and its routing protocol will having effects on other layers. Yi's proposal is an improvement of the Zhou's with a certificate revocation mechanism. But the problems of low rate of successful authentication and certificate-update delay still exist. Kong's scheme is a full distributed key management framework, that is to say, every node in the network is a server. This method improves the efficiency of authentication, but it reduces the security of the network, since the adversary can easily compromise arbitrary t nodes and gain the system's private key. Note that any threshold cryptography based methods will be existed the problem of the balance of the efficiency and security.

Hubaux obeys the ad hoc networks' nature that all nodes are in haphazard manner. But there still exists some problems. During the authentication, the certificate chains are possible not to be found. Because of the lack of trust authority, the longer certificate chains are trend to be unreliable. Malicious nodes can destroy the security of the system by fabricating a lot of false certificates. Furthermore, Hubaux's scheme doesn't provide an effective algorithm to manage the certificates, thus causing a number of redundancies. Gokhale use troups instead of certificates. But the weakness is the same to Hubaux. And it can't resist active attacks.

Table 1. The comparisons of different comparisons

	Storage	Security	Efficiency	Certificate update	Revocation mechanism
Zhou	Nodes: little	high	low	yes	no
	Servers:a lot				
Yang	little	low	high	yes	yes
Yi	little	high	low	yes	yes
Kong	little	low	high	yes	yes
Hubaux	A lot	low	low	yes	yes
Gokhale	little	low	low	no	no
Khalili	little	high	low	no	no
Lv	little	high	high	no	no
Venkatramen	little	low	high	no	no
Li, Liu and Lu	little	high	high	yes	yes
Xu	little	high	high	no	no

The id-based schemes are based on elliptic-curve cryptography, which have very short ciphertexts/signatures and efficient computation times. But it is vulnerable to man-in-the-middle attacks. The schemes also lack the certificate update mechanisms and the deletion of the malicious nodes. Khalili choose only n nodes to format the system private key while Lv distributes it to the whole networks. So the id-based schemes also have the weaknesses of the threshold cryptography schemes.

In Venkatraman's proposal, every node in the network knows the system key pair, so the cluster key is easy to be known to the malicious nodes. When joins a cluster, a mutual authentication is performed by the new node and the existing nodes or the cluster heads using the system key pair. The mutual authentication by sending a challenge and receiving a response is pretty cost. And the scheme doesn't detect and deal with the malicious nodes.

Compare to Venkatraman's scheme, Li, Liu and Lu's usage of threshold cryptography and identity based signcryption algorithm greatly increase the security of the system and reduce the computation costs of the public key. Liu has the malicious detection mechanism while Lu's is more scalable.

In Xu's system, there is no need to keep certificates and easy to deal with malicious nodes. But it is not complete because it assumes that every node has a public/private key pair and the CHs hold the correct id list. But how to identify the nodes that the CHs hold is legal is also a problem. Furthermore, if the scale of the network is very large, there may be a great number of sessions that is to be initiated by the same time. There will be a very high computational capabilities requirement for the CHs.

Besides those characteristics mentioned above, we trend to pay an attention on the authentication efficiency of them.

Zhou didn't give the process of authentication. He use (n, t + 1) threshold cryptography to accomplish the service. So for a joining node, it must to broadcast requests to the servers and get at least (t + 1) partial certificates to recover a correct certificate. The requests would reach the server though multi hops, that will cause a low efficiency. Yi is similar to Zhou. Their efficiency is the same.

Yang and Kong have some improvement compares to Zhou. They are easy to contact enough servers. Yang let a server replace the node to acquire the partial certificates wile Kong just needs to contact the neighboring nodes.

The authentication process of Khalili is same to Zhou and Lv is same to Kong. The only difference is the computing methods of certificates. This may cause a bit influence on efficiency.

The cluster-based schemes are analogical. In every cluster, the CH acts as CA. The authentication is like traditional centralized networks.

Hubaux and Gokhale are different. For Hubaux, when authenticating, one has to merge his certificate repository with the other whom he want to communicate with and try to find a chain. This chain represents the trust relationship between them. If it is found, the authentication is finished. This is not always successful. So the efficiency is not high. Gokhale is similar to Hubaux. But Gokhale uses troups instead of certificates and Gokhale uses a zero-knowledge proof to accomplish the membership verification. That cost a lot. So the Hubaux's scheme is more efficient than Gokhale's.

4 Further Study

We have introduced many schemes above. Each one has some advantages and drawbacks. We can conclude that the schemes that based on threshold cryptography, identity encryption and clustering structure are sufficient. There are some good proposals too. But the self-organized schemes are relatively less, while in some ways the organized schemes are more adaptable to the ad hoc network. We can do the researches on this way. Here we provide two possible improvements: one is a bidirectional model, the other is a trust model with parameter.

These two models are all based on the self-organized public-key management of Hubaux. As it shows, the Hubaux's scheme has two obvious flaws. One is sometimes it may be hard to find the certificate chains, that means, a low authentication success rate. Another is when the chains become too long, the credibility reduces. On the basis of these analyses, we come up some ideas. These two models are the trials.

4.1 A Bi-directional Trust Model

As we can see, Hubaux describes the trust relationship through a certificate graph G(V, E). While V stands for a public key and E stands for a certificate. When A trust B, A signs B a certificate with its private key. In another word, there exists an arrow from A to B in the graph G.

In our model, we also apply the concept of graph G(V, E). This graph is defined as the trust relationships of the whole network. While V represents the collection of Vertexes and E represents the collection of the edges. A vertex stands for a node. An edge stands for the trust relationship between two nodes. Different from Hubaux, we have no certificates. Because the trust relationship is bi-directional in our model, a certificate can't describe this kind of relationship. This can simply exhibit on the graph, shown as Fig. 3. Obviously, this is an undirected graph.

As Fig. 3 shows, if v_1 trust v_2 and v_2 trust v_1 too. Then v_1 can establish a relationship with v_2. There will be a link between v_1 and v_2 in the graph. Every node holds a sub graph according to their storage capacity. When v_u wants to communicate with v_k, they try to find a pathway between them to accomplish the authentication.

Because the graph is similar to the topology graph of mobile network, we can take the advantages of the existing routing protocols to find the path between two nodes more efficient.

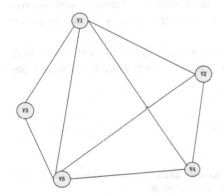   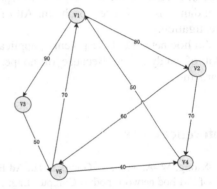

Fig. 3. The trust relationship graph   **Fig. 4.** Trust relationship graph with weight

4.2   A Trust Model with Parameter

The other model we provide is similar to Hubaux's. We still apply a graph G(V, E), while V and E are the collections of vertexes and edges, respectively. A vertex stands for a node and an edge stands for the relationship between two nodes. But we introduce a parameter to measure the extent of the trust. As we can see in Fig. 4, this graph is digraph.

In this model, every node can choose to trust one else or not with a parameter w. This parameter represents the weight of the edges on the graph. It implies the extent of trust. The parameter w ranges from 0 to 99. When w = 0, it represents full trust. The extent of trust decrease when the value of w grows. As shown in Fig. 4, there is a narrow from v_1 to v_2 with a weight of 80. That is to say, v_1 trust v_2 with only a percentage of 20, which is pretty low. When v_1 want to authenticate v_2, they have to try to find at least one path that the addition is below the fix threshold value. If not, the authentication failed. In a graph, there are algorithms can easily to find the shortest distance between two nodes. We use a trust matrix to replace the certificate.

5 Conclusions

In this paper, we introduce many kinds of security schemes for ad hoc network and compare their strengths and weaknesses. Among those the self-organized threshold mechanism scheme is the most adaptable to the ad hoc networks' nature so that we propose two trust models through the improvement of Hubaux's model. One is the bidirectional trust model which uses two-way trust instead of one-way trust. This can greatly improve the authentication success rate and reduce the storage cost. The other model, with a trust weight, well resolves the problem of low confidence caused by long certificate chains in Hubaux's.

But some problems still remain. For the latter, the matrix will be large in order to attain enough information in a large network. The storage cost is nearly as much as Hubaux's. And for the former, how to represent the bidirectional trust as well as avoid redundancy is the biggest problem. All of these problems require solutions and more investigation.

Ad hoc networks have potential applications in a recent future. That allows us to do a lot of study on it. Because of no perfect schemes, further study is urgent and promising.

References

1. Xiong, W.-A., Kun, S., Gong, Y.-H.: Ad Hoc Security authentication mechanism overview of Ad hoc network nodes. Comput. Eng. Appl. 44(13) (2008)
2. Desmedt, Y.: Threshold cryptography. Eur. Trans. Telecommun. 5(4), 449–457 (1994)
3. Zhou, L., Hass, Z.J.: Securing ad hoc networks. IEEE Netw. 13(6), 24–30 (1999)
4. Yi, S., Kravets, R.: MOCA: mobile certificate authority for wireless ad hoc networks. In: Proceedings of the 2nd Annual PKI Research Workshop (PKI 2003), April 2003. http:// mobius.cs.uiuc.edu/~seungyi/
5. Yi, S., Kravets. R.: Key management for heterogeneous ad hoc wireless networks. Poster Presentation, ICNP 2002. http://www-sal.cs.uiuc.edu/~rhk/pubs/tr-2290-1734.pdf
6. Xia, Y., Xiaozhu, J., Han, Z.: A new key management scheme based on threshold mechanism of Ad Hoc network. Journal of QingDao University (Natural Science Edition) 23 (4) (2010)
7. Kong, J., Zerfos, P., Luo, H., Lu, S., Zhang, L.: Providing robust and ubiquitous security support for mobile ad-hoc networks. In: Proceedings of the 9th IEEE International Conference on Network Protocols (ICNP 2001) (2001)
8. Hubaux, J.P., Buttyan, L., Capkun, S.: Self-organzied public-key management for mobile ad hoc networks. Trans. Mobile Comput. 2, 52–64 (2003)
9. Hubaux, J.P., Buttyan, L., Capkun, S.: The quest for security in mobile ad hoc networks. In: Proceedings of MobiHOC, October 2001
10. Zimmermann, P.: The Official PGP User's Guide. MIT Press, Cambridge (1995)
11. Gokhale, S. Dasgupta, P.: Distributed authentication for peer-to-peer networks. In: Proceedings of the 2003 Symposium on Applications and the Internet Workshops 2003, January 2003

12. Camenisch, J.L., Michels, M.: Proving in zero-knowledge that a number is the product of two safe primes. In: Stern, J. (ed.) EUROCRYPT 1999. LNCS, vol. 1592, pp. 107–121. Springer, Heidelberg (1999)

13. Shamir, A.: Identity-based cryptosystems and signature schemes. In: Blakely, G.R., Chaum, D. (eds.) CRYPTO 1984. LNCS, vol. 196, pp. 47–53. Springer, Heidelberg (1985)

14. Desmedt, Y.G., Quisquater, J.-J.: Public-key systems based on the difficulty of tampering. In: Odlyzko, A.M. (ed.) CRYPTO 1986. LNCS, vol. 263, pp. 111–117. Springer, Heidelberg (1987)

15. Tsuji, S., Itoh, T.: An ID-based cryptosystem based on the discrete logarithm problem. IEEE J. Sel. Areas Commun. 7(4), 467–473 (1989)

16. Maurer, U.M., Yacobi, Y.: Non-interative public-key cryptography. In: Davies, D.W. (ed.) EUROCRYPT 1991. LNCS, vol. 547, pp. 498–507. Springer, Heidelberg (1991)

17. Boneh, D., Franklin, M.: Identity-based encryption from the Weil pairing. In: Kilian, J. (ed.) CRYPTO 2001. LNCS, vol. 2139, pp. 213–229. Springer, Heidelberg (2001)

18. Khalili, A., Katz, J., Arbaugh, W.A.: Toward secure key distribution in truly ad hoc networks. In: Proceedings of IEEE Workshop on Security and Assurance in Ad hoc Networks (2003)

19. Lv, X., Cheng, G., Xu, F.: Threshold authentication scheme of ad hoc network based on bilinear pairings. Comput. Eng. 35(1), 147–149 (2009)

20. Venkatraman, L., Agrawal. D.P.: A novel authentication scheme for ad hoc networks. In: IEEE Conferences on Wireless Communications and networking, WCNC, vol. 3, pp. 1268–1273 (2000)

21. Li, G.S., Han, W.-B.: Cluster-based key management in ad hoc networks. Comput. Sci. 33 (2) (2006)

22. Li, G.S.: Resarch for Mobile Ad Hoc Security. The PLA Information Engineering University (2005)

23. Liu, Z.-L., Xin, Y., Zhu, H.-L.: A cluster-based key management scheme for ad hoc networks. Netinfo Secur. 10 (2012)

24. Lu, W.: An Identity-based Hierarchical Key Management Scheme for Wireless Mesh Network. Xidian Univerity (2013)

25. Xu, S.: Research of Key Management and Authentication Mechanisms for Ad Hoc Network. Ji'nan University (2013)

26. Rajamanickam, M., Murugesan, S., Mariappan,V.: A Node Authentication Clustering Based Security for ADHOC Network, 2014ICCSP, 03–05 April 2014

Trust Computing and Privacy Protection

Structural Analysis of IWA Social Network

Wenpeng Liu, Yanan Cao[✉], Diying Li, Wenjia Niu, Jianlong Tan,
Yue Hu, and Li Guo

Institute of Information Engineering, Chinese Academy of Sciences, Beijing, China
{liuwenpeng,caoyanan,lidiying,niuwenjia,tanjianlong,
huyue,guoli}@iie.ac.cn

Abstract. Internet Water Army (IWA), a special group of online users, has more and more engaged our attention due to the negative effects caused by their irresponsible comments or articles. While most of related work focused on how to detect IWA using a classifier, there is a lack of analysis about the distribution and behavior characteristics of the special group. To address this issue, this paper constructs an IWA social network in which IWAs are core nodes, and preliminarily studied the network from its traits of structure and composition. Firstly, we crawled IWAs from a task posting website and extracted the relations between them and normal users from a social network site. Then, we applied two classical community detection algorithms FN and CPM on the IWA social network, and analyze the community detection result. Experimental results show that IWA social network is deserved to analyze and discuss, and we found some interesting phenomena which are very helpful to better understanding and monitoring the IWA accounts.

Keywords: Internet water army · Social network · Community detection · Community structure · Sina micro-blog

1 Introduction

As the rise of the domestic social media such as forum and micro-blog, an increasing number of Internet users joined social network platform. However, the openness and rapid spread of social platform also generated an interest-driven group called hidden paid posters, or termed Internet Water Army (IWA)[1], in China. IWA attracting more attentions since their negative impact causing by their public guidance of irresponsible opinions. IWA Refers to "the large number of people who are well organized to flood the Internet with purposeful comments and articles." [4] Driven by economic interests or other purpose, companies and individuals preferred to hire online users to make comments to create hot and trending topics so as to gain popularity. By this means, the articles or remarks posted from this purposive users result in a one-sided attitude and influence common users' recognition or decisions. So many sensational cases caused by water army reflect wicked effect of IWA, such as the framed incident of Mengniu to Yili, film critics of "Hong Men Yan". In general, IWA take all kinds of post tasks in

---

[1] http://en.wikipedia.org/wiki/Internet_Water_Army.

© Springer-Verlag Berlin Heidelberg 2015
W. Niu et al. (Eds.): ATIS 2015, CCIS 557, pp. 141–152, 2015.
DOI: 10.1007/978-3-662-48683-2_13

normal state and commonly known as web hyper. Furthermore, they are the most probably potential crowd that wide spreading negative rumors. Consequently, it has a great significance that building a blacklist library of IWA to accumulate related data and learning characterize of IWA structure and behavior rules.

Previous studies on Internet Water Army mainly concern problem of water army detection, while, our research focus on the analysis of the structure of water army network. Empirically, IWA have a lot of members and each member takes control of a good few accounts that have lots of fans. What's more, primary accounts of member have communication with other water army users or normal users to hidden identities of IWA. With such phenomena, we suppose that it is meaningful to diagnose relationships between IWA and normal users. Generally acknowledged, community structure is considered to be a significant property of real-world and virtual world as it often reveals interrelationships among nodes within a network. On the general question of community structure detection, various scholars have studied on the issues for a few years and have good results. The summarization of relevant research will be described in next section. For a better analysis of IWA, we propose a concept of IWA social network.

The IWA social network is an unnatural social network totally different from natural social network. Note that natural social network we mentioned means in which members connect others (by means of following, forwarding et.) since they have same interest or work in the same company or other common intrinsic properties. While IWA social network we proposed here refers to the special group in which members are expanded based on IWA. In other words, they gathered owing to taking over some tasks that bring them economic interests.

We get thousands of accounts of Sina Micro-blog which are proven exactly water army by crawling from a task posting website. On this website, employers post tasks accompanied with reward, meanwhile hyper choose tasks to accomplish and upload pictures of proof to get paid. Afterwards, we filtered data among these accounts in terms of some rules. Based on these filtered accounts, we crawl more accounts have links with them in Sina Micro-blog. Subsequently, we do community detection to all these nodes by two typical methods. After the experiments, we could observe that the IWA social network we discovered are special in community structure in contrast to natural network studied by previous research.

2 Related Work

Previous work about Internet water army mostly focused on water army detection or similar identification like forum and blog spammers. Most studies detect water army through establish classifier. Shin et al. [2] develop light-weight features on spammers' IP, commenting activity and some characteristics to train SVM classifier and achieve a good result in identifying forum span. Chen et al. [4] design a new detection mechanism using both non-semantic analysis and semantic analysis. They trained the classifier with Sina dataset and showed a promising performance by used it test Sohu dataset. Recently, Xu et al. [5] propose a novel bursty topic classification algorithm based on SVM active learning, which in light of the discovery that the topics driven by water army exhibit the characteristics different from general topics in their latency stage. There are still some researchers exploring this issue without use of classifier. On the issue of identification on forum and blog spammers, Li et al. [1] take advantage of text sentiment analysis to discern the net cheaters. They analysis the emotional tendencies of information publisher and then to determine authorship by calculating the ratio of positive and negative. In work [3], the authors focused on label groups and found that labeling groups of spammers could be detected if the spammers had similar behavior when they wrote reviews for products.

With all that said, previous work have done a good job on spammers, fortunately, most of methods and techniques could be still used for water army detection. Still, there are some problems need to be aware of and improved. Even though new method which combining all sorts of methods and analysis techniques achieved more satisfying effect in detecting water army, the features and thresholds are selected too subjective. Besides, since the identity of water army cannot be proved, the dataset they used are either uncertain (label by individual experience) or too small, let alone testified.

In order to solve the two aforementioned questions, we attempt to make thorough analysis on the structure and behavior of water army. Besides, further study like impact analysis and propagation prediction of IWA could continue. As we known, only when water army acting collectively, could they guide and influence public opinion upon their willingness. Therefore, we are curious about interactions in water army and try to find some communities between them like natural social network. Community structure is considered to be a significant property of real-world and virtual world as it often reveals interrelationships among nodes which constitute the network. Consequently, we'll apply some community detection algorithms on water army network.

With the rapid rise of large-scale social network, such as Facebook, Twitter and Sina Microblog, social network analysis has become a hot issue. Many kinds of community detection algorithms have been created and becoming complete and mature. In general, the relevant algorithms in networks could be divided into two categories: non-overlapping community detection (also known as traditional community detection) and overlapping community detection. As for traditional community detection, all types of algorithms have been developed quite mature. The most popular algorithm of divisive algorithms is that proposed by Girvan and Newman [10]. Meanwhile, the significant new concept of modularity has been proposed. Accordingly, many optimization modularity algorithms pertain to Modularity-based methods emerged. For example, FN algorithm proposed by Newman [9], which we used to analysis network structure of IWA in this paper, is one of the greedy techniques in Modularity Optimization methods. With regard to overlapping community detection, is a research hotspot in recent years since it is closer to reality. One of the most popular and most original technique is the Clique Percolation Method (CPM) [7]. "It is based on the concept that the internal edges of a community are likely to form cliques due to their high density." [12] It's obviously that CPM cannot partite sparse network well.

3 Our Approach

3.1 Basic Concept of IWA Social Network

In previous studies of social network, most of researchers focused on the community or organization in which members gathered spontaneously owing to their intrinsic characteristics. We call it natural social network. For example, persons could be partitioned into a community on account of their same hobbies (such as football, a film star or a drama) or the same organization they participate in (such as the same school or company).

In order to deeply study the distribution and behavior characteristics of IWA, we propose a novel social network, called IWA social network. This special network consists of two kinds of nodes: IWAs as the core nodes, and normal users which communicate with IWAs as the expanded ones. That is to say, the unnatural social network in which core nodes have connections with others due to their economic interests or purposive interaction. Moreover, these economic interests achieved by accomplish some promotion tasks of publishing fake statement.

In point of characteristics of IWA social network, several points can be concluded for now. We presume that IWA contains a group of members and each member takes control of a good few accounts that have lots of fans. To maintain transmission and disguised as ordinary, among these accounts exist water army member's primary accounts which contact with others include both water army users and normal users. In this manner, IWAs could have relations with normal users. Nevertheless, statements above are hypothesis based on our survey on IWA. A series of experiments later will confirmed our hypotheses.

For now, we present basic definition that will be used throughout the article.

Definition 1. Given a IWA social network $WAG = \{E, V\}$

- $V = \{v_1, v_2, \ldots, v_n\}$ is a set of n nodes, which denote IWAs and their related normal users;
- $E = \{e_1, e_2, \ldots, e_m\}$ is a set of m edges, which denote the relations between nodes.

WAG is an undirected unweight sparse graph. The network structure is defined by the $n \times n$ adjacency matrix A. Each element A_{ij} of A is equal to 1 if there is an edge connecting nodes i and j. In unnatural social network, V is a set of nodes consists of watery army accounts and their connecting accounts, A_{ij} equal 1 if there has connection (follow and follower) between account i and j.

3.2 IWA Social Network Construction

The IWA social network is an unnatural social network different from natural social network. The construction of UNSN usually takes place in three stages and will be introduced in this subsection.

Data Crawler. Firstly, we need to get a number of data contains accounts which are proven to be water army.

After a period of investigate and survey, we found some websites used to publish tasks by employer. And then hyper (short for water army member) will complete and submit the task on this site to get paid. From the task list, we could glance over titles of 50 tasks on each page sorted from newest to oldest. Click into each task subject, we can acquire all the detailed information of it like task requirements, complete status of each response from hyper. It's very gratifying that all the hyper disclose their account and posting address in Sina so as to task checking.

Based on this discovery, we could crawl data as we like. In the crawl stage, multi-threading and distributed techniques are used to improve the performance and responsiveness of crawler program. Besides, in order to avoid blocked, we take use of proxy IP switching to crawl data. Proxy IP we used are selected from IP agent pool in turn which we build for other project before.

Data Cleaning. We plan to filter the data in this stage for fear of accounts we crawled in first phase are isolated.

For now, we've got large amounts of accounts that participated in promotion tasks of IWA. We're forecasting most of accounts we crawled are isolated in the network. In other words, many hyper have few interactive behaviors with other users in social network. Obviously, it has no means to partite those isolated nodes and their related nodes. Such being the case, we make a rule to filter raw data.

For this purpose, we build a structural model of activity evaluation and judgement matrix to judge node's activity. Setting threshold value V_0 for filtering baseline, and then remove those nodes whose V_i lower than V_0. After filtering the raw data, left nodes preserved as source nodes in prepared to be expanded.

Data Expansion. Up to now, we have some accounts that take part in tasks of water army and have normal activity-degree. The next step that we plan to do is to enlarge our IWA social network based on these special nodes.

Similar to the work in 3.1, this phase of work are accomplished by means of crawler. While, the difference is that the major information we crawled here are edges between nodes rather than the information of node itself. Also, it's important to determine how to judge an edge existing or not between two nodes. For example, extended nodes can be crawled along comment, forwarding and following, followers of source nodes which belonging deep and breadth direction respectively.

After completion this phase, the construction of an IWA social network has been finished.

3.3 Community Detection Algorithm

Non-overlapping community detection and overlapping community detection are both used to test our network for full analysis. FN algorithm have a good accuracy and efficiency as classical method based on modularity optimization. Moreover, FN could partite any network no matter dense or sparse graph. Therefore, we prefer to choose a strict requirement community detection as a comparison experiment. Accordingly, we select FN algorithm and CPM algorithm which belong to non-overlapping and over-lapping community detection respectively as our experimental algorithms. And then these two methods will be reviewed in prepared to do experiment.

FN Algorithm. FN algorithm is based on the idea of modularity optimization. A detailed account of which is given in [9]. We simplified algorithms as following steps.

- Starting with a state in which each vertex is the sole member of one of n communities, k is initialized to n.
- Step 1: Calculate the Q value of all communities refer to quality function or "modularity". e_{ij} is the fraction of edges in the network that connect vertices in group i to those in group j, and $a_i = \sum_j e_{ij}$, then Q is defined as

$$Q = \sum_i (e_{ii} - a_i^2)$$

- Step 2: Choosing community i and j that result in the greatest increase in Q, which we defined as $\Delta Q = e_{ij} + e_{ji} - 2a_i a_j = 2 \left(e_{ij} - a_i a_j \right)$
- Step 3: Merging group i and j into a new group. Meanwhile, k plus one.
- Termination condition is k equals 1, otherwise jump to step 1.

In Fig. 1, we show the dendrogram derived by feeding the "karate club" network into FN algorithm. The peak modularity is Q = 0.381 and corresponds to a split into two groups.

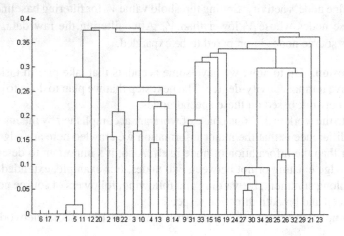

Fig. 1. Dendrogram of the communities found by FN in the "karate club" network in [10].

CPM Algorithm. The Clique Percolation Method (CPM) is based on the assumption that a community consists of overlapping sets of fully connected subgraphs and detects communities by searching for adjacent cliques. You can get a full description in [7], and a simple illustration is given in Fig. 2. For brevity, we also simplify the process and describes them below:

- First extract all complete subgraphs of the network that are simply called *cliques*.
- Preparing the clique-clique overlap matrix, in which the matrix elements are equal to the number of common nodes between the corresponding two cliques.
- Replacing every off-diagonal entry smaller than k−1 and every diagonal entry smaller than k by 0, the remaining elements by 1.

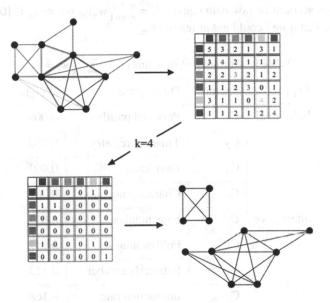

Fig. 2. A simple illustration of the extraction of the k-clique-communities at k = 4 using the clique-clique overlap matrix [7].

4   Experiment

4.1   Data Setting

As one of the most popular online social network, Sina Micro-blog have already over 5 billion users active on it. It has amassed a tremendous amount of data to mining and analysis include water army. Therefore we'll focus on it to crawl data and experiment.

In that task posting website, we concentrate attention on the task block of Sina and start data crawling. After ten days of crawling, we've got nearly 23,000 accounts and 1.2 million task records exists in the database. Some samples provided at http://202.43.148.168:18080/washow/servlet/Show. This wealth of IWA data are conclusive evidence for identification of water army accounts.

We've got 23,000 accounts which participated in promotion tasks of IWA. However, most of accounts we crawled are isolated in the network so we make a rule to filter raw data. Make it clearly that our goal is to find out those accounts have few social behaviors and remove them. For this purpose, we build a structural model of activity evaluation and judgment matrix to identify target nodes. Combined this structural model and judgment matrix, we get every weight of 8 attributes of structural modes by using analytic hierarchy software yaahp. All attributes and their weights shown in Table 1. In which C_8 denotes Interactive rate equals N1/N2, N1 refers to number of posts user i comments or reply to other users, N2 refers to the number of posts comment or response by the user i. Set threshold value for each property and normalized them. Compute activity value for each account of raw data equals $V_i = \sum_{n=1}^{8} w_n v_n$, where $v_n \in [0, 1]$ indicates the rate value that note i could get at feature C_n.

Table 1. Attributes of structural model $\sum_{i=1}^{8} w_i = 1$

Type	Feature	Description	Weight
Individual	C_1	Personal profile	0.008
	C_2	Time for registry	0.063
	C_3	User level	0.401
	C_4	Character tag	0.203
Interactive	C_5	Fans number	0.032
	C_6	Follow number	0.012
	C_7	R-friends number	0.113
	C_8	Interaction rate	0.168

Then, we could remove those nodes whose V_i lower than threshold V_0. After filtering the raw data, about 50 accounts preserved as source nodes in prepared to be expanded.

For now, we've got 50 accounts that take part in tasks of water army and have normal activity-degree. Afterwards, enlarging our IWA social network based on these special nodes. The major information we crawled here are edges between nodes rather than the information of node itself. Extended nodes are crawled along comment, forwarding and following, followers of source nodes which belonging deep and breadth direction respectively. 9,000 nodes and 15,000 edges acquired through crawling data based on 50 accounts of water army in a few days.

4.2 Experimental Results and Analysis

We've got a network of 9,000 nodes and 15,000 edges, especially, in which 50 accounts are exactly proved to be identity of water army. In this section, two classical algorithms reviewed in part 2.2 are used to partite this IWA social network. In the meanwhile, we'll describe our findings and attempt to explain the phenomena.

First of all, the result of community partition has vast difference between FN and CPM methods as shown in Fig. 3(a). We got 26 communities by using FN algorithm while only 11 communities using CPM algorithm. Moreover, each community partitioned by FN has much more members than that of CPM. It's not difficult to understand that FN is much more prone to partition larger scale community than CPM owing to their principle of community detection, especially for sparse network like this IWA social network we build. On the other hand, we could observe that most of nodes in the network are not partitioned into any community when applying CPM method. Moreover, in experimental results, communities can only be found by k = 3 as shown in Fig. 4(a). Therefore, we fully recognized that most water army have not integrate social circuit. Only a fraction of water army contact close with others to form a community.

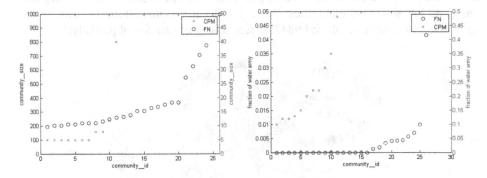

Fig. 3. Community detection by FN and CPM. (a) number distribution of nodes in each community; (b) fraction distribution of water army accounts in each community.

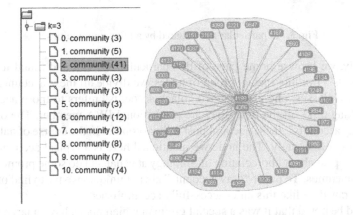

Fig. 4. Community detection by CPM. (a) communities can only be found by k = 3; (b) member's structure of one community.

Secondly, from the statistical result illustrated in Fig. 3(b), we could observe the fraction of water army accounts in each community in the divided result of FN and CPM. Tracking observation all the water army accounts in the maximum fraction, we found an amazing phenomenon. The content in home page of these accounts are very similar with each other. There exist many similar or even same posts or forwarding in similar time in their micro-blog. We could imagine two kinds of cases, one is they belong in a same group of IWA, the other is that these similar accounts are held by one people. In order to confirm the generality or contingency of this phenomenon, we monitored other high fraction IWA accounts, the result is the same.

It's not too difficult to explain it depend our experience. Once those accounts in a same IWA group are crawled, they should be partitioned in one community due to their connections, accordingly their community has a high fraction of unnatural accounts. On the other side, the posters in low fraction community are usually completing tasks individual.

Finally, take a close look at the community detection results by using CPM algorithm. We concentrated more on overlapping nodes in CPM's result since it could partite one node into several communities. What surprise us was that all the 11 communities have one shared node numbered 9847. Figure 5 is an illustration of partially.

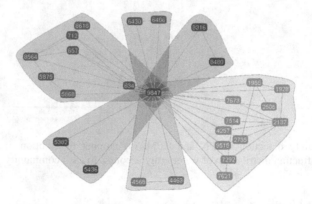

Fig. 5. A particular node shared by all the communities.

Similarly, we browse home page of this particular account and found it is one of "gray accounts". For this special group of nodes, we divide all these accounts that take tasks into two classes, one class named "black accounts" refers to those accounts are detected taking tasks all the time, they are professional IWA member. The other class termed "gray accounts", these account post normal content in the course of nature while pick up tasks occasionally. The node we mentioned here is a typical account of "gray accounts", he post about appreciation of Sinology at usual and do some promotion tasks as poster sometimes. To proof "gray accounts" are not unique, we try to find other more accounts in raw data like this and successfully accomplished.

It should be noted that it was a special group in which nodes have a large followers and high influence in the network. What this amounts to is that once these "gray accounts" forwarding or updating a post for economic benefit, it has a higher probabilistic to influence their followers and spreading rumors further. Concluded, these inconspicuous part-time IWA accounts have more clout and higher propagation force than those full-time. Even more frightening, they are more difficult to identity and supervised owing their ambiguity of actions.

5 Conclusion

With the advent of Web 2.0 era, Internet public opinion play a special role in guiding social discussion. Therefore, a fully analysis of IWA social network structure and their transmission routes is of great significance. In this paper, we proposed a concept of IWA social network which is an unnatural social network and mainly analysis the structural characteristics of this network. Then, some meaningful appearance are represented and we attempt to explain them by human thoughts. In concluded, we summarize them as follows:

- IWA social Network is a sparse network with only a few water army have shaped social circles.
- Both FN and CPM algorithms could help finding communities with high fraction of water army and their content are surprising similarity.
- "Gray accounts", which post normal content under normal circumstances while pick up tasks occasionally, are discovered as a special group which have more influence and spreading capacity than other water army.

The present experiments shows that the network of IWA is worthy of analyzed and some meaningful phenomenon could be mined after a series of analyses. Next, we intended to study on the influence of these accounts (especially those "gray accounts") and prediction of transmission.

Acknowledgements. This work was supported by the National Natural Science Foundation of China grant (NO. 61403369), the Strategic Leading Science and Technology Projects of Chinese Academy of Sciences (No. XDA06030200), Beijing Key Lab of Intelligent Telecommunication Software and Multimedia (ITSM201502) and Guangxi Key Laboratory of Trusted Software (KX201418).

References

1. Guangzeng, L.G.G.T.K.: Recognition of Net-cheaters Based on Text Sentiment Analysis. Libr. Inf. Serv. 8 (2010). School of Information Management of Wuhan University, Wuhan 430072
2. Shin, Y., Gupta, M., Myers, S.: Prevalence and mitigation of forum spamming. In: INFOCOM, 2011 Proceedings IEEE, pp. 2309–2317. IEEE, April 2011
3. Mukherjee, A., Liu, B., Glance, N.: Spotting fake reviewer groups in consumer reviews. In: Proceedings of the 21st International Conference on World Wide Web, pp. 191–200. ACM, April 2012
4. Chen, C., Wu, K., Srinivasan, V., Zhang, X., Chen, C., Srinivasan, V., et al.: Battling the internet water army: detection of hidden paid posters. In: IEEE/ACM International Conference on Advances in Social Networks Analysis & Mining, pp. 116–120. IEEE (2013)
5. Xu, H., Cai, W., Chen, G.: Forum-oriented research on water army detection for bursty topics. In: 2014 9th IEEE International Conference on Networking, Architecture, and Storage (NAS), pp. 78–82. IEEE, August 2014
6. Xie, J., Kelley, S., Szymanski, B.K.: Overlapping community detection in networks: the state-of-the-art and comparative study. ACM Comput. Surv. (CSUR) 45(4), 43 (2013)

7. Palla, G., Derenyi, I., Farkas, I., Vicsek, T.: Uncovering the overlapping community structure of complex networks in nature and society. Nature **435**(7043), 814–818 (2005)
8. Pollner, P., Palla, G., Vicsek, T.: Preferential attachment of communities: the same principle, but a higher level. EPL (Europhys. Lett.) **73**(3), 478 (2006)
9. Newman, M.E.: Fast algorithm for detecting community structure in networks. Phys. Rev. E **69**(6), 066133 (2004)
10. Girvan, M., Newman, M.E.: Community structure in social and biological networks. Proc. Natl. Acad. Sci. **99**(12), 7821–7826 (2002)
11. Cho, E., Myers, S.A., Leskovec, J.: Friendship and mobility: user movement in location-based social networks. In: Proceedings of the 17th ACM Sigkdd International Conference on Knowledge Discovery and Data Mining, pp. 1082–1090. ACM, August 2011
12. Fortunato, S.: Community detection in graphs. Phys. Rep. **486**(3), 75–174 (2010)
13. Kausar, M.A., Dhaka, V.S., Singh, S.K.: Web crawler: a review. Int. J. Comput. Appl. **63**(2), 31–36 (2013)

A Differentially Private Method for Reward-Based Spatial Crowdsourcing

Lefeng Zhang[1]($\boxtimes$), Xiaodan Lu[1], Ping Xiong[1], and Tianqing Zhu[2]

[1] School of Information and Security Engineering,
Zhongnan University of Economics and Law, Wuhan, China
lefeng.e.zhang@gmail.com, lxd0937@126.com, pingxiong@znufe.edu.cn
[2] School of Information Technology, Deakin University, Geelong, Australia
tianqing.e.zhu@gmail.com

Abstract. The popularity of mobile devices such as smart phones and tablets has led to a growing use of spatial crowdsourcing in recent years. However, current solution requires the workers send their locations to a centralized server, which leads to a privacy threat. One of the key challenges of spatial crowdsourcing is to maximize the number of assigned tasks with workers' location privacy preserved. In this paper, we focus on the reward-based spatial crowdsourcing and propose a two-stage method which consists of constructing a differentially private contour plot followed by task assignment with optimized-reward allocation. Experiments on real dataset demonstrate the availability of the proposed method.

Keywords: Spatial crowdsourcing · Location privacy · Differential privacy

1 Introduction

Spatial Crowdsourcing (SC) [7] has become a successful model for performing location-based tasks due to the popularity of smart devices and the higher network quality. It is a special case of crowdsourcing that people (termed *workers*) must physically travel to a location to perform an assigned task, such as collecting various types of data instantaneously including picture, video, audio, location, time, speed and direction acceleration [13].

Typically, a *requester* uploads his/her spatial tasks to a centralized Spatial Crowdsourcing server (*SC-server*), then the SC-server assigns the tasks to a set of workers. However, in practise, workers are generally required to report their exact locations to the SC-server. Then the SC-server can select the best-suited workers for each task to achieve a desired assignment success rate. Thus, it poses a privacy threat since the SC-server may not be trusted. Studies have shown that sophisticated adversaries can infer an individual's home location, political views, religious inclinations by exploiting the location information [1].

Besides of the privacy issue, *Assignment Success Rate* (ASR) is another key metric for the most of SC applications. It refers to the ratio of tasks accepted by

© Springer-Verlag Berlin Heidelberg 2015
W. Niu et al. (Eds.): ATIS 2015, CCIS 557, pp. 153–164, 2015.
DOI: 10.1007/978-3-662-48683-2_14

workers to the total number of task requests [13]. In this paper, we focus on a particular type of SC, *reward-based SC*, in which workers solve tasks in order to receive rewards [7]. In this scenario, whether a worker is likely to accept a task, is determined by two factors: the travel distance for performing the task, as well as the amount of the reward for the task. On one hand, when distance is short, a worker would like to accept a task even the reward is low to some extent. On the other hand, long distance may be acceptable as long as the reward is attractive.

Thus, the goal of this paper is to propose an optimization approach for spatial task assignment with *differential privacy* (DP for short) guarantee in reward-based SC. As a strong and provable privacy definition, DP is generally achieved by introducing a great deal of noise to hide individual's information. But when workers' locations are hidden by DP mechanism, it increases the complexity of the task assignment process and poses challenges as follows:

- The first challenge is, a large amount of noise has to be introduced to achieve DP. Existing methods generally split privacy budget to small parts for multiple DP processes, and small budget causes significant noise.
- Distance is a major metric for achieving a high task assignment ratio because workers are generally willing to accept those nearby tasks. But with privacy concern, exact locations are replaced by noisy statistics or cloaked regions. In this scenario, estimating the distance between a worker and a task is significantly complicated by the uncertainty of locations.
- The third challenge is modeling the willingness of a worker to accept a task. People are likely to accept the tasks with short distance and high reward. But in practice, how to represent the willingness by a probability model which is characterized by distance and reward is a challenge.

While a very limited works have investigated the privacy issues in SC as well as the efficiency of task assignment [8,12,13], these studies can only solve parts of these challenges, especially when privacy and reward are considered simultaneously. In this paper, we aim to fill the void by addressing those challenges.

The rest of this paper is organized as follows. We introduce the background and related work of SC in Sect. 2. Then a differentially private method for reward-based SC is presented in Sect. 3. Section 4 presents the experimental results, followed by the conclusion in Sect. 5.

2   Related Work and Background

2.1   Related Work

Spatial Crowdsourcing [7] can be classified to two categories, *Worker Selected Tasks (WSD)* mode and *Server Assigned Tasks (SAT)* mode.

In *WSD* mode, SC-server publishes spatial tasks without any background information about workers. *WSD* is very simple to perform, but its drawback is lack of control over the task assignment process.

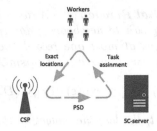

Fig. 1. An framework for private spatial crowdsourcing

In contrast, with *SAT* mode, workers should report their locations to SC-server firstly, then SC-server selects the best-suited workers for each task. Obviously, it poses a privacy threat because of the exposure of workers' locations. Our focus in this paper is on *SAT* mode.

Actually, location privacy preserving has been widely studied in literature. Various methods have been proposed to address the issue, such as spatial cloaking [11] and dummy-based methods [9]. So, it is natural to apply these methods in SC. Pournajaf et al. [12] proposed a two-stage optimization approach for spatial task assignment. Workers submit cloaked regions to SC-server instead of exact locations to achieve privacy preserving. However, spatial cloaking methods have their own inherent drawbacks that the background knowledge of the adversary must be assumed in order to demonstrate the privacy guarantees [2].

As a result, stronger privacy models that abstract from adversary's background knowledge, for instance, DP [3,4], are supposed to be a better solution. To et al. [13] proposed a framework for achieving DP in SC. The basic idea of the framework is to connect the SC-server and workers by a third trusted party, *cell service provider* (CSP), as shown in Fig. 1. CSP performs a private spatial decomposition (PSD) algorithm to generate a sanitized release of location distribution, which is used for task assignment at SC-server side subsequently. As a follow-up study, To et al. [14] also proposed an interactive visualization and tuning toolbox, *PrivGeoCrowd*, to help system designers tune multiple parameters for getting satisfactory results. However, the DP algorithm used in their method divides the privacy budget into two parts for performing a two-stage DP process. Accordingly, small privacy budget will introduce a great deal of noise which dramatically decreases the utility of the sanitized release. Thus in this paper, we present a novel contour-plot based method to generate a sanitized location distribution while achieving DP with less magnitude of noise.

2.2 Differential Privacy

To achieve strong protection guarantees for workers' location privacy, we apply the DP model in our proposed method. DP requires that releasing an aggregated report should not reveal too much information on any individual [3].

Definition 1 (ε-*Differential Privacy* [5]). *A randomized mechanism $\mathcal{M}$ gives ε-differential privacy for any pair of neighboring datasets D and D', where their symmetric difference contains at most one record (i.e., $|D \Delta D'| \leq 1$), and for every set of outcomes Ω, the randomized mechanism $\mathcal{M}$ satisfies:*

$$Pr[\mathcal{M}(D) \in \Omega] \leq \exp(\epsilon) \cdot Pr[\mathcal{M}(D') \in \Omega], \tag{1}$$

where ϵ is the privacy budget; the less the budget is, the higher the privacy level.

The *Laplace* mechanism [6] is usually utilized to achieve DP.

Definition 2 (*Laplace* Mechanism). *Given a function $f : D \to \mathbb{R}$, the mechanism,*

$$\mathcal{M}(D) = f(D) + Laplace(\frac{S}{\epsilon}), \tag{2}$$

provides the ϵ-differential privacy, where S is the maximal change on the result of function f, termed sensitivity.

The *parallel composition* of privacy budget is widely used in the design of DP mechanisms [10].

Definition 3 (*Parallel Composition*). *Given a set of privacy steps $\mathcal{M} = \{\mathcal{M}_1, ...\mathcal{M}_m\}$, if $\mathcal{M}_i$ provides ϵ_i privacy guarantee on a disjointed subset of the entire dataset, the parallel of $\mathcal{M}$ will provide $\max\{\epsilon_1, ..., \epsilon_m\}$-differential privacy.*

In this paper, we use the *Laplace* mechanism with *parallel composition* to construct a contour plot which represents the workers' location distribution. The contour plot is generated at the CSP side and published to the SC-server.

3   Differentially Private Method

In this section, we propose a two-stage method for task assignment that consists of (*i*) constructing a contour plot and (*ii*) determining assignment radius for a each task according to the contour plot.

We apply a similar framework to the one shown in Fig. 1. Specifically, the CSP collects exact worker locations, then generates a contour plot and publishes it to the SC-server. The SC-server will estimate a circle for each task. All the workers in the circle will be notified to perform the task.

3.1   Problem Definition

Task assignment in crowdsourcing aims to assign a set of tasks to a group of workers while ensuring a high *Assignment Success Probability* for each task.

Definition 4 (*Assignment Success Probability*). *Given a task t that is assigned to a set of workers P, Assignment Success Probability (ASP) is the probability that the task t is accepted by at least one worker in P.*

Obviously, to calculate ASP, the probability that the task t is accepted by a worker in P should be evaluated at first. For simplicity, t is also used to denote the location of the task t.

Definition 5 (*Acceptance Probability*). *Acceptance probability, denoted by θ, is the probability that a worker p accepts a task t. $\theta = Pr(p$ accepts $t)$.*

We assume θ is influenced by the reward w as well as the Euclidean distance between t and p. Given a fixed reward, shorter distance leads to higher θ. Meanwhile, for a fixed distance, the more the reward, the higher θ.

To achieve a satisfactory global assignment success rate, we predefine *Expected Assignment Success Probability*, denoted by E_{ASP}, as the threshold that each task should meet with. As SC-server has only a contour plot instead of the exact workers' locations, it can not assign a task to particular workers. Alternatively, SC-server will assign a task to a group of workers in a circle.

Thus, the problem of task assignment of SC in this paper is that, given a total amount of reward W, we specify a circle region with radius r for each task t with a piece of reward w while ensuring the ASP of t is no less than E_{ASP}.

3.2 Building Contour Plot with DP

Many algorithms can be applied to construct private synopsises of spatial datasets, such as *DPCube* [15] and *AG* [8]. While these algorithms work well for answering range queries, there are some weaknesses for using them in SC.

Firstly, existing methods generally assume that locations are distributed uniformly in a cloaked region. However, in spatial datasets, this assumption works only when the region is relatively small. In reality, people tends to be clustered around a tiny residential areas for sociality. Thus, for cells with large size, large errors will be caused when evaluating the worker density for task assignment.

Secondly, most of the existing algorithms divide the privacy budget ϵ into two parts, for example, $\epsilon_1 = \epsilon_2 = 0.5\epsilon$, where ϵ_1 is used for decomposing data domain with differentially privacy and ϵ_2 for adding noises. Thus, because only a part of budget is used for adding noise, the magnitude of noise increases dramatically.

Actually in SC, a differentially private synopsis of worker distribution is used for evaluating the worker densities around particular task locations, instead of answering range queries. Fine-grained grid with accurate count in each cell is crucial for archiving efficient task assignment.

In this paper, we apply a contour plot to demonstrate the density distribution of workers. We firstly predefine the size of an unit cell, for instance, $0.04\,km^2$. Then the unit cell is defined as a square with $0.2\,km \times 0.2\,km$. Using the simple uniform-grid method, the data domain is decomposed to a $m \times n$ grid and each grid cell is an unit cell. After counting the workers in each cell, independent Laplace noise is then added to each count using the full budget ϵ. According to the Definition 3 of *Parallel Composition*, the uniform-grid method provides the ϵ-*differential privacy* because all the cells are disjointed subsets of the entire dataset. The noisy count of $m \times n$ cells compose a $m \times n$ matrix. Finally, we

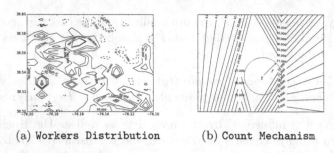

(a) Workers Distribution   (b) Count Mechanism

Fig. 2. Work distribution and count mechanism

consider each entry of this matrix as altitude, a contour plot can be created accordingly. As an instance, the contour plot of the experimental dataset in this paper is shown in Fig. 2a.

3.3 Task Assignment

In this subsection, we firstly model the *Acceptance Probability* and *ASP*, then present the method for calculating r and w based on the models.

Modeling Acceptance Probability and ASP. We consider acceptance probability θ ($0 \leq \theta \leq 1$) as a function f with variables w and d, i.e., $\theta = f(w, d)$. Considering the relationship in reality among acceptance probability, distance and reward, function f should meet with the following requirements:

* $\theta \in [0, 1]$ for all the w and d;
* If $w < w_0$ or $d > MTD$ (*maximum travel distance*), then $\theta = 0$;
* Given a specific $w \geq w_0$, θ increases with the decrease of d;
* Given a specific d, θ increases with the increase of w ;
* When d increases or decreases, changing w accordingly can guarantee that θ stays the same level.

To model θ, we introduce the hyperbolic tangent function, as shown in Fig. 3,

$$y = \mathrm{th}x = \frac{e^x - e^{-x}}{e^x + e^{-x}}.$$

The hyperbolic tangent function is a framework of the objective function f, but it converges to 1 too fast with the increase of x. Thus we define the function as $f = \mathrm{th}(c_1 x)$, where c_1 is the parameter that controls function scalability.

To characterize the combined effect of distance d and reward w, we define $\mu = c_2 \cdot \frac{w}{d}$ as the ratio of reward w and distance d, where c_2 controls the scale of w and d. When $w \geq w_0$, it can be deduced that

$$y = \mathrm{th}(c_1 \cdot \mu) = \mathrm{th}(c_1 \cdot c_2 \cdot \frac{w}{d}) = \mathrm{th}(c \cdot \frac{w}{d}),$$

where $c = c_1 \times c_2$, c is the only parameter of proposed function.

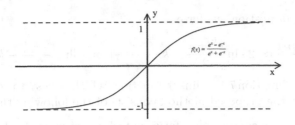

Fig. 3. Hyperbolic tangent function

Then, we formally define the acceptance probability as

$$\theta = f(w, d) = \begin{cases} \text{th}(c \cdot \frac{w}{d}), & \text{if } w \geq w_0; \\ 0, & \text{otherwise.} \end{cases} \quad (3)$$

Inspired by To et al. [13], we develop the analytical ASP probability model for a task t in the circle area $\odot_r^t$ as follows,

$$ASP = 1 - (1 - \theta)^n. \quad (4)$$

Solving r with Taylor Formula. Efficient task assignment aims to ensure the ASP of each task no less than E_{ASP}. Therefore, we can calculate the minimum radius r by setting the ASP of a task t equals E_{ASP}.

To solve Eq. 4, the SC-server need to estimate the distance d between task t and worker p, as well as the number of the workers n in $\odot_r^t$. Suppose a worker p has the coordinates (x, y), then the expectation of $\sqrt{(x^2 + y^2)}$ can be regarded as the best estimation of d, i.e.,

$$E(r) = \iint\limits_{\odot_r^t} \sqrt{(x^2 + y^2)} \cdot \frac{1}{\pi r^2} \, \mathrm{d}x \, \mathrm{d}y = \frac{2}{3}r. \quad (5)$$

Given a contour plot, the worker density den in $\odot_r^t$ can be estimated. If a task t is exactly on a contour line, then we can get the density directly. Otherwise, when t is between two contour lines, for simplicity, we approximate the density with the mean of the two contour values. Thus, the number of workers in $\odot_r^t$ can be estimated by $n = \pi r^2 \cdot den$, as shown in Fig. 2b. Combining Eqs. 3–5, it can be verified r satisfies the following equation,

$$-\frac{\ln(1 - E_{ASP})}{\pi \cdot den} = r^2 \cdot \ln\left(\frac{e^{\frac{3cw}{r}} + 1}{2}\right) \quad (6)$$

Equation 6 is a transcendental equation, we cannot solve it without losing any accuracy. We approximate the right side of Eq. 6 with a *linear* function, then solve the simplified equation to get solution r.

Consider the right side of Eq. 6 as $h(r)$, for a simpler presentation, set $r_0 = 1$, from *Taylor* formula, it is easy to know that

$$h(r) \approx h(r_0) + h'(r_0)(r - r_0).$$

Therefore, after derivation, we have

$$-\frac{\ln(1 - E_{ASP})}{\pi \cdot den} \approx [2 \cdot \ln \frac{e^k + 1}{2} - k \cdot \frac{e^k}{e^k + 1}] \cdot r - [\ln \frac{e^k + 1}{2} - k \cdot \frac{e^k}{e^k + 1}] \quad (7)$$

where $k = 3cw$. Equation 7 is a linear function, which is easy to solve.

Conclusively, the proposed method consists of the following three steps:

1. Given E_{ASP} and a contour plot, for each task t_i, set $w_i = W/|T|$ and evaluate the worker density den_i around t_i;
2. For each task t_i, compute r_i with Eq. 7;
3. Set $w_i = w_0 + \frac{r_i}{\sum_{i=1}^{|T|} r_i}(W - w_0|T|)$, repeat step 2 and output w_i and r_i.

4   Experiments

4.1   Settings

We use the real world dataset Gowalla in our experiments. Gowalla consists of the check-in location information of users in a location-based social network. For our experiments, we use the check-in data in the area around Washington DC. We sample about 76000 records and assume each check-in point represents a worker in SC system. The locations of tasks are randomly selected within the geographic coordinates $38.04\,°-39.04\,°N$ and $76.52\,°-77.52\,°W$.

We define several metrics, *Distance Error (DE)*, *Reject Ratio (RejR)* and *Execution Cost (EC)* to evaluate the performance of the proposed method.

DE is used to evaluate the total errors caused by noises. Suppose in the scenario without noise, SC-server specify r_i to task t_i, and r_i changes to r_i' with the noise introduced. Therefore, *DE* can be calculated by

$$DE = \sum_{i=1}^{|T|} |n_i \times \frac{2}{3} r_i - n_i' \times \frac{2}{3} r_i'| \quad (8)$$

where n_i and n_i' are respectively the number of workers in $\bigodot_{r_i}^{t_i}$ and $\bigodot_{r_i'}^{t_i}$.

EC is used to measure the cost for executing all the tasks. Given task t with distance d and reward w, there is a contradictory relationship between d and w that d decreases with the increasing of w, and vice versa. We need to find the tradeoff between them to minimize the execution cost of the tasks. Thus we define the total execution cost as

$$EC = \sum_{i=1}^{|T|} (n_i \times \frac{2}{3} r_i \times w_i). \quad (9)$$

We define *Reject Ratio* to measure the ratio of tasks rejected by workers to the total number of tasks. For those tasks with very low worker densities, SC-server would specify them with large circles that containing enough amount of workers for achieving E_{ASP}. In practise, We assume that a task with distance greater than MTD is impossible to be performed.

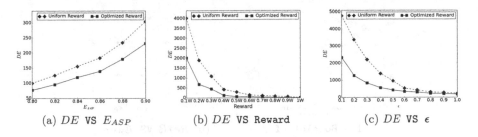

(a) DE vs E_{ASP} (b) DE vs Reward   (c) DE vs ϵ

Fig. 4. Estimation of DE

4.2   Experiment Results and Comparisons

We randomly generate 10000 tasks and measure the performance of the proposed methods. To demonstrate the efficiency of optimized-reward allocation strategy, we use the naive reward allocation as a benchmark that tasks are assigned with the same reward $W/|T|$. The MTD is set to be the 90 % distance percentile value. In our experiments, we study the effect of different parameters such as privacy budget ϵ, E_{ASP} and the total reward W. We consider $\epsilon \in [0.1, 1.0]$, $E_{ASP} \in [0.80, 0.90]$. The total reward ranges from $0.1W$ to $1.0W$.

Evaluation of DE. The variation tendencies of DE with different E_{ASP}, W, ϵ are shown in Fig. 4. Figure 4a captures the effect of E_{ASP} on distance error DE. With the increase of E_{ASP}, DE increases regardless of the reward allocation. Larger E_{ASP} potentially requires more workers participate in task assignment, therefore causes more distance error. As optimized reward shrinks radius distribution, the DE for optimized reward is always less than uniform reward. This means the optimized reward allocation benefits task assignment.

Figure 4b presents the result with various rewards. It is obvious that with higher reward, workers are more willing to accept a task. The higher reward, the less workers needed and the smaller radius. Therefore, there is a sharp decrease of DE with W increases. But after increasing to some levels, reward is not a dominating factor in DE, the curve goes flat. As optimized reward restricts the radius in a small range, the optimized curve is always lower than uniform curve.

Figure 4c shows the variation tendency between DE and privacy budget ϵ. ϵ is an influential factor when generating the contour plot. Small ϵ means more noises added in each cell. Therefore, the smaller ϵ, the larger distance error DE. Because the optimized radiuses aggregate in a small interval, the impact of noise is limited as well, thus the DE for optimized reward is always smaller.

Evaluation of $RejR$. In this experiment, we look into the $RejR$ with the impact of E_{ASP}, W and ϵ. Figure 5b reveals the variation tendency of $RejR$ with the change of E_{ASP}. In this experiment, we set total reward $W = 0.1W$, and privacy budget $\epsilon = 0.3$, the expected assignment success rate E_{ASP} is arranged from 0.80 to 0.90. In Fig. 5b, the $RejR$ of optimized reward always keeps lowest while E_{ASP} changes, i.e., none of the assignment radiuses exceeds workers' MTD.

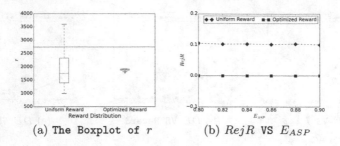

(a) The Boxplot of r (b) $RejR$ VS E_{ASP}

Fig. 5. $RejR$ with E_{ASP}

Specifically, Fig. 5a illustrates the condition where $E_{ASP} = 0.90$. Figure 5a shows that all the radiuses with optimized reward are located beneath the MTD threshold, as presented by the horizontal line.

The results for W and ϵ are similar as Fig. 5b. With total reward varies from $0.1W$ to $1.0W$, and ϵ varies from 0.1 to 1.0, the $RejR$ of optimized reward invariably keeps 0. It means the optimized reward indeed improves task assignment, but different amounts of total reward do not influence $RejR$ much. Moreover, the privacy budget ϵ controls the noise added in each cell, and influences the absolute value of radius, but it does not affect the proportion of radiuses within MTD threshold. Therefore the $RejR$ still keeps 0 when ϵ changes.

Evaluation of EC. In this section, we estimate the execution cost EC with various parameters, as shown in Fig. 6. Figure 6a illustrates the execution cost EC as a function of E_{ASP}, with $\epsilon = 0.2$ and $W = 0.1W$. EC increases with E_{ASP} increases. This is because, high E_{ASP} requires more workers participate in a task, enlarging the assignment radius. With the same E_{ASP}, the radius of optimized reward varies in a small range, leading to a relatively small EC.

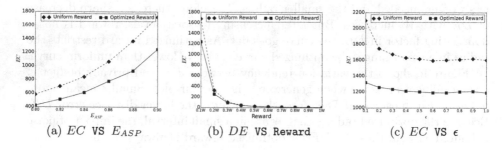

(a) EC VS E_{ASP} (b) DE VS Reward   (c) EC VS ϵ

Fig. 6. Estimation of EC

Figure 6b shows the impact of W on distance error DE. It demonstrates when W doubled or trebled, EC has a sharply decrease, as high reward always attracts more workers. However, with W increases continually, EC goes flat, because reward is not a main influential factor when it comes some levels.

The behavior of EC with different ϵ is shown in Fig. 6c. In this experiment, E_{ASP} is set to 0.9 and $W = 0.1W$. As ϵ mainly influences the added noise in contour plot, EC does not change much a as ϵ increases. With the same ϵ, optimized reward leads to a small radius range, therefore, the EC for optimized reward is always less than uniform reward.

5 Conclusions

In this paper, we investigate the privacy issue in Spatial Crowdsourcing and propose a differentially private method for task assignment in reward-based SC. To achieve DP, we construct a contour plot to represent the distribution of workers with differential privacy guarantee. In addition, to achieve an expected global task assignment ratio, we construct models for *Assignment Success Probability* and *Acceptance Probability* by introducing a hyperbolic tangent function. On the basis of these models, we present the method of calculating a radius of circle area for each task to ensure the ASP is no less than the given E_{ASP}. The experimental results show that contour plot is an effective representation of location distribution. Besides, the comparison between optimized-reward and naive-reward allocation strategies shows that the task acceptance ratio can be increased significantly by tuning the amount of reward for each task according to the travel distance.

Acknowledgements. This work is supported by the Natural Science Foundation of HuBei province (China) under Grant No. 2014CFB354 and the Fundamental Research Funds for Central Universities of China under Grant No. 31541511301.

References

1. Andrés, M.E., Bordenabe, N.E., Chatzikokolakis, K., Palamidessi, C.: Geo-indistinguishability: differential privacy for location-based systems. In: Proceedings of the 2013 ACM SIGSAC Conference on Computer; Communications Security, CCS 2013, pp. 901–914. ACM, New York (2013)
2. Dewri, R.: Local differential perturbations: location privacy under approximate knowledge attackers. IEEE Trans. Mob. Comput. **12**(12), 2360–2372 (2013)
3. Dwork, C.: Differential privacy. In: Bugliesi, M., Preneel, B., Sassone, V., Wegener, I. (eds.) ICALP 2006. LNCS, vol. 4052, pp. 1–12. Springer, Heidelberg (2006)
4. Dwork, C.: Differential privacy: a survey of results. In: Agrawal, M., Du, D.-Z., Duan, Z., Li, A. (eds.) TAMC 2008. LNCS, vol. 4978, pp. 1–19. Springer, Heidelberg (2008)
5. Dwork, C.: A firm foundation for private data analysis. Commun. ACM **54**(1), 86–95 (2011)
6. Dwork, C., McSherry, F., Nissim, K., Smith, A.: Calibrating noise to sensitivity in private data analysis. In: Halevi, S., Rabin, T. (eds.) TCC 2006. LNCS, vol. 3876, pp. 265–284. Springer, Heidelberg (2006)

164   L. Zhang et al.

7. Kazemi, L., Shahabi, C.: Geocrowd: enabling query answering with spatial crowd-sourcing. In: Proceedings of the 20th International Conference on Advances in Geographic Information Systems, SIGSPATIAL 2012, pp. 189–198. ACM, New York (2012)

8. Li, N., Yang, W., Qardaji, W.: Differentially private grids for geospatial data. In: Proceedings of the 2013 IEEE International Conference on Data Engineering (ICDE 2013), pp. 757–768. IEEE Computer Society, Washington, D.C. (2013)

9. Lu, H., Jensen, C.S., Yiu, M.L.: Pad: privacy-area aware, dummy-based location privacy in mobile services. In: Proceedings of the Seventh ACM International Workshop on Data Engineering for Wireless and Mobile Access, MobiDE 2008, pp. 16–23. ACM, New York (2008)

10. McSherry, F., Talwar, K.: Mechanism design via differential privacy. In: Proceedings of the 48th Annual IEEE Symposium on Foundations of Computer Science, FOCS 2007, pp. 94–103. IEEE Computer Society, Washington, D.C. (2007)

11. Pan, X., Xu, J., Meng, X.: Protecting location privacy against location-dependent attack in mobile services. In: Proceedings of the 17th ACM Conference on Information and Knowledge Management, CIKM 2008, pp. 1475–1476. ACM, New York (2008)

12. Pournajaf, L., Xiong, L., Sunderam, V., Goryczka, S.: Spatial task assignment for crowd sensing with cloaked locations. In: Proceedings of the 2014 IEEE 15th International Conference on Mobile Data Management, MDM 2014, vol. 01, pp. 73–82. IEEE Computer Society, Washington, D.C. (2014)

13. To, H., Ghinita, G., Shahabi, C.: A framework for protecting worker location privacy in spatial crowdsourcing. Proc. VLDB Endow. 7(10), 919–930 (2014)

14. To, H., Ghinita, G., Shahabi, C.: Privgeocrowd: a toolbox for studying private spatial crowdsourcing. In: Proceedings of the 31st IEEE International Conference on Data Engineering (2015)

15. Xiao, Y., Gardner, J., Xiong, L.: Dpcube: releasing differentially private data cubes for health information. In: Proceedings of the 2012 IEEE 28th International Conference on Data Engineering, ICDE 2012, pp. 1305–1308. IEEE Computer Society, Washington, D.C. (2012)

Do Applications Perform Its Original Design? A Preliminary Analysis from Internet Big Data

Lei Qian[1,2], Yinlong Liu[1(✉)], and Yanfei Zhang[3]

[1] Institute of Information Engineering, Chinese Academy of Science,
Beijing, People's Republic of China
lqia012@aucklanduni.ac.nz, liuyinlong@iie.ac.cn
[2] Department of Computer Science, The University of Auckland,
Auckland, New Zealand
[3] Department of ITSS, East China Normal University, Shanghai
People's Republic of China
yfzhang@admin.ecnu.edu.cn

Abstract. Transmission Control Protocol (TCP) is the most widely used Internet protocol in today's Internet. More and more applications are operating towards over TCP. Every application layer protocol is designed to perform a specific purpose, for example File Transfer Protocol (FTP) is designed for file transfer. Therefore every application layer protocol has different performance expectations. In this paper, we try to observe that whether characteristics existence in different application layer protocols by illustrating our performance evaluation result of five different application layer protocols (HTTP, HTTPS, FTP, SMTP, and SSH) in individual flow level from over 10 years IP packets trace files collected from two different locations. Our results show that the performance of application layer protocol is still in chaotic and some result is difficult to find a reasonable explanation. We believe that this report is a starting point for both researchers and Internet participators to explore possible reasoning behind of the results.

1 Introduction and Motivations

The usage of Internet has been explosively increased in last two decades. More and more services are now migrating towards the Internet. Transmission Control Protocol (TCP) is the most popular transport layer protocol which is over IP. Researches show that more than fifty percent Internet traffic is either TCP traffic or traffic over TCP. Studies also indicate that streaming protocols, which original designed over User Datagram Protocol (UDP) is now moving towards HTTP which is over TCP in [1, 2].

Internet measurement has been considered as a vital tool for understanding behaviors of the Internet [6, 7] which includes but not limited to performance evaluation, security issue detection, traffic management and many other perspectives. A flow contains six different attributes, called six-tuples, which are IP versions, source IP, destination IP, source port, destination port, and protocol. There are a number of research works to observe Internet performance from different perspectives [1–5, 11, 12]. Researches in [1, 11, 12] conduct analysis of flow lifetime indicate that most TCP have very short flow

© Springer-Verlag Berlin Heidelberg 2015
W. Niu et al. (Eds.): ATIS 2015, CCIS 557, pp. 165–176, 2015.
DOI: 10.1007/978-3-662-48683-2_15

lifetime. However, research in [2] illustrates a long duration individual flows' behavior analysis from TCP Round Trip Time (RTT) and RTT variation, and observed that some long lifetime TCP flows "may have regular patterns of RTT distribution, some apparently have self-similar RTT distribution [2]".

The motivations of this report are firstly, we are attempting to explore whether particular characteristics existence for a certain application layer flows. Secondly, we are attempting to find out whether application flows' performance in RTT and RTT variation match its expectations (application's original design). Last but not least, we are aiming to explain possible causes behind of it.

The rest of paper is organised as follows. In Sect. 2, we first introduce measurement data sets we used in this report, it followed by illustrating our measurement metrics and measurement framework. Section 3 illustrates our example analysis results with discussion. Section 4 concludes our research work included in the paper followed by possible interesting future investigations.

2 Measurement Methodology

This section introduces our measurement methodology. Section 2.1 first introduces data sets we used to conduct our analysis, and Sect. 2.2 listed measurement metrics we selected to apply for analysis. Section 2.3 introduces our measurement framework and flow extraction methodology.

2.1 Overview of Data Sets

Analysis of large amount data is the compulsory requirement for a reasonable performance evaluation of individual flows on application layer. Fortunately we are able to use identical data sets used in [1, 2] which captured outside the firewalls at the University of Auckland and the University of Waikato (WITS) [1, 2] since the data is still stored in our measurement servers. Table 1 lists basic statistics of data sets [1, 2]. The reported work includes the analysis of more than 3 Terabytes of Internet traffic which has around 5.0 billion packets [2].

Table 1. Overview of network traffic data sets used for measurement [1, 2].

Trace file	Start time	Duration	TCP flows (Million)
AKL-2003	2003-Dec-04 [00:00]	24.00 h	103.07
AKL-2005	2005-Aug-16 [14:00]	3.00 h	3.55
AKL-2006	2006-July-27 [13:00]	24.00 h	130.22
AKL-2007	2007-Nov-01 [13:00]	24.00 h	200.05
AKL-2009	2009-Aug-03 [08:00]	11.00 h	40.58
WITS-2004	2004-Mar-01 [00:00]	24.00 h	4.05
WITS-2005	2005-May-12 [00:00]	24.00 h	5.59
WITS-2006	2006-Oct-30 [00:00]	24.00 h	4.89

2.2   Measurement Metrics

Round Trip Time (RTT): We compute Round Trip Time (RTT) as the time difference between a TCP packets and its corresponding Acknowledgement been seen. This can be computed from corresponding TCP packets acknowledgement/sequence number information and the time stamp value stored in packet trace files [2].

Round Trip Time Variation (RTTV): We apply similar definition as IP delay variation [13] in this study. The RTT Variation defines as the time round trip time difference between two consecutive TCP packets which belongs to an identical application flow [2].

Application Flow Classification: There are five different application layer protocols included in this analysis, which are Hypertext Transfer Protocol (HTTP, port 80), HTTP Secure (HTTPS, port 443), Simple Mail Transfer Protocol (SMTP, port 25), File Transfer Protocol (FTP, port 21), and Secure Shell (SSH, port 22). We use destination port to determine applications in this report, corresponding packets belongs to a same application flows information is extracted and stored separately for further detailed analysis. "Application flows" will be used for short in rest of paper.

Sorting of Application Flows: Table 1 illustrates that there are more than 500 million of flows in all eight packet trace files and it is impossible to analysis all of them individually. We decided to use longest 40 flows extracted from each packet trace file, because firstly long duration flows can be very interesting since most flows are very short [1, 2, 11, 12]. Secondly, previous studies have already shown interesting long duration flows' behavior at transport layer [2]. Therefore we decide to analysis of long duration flows in this report.

2.3   Measurement Framework

We have an Intel i7-4712HQ CPU @ 2.30 GHz processor with 16 GB memory hardware to perform data sets analysis. There is a Java based library design for packet analysis called java jpcap [14] which is suitable for packet analysis. Our measurement framework requires to run each trace files twice. Flows information will be extracted and descending ordered by its duration after finish running of the first round. Our selected longest 40 applications flows in each trace files are ready for plotting after finish of second round running of trace files.

3   Measurement Result

In this section, we present results showing unusual phenomena in both RTT and RTT variation time series plots and CDF distributions. The presented plots are only selected examples which have been carefully picked from over 1600 individual application layer flows plots, due to page limitations. Each plot in this section contains four

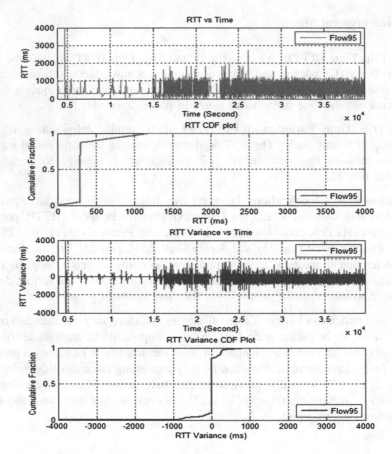

Fig. 1. Shows a HTTPS flow with flow ID = 95 extracted from AKL-2009 trace files. Lifetime of this HTTPS flow is longer than 30000 s (~500 min) with multiple level packet transmission rates.

subplots, as our previous study in [2], the top subplot shows the time series of RTT, second subplot shows the CDF distribution of RTT, the third subplot shows the time series plot of RTT variation, and bottom one illustrates the CDF distribution of RTT variation.

3.1   HTTP and HTTPS Performance

Section 3.1 illustrates two examples of HTTP or HTTPS results. Merging HTTP result with HTTPS result together because both HTTP and HTTPS have very similar designation (except HTTPS with encryption/SSL). Figure 1 shows a HTTPS flow with longer than 500 min lifetime. The transmission rates of are various, few packets transmitted on the first 10000 s but transmission rate suddenly getting busy on next ~ 8000 s. It could be some management flows over HTTP/HTTPS, and also large file sharing protocol which is over HTTPS. The RTT variation seems to be relatively stable in this situation from the CDF distribution in RTT variation.

Figure 2 illustrates a HTTP flow with more than 33 min lifetime and transmitted fairly busier than the flow shown in Fig. 1. However, there is a very long RTT value observed in this plot. The CDF distribution of RTT shows that there are only around 50 % of packet with RTT shorter than 2000 ms, and RTT variation is spread widely from −1000 ms to 1000 ms.

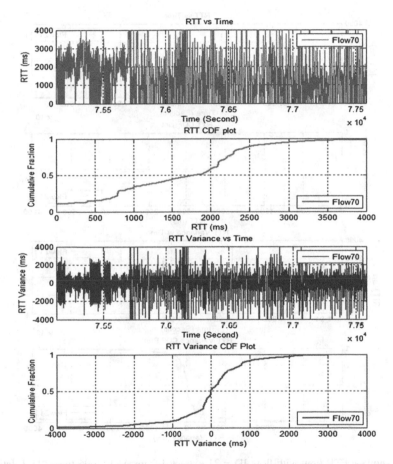

Fig. 2. Shows a HTTP flow with flow ID = 70 extracted from AKL-2003 trace file. Lifetime of this HTTP flow is around 2000 s (~ 33 min) with extremely long RTT value.

3.2   FTP Performance

Section 3.2 includes two examples of FTP flows extracted from eight trace files. Figure 3 illustrates a long FTP flow with 196500 s (around 349 min) lifetime. Overall RTT value seems reasonable from CDF distribution of RTT, shows that more than 80 % of packets with RTT shorter than 250 ms. However, RTT variation spread widely as well. FTP is original designed for transferring files; therefore a large number of packets with large packet size transmitted are expected. The interesting spotted in Fig. 3 is that it does not have large amount of packets transmitted.

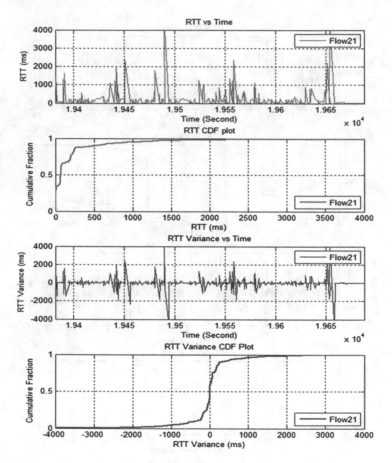

Fig. 3. Shows a FTP flow with flow ID = 21 extracted from AKL-2006 trace file. Lifetime of this FTP flow is around 19650 s ($\sim$349 min) not many packets transmitted.

Figure 4 provides a extreme example of a FTP flow with few packets transmitted but have long RTT value. A FTP flow with over 8000 s lifetime but very few packets transmitted through the duration. However this flow have extremely long RTT value, the RTT CDF distribution also indicate that around only 10 % of packets been acknowledged within 1000 ms, which is considered as a very long RTT value. Only around 50 % packets have RTT value within 2000 ms. Both cumulative distribution of RTT and number of packets transmitted indicates a very unusual performance of FTP we expected.

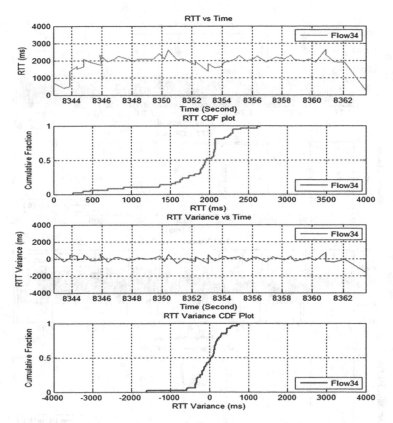

Fig. 4. Shows a FTP flow with flow ID = 34 extracted from WITS-2005 trace file. Lifetime of this FTP flow is longer than 8300 s ($\sim$138 min) with extremely long RTT value.

The most interesting point behind the illustrated result shown in this sub section is the cause of this phenomenon. Network congestion might be a possible explanation, but other possibilities need to be explored.

3.3 SSH Performance

Section 3.3 illustrates two examples of SSH flows RTT and RTT variation plots. Secure Shell, or SSH is designed to remote to computers using encrypted to increase its security level. Therefore short packets, but quick response time is expected [10] otherwise users might suffer from long response time. Moreover, long duration flows are also possible since remote service might last for long period.

Figure 5 shows a reasonable SSH looking plot from both RTT and RTT variation distribution perspectives. Time series RTT plot shows that flow contains reasonable amount of packet with relatively short RTT value, which over 90 % of packets.

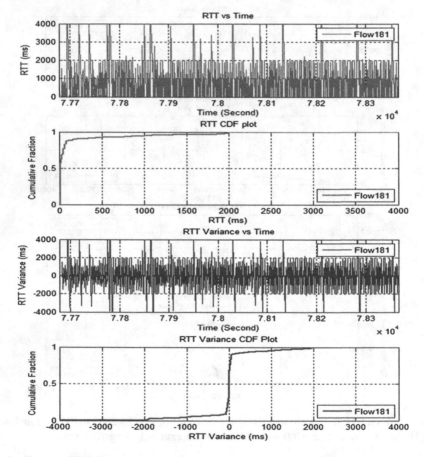

Fig. 5. Shows a SSH flow with flow ID = 181 from AKL-2003 trace file, with traffic transfer frequency, short RTT value and stable RTT variation.

Figure 6 shows a SSH flow with flow ID = 178 extracted from AKL-2009 trace file. Surprisingly, more than 70 % of packets are acknowledged longer than 250 ms, which is long RTT for interactive traffic. Moreover, the CDF distribution of RTT variation

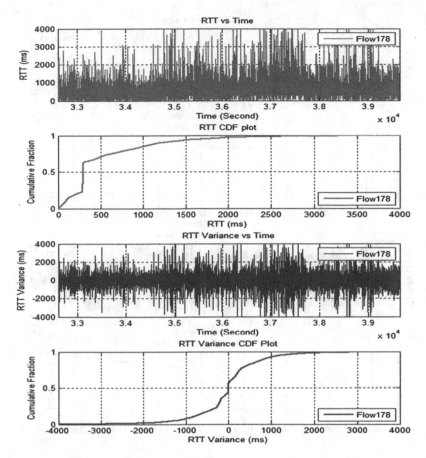

Fig. 6. Shows a SSH flow with flow ID = 178 from AKL-2009 trace file, with a large volume of packets transmitted, with long RTT value, and widely spread RTT variation value.

also spread widely from −2000 to 2000 ms, which implies the instability of the network. One possible cause of this phenomenon is network congestion occurs; therefore users' experience might be very poor in this case.

3.4 SMTP Performance

Simple Mail Transfer Protocol (SMTP) was original designed for email transmission. Therefore a short flow life time with medium/high level of packets number transmitted are expected.

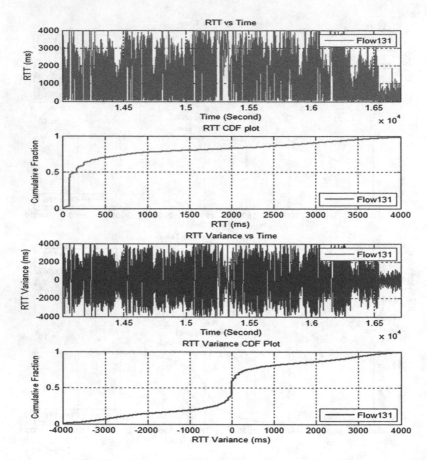

Fig. 7. Shows a SMTP flow with flow ID = 131 extracted from AKL-2009 trace file, with long lifetime and packets keep transmitting throughout this flow.

Figure 7 shows a SMTP flow extracted from our AKL-2009 trace files with extremely long lifetime, with at least longer than 2000 s. Interestingly, there are always packets transmitted observed in this particular flow. It is an unusual SMTP flow illustrated in Fig. 7, one possible explanation would be packet retransmission due to the large spread of RTT variation, which lead to email resending.

Figure 8 shows another extreme case of SMTP flows. In Fig. 8, there are only few packets transmitted through around 300 s. It is possible if the email only contains little information therefore not many packets transmitted, however it is strange that a SMTP flow last for long time. On the other hands, the CDF distribution of RTT also show that over 70 % of packets have been acknowledged within 500 ms, which should not cause large proportion of packets retransmission. The CDF distribution of RTT variation also indicates that the variation does not widely spread (from −1000 to 1000 ms).

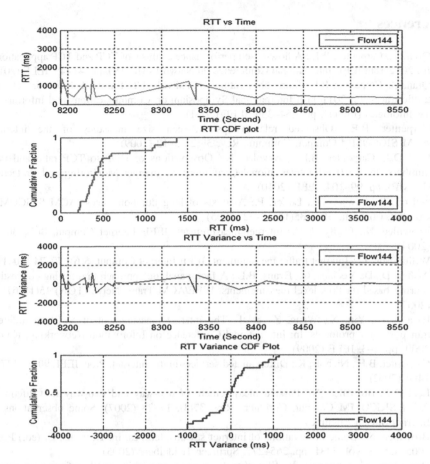

Fig. 8. Shows a SMTP flow with flow ID = 144 extracted from WITS-2006 trace file, with long lifetime but few packets transmitted this flow.

4 Conclusion and Future Works

In this paper, we reported a preliminary analysis of the performance of individual flows at application layer to determine whether application level flow performance matches application protocol's original design. We surprisingly found long duration application flows with unusual pheromones existence. For example, a long FTP flow with more than ~ 138 min flow lifetime has only few packets transmitted. Moreover, SMTP, which normally used for mail transfer purpose has more than 4 h 30 min lifetime with large number of TCP packets transferred.

This report is just a starting point of application layer level individual flow analysis. The result included in this paper leaves many interesting questions for further investigation. What causes the application layer flow performance in chaotic? Does it because of security issues or use of port number with other purpose?

References

1. Qian, L., Carpenter, B.E.: A flow-based performance analysis of TCP and TCP applications. In: 2012 18th IEEE International Conference on Networks (ICON), pp. 41–45. IEEE (2012)
2. Qian, L., Carpenter, B.E.: Some observations on individual TCP flows behavior in network traffic traces. In: 2011 11th International Symposium on Communications and Information Technologies (ISCIT), pp. 354–359. IEEE (2011)
3. Carpenter, B.E.: Observed relationships between size measures of the internet. ACM SIGCOMM Comput. Commun. Rev. 39(2), 5–12 (2009)
4. Lee, D.J., Carpenter, B.E., Brownlee, N.: Observations of UDP to TCP ratio and port numbers. In: 2010 Fifth International Conference on Internet Monitoring and Protection (ICIMP), pp. 99–104. IEEE (2010)
5. Nelson, R., Lawson, D., Lorier, P.: Analysis of long duration traces. ACM SIGCOMM Comput. Commun. Rev. 35(1), 45–52 (2005)
6. Brownlee, N., Claffy, K.C.: Internet measurement. IEEE Internet Comput. 8(5), 30–33 (2004)
7. Williamson, C.: Internet traffic measurement. IEEE Internet Comput. 5(6), 70–74 (2001)
8. Arifler, D., De Veciana, G., Evans, B.L.: A factor analytic approach to inferring congestion sharing based on flow level measurements. IEEE/ACM Trans. Netw. (TON) 15(1), 67–79 (2007)
9. Hwang, H., Yin, X., Wang, Z., et al.: The internet measurement of VoIP on different transport layer protocols. In: International Conference on Information Networking, ICOIN 2009, pp. 1–3. IEEE (2009)
10. Carpenter, B.E., Nichols, K.: Differentiated services in the Internet. Proc. IEEE 90(9), 1479–1494 (2002)
11. Lee, D.J., Brownlee, N.: Passive measurement of one-way and two-way flow lifetimes. ACM SIGCOMM Comput. Commun. Rev. 37(3), 17–28 (2007). Some observations of Internet Stream Lifetimes
12. Brownlee, N.: Some observations of internet stream lifetimes. In: Dovrolis, C. (ed.) PAM 2005. LNCS, vol. 3431, pp. 265–277. Springer, Heidelberg (2005)
13. Demichelis, C., Chimento, P.: IP packet delay variation metric for IP performance metrics (IPPM). RFC3393, IETF (2002)
14. jpcap network packet capture library. http://jpcap.sourceforge.net/

Trust Prediction with Trust Antecedent Framework Regularization

Haiyang He$^{(\boxtimes)}$, Yong Wang, and Guoyong Cai

School of Computer Science and Engineering,
Guilin University of Electronic Technology, Guilin 541004, Guangxi, China
{haiyang0902, ccgycai}@gmail.com, hellowy@126.com

Abstract. In recent years, many discipline theories are developed for under-standing trust and solving the data sparse problem. Trust Antecedent framework is an integrative and well-known model in management science, which takes ability, benevolence and integrity as three key factors to explain how trust relations are established between a trustor and a trustee. In this paper, we propose a new trust prediction model based on Trust Antecedent framework (TA) and matrix factorization. We focus on how the factors of TA affect user's trust in online social networks. TA is incorporated into a matrix factorization with a regularization term to enhance the trust prediction performance. Our experiments conducted on a real-word dataset from Ciao demonstrate that our approaches outperform other state-of-the-art methods in trust prediction.

Keywords: Trust prediction · Matrix factorization · Trust antecedent framework · Regularization

1 Introduction

With the pervasive of online social network, the content that user generated increases at an unprecedented rate, that makes the problem of information overload increasingly severe. Trust, which reflects a comprehensive evaluation of another user's behavior and the ability of a user, plays an important role in helping online users collect reliable information, and make decisions [9–11]. However, trust is known to be a complex and abstract concept influenced by many factors. It is difficult to find an accurate model for trust in online social network. There are mainly two challenges:

Firstly, trust is known to be a complex and ambiguous concept in various contexts. It is hard to find the real factors that lead to the interpersonal trust between users.

Secondly, explicit trust relationships are extremely sparse, and in social network only a small percentage of users specify many trust relationships while a large proportion of users specify a few trust relationships, making the online trust relationships follow a power law distribution.

Trust Antecedent framework is an integrative trust model and well studied in the management and social science discipline, which is proposed by Mayer [14]. As show in Fig. 1, three key factors of trustee are generalized by the framework, which explain a major portion of the trustee's trustworthiness. These three factors provide a solid and parsimonious foundation for the empirical study of trust for trustors. Recently, matrix

© Springer-Verlag Berlin Heidelberg 2015
W. Niu et al. (Eds.): ATIS 2015, CCIS 557, pp. 177–188, 2015.
DOI: 10.1007/978-3-662-48683-2_16

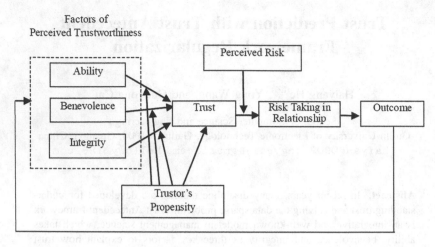

Fig. 1. Trust Antecedent framework

factorization becomes a very popular technology in data mining to address the data sparse problem [2, 4, 9]. In Sect. 3, we will introduction matrix factorization in detail.

Motivated by the benefits of Trust Antecedent framework and matrix factorization, we exploit the Trust Antecedent Framework effect in trust relations prediction by modifying matrix factorization. Our main contributions are summarized as the following:

- Propose an unsupervised framework, tafTrust, to prediction trust relations between users by incorporating matrix factorization and Trust Antecedent Framework;
- Evaluate tafTrust real-world dataset Ciao, and elaborate the importance of trust antecedent factors in trust prediction.

The rest of the paper is organized as follows. In Sect. 2, we briefly introduce some related works. Section 3 introduces how to use the low-rank matrix factorization method for trust prediction. The Trust Antecedent Framework regularization framework is presented in Sect. 4. The experimental evaluation and results are presented in Sect. 5. Finally, we finally conclude and present the future work in Sect. 6.

2 Related Work

In recently years, many researchers have studied the trust prediction problem in online social network, and have proposed some methods to deal with the problem. Existing methods can be mainly classified into two categories: supervised methods [11, 13, 18] and unsupervised methods [9, 16, 17].

Supervised methods first construct features from available source and then train a binary classifier based on these features by considering existing trust relations as labels. Nan Ma et al. [13] predict trust relations using user and interaction features generated from users rating other users' reviews by building classifier. Nikolay Korovaiko et al. [14] focus on a case where the background data are user ratings for online product reviews and show state-of-the-art classifiers can do an impressive job in predicting trust based on extracted features. However, in general online social network trust relations follow a power law distribution, making the classification problem extremely unbalanced [9] and thus affecting the accuracy of classification.

Most existing unsupervised trust prediction methods are mainly based on trust propagation, which propagate trust through finding reliable trust paths or combining multiple trust paths from a source user to an unknown target user in a web of trust. In [16], several atomic strategies of trust relationship propagation are proposed such as direction propagation, transpose trust, co-citation, and trust coupling. They also discussed distrust relationship propagation for trust prediction. Tang et al. [9] develop an approach to exploit homophily effect in trust relations via homophily regularization to alleviate the sparsity problem as well. Jin Huang et al. [17] propose a robust rank-k matrix completion (RRMC) method, which explicitly guarantees the low-rank of the recovery matrix and minimizes the influence of noisy observations. However, in most social network the explicit trust relationships that user specified are usually small, making the trust network very sparse. So these methods may not have a good performance.

3   Matrix Factorization Model for Trust Prediction

In this section, we introduce basic trust prediction algorithm based on Nonnegative Matrix Factorization (NMF) that we used in this paper. NMF is first brought into machine learning and data mining fields by Lee and Seung [5, 6], and has been widely employed in various applications such as recommender system [1, 4, 7, 12] and pattern recognition [8]. Given a non-negative matrix $X \in \mathbb{R}^{m \times n}$, NMF aims to find two non-negative matrix factors $U \in \mathbb{R}^{m \times d}$ and $V \in \mathbb{R}^{n \times d}$ which minimize $\|X - UV\|_F^2$ where d represents the number of latent features with $d \ll m, n$ and $\|.\|_F^2$ denotes the matrix Frobenius norm of a matrix.

In online social network, we have a set of users u = $\{u_1, u_2, ..., u_n\}$ where n is the number of users. And we set the matrix $G \in \mathbb{R}^{n \times n}$ represent the trust relationship between users where $G(i, j) = 1$ if u_i trusts u_j, $G(i, j) = 0$ otherwise.

In this paper, we consider the $n \times n$ trust ratings matrix G describing n trustors's numerical rating on n trustees. However, in the real world, each user only specifies a few trust relationships, resulting in G very sparse and low-rank. We harness non-negative matrix factorization to model trust prediction. Our task, then, is to find two matrices U and V such that their product approximates G:

$$G \approx UV^T = \hat{G} \tag{1}$$

where $U \in \mathbb{R}^{n \times d}$ is the trustor-specific matrix, $V \in \mathbb{R}^{n \times d}$ is the trustee-specific matrix with $d \ll n$.

Next, we have to find a way to obtain U and V. The matrix factorization model seeks a low-rank representation by minimizing

$$\frac{1}{2}\|G - UV^T\|_F^2 \tag{2}$$

where $\|.\|_f^2$ is the matrix Frobenius norm. As we all known, G is an extremely sparse matrix and contains a large number of missing values. So, Eq. 2 is changed to:

$$\min_{U,V} \frac{1}{2} \sum_{i=1}^{n} \sum_{i=1}^{n} I_{ij}(G_{ij} - U_i V_j^T)^2 \tag{3}$$

where I_{ij} is the indicator function. $I_{ij} = 1$ if user i (trustor) trust user j (trustee), otherwise, $I_{i,j} = 0$. Regularization technique is often used to avoid over-fitting. Therefore, two smoothness regularization terms are appended to the Eq. 3. Then we have:

$$\min_{U,V} \frac{1}{2} \sum_{i=1}^{n} \sum_{i=1}^{n} I_{ij}(G_{ij} - U_i V_j^T)^2 + \frac{\lambda_1}{2} \|U\|_F^2 + \frac{\lambda_2}{2} \|V\|_F^2 \tag{4}$$

where $\lambda_1, \lambda_2 > 0$. One approach to minimizing Eq. 4 is gradient descent. Once the two matrices U and V are obtained, the missing values in trust rating matrix G can be determined.

4 Modeling Trust Antecedent Framework for Trust Prediction

In this section, we introduce the trust antecedent framework and analysis of three key factors of the framework that affect trust between trustor and trustee in detail. Then, we will introduce how to integrate the trust antecedent framework into the matrix factorization as a regularization item.

4.1 Factors of Perceived Trustworthiness

For individuals, a better understanding of their social networks can help them share and collect reliable information more effective and efficient [10]. In this subsection, we introduce the three key factors that lead to user inter-personal trust.

Ability: In real life, people are more likely to establish trust with persons who have competence and skills. Similarly, in online social network, for candidate trustor-trustee pair, the higher ability of candidate trustee, the higher trust level between the trustor-trustee pair. In this paper, we define *ability(i, j)* as the *ability coefficient* between u_i and u_j. To compute the *ability(i, j)* value of the candidate trustor-trustee (u_i, u_j), we adopt the calculation method introduced in Nguyen et al. [15] which using the average rating u_j received from u_i and the interaction intensity from u_i to u_j represent the ability of the user pair (u_i, u_j). Obviously, the *ability*(i, j) satisfy three conditions: (1) *ability* $(i, j) \in [0, 1]$; (2) *ability*$(i, j) \neq$ *ability*(j, i); (3) the larger the *ability*(i, j) is, the higher trust level between u_i and u_j. Correspondingly, in low-rank space, A larger value of *ability*(i, j) indicates that the distance between user-specific vectors U_i and U_j should be smaller, while a small value means that the distance between the user-specific vectors should be larger. Hence we add the ability regularization term to impose constraints between one user and their trustees:

$$\sum_{i=1}^{n} \sum_{f \in F^+(i)} ability(i, f) \|U_i - U_f\|_F^2 \tag{5}$$

where $F^+(i)$ is the set of trustees who, at least, have a trust path connected from trustor i.

Benevolence: In trust antecedent framework, benevolence is an important trust factor which expresses that a trustee wants to do good with a trustor. Similar with the ability, we use *benevolence*(i, j) as the *benevolence coefficient* between u_i and u_j. Nguyen et al. [15] associate it with user's leniency in giving ratings. As we all known, users with high leniency tend to give high ratings whereas users with low leniency tend to give low ratings. In this paper, we employ the same method. For the candidate trustor-trustee pairs u_i and u_j, the local leniency l_{ij} is measured by the relative difference between the u_i ratings on the reviews written by u_j and the quality of these reviews:

$$l_{ij} = \frac{1}{|W_{i,j}|} \sum_{w_k \in W_{i,j}} \frac{r_{ik} - q_k}{r_{ik}} \tag{6}$$

where $W_{i,j}$ is the set of reviews written by u_j and rated by u_i, and r_{ik} is the rating score that u_i give the review w_i. q_k denotes the quality of a review w_k in $W_{i,j}$, and q_k is defined as the follow:

$$q_k = \omega(|U_{i,p}|, \alpha', \mu') \cdot \frac{1}{|U_{i,p}|} \sum_{u \in U_{i,p}} (r_{ik} \cdot (1 - \theta \cdot l_{up})) \tag{7}$$

where $U_{i,p}$ is the set of users who rated review w_i written by user u_p. A review w_i with more ratings is more likely to have better quality. So, $\omega(|U_{i,p}|, \alpha', \mu')$ accounts for the effect of number of ratings received by review w_i, given by:

$$\omega(x, \alpha, \beta) = \frac{1}{1 + e^{-\alpha(x-u)}} \tag{8}$$

where $\theta = 0.5, \alpha' = 0.1, \mu' = 5$, as suggested in [15].

Iterative computation is used to calculate the leniency and quality values in Eqs. 7 and 8. The iterative algorithm is shown in Algorithm 1.

Algorithm 1. computation of local leniency

Input: Users U, Reviews W, Ratings R

Output: User's local leniency l_{ij}

1: initialized local leniency l_{ij}=0

2: **while** not convergent **do**

3:   **for** each review w_i in W **do**

4:   calculate review quality q_i by Equation 7;

5:   **for** each user u_i in U **do**

6:    **for** each u_j in U **do**

7:     update local leniency l_{ij} by Equation 6;

8:     l_{ij} for all users

Finally, in order to limit the value of *benevolence*(i, j) within $[0, 1]$, using the Eq. 9:

$$benevolence(i,j) = \frac{l_{ji} - \min l}{\max l - \min l} \tag{9}$$

Similarity with ability, the benevolence regularization term is added to impose constraints between one user and their trustees:

$$\sum_{i=1}^{n} \sum_{f \in F^+(i)} benevolence(i,f) \|U_i - U_f\|_F^2 \tag{10}$$

Integrity: Integrity often refers to the consistency of trustee's behaviors to fulfill a set of moral principles. To evaluate the trustee's integrity that trustor perceived, using the number of trust statements the trustee received. We employ the Eq. 8 to bound the range of *integrity coefficient* into $[0, 1]$:

$$integrity(i,j) = \omega(|T_{*j}|, \alpha'', \mu'') \tag{11}$$

where the parameters α'' and μ'' are set following the same value with Eq. 7. The integrity factor have the same value range and trend with the above two factors, so the integrity regularization term is added to impose constraints between one user and his trustees:

$$\sum_{i=1}^{n} \sum_{f \in F^+(i)} integrity(i,f) \|U_i - U_f\|_F^2 \tag{12}$$

In this subsection, three trust antecedent factors of Trust Antecedent Framework are analyzed in detail and the quantitative methods about the three factors are given. The three factors in Trust Antecedent Framework have the same trend that a person is more likely to establish trust relation with another if the latter has high ability, benevolence and integrity. We define the $TAF(i, j)$ as the integral Trust Antecedent Framework coefficient which consider all the three trust antecedent factors. And the $TAF(i, j)$ can be formulated as:

$$TAF(i,j) = \zeta_1 ability(i,j) + \zeta_2 benevolence(i,j) + \zeta_3 integrity(i,j) \tag{13}$$

where ζ's are the weight coefficients. In our model, we treat the three factors equally important. Hence, we set all the coefficients are equal.

For the given candidate trustor-trustee pair u_i and u_f, with the $TAF(i, f)$, the integrated Trust Antecedent Framework regularization is formulated as:

$$\frac{\gamma}{2} \sum_{i=1}^{n} \sum_{f \in F^+(i)} TAF(i,f) \left\| U_i - U_f \right\|_F^2 \tag{14}$$

where $\gamma > 0$, which is used to control the influence of TAF coefficient, $F^+(i)$ is the set of trustees who, at least, have a trust path connected from trustor i. A larger value of $TAF(i, f)$ indicates that the distance between user-specific vectors U_i and U_f should be smaller, while a small value means that the distance between the user-specific vectors should be larger.

4.2   The Proposed Framework: tafTrust

In the previous subsection, we review the three key factors that lead to user interpersonal trust and give the definition of Trust Antecedent Framework regularization. With the definition of Trust Antecedent Framework regularization, we proposed our framework, tafTrust, based on Nonnegative Matrix Factorization (NMF) while exploiting Trust Antecedent factors effect for trust prediction. Finally, tafTrust can be formulated as:

$$\min_{U,V} L(G, U, V) = \frac{1}{2} \sum_{i=1}^{n} \sum_{j=1}^{n} I_{ij} \left(G_{ij} - U_i^T V_j \right)^2$$
$$+ \frac{\lambda_1}{2} \|U\|^2 + \frac{\lambda_2}{2} \|V\|^2 \tag{15}$$
$$+ \frac{\gamma}{2} \sum_{i=1}^{n} \sum_{f \in F^+(i)} TAF(i,f) \left\| U_i - U_f \right\|_F^2$$

In our model, the $TAF(i, f)$ is used to control the distance between u_i to u_f in low-rank space. If user u_i is more likely to establish trust relation with user u_f, and $TAF(i, f)$ is larger, then the distance between u_i and u_f is smaller in low-rank space and vice versa. In most case, $TAF(i, f) \neq TAF(f, i)$, indicating that the trust value from user u_i to user u_f is not equal to that from user u_f to user u_i in general.

In addition, trust propagation plays an important role in trust prediction, suggesting that if user u_i trust u_f and user u_f trust u_g (suppose u_i does not trust u_g), the distance between feature vectors U_i and U_f is minimized when we minimize $TAF(i,f)\|U_i - U_f\|_F^2$ and $TAF(f,g)\|U_f - U_g\|_F^2$.

A local minimum value of the objective function (15) can be acquired by using gradient descent methods in latent factors of U_i and V_j:

$$\frac{\partial L}{\partial U_i} = -\sum_{j=1}^{n} I_{i,j}(G_{ij} - U_i^T V_j)V_j + \lambda_1 U_i$$
$$+ \gamma \sum_{f \in F^+(i)} TAF(i,f)(U_i - U_f) \qquad (16)$$
$$+ \gamma \sum_{g \in F^-(i)} TAF(g,i)(U_i - U_g),$$

$$\frac{\partial L}{\partial V_i} = -\sum_{i=1}^{n} I_{i,j}(G_{ij} - U_i^T V_j)U_j + \lambda_2 V_i \qquad (17)$$

5 Experiments

In this section, we design some experiments to evaluate the performance of our proposed trust prediction model tafTrust and compare it with other popular methods.

5.1 Dataset

To evaluate our proposed method, we applied our model to a real-word dataset which obtains from a product review site, i.e., Ciao which is widely used in various academic research such as trust prediction [9, 15]. In this sites, users can write textual reviews and rate reviews written by other users with numerical ratings. In addition, each user in Ciao has a trust list to maintain his/her trust users based on previous experience.

Similar with [9], in order to obtain datasets that are large enough and have sufficient historical information for the purpose of evaluation, we filter the users with less than one trustor and rating for the Dataset.

Finally, we have two datasets and summary statistics of the datasets are in Table 1. On average, users of Ciao have 4.705 trust relations.

Table 1. Statistics of the datasets

Statistics	Ciao
# of users	4,138
# of reviews	71,633
# of rating	1,625,480
# of trust relations	19,470
Trust network density	0.00114

5.2 Evaluation Metrics

The task of trust prediction is inferring unknown trust relations among pairs of users. So, two popular metrics, the Mean Absolute Error (MAE) and the Root Mean Square Error (RMSE) are used to measure the prediction accuracy, which widely used in evaluate the matrix completion [2, 3, 4, 17]. These two metrics are commonly used form matrix completion evaluation. In the experiment, trust rating data is divided into two sets G_1 and G_t. The first data sets G_1 is used to train and G_t is used to test. The metric MAE is defined as:

$$MAE = \frac{1}{|G_t|} \sum_{i,j} |G_{ij} - \hat{G}_{ij}| \tag{18}$$

where G_{ij} denotes the real trust ratings that user u_i gives to user u_j, $\hat{G}_{ij}$ represents the trust ratings that user u_i will gives to user u_j as predicted by a method, and T denotes the number of trust ratings in the training data. The metric RMSE is formulated as:

$$RMSE = \sqrt{\frac{1}{G_t} \sum_{ij} \left(G_{ij} - \hat{G}_{ij}\right)^2} \tag{19}$$

We can see that the smaller MAE or RMSE value means a better performance of the prediction accuracy.

5.3 Comparison Methods and Details

In this subsection, we compare the proposed framework with various trust prediction methods as follows,

- *SIM:* this method only use the user similarity to represent the estimate trust rating between trustor and trustee [9]. Here we use the Pearson Correlation Coefficient to measure user's similarity.
- *NMF:* this method decomposes the original matrix into two non-negative factor matrices to seek a low-rank approximation. It only uses trust rating matrix for prediction [19].
- *MF-ISR:* this method is proposed by Ma et al. [4]. It adds social regularization into matrix factorization by introducing individual-based social regularization term. User's similarity is used to control the distance between neighbor users in low-rank space.

For the dataset, we use different training data settings (80 %, 60 %) to test the methods. Training data 80 %, for example, means we randomly select 80 % of trust rating from the trust rating matrix as the training data to prediction the remaining 20 % of trust rating and the experimental results are shown in Table 2. In all the experiments conducted in this paper, the values of parameters λ_1 and λ_2 are set to a trivial value 0.01, the Trust Antecedent Framework coefficient is set as $\gamma = 0.003$. The impact of the

Table 2. Performance comparisons of different methods (Dimensionality = 10)

Dataset	Training	Metrics	SIM	NMF	MF-ISR	tafTrust
Ciao	80 %	MAE	0.4309	0.3234	0.2979	0.2947
		RMSE	0.5373	0.4517	0.4371	0.4323
	60 %	MAE	0.4283	0.3637	0.3467	0.3412
		RMSE	0.5352	0.5038	0.4912	0.4873

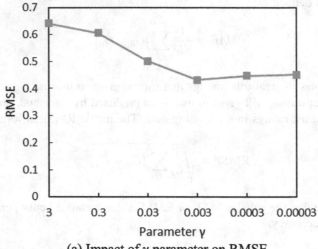

(a) Impact of γ parameter on RMSE

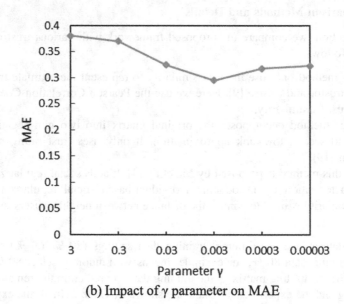

(b) Impact of γ parameter on MAE

Fig. 2. Impact of parameter γ (Dimensionality = 10)

parameter γ will be discussed in the Subsect. 5.4. The experimental results using 10 dimensions to represent the latent features. So the value of d is set as $d = 10$.

In order to make the MAE and RMSE value is credible, each experiment is repeated 5 times and the final MAE and RMSE value is set the average value. Table 2 presents the MAE and RMSE performance of different methods. We can observe that our method consistently outperform other approaches.

5.4   Impact of Parameter γ

In the proposed trust prediction framework, parameter γ is used to control the impact of TAF coefficient, the larger the γ values, the greater effect. Hence, we conduct another experiment to study the influence of parameter γ on the system.

Figure 2 illustrate the impacts of γ on RMSE and MAE in our model. We observe that the value of γ impacts the results significantly. From the results, we can see that no matter using which training data setting, as γ increases, the RMSE and MAE values decrease at first, but when γ goes below a certain threshold like 0.003, the RMSE and MAE values increase with further increase of the value of γ.

6   Conclusion and Future Work

In this paper, we exploit trust antecedent framework for trust prediction based on matrix factorization. With the trust antecedent framework regularization, an unsupervised trust prediction framework, tafTrust, is proposed which incorporates three key factors that lead user inter-personal trust. Experiments conducts on real-world datasets show that the proposed framework have a better performance in prediction accuracy. The quantitative of trust factors in our paper plays an important role in control the distance between users in low-rank space. In the future, we would like to design more accurate representations for trust antecedent factors using more information about users. The distrust relation is also an important information, another direction of our future work is to integrate the distrust relation to our framework.

Acknowledgments. This work is supported by Guangxi Key Laboratory of Trusted Software KX201408 and the Graduate Innovation Project GDYCSZ201469.

References

1. Mnih, A., Salakhutdinov, R.: Probabilistic matrix factorization. In: Advances in Neural Information Processing Systems, pp. 1257–1264 (2007)
2. Koren, Y., Bell, R., Volinsky, C.: Matrix factorization techniques for recommender systems. Computer **8**, 30–37 (2009)
3. Salakhutdinov, R., Mnih, A.: Bayesian probabilistic matrix factorization using Markov chain Monte Carlo. In: Proceedings of the 25th International Conference on Machine Learning, pp. 880–887. ACM (2008)

4. Ma, H., Zhou, D., Liu, C., et al.: Recommender systems with social regularization. In: Proceedings of the Fourth ACM International Conference on Web Search and Data Mining, pp. 287–296. ACM (2011)
5. Lee, D.D., Seung, H.S.: Learning the parts of objects by non-negative matrix factorization. Nature **401**(6755), 788–791 (1999)
6. Lee, D.D., Seung, H.S.: Algorithms for non-negative matrix factorization. In: Advances in Neural Information Processing Systems pp. 556–562 (2001)
7. Jiang, M., Cui, P., Wang, F., et al.: Scalable recommendation with social contextual information. IEEE Trans. Knowl. Data Eng. **26**(11), 2789–2802 (2014)
8. Long, X., Lu, H., Peng, Y., et al.: Graph regularized discriminative non-negative matrix factorization for face recognition. Multimedia Tools Appl. **72**(3), 2679–2699 (2014)
9. Tang, J., Gao, H., Hu, X., et al.: Exploiting homophily effect for trust prediction. In: Proceedings of the Sixth ACM International Conference on Web Search and Data Mining, pp. 53–62. ACM (2013)
10. Tang, J., Chang, Y., Liu, H.: Mining social media with social theories: a survey. ACM SIGKDD Explor. Newsl. **15**(2), 20–29 (2014)
11. Korovaiko, N., Thomo, A.: Trust prediction from user-item ratings. Soc. Netw. Anal. Min. **3**(3), 749–759 (2013)
12. Jamali, M., Ester, M.: A matrix factorization technique with trust propagation for recommendation in social networks. In: Proceedings of the Fourth ACM Conference on Recommender Systems, pp. 135–142. ACM (2010)
13. Ma, N., Lim, E.P., Nguyen, V.A., et al.: Trust relationship prediction using online product review data. In: Proceedings of the 1st ACM International Workshop on Complex Networks Mmeet Information and Knowledge Management, pp. 47–54. ACM (2009)
14. Mayer, R.C., Davis, J.H., Schoorman, F.D.: An integrative model of organizational trust. Acad. Manag. Rev. **20**(3), 709–734 (1995)
15. Nguyen, V.A., Lim, E.P., Jiang, J., et al.: To trust or not to trust? Predicting online trusts using trust antecedent framework. In: Ninth IEEE International Conference on Data Mining, ICDM 2009, pp. 896–901. IEEE (2009)
16. Guha, R., Kumar, R., Raghavan, P., et al.: Propagation of trust and distrust. In: Proceedings of the 13th International Conference on World Wide Web, pp. 403–412. ACM (2004)
17. Huang, J., Nie, F., Huang, H., et al.: Social trust prediction using rank-k matrix recovery. In: Proceedings of the Twenty-Third International Joint Conference on Artificial Intelligence, pp. 2647–2653. AAAI Press (2013)
18. Zolfaghar, K., Aghaie, A.: A syntactical approach for interpersonal trust prediction in social web applications: combining contextual and structural data. Knowl.-Based Syst. **26**, 93–102 (2012)
19. Zhu, S., Yu, K., Chi, Y., et al.: Combining content and link for classification using matrix factorization. In: Proceedings of the 30th Annual International ACM SIGIR Conference on Research and Development in Information Retrieval, pp. 487–494. ACM (2007)

Trust Prediction Based on Interactive Relations Strength

Guoyong Cai[✉], Liyuan Wang, and Haiyang He

School of Computer Science and Engineering,
Guilin University of Electronic Technology, Guilin 541004, Guangxi, China
{ccgycai,haiyang0902}@gmail.com, 745922484@qq.com

Abstract. In online social network, trust is the basis of reliable interaction among users, and interaction relations also affect trust establishment. Although many researchers have studied approaches of trust model and prediction, most trust prediction methods are based on the existing trust network, and lack the in-depth study of user interaction and contents; therefore, it is not conducive to implement those trust prediction models, at the same time it also limits the scope of their applications. To deal with these issues, this paper presents a novel trust prediction framework based on both a trust network and the interactive contexts between users, and a kind of measurement mechanism is put forward to evaluate the strength of interaction relations. Combined with the existing trust network, a trust prediction threshold value is learned and used to predict unknown trust relations. Empirical experiments conducted on Epinions dataset show that the unknown trust relations can be effectively predicted combining with the user's interaction behaviors, and the proposed method can improve the performance of the trust prediction model.

Keywords: Online social network · Trust prediction · Interaction behavior · Relational strength

1 Introduction

With the rapid development of Web 2.0 technologies, online social networks have become the main tool for online users to express opinions, exchange experiences, and share resources. However, its popularity also has brought a series of problems, such as information overload and the lack of reliable data. Trust, as the foundation of inter-action, plays an important role in helping online users collect reliable information and make a decision [1]. For example, the online users in electronic commerce are more inclined to collect useful information from users they trust. Therefore, trust mechanism is widely used in online e-commerce, like Epinions, its provider implements the trust mechanism by allowing users to add their trust users, to publish his ratings and reviews for items, and to rate another users' ratings again. But in the actual world, the explicit trust network is sparse. Only a few of users specify many trust relations, and most of users don't specify their explicit trust relations. Therefore, it is necessary to predict whether there will establish a trust relation between two users.

© Springer-Verlag Berlin Heidelberg 2015
W. Niu et al. (Eds.): ATIS 2015, CCIS 557, pp. 189–200, 2015.
DOI: 10.1007/978-3-662-48683-2_17

In recent years, many domestic and foreign scholars have conducted a series of studies on trust prediction [2–14]; however, these studies are usually based on the original trust relation network. For example, paper [2, 3] proposed EigenTrust and TidalTrust model, which are carried out based on a trust network. Instead, paper [4] applies user's interaction behavior or shared information to infer trust relations. In order to have a better prediction, a new trust relation prediction method is presented in this paper. The method exploits both existing trust network and interactive behaviors between users.

The main contributions of this paper are: (1) a new trust prediction framework is proposed, it predicts unknown trust relations by learning a relational strength threshold; (2) a method is proposed to compute the trust relation strength between users based on reviews. The method builds an interactive reviews network structure between users and fields, and utilizes the diffusion theory to compute the strength.

The rest of the paper is organized as follows: In Sect. 2, related work is reviewed and some limitations of them are discussed. Section 3 introduces the details about our proposed framework. Section 4 presents experimental results and analysis. Finally, Sect. 5 concludes this study with future work.

2   Related Work

In recent years, along with the in-depth research on trust, a series of trust models [5] have been proposed. They are mainly based on probability and statistics [6], machine learning, network structure and semantic reasoning. Of which the statistics and machine learning technology focus on learning a trust prediction model; the network structure and semantic reasoning focus on implementing a static model of trust computing.

From the aspects of machine learning, existing trust prediction algorithms can be divided into two categories: supervised methods [3, 4] and unsupervised methods [5, 6]. Liu et al. [7] proposed a SVM-based prediction model which can infer the trust relation between two users based on their individual actions and interactions in an online community. Zolfaghar et al. [8] determined the link tag of trust and distrust relationships in trust networks through the investigation, and then using the integrated learning method to establish the trust prediction framework, of which the features of trust relationship included the knowledge of the social trust, reputation, similarity, and the personal trust. Korovaiko et al. [4] think that the trust relationships between users are notoriously hard to model, so they use the similarity between the trust users to predict trust. They consider from eight aspects, and put forward a personalized trust prediction model. The above mentioned work neglected the theme feature of trust relations between users. As we know that trust relationships of users in different fields are usually different.

In order to overcome the extreme imbalance problems of supervised learning method, unsupervised algorithm has been proposed. And most unsupervised methods are based on trust propagation. In [10], Guha et al. utilized the original trust network and four atomic propagations to mine the unknown trust relations. The atomic propagations include direct propagation, co-citation propagation, transpose propagation and trust coupling propagation. And in [11], Borzymek et al. proposed a method which exploited rating similarity to enrich traditional trust propagation methods. The experimental results demonstrate that the method combined the trust network with rating similarity can improve the prediction accuracy. Xiang et al. [12] developed an unsupervised model that estimates relationship strength mainly from interaction activity (e.g., communication, tagging) and user similarity with the goal of automatically distinguishing strong relationships from weak ones. However the model also ignored user's field information. Jiliang Tang et al. [13] proposed an unsupervised framework combined low-rank matrix factorization techniques with homophily regularization for trust prediction. But the method only exploits the higher ratings in the 5-stars systems, and ignores the lower ratings.

From the aspects of network structure and semantic reasoning, Zhang et al. [14] used the Semantic Web technology to create a field ontology in order to share the resource, at the same time, they utilize the reasoning function based on personality and behavior to infer implicit trust relations, but the method did not consider the unstructured data that user generated and the difference of trust relation strength between users.

In summary, trust prediction in the online social network has been preliminary studied. However, online users may not clearly label all the trust relationship, how to predict the unknown trust relations more accuracy is still an open problem. In order to address this trust prediction problem, a novel trust prediction framework is proposed, this framework utilizes the trust relationship strength in fields and the existing trust relations to predict unknown trust relations.

3 Trust Prediction Framework

In order to research the prediction problem, the data on Epinions are collected. The website provide users with detailed goods reviews and recommendation, and consequently it can help consumers make decisions. Figure 1 shows someone's homepage information in Epinions. It includes this user's trust list (i.e. who trust) and the trusted list (i.e. who is trusted by), and the two lists together build the user's trust network (i.e. Web of Trust). The lower right corner shows the user's rating behavior, mainly includes the user's rating for the items (i.e. Product Rating) and the reviews' effectiveness rating by other users (i.e. Review Rating). The prediction models proposed often apply the user's trust network and user's rating behavior.

Seen from Fig. 1, the trust relationship strength between the registered users is unknown, and the context of the trust relationship is unclear. Considering this limitation, this paper proposes a new framework shown in Fig. 2 to predict trust; it includes four parts outlined below:

(I) Extraction of feature vector of field behavior. In order to further dig out the hidden user features, three attributes are extracted from the dataset, which are used to characterize the strength of the trust relationship, namely the degree of engagement of users, user's reputation and the degree of fields' attention. The degree of engagement represents the degree of users' activity in some fields; user's

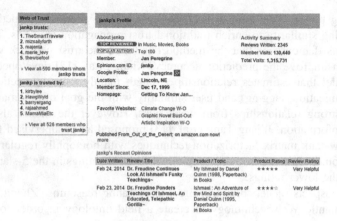

Fig. 1. A user's homepage information in Epinions

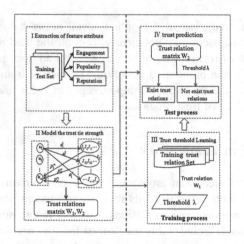

Fig. 2. Trust prediction framework

reputation is the user's trusted value. Commonly, the more objective user's reviews are, the easier the user gains recognitions from others, and thus the higher credibility of the user gets; the degree of fields' attention denotes the recognized degree of a user in a field, where the fields are the item's categories which is referred in a user's interaction behavior, such as clothes belong to clothing category, basketball belongs to ball fields.

(II) Modeling the trust relation strength. This part exploits the network structure G between users and fields and the substance diffusion theory [15] of complex networks to compute the trust relationship strength matrix W_1. See in Sect. 3.1.

(III) Trust threshold learning. Trust relationship strength threshold λ is learned by continuous iteration learning method, which is based on the existing trust relations matrix W_t and the corresponding trust relationship strength matrix W_1.

(IV) Trust prediction. The test dataset is needed to execute step (I) and step (II) again, and produce a trust relationship strength matrix W_2, then combining with the trust relationship strength threshold λ, the unknown trust relations can be predicted.

3.1 Modeling Relational Strength in Fields

In the users' interaction behaviors dataset, most users' rating behavior is very sparse, so the interaction behavior description based on items will arouse serious data sparseness problem. This paper elevates an item behavior description to a field behavior description, thus to mitigate the impact of data sparseness. The network structure (denoted by G) between users and fields is presented in Fig. 3.

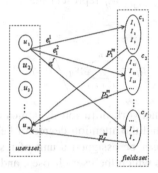

Fig. 3. Interactional behaviors among users and fields

Figure 3 shows three sets, respectively the user set $U = \{u_1, u_2, ... u_m\}$, the field set $C = \{c_1, c_2, ..., c_f\}$, and the item set $I = \{I_1, I_2, ... I_n\}$. Where each field includes lots of items, such as the electronic field contains mobile phone, computer, tablet, and other goods, i.e. $I_x \in c_y$; each item is paid attention by one or more users, so there is a certain kind of relation between users and fields. If user u_i commented item I_j and the item belongs to field c_f, a directed edge e_i^f will exist from user u_i to field c_f. On the contrary, if a similar item I_n which belongs to field c_f is concerned by user u_j, another directed edge p_j^f will exist from field c_f to user u_j. These denote two kinds of relations between users and fields, namely the degree of users' engagement and the attention degree of fields respectively. The former denotes a user's activity degree in a field; the latter indicates the degree of a field recognized by users. Due to the difference of the number of items within each field and the users' rating, the edges' weights are different.

In Epinion's rating system, users are allowed to give five stars rating to items. The higher the rating is, the more recognition the item gains. In order to distinguish the rating rank, that is, the user preference for items, each edge between users and items will be assigned a weight w. When user u_i commented item I_j, and the rating is greater than or equal to 3, then set $w_{ij} = 1$; if user u_i commented on item I_j but the score is less than 3, then set $w_{ij} = 0.5$; If user u_i does not comment on item I_j, then set $w_{ij} = 0$.

The degree of engagement e_i^f between user u_i and field c_f can be expressed as a proportion between the edge weight from user u_i to field c_f and the total edge weight of user u_i, which is shown in formula (1). Where $d(u_i) = \sum_{j=1}^{n} w_{ij}$ denote the sum of edges' weight between user u_i and all items.

$$e_i^f = \sum_{j=1, j \in f}^{n} w_{ij} \Big/ d(u_i) \tag{1}$$

The attention degree p_i^f also can be described as a proportion between the edge weight from field c_f to user u_i and the total weights of edges in field c_f, as shown in Eq. (2). Where $o(c_f) = \sum_{i=1}^{m} \sum_{j=1, j \in f}^{n} w_{ij}^f$ represent the sum of edge's weight between field c_f and all users.

$$p_i^f = \sum_{j=1, j \in f}^{n} w_{ij} \Big/ o(c_f) \tag{2}$$

Inspired by the complex network diffusion dynamics theory, we assume that the engagement degree of users and the attention degree of fields also can spread along a network. Assume that each user be assigned a unit of resource, then the resource is equally spread to all the items which the user chooses, and next each item spreads the resource that it receives to users who concerns it. Assume that a certain amount of substance exists between any two user u_α and u_β, $S_{\alpha\beta}$ denotes the substances ratio from user u_β to user u_α, i.e. the trust value by user u_β to user u_α, is defined in formula (3).

$$S_{\alpha\beta} = H(\beta) \times \sum_{f=1}^{|f|} e_\beta^f \cdot p_f^\alpha \tag{3}$$

where $H(\beta)$ indicates the average reputation of user u_β, which is defined as $H(\beta) = \sum_{j=1}^{n} f\_rating(I_j)/k$, where $f\_rating(I_j)$ is the feedback rating from system to the review written by user u_β to item I_j; k represents the numbers user u_β commented on items, n is the number of items, $|f|$ is the number of fields, e_β^f and p_α^f denotes the field engagement degree of user u_β and the attention degree of field c_f. $\sum_{f=1}^{|f|} e_\beta^f \cdot p_\alpha^f$ represents the spreading coefficient between user u_β and u. As a result, the trust relations strength matrix W_1 is computed by Algorithm 1.

Algorithm 1. Computing the trust relations strength matrix W_1

Input: user rating matrix R between users and items, contextual matrix B between fields and items, the helpful rating matrix H of users' reviews

Output: relationship strength matrix W_1 between users

// the initialization part

1: Compute user Set U and field Set C from matrix R and B respectively
2: initialize the number of reviews $k_i=0$, written by user u_i's
3: initialize user u_i's reputation $h_i=0$
4: $For(i=0; i<m; i++)$ // rating matrix normalized processing
5:     $For(j=0; j<n; j++)$
6:         if $r_{ij} \geq 3$ then $\hat{r}_{ij} = 1$
7:         Else if $0 < r_{ij} < 3$ then $\hat{r}_{ij} = 0.5$
8:         Else $\hat{r}_{ij} = 0$
9:     End for
10: End for

// computing the user's reputation h_i using the feedback rating matrix H

11: $For(i=0; i<m; i++)$
12:     $For(j=0; j<n; j++)$
13:         if (exist user u_i in user set U && $h_{ij} \geq 1$)   // h_{ij} is the element of H
14:             $h_i += h_{ij}$; $k_i ++$;   // k_i is the number of reviews by user u_i
15:     End for
16:     $h_i = h_i / k_i$ //user's reputation, i.e. the average of feedback ratings
17: End for

// compute the weight, b_{jf} denotes that the field c_f contains lots of items I_j

18: $For(i=0; i<m; i++)$
19:     $For(j=0; j<n; j++)$
20:         if (exist user u_i in user set U)
21:             $d(i) = \sum_{j=1}^{n} \hat{r}_{ij}$ // calculate the user u_i's rating for all items
22:         $For(f=1; f<|C|; f++)$
23:             if (exist user u_i in user set U && $b_{jf} == 1$)   // $b_{ij} \in \{0,1\}$
24:                 $w(i, f) = \sum_{j=1}^{n} \hat{r}_{ij}$ //calculate the user u_i's rating for field f
25:             if (exist field f in field set C && $b_{jf} == 1$)   //C is field set
26:                 $d(f) = \sum_{i=1}^{m} \sum_{j=1,j=f}^{n} \hat{r}_{ij}$ //calculate all users rating for field f
27:         End for
28: End for

// compute the trust value matrix

29: $For(i=0; i<m; i++)$
30:     $For(j=0; j<m; j++)$
31:         $For(f=1; f<c; f++)$
32:             $W_1^{(t)} += h_j * [w(j, f)/d(j)] * [w(i, f)/o(f)]$
33:         End for
34:     End for
35: End for

//compute the trust relation strength matrix S'

36: $W_1^{(t)} = W_1^{(t)} / h_j$
37: return W_1

3.2   Trust Prediction Model

Trust prediction model can be viewed as classification problem. But different from previous trusted prediction models, the paper utilizes the existing trust network and trust relation strength matrix W_I to predict the unknown trust relations. Interactional strength between users can be characterized to some extent the existence of a trust relationship between users [5]. Because the interactional intensity is a series of discrete values which cannot clearly distinguish relational types of users, firstly we learn a strength threshold λ_w to trust relationship. The learning process is shown in Algorithm 2, where $r(\lambda)$ is the trust relation coverage when the threshold equal to λ.

Algorithm 2.   Learning the trust relation strength threshold λ_w

Input: the existing trust relation matrix W_t, relation strength matrix between users W_I

Output: trust relation strength threshold λ_w

1: initialize the step width of the trust relation strength $\Delta = 0.01$
2: initialize the trust relation coverage $r_0 = 0$
3: initialize the number of trust relations $n_t = 0$
4: initialize the number of trust relations $n_d = 0$
5: *for*$(\lambda=0;\ \lambda<1;\lambda+=\Delta\ )$
6:   *for*$(i=0;\ i<m;\ i++)$
7:    *for*$(j=0;\ j<n;\ j++)$
8:      *if* $w_1^{(ij)} \geq \lambda\ \&\ \&w_t^{(ij)} = 1$
9:         $n_t \leftarrow n_t +1$
10:      *if* $w_1^{(ij)} < \lambda\ \&\ \&w_t^{(ij)} = 1$
11:         $n_d \leftarrow n_d +1$
12:   *End for*
13: *End for*
14:   $r(\lambda)= n_t/\ (n_t +n_d)$
15:   *if* $r(\lambda)>r_0$
16:     $r_0 \leftarrow r(\lambda)$
17:     $\lambda_w \leftarrow \lambda$
18:   else return λ_w
19: *End for*
20: return λ_w

The trust relation coverage is defined as a ratio between the numbers of trust relation that the relation strength is not less than the specify threshold and all the trust relations, it can be computed in formula (4) as follow.

$$r(\lambda) = \sum_{x \geq \lambda} num_t^x \Big/ num_t \qquad (4)$$

where num_t^x denotes the number of trust relations that the relation strength is not less than λ; num_t denotes all the number of trust relations. To obtain the best strength threshold for trust relationships, we utilize an iterative method that is based on coverage rate of all trust relationships.

Finally, the unknown trust relations are predicted by using the interactional strength threshold learned by Algorithm 2. That is, when the relational strength is not less than the threshold, a trust relation is set for the two users; otherwise, there is no trust relation between the two users.

4 Experiments and Evaluation

4.1 Dataset and Evaluation Method

This paper chooses Epinions dataset to validate the algorithm. The dataset includes user's rating and trust relations between users. Statistical characteristics of the experiment Epinions dataset are shown in Table 1.

Table 1. Statistics of Epinions dataset

Description	Value	Range of values
# Users	22165	[1, 22165]
# Items	296277	[1, 296277]
# Categories	27	[1, 27]
# Ratings	359016	[1. 5]
# Helpful	359016	[1, 6]
# Trust link	155323	1

The dataset includes 359016 ratings information which generated by 22165 users with 296277 products and 155323 trust relations exist (no distrust relations). Where Helpful denotes the rating level for a user's review, it can be divided into 6 levels, namely Very Helpful, Most Helpful, Helpful, Off Topic, Not Helpful and Somewhat Helpful. The higher the rating grade is, the higher recognition and affirmation the user as a reviewer is.

To verify the proposed algorithm, this paper employs a common metric [16] to evaluate the performance of trust prediction. We choose $x\%$ of trust set as training trust relations C and the remaining $1 - x\%$ as testing trust relations N to predict. x is varied as $\{50, 60, 65, 70, 80, 90\}$ in this paper and repeating the experiments 5 times for each x and reporting the average performance. The common metric is calculated in formula (5).

$$PA = \frac{|N \cap P|}{|N|} \tag{5}$$

Where N denotes the actual trust relation set, P indicates the predicted trust relation set. $|\cdot|$ denotes the size of a set. If the value is larger, the performance with this algorithm is better.

4.2   Comparison of Different Trust Predictors

In this subsection, we compare the proposed framework with various baseline methods, namely *TP, TP+Similar, Random.*

TP: it utilizes four types of atomic propagations, i.e., direct propagation, co-citation, transpose trust and trust coupling to predict trust relations [10]

TP+similar: a combination of similar and TP, integrating both the existing trust network and rating or profile similarity [11]

Random: it is a baseline method which randomly suggests trust relations to pairs of users [6].

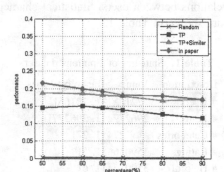

Fig. 4. Performance comparisons for different trust predictors

The evaluation results are shown in Fig. 4. It shows that with the increase of x, the performance of all methods reduces. In general, with more training trust relations, we obtain better performance for the same set of testing trust relations. However, in our experiments, the sets of testing trust relations are different for different $x\%$ s. To clarify the confusion, we conduct a validation experiment by fixing the set of testing trust relations to 10 % and the experimental results are shown in Table 2.

Table 2. Performance of different prediction methods

Datasets		Random	TP	TP + Similar	In paper
Epinions	50 %	0.0027	0.1201	0.1276	0.1304
	60 %	0.0025	0.1335	0.1357	0.1411
	65 %	0.0024	0.1437	0.1481	0.1548
	70 %	0.0017	0.1473	0.1502	0.1689
	80 %	0.0015	0.1521	0.1557	0.1846
	90 %	0.0016	0.1558	0.1702	0.2014

In Table 2, it is clear that with the increase of trust relations, the performance does increase in our expectation. We also note that when x is from 90 to 50, the method proposed in this paper is more accuracy than *TP, TP+Similar.*

5 Conclusions

Due to the information overload in social networks, it is difficult for users to find reliable information and make a decision. To address this problem, this paper proposed a new method to incorporate users' interactional strength with explicit trust relations to predict implicit trust relations. We use a supervised learning method for building trust predictors from structural attributes of a trust network and interactional relation strength which is computed based on factors extracted from user behavior and field information. To achieve good prediction accuracy, critical factors which consist of participation, popularity, reputation and similarity, are employed to model trust relation strength. The experiment results on Epinions dataset showed that interactional relation strength influences the trust relation establishment. The proposed prediction framework is verified with Epinion's data set. For a future work, we would like to further exploit the contextual information and proposed more fine-grain trust prediction models.

Acknowledgments. This work is supported by the Software Innovative Team of Guilin University of Electronic Technology and Graduate Innovation Project GDYCSZ201469.

References

1. Liu, G., Wang, Y., Orgun, M.A.: Social context aware trust network discovery in complex contextual social networks. In: AAAI (2012)
2. Sherchan, W., Nepal, S., Paris, C.: A survey of trust in social networks. ACM Comput. Surv. (CSUR) **45**(4), 47 (2013)
3. Zolfaghar, K., Aghaie, A.: A syntactical approach for interpersonal trust prediction in social web applications: combining contextual and structural data. Knowl.-Based Syst. **26**, 93–102 (2012)
4. Korovaiko, N., Thomo, A.: Trust prediction from user-item ratings. Soc. Netw. Anal. Min. **3** (3), 749–759 (2013)
5. Oh, H.-K., Kim, J.-W.; Kim, S.-W., Lee, K.: A probability-based trust prediction model using trust message passing. In: Proceedings of the 22nd International Conference on World Wide Web Companion, pp. 161–162. International World Wide Web Conferences Steering Committee (2013)
6. Tang, J., Gao, H., Hu, X., Liu, H.: Exploiting homophily effect for trust prediction. In: Proceedings of the Sixth ACM International Conference on Web Search and Data Mining, pp. 53–62. ACM (2013)
7. Liu, H., Lim, E.-P., Lauw, H.W., Le, M.-T., Sun, A., Srivastava, J., Kim, Y.: Predicting trusts among users of online communities: an Epinions case study. In: Proceedings of the 9th ACM Conference on Electronic Commerce, pp. 310–319. ACM (2008)
8. Zolfaghar, K., Aghaic, A.: Mining Trust and Distrust Relationships in Social Web Applications. Institute of Electrical and Electronics Engineers, Austin (2010)
9. Wang, D., Pedreschi, D., Song, C., Giannotti, F., Barabási, A.: Human mobility, social ties, and link prediction. In: Proceedings of the 17th ACM SIGKDD International Conference on Knowledge Discovery and Data Mining, pp. 1100–1108. ACM (2011)

10. Guha, R., Kumar, R., Raghavan, P., Tomkins, A.: Propagation of trust and distrust. In: Proceedings of the 13th International Conference on World Wide Web, pp. 403–412. ACM (2004)
11. Borzymek, P., Sydow, M., Wierzbicki, A.: Enriching trust prediction model in social network with user rating similarity. In: International Conference on Computational Aspects of Social Networks, pp. 40–47. IEEE (2009)
12. Sydow, M.: Towards using contextual information to learn trust metric in social networks: a proposal. In: Lenzini, G., et al. (eds.) Proceedings of the 2nd Workshop on Combining Context and Trust, Security and Privacy, CEUR Workshop Proceedings, vol. 371, pp. 11–16, Trondheim, Norway. Accessed 16 June 2008. ISSN 1613-0073
13. Xiang, R.J., Neville, J., Rogati, M.: Modeling relationship strength in online social networks. In: Proceedings of the International Conference on World Wide Web, pp: 981–990. Raleigh, USA (2010)
14. Zhang, Y., Yu, T.: Mining trust relationships from online social networks. J. Comput. Sci. Technol. 27(5), 529–538 (2012)
15. Pan, X., Deng, G.S., Liu, J.G.: Weighted bipartite network and personalized recommendation. Phys. Procedia 3(5), 1867–1876 (2010)
16. Xiao, Z.Y., Yuan, L.L.: Evaluation metrics for recommender systems. J. Univ. Electron. Sci. Technol. China 41(2), 164–175 (2012)

Cloud Security and Applications

You Can't Hide: A Novel Methodology to Defend DDoS Attack Based on Botcloud

Baohui Li[1,2], Wenjia Niu[2], Kefu Xu[2(✉)], Chuang Zhang[2],
and Peng Zhang[2]

[1] School of Computer Science, Beijing University of Posts
and Telecommunications, Beijing 100876, China
delibh@126.com
[2] Institute of Information Engineering, Chinese Academy of Sciences,
Beijing 100093, China
{niuwenjia,xukefu,zhangchuang,zhengpeng}@iie.ac.cn

Abstract. In recent years, Distributed Denial of Service (DDoS) attack without
employing spoofing source addresses (e.g., SMTP Flood, HTTP/GET Flood [1])
becomes increasingly pervasive. Specially, the advent of cloud computing has
exacerbated this situation, increasing the power of distributed massive attacks
while involving the responsibility of cloud service provider (CSP) that do not
own appropriate solutions. Therefore, we present a novel defense method
srcTrace, leveraged by CSPs, to traceback malware residing in cloud-bots.
srcTrace begins with identifying attack flows, then tracebacks the malicious
processes based on attack flows' address information. Experimental results and
analysis show that *srcTrace* can correctly traceback malware in *ms* time level,
reducing the impacts both upon cloud tenants and attack targets.

Keywords: DDoS Attack based Botcloud · Chase Cloud-bot · Information
entropy · Traceback malicious process · Virtual machine introspection

1 Introduction

Recently, an increasing number of DDoS attackers send seemingly legitimate packets
without employing spoofing IP. In addition to deeply hiding technologies (e.g.,
Fast-Flux [2]), cloud computing largely exacerbates this phenomenon, for that DDoS
attack power in cloud, which was called botcloud in [3], can be setup on demand and at
very large scale without requiring a long dissemination phase nor expensive deployment costs. Beyond the numerous exploiting cases [4, 5], experimental study [6] also
showed that five of the most famous CSPs could be easily exploited to launch DDoS
attack.

To the best of our knowledge, while prior researches have tried to detect DDoS
attack based on botcloud from the position of CSPs [7, 8], very little effort has been
spent on defending this attack. It is obvious that tracebacking and hunting down the
malware sending attack packets is essential in solving this DDoS attack challenge.
However, such a goal is highly challenging for the reasons as follows:

© Springer-Verlag Berlin Heidelberg 2015
W. Niu et al. (Eds.): ATIS 2015, CCIS 557, pp. 203–214, 2015.
DOI: 10.1007/978-3-662-48683-2_18

(1) Malware always hide themselves through invading kernels or other modules, and CSPs do not have any privilege to log in suspicious cloud-bots. Hence, our proposed method should effectively identify these hidden processes without logging in suspicious cloud-bots.

(2) The implementation of the proposed method should bring no modifications on current software and hardware, otherwise, CSPs are reluctant to deploy our method.

In this paper, we propose a novel defense method *srcTrace*, aiming at tracebacking the malicious processes, providing a prerequisite to suppress this attack directly at source end. *srcTrace* (i) identifies DDoS attack flows, (ii) extracts their corresponding source IP and port, (iii) chases cloud-bot using source IP, and (iv) tracebacks malicious process based on source port. To summarize, the main contributions of this paper are as follows:

(1) We proposed a method to identify attack flows, taking advantages of entropy variation. Our proposed method can work independently as an additional module on egress routers for monitoring and recording flow information, thus has high adaptability in cloud environment.

(2) We designed a method of identifying malware without entering cloud-bots. Further, this method can effectively detect hidden process without any help from cloud-bots.

(3) We have implemented a prototype using *Openstack* and *Xen*. Experimental results showed that out method is adaptive with cloud computing environment.

This paper proceeds as follows. Section 2 gives a overview of related works. Then we elaborate our novel tracebacking method *srcTrace* in Sect. 3, giving experimental results and analysis in Sect. 4. Finally, we conclude our work in Sect. 5.

2 Related Works

Even if very little work has been spent on defending DDoS attack based on botcloud, the problem in ordinary network environment was extensively studied in the last decade. Therefore, we present a brief overview of related works, mainly focusing on defense measures at intermediate network and at source-end.

Several schemes focus on selective packet discarding based on attack characterization at intermediate network, preventing attack packets from reaching intended victims [9, 10]. For example, PacketScore [9] prioritize packets based on a per-packet score which estimate the legitimacy of a packet given the attribute values it carries. Once the score of a packet is computed, they perform score-based selective packet discarding where the dropping threshold is dynamically adjusted based on the score distribution of recent incoming packets and the current level of overload the system.

Since a successful source-end DDoS defense enables early suppression of the attack and minimizes collateral damage, numerous research works commit to defend DDoS attack at source-end [11, 12]. Take [11] as an example, D-WARD performs autonomous detection and suppression of DDoS attacks originating from the deploying network while guaranteeing good service to existing legitimate connections to the victim of the attack. To meet the requirement for liberal response, D-WARD applies rate-limiting, rather than filtering, to the attack flow.

Based on above analysis, we can conclude that most defense works generally discarding packets passively, utilizing dropping decisions in high implementation complexity. More seriously, CSPs are reluctant to take such measures because they consume considerable cloud resources. Therefore, we designed a novel defense method *srcTrace*, focusing on tracebacking malware in cloud. Moreover, we can proactively eliminate or suppress the malicious processes, without non-stop passive defending.

3   A Novel Methodology of Defending DDoS Attack Based on Botcloud

Figure 1 illustrates the workflow of *srcTrace*, comprised of *Bot_Chase* and *Mp_Trace*. *Bot_Chase* first identifies the attack flows and their corresponding source addresses, chases cloud-bots using source IPs. Successively, *Mp_Trace* tracebacks the malicious program sending attack packets based on source ports. Following this brief overview, we discuss the important steps of *srcTrace* in more detail.

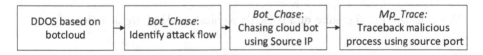

Fig. 1. Workflow of *srcTrace*.

3.1   Identifying Attack Flows

Definition 1. A **Flow** is a collection of data packets with the same destinations (destination IP) sent from cloud computing.

Since DDoS attack without employing spoofing IP mainly locate with Layer 7, we only analyze traffic with established connections. *Bot_Chase* is deployed in cloud center's egress router. When received an alarm generated by any detection methods, such as [8], *Bot_Chase* first identifies attack flows to obtain their source addresses. To make the subsequent analysis simple and clear, this section presents the following assumptions.

Hypothesis 1. During a short time interval, the number of flows and the size of each flow are relatively stable. Although the peak of web services in cloud often arises, each peak period lasts a few minutes or even longer. If we dived this dramatic change into a number of small fragments, such as seconds, the changing rate of a flow is still relatively smooth.

Hypothesis 2. Transmission rate of attack flow is not smaller than legitimate flow's, and the similarity of attack flows is much higher than the similarity among legitimate flows (e.g., flash crowds) [10]. Obviously, attacker can avoid detection through sending small traffic in each connection, however, the convergence at egress routers are usually huger than legitimate flow. Therefore, this assumption is reasonable for the majority of DDoS attacks.

We denote *win_size* as the count number of packets going through *Bot_Chase* during time interval t, which were treated as a sample. And we describe each sample in two dimensions, the size distribution of data streams and the payload distribution. Further, we utilize flow entropy *f_entr* and payload entropy *c_entr* to quantify above two distributions, respectively. *sum_entr* is the sum of *f_entr* and *c_entr*.

Let N_f denote the number of packets with regard to flow f in a sample. Based on the large number theorem, the probability of flow f at *Bot_Chase* is

$$p_f = N_f/win\_size, \tag{1}$$

where, $\sum_{f=1}^{n} N_f = win\_size$, $\sum_{f=1}^{n} p_f = 1$, and n represents the size of different flows in this sample. Let F be the random variable of the number of flows in a sample, therefore, we define flow entropy $f\_entr(F)$ for a sample as follows:

$$f\_entr(F) = -\sum_{i=1}^{n} p_i \log(p_i). \tag{2}$$

We calculate the signature of a packet's payload *payload_sig* as follows:

$$payload\_sig = \sum_{i=1}^{l} binary[i], \tag{3}$$

where *binary* denotes the binary representation of the packet payload, l is the length of *binary*. Let m represent the largest payload signature for a sample, S_i denotes the number of packets with payload signature equals with i. Therefore, the probability of packets with payload signature equals with i in a sample is calculated as follows:

$$p_i = S_i/win\_size, \tag{4}$$

where $\sum_{i=1}^{m} S_i = win\_size$. Let L be the random variable of largest payload signature in a sample, therefore, we define payload entropy $c\_entr(L)$ for a sample as follows:

$$c\_entr(L) = -\sum_{i=1}^{m} p_i \log(p_i). \tag{5}$$

We divide our timeline into two segments for the following investigation: before DDoS attack and under DDoS attack. The entropy in *Bot_Chase* is, therefore, denoted by A^-, A^+, respectively. For example, f_entr^- denotes the flow entropy before DDoS attack, and f_entr^+ represents the flow entropy under DDoS attack.

Let C be the mean value of sum_entr^-, and the standard variation of is θ. Since the number of flows and each flow's transmission rate is stable in a short time interval (Hypothesis 2), therefore, we can justify a reasonable threshold ψ to make the following equation holds with high probability:

$$|sum\_entr^- - C| \leq \psi. \tag{6}$$

In order to make our method adapting to changes of network traffic, we update mean C and standard variation θ as formula (7).

$$C[n] = \sum_{i=1}^{m} \alpha_i C[n-i], \sum_{i=1}^{m} \alpha_i = 1$$

$$\theta[n] = \sum_{i=1}^{m} \beta_i \theta[n-i], \sum_{i=1}^{m} \beta_i = 1 \tag{7}$$

where, $C[n]$ represents the current mean of sum_entr, $C[n-i]$ is the ith sample instance in the near past, and α_i, $i = 1, 2, ..., n$, are the weights for n past samples, respectively. In order to reflect the nearest changes, let $\alpha_i > \alpha_j$ for $i < j$, $i, j \subset I$. The values of α_i ($i = 1, 2, ..., n$) are decided by the experiments of non-attack cases. The same for $\theta[n]$, $\theta[n-i]$, β_i, $i = 1, 2, ..., n$, respectively. We will continuously update C and θ in non-attack case.

Theorem 1. Compared with the non-attack situation, the entropy drops dramatically when attack flows are passing through out *Bot_Chase*, in other words, $sum\_entr^- \gg sum\_entr^+$ holds.

Proof. Let's first proof $f\_entr^- \gg f\_entr^+$. Let $f(x) = x\log x$, $x >= 0$. We know that $f(x)$ is a monotonically increasing convex function. Therefore, $-f(x) = -x\log x$, $x >= 0$, is a monotonically decreasing concave function. Let X be the random variable for the flow distributions. Applying Jensen's inequality [14] to $f(x)$, we have $Ef(x) \geq f(Ex)$, and further $-Ef(x) \leq -f(Ex)$ holds.

Let $P(X_0) = \{p_1^0, ..., p_n^0\}$ be the distribution of flows for non-attack case, and $P(X_1) = \{p_1^1, ..., p_m^1\}$ be the distribution when attack flows are passing through our detecting module. Since attack flows contain more packets than normal, $EX^0 \ll EX^1$ holds, further, $-f(EX^0) \gg -f(EX^1)$ holds, in other words, $-\sum_{i=1}^{n} p_i^0 \log p_i^0 \gg -\sum_{i=1}^{m} p_i^1 \log p_i^1$ and $f\_entr^- \gg f\_entr^+$ hold.

Now, let's proof $c\_entr^- > c\_entr^+$. Let $P(Y_0) = \{p_1^0, ..., p_n^0\}$ be the distribution of payload signature for non-attack case, and $P(Y_1) = \{p_1^1, ..., p_m^1\}$ be the distribution when DDoS attack flow are passing through the our tracebacking module. We can infer from formula (6) that c_entr reaches maximum, $\log n$, when the distribution is even, namely $p_1^0 = p_2^0, ..., = p_n^0$, and it reaches the minimum 0, when the distribution is extremely uneven, say, $p_1^0 = 1 (1 \leq i \leq n)$, $p_k^0 = 0$ ($k = 1, 2 \cdots n$, $k \neq i$). We also know that *c_entr* is a monotonic function, therefore, it is clear that when a DDoS attack occurs, the distribution moves toward the extreme uneven point; as a result, the upper bond of *c_entr* drops. That is to say, $c\_entr^- > c\_entr^+$ holds.

Since *sum_entr* is the sum of *f_entr* and *c_entr*, $sum\_entr^- \gg sum\_entr^+$ holds. □

Based on Theorem 1, we can infer that formula (8) holds with high probability, for that attack flows have higher packet transmission rate and payload similarity.

$$|sum\_entr^+ - C| \geq \psi. \tag{8}$$

When any DDoS detection algorithms determine the presence of DDoS attack, we sort flows by packets number and *c_entr* from big to small, then remove the top flow until (6) holds. The working process for malicious flows identification is shown in Program 1.

Pogram 1. Pseudocode for identifying malicious flows

```
{Assuming Bot_Chase receives a alarm that DDoS attack
 is ongoing};
var f:0..Maxlength, C, θ, t, Ψ,i;
begin
  capture packets during the interval t;
  classify and sort sample S into flows f₁, f₂, …,fₙ;
  i := 1;
  repeat
    calculate sum_entr(S\fᵢ) after eliminating flow fᵢ
    if (|sum_entr⁻ - C|≤ψ) {
      break;
    else
      extract srcIP, srcPort of this flow;
    }
    i := i + 1;
  until i>n
end
```

As is illustrated by Program 1, a flow f would be distinguished as an attack flow, only if formula (8) holds after eliminate this flow. Based on the above description, we can conclude that our method is easy to be deployed in cloud computing, since it needs no changing of software and hardware in cloud.

Since CSPs have complete control over botcloud, we can easily identify cloud-bots based on source IPs. Due to space limitations, we do not detail the method for chasing cloud-bots.

3.2   Tracebacking Malicious Processes

After we identify cloud-bots based on source IPs, *Mp_Trace* tracebacks the malicious process related with the source port. Since Xen [13] is widely used in cloud computing, such as EC2, IBM SoftLayer, Linode, Rackspace Cloud and other mainstream manufactures. Therefore, we take Xen as our experimental scene. *Mp_Trace* was deployed in Dom0, distributed among the whole cloud. Obviously, how to identify the process related with specified port number is the core task to *Mp_Trace*. Thus, we focus on detailing virtual machine introspection technology used to accomplish this key task.

As is shown in the left side of Fig. 2, linux operating system uses doubly linked list to organize processes' descriptors *task_struct*, and each *task_struct* stores information on opened files. Linux kernel encapsulates sockets as file descriptors, and the relationship between port number and processes are illustrated by the right side of Fig. 2. Based on above analysis, we can get the malicious processes related with specified port through traversing the doubly linked list and analyzing each process's opening file information.

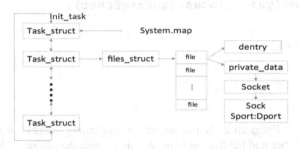

Fig. 2. Relationship between *task_struct* and port.

Although *Xen* provides functions to access DomU's memory from Dom0 with specified address, there is a gap between the obtained information in binary form and the semantic we needed [15]. For example, binary string 01100111 01100101 01110100 01110100 01110100 01111001 is obtained from the virtual address fff-f880039384c78 of our experimental platform,we do not know the specific meaning of this binary string. Only after semantic reconstruction, we can see that it is a process's name *gettty*, corresponding to process identifier 1068. In order to fill this gap, we designed a method of reconstructing the semantics needed by our tracebacking module, with the help of the way of reconstructing semantic provided by [15]. We traverse the whole linked list to analyze each process, which is shown in Program 2.

Program 2. Tracebacking malicious process

```
    var     array_port : 0..Maxlength, port_id,, addr,
            offset, next_addr,list_head;
  begin
    init();
    addr:=xa_access_kernel_symbol
                    ("System.map","init_task", &offset);
    memcpy(&next_addr, addr + offset);
    list_head:=next_addr;
    while(1){
      addr:=xa_access_virtual_address(next_addr,
                &offset);
      memcpy(&next_addr,addr+offset);
      array_port:=analysis_port(addr+offset);
      if (list_head == next_addr) {break;}
      if (port_id in array_port){
        analysis_process(addr+offset);
      }
    destroy();
    }
  end
```

As illustrated in Program 2, firstly, we get the beginning address of this linked list using *init_task* symbol and file *System.map*. We also obtain the offsets within *task_struct* needed to access information such as *next* pointer and the process name. In this way, we traverse the whole linked list and analyze each process's ports. Since the linked list is circular, the code ends when it finds a pointer back to the head of the list.

Malicious programs usually hide themselves by subverting the puppet machine's kernel or other software, denying anti-virus software from obtaining reliable information. However, *Mp_Trace* utilizes the semantics reconstructed by Program 2, without the auxiliary of puppet machines under detecting. Therefore, in this sense, our method can effectively detect hidden processes. In addition, our method can avoid direct attacks, since *Mp_Trace* is independent of malware residing in cloud-bots.

4 Experiments and Analysis

4.1 Experimental Setting

Since real world data from IaaS cloud providers were not accessible, we build a private cloud using *Openstack* and *Xen*, providing of an Infrastructure as a Service (IaaS). The operating systems in Dom0 and DomU are all Ubuntu 14.04 (kernel version 3.13.0-24-generic), and the detailed experimental configurations are listed in Table 1.

Table 1. Experimental environment configurations.

Options	Size
Number of VCPUs in Dom0	4
Dom0 virtual memory	2048 M
Number of VCPUs in DomU	1
DomU virtual memory	1024 M

4.2 Experimental Results and Analysis

Our analysis mainly focuses on the effectiveness and efficiency of *strTrace*. The first three experiments aim at verifying the effectiveness of our approach to identify attack flows, and the fourth experiment test the performance of the method of tracebacking malicious processes based on virtual machine introspection.

Experiment 1. *sum_entr*'s variation with increasing number of flows in non-attack scenario.

Since flows in line with Poisson distribution or Gaussian distribution are deemed as normal by most researchers, we simulate above two types of flows. Each simulation flow in our experiment lasts for 5–10 min, and its packet transmission rate is 100 packets per second (short for *pps*). We set the size of time window for each sample 3 s. In addition, to verify the changing state of *sum_entr* in actual environment, we also tested the actual traffics generated by communications with external servers, such as www.baidu.com, www.github.com and so on. Figure 3 shows the variation of *sum_entr* by increasing number of data streams.

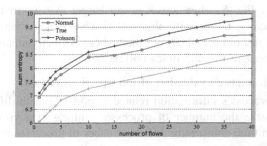

Fig. 3. *sum_entr*'s value by increasing number of flows.

As we can see from Fig. 3, the value of *sum_entr* increases slowly as the number of flows increases. From this, we can find that the value of *sum_entr* is relatively stable with non-attack situation, in a short time interval.

Experiment 2. *sum_entr*'s variation when flow's transmission rate fluctuating wildly.

To test the stability of *sum_entr* when flows' transmission rate fluctuating wildly, we simulate the two types of flows with average transmission rate of 100 *pps*. Specially, one's standard deviation is 25 *pps*, and the other's 50 *pps*. Figure 4 illustrates the changing of *sum_entr*'s standard variation by increasing number of flows.

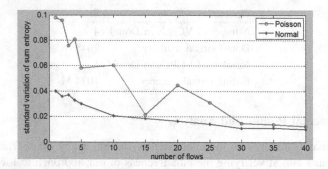

Fig. 4. Value of *sum_entr*'s Standard variation by increasing number of flows.

Figure 4 illustrates that, with the increasing of number of flows, the standard variation of *sum_entr* fluctuates smaller, substantially, and the fluctuation range is less than 0.07. In other words, the *sum_entr* is also stable when services' peaks arise. If we set threshold ψ to 0.07, our approach of identifying attack flows can distinguish between services' peak and DDoS attack.

Experiment 3. Changing of *sum_entr* under DDoS attack.

In order to test the impact of DDoS attack against *sum_entr*, we simulate five normal data flows and one attack flow of HTTP Get flood. The normal flows' constant transmission rate is 100 *pps*, and in contrast, the attack flow is one to seven times bigger than normal flows'. The changing of *sum_entr*, by increasing attack strength, is shown in Fig. 5.

As is showed by Fig. 5, when attack power bigger than normal flows, *sum_entr* decreased nearly linearly, falling with almost 0.45 when attack strength adds 100 *pps*. Assuming that the threshold ψ is 0.07, our method can correctly identify an attack flow when its transmission rate was 2.5 times normal flow's.

Experiment 4. Performance evaluation of introspecting method.

We introspect the process's information related to port 631 with different number of processes. We increase the number of processes running in a virtual machine, the relationship between time-consuming and the number of processes is shown in Fig. 6.

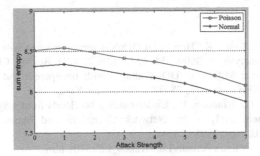

Fig. 5. Value of *sum_entr* with increasing attack strength.

As we can see from Fig. 6, the time consumming in tracebacking malicious process is in *ms* level, and increases sub-linearly by increasing number of processes. It is obvious that *Bot_Chase* can adapt well to cloud computing in performance requirement.

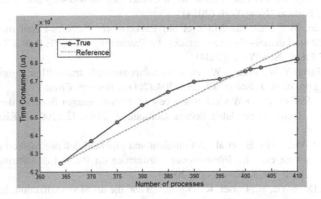

Fig. 6. Time consumed in introspecting with increasing number of process.

5   Conclusion and Future Works

DDoS attacks based on botcloud have posed great threat both on victims outside of cloud and puppet machines in cloud. To effectively defend this attack without employing spoofing IP, we proposed and designed a novel defense method *srcTrace*, compose of and *Mp_Trace*, preventing cloud computing from changing into DDoS attack vector. We also implemented a prototype for *strTrace*, experiments and analysis show that *strTrace* has the following advantages:

(1) *Bot_Chase* can run without changing any software or hardware in cloud. Therefore, it is easy to be deployed in cloud.
(2) Hidden processes can be effectively identified by *Mp_Trace* needing no help of cloud-bots. Hence, our method can meet the needs of CSPs.

References

1. Wang, J., Yang, X., Long, K.: Http-flood DDoS detection scheme based on large deviation and performance analysis. J. Softw. **34**, 1272–1280 (2012). Beijing, China
2. Lua, R., Yow, K.C.: Mitigating DDoS attacks with transparent and intelligent fast-flux swarm network. IEEE Netw. **25**, 28–33 (2011). New York
3. Badis, H., Doyen, G., Khatoun, R.: Understanding botclouds from a system perspective: a principal component analysis. In: Network Operations and Management Symposium, pp. 1–9. IFIP/IEEE, New York (2014)
4. Linuxidc. http://www.linuxidc.com/Linux/2009-12/23401.htm
5. Current Cyber Security News (2011). http://cyberseecure.com/2011/07/cybercriminals-find-an-edge-in-cloud-computing-newsfactor/
6. Pedram, H., Jia, J., Daria, R.: Botcloud an emerging platform for cyber-attacks (2012). http://baesystemsdetica.blogspot.fr
7. Hammi, B., Guillaume, D., Khatoun, R.: A collaborative approach for a source based detection of botclouds. In: 2015 IFIP/IEEE International Symposium on Integrated Network Management (IM), pp. 906–909. IEEE Press, New York (2015)
8. Hammi, B., Khatoun, R., Doyen, G.: A factorial space for a system-based detection of botcloud activity. In: 2014 6th International Conference on Mobility and Security (NTMS), pp. 1–5. IEEE Press, New York (2014)
9. Kim, Y., Lau, W.C., Chuah, M.C., et al.: Packetscore: statistics-based overload control against distributed denial-of-service attacks. In: Proceedings of IEEE INFOCOM, pp. 2594–2604. IEEE Press, New York (2004)
10. Sun, Z.X., Tang, Y.W., Zhang, W., et al.: A router anomaly traffic filter algorithm based on character aggregation. J. Softw. **17**, 295–304 (2006). Beijing, China
11. Mirkovic, J., Reiher, P.: D-WARD: a source-end defense against flooding denial-of-service attacks. IEEE Trans. Dependable Secure Comput. **2**, 216–232 (2005). IEEE Press, New York
12. He, Y., Chen, W., Xiao, B., et al.: An efficient and practical defense method against DDoS attack at the source-end. In: International Conference on Parallel & Distributed Systems, pp. 265–269. IEEE Press, New York (2005)
13. Barham, P., Dragovic, B., Fraser, K., et al.: Xen and the art of virtualization. In: Proceedings of the 19th ACM Symposium on Operating Systems Principles, pp. 164–177. ACM Press, New York (2003)
14. Cover, T.M., Thomas, J.A.: Elements of Information Theory. Wiley-Interscience, New York (2007)
15. Payne, B.D., De Carbone, M.D.P., Lee, W.: Secure and flexible monitoring of virtual machines. In: Twenty-Third Annual Computer Security Applications Conference, pp. 385–397. IEEE Press, New York (2007)

Quantitative Evaluation Method
of Cloud Security

Xinlong Zhao[1], Weishi Zhang[1], and Wei Ma[2(✉)]

[1] Department of Information Science and Technology,
Dalian Maritime University, Dalian 116026, China
zhaoxl@dl.cn, teesiv@dlmu.edu.cn
[2] Institute of Information Engineering, CAS, Beijing 100093, China
mawei@iie.ac.cn

Abstract. As cloud computing technology has been widely used in the world, the security assessment of cloud computing platform has caught lots of attention. Based on the characteristics of cloud computing platform, this article presents an indicator system to evaluate the security of cloud computing. The system makes use of fuzzy membership function to express the subjective evaluation elements and adopt G.A. Miller theory to quantify the overall security of cloud computing platform. The method in the paper not only helps to get the optimal weight, but also takes both the experts' preference to assessment program and optimal ranking into account. And the example shows that the methodology in this paper is operable and reasonable for the assessment of cloud computing platform security.

Keywords: Security assessment · Cloud computing

1 Introduction

With the rapid development of global computer technology, cloud computing technology has become the key of new technological revolution, and has been widely used in government, business, education, data center and so on [1]. Cloud platform provides users with the convenience of service, rapid expansion of storage space and computing power and a lower cost of deployment. However, the adoption of cloud computing means that the core data and business of users is out of the control of their owns. Thus the security problems of cloud platform have been concerns for lots of people [2, 3]. Cloud computing platforms break out of the border of traditional information systems and run at the shared IT infrastructure, which means that the old security assessment methods, based on the border guard, can not play a role any more [4, 5]. It has become an important subject of study to evaluate the security of cloud computing platform and provide users the quantified and evaluable indicators. In recent years, the security protection technology for cloud platforms, especially the data security technology, has become a focal point of research at home and abroad [6]. And the assessment method of overall cloud platform security has also aroused the interests of researchers [4, 7]. However, the widely recognized assessment program about cloud security has not yet been found since that cloud security-related standards have not been established, and

W. Niu et al. (Eds.): ATIS 2015, CCIS 557, pp. 215–225, 2015.
DOI: 10.1007/978-3-662-48683-2_19

there is no systematic assessment and quantitative methods in cloud security. Based on the characteristics of cloud computing platform, this article presents a methodology to establish an indicator assessment system for cloud computing security. The system makes use of fuzzy membership function to express the subjective evaluation elements and adopted G.A. Miller theory to quantify the overall security of cloud computing platform. Besides, the example in the article shows a comprehensive procedure of evaluating the cloud platform security and proves the method operable for builders and users.

2   Related Work

Cloud computing platform provides dynamic and scalable virtual resources through the Internet. With the characteristics of distributed computing, parallel processing, storage, and powerful computing, it belongs to the specific information system patterns in the age of big data. However, cloud security issues are also increasingly prominent which restrict the in-depth development of cloud computing technology in spite of its convenient service. There have been a lot of research works for cloud computing security issues. For example, Feng et al. [2] think the security problem should be taken into account in cloud computing platform; Chen et al. [1] come up with a more comprehensive cloud computing security system, and Lin and others [3] present us a cloud computing security architecture.

On the other hand, in order to improve information and network security, we have established information security rating system and have developed a series of security standards. Nevertheless, the security rating system points at the issues for traditional information systems and does not involve the boundaries blur of cloud computing platform. There are also some works to study the security assessment programs considering the particularity of cloud platform. For examples, Chen et al. [4] give us a security evaluation methodology based on level protection; Jiang [7] build a security assessment model based on level protection. However, these evaluation methods often focus on how to make the cloud assessment compatible with the existing assessment system, and do not propose a suitable and quantifiable method for cloud platform security assessment.

Therefore, this paper presents an indicator system for cloud computing platform, as well as the metrics of quantified expression and the overall methodology. The approach in the paper has a positive effect on the assessing of cloud computing security and helps users choose the appropriate cloud service, which promotes the healthy development of cloud computing industry.

3   Cloud Security Indicator System

A qualitative assessment method can be considered in cloud computing security indicator system. A list can be used firstly to record all cloud computing security indicators to assess, and then the indicator is to be reviewed one by one. If all of the indicators meet the benchmarks, the tested can pass. If the requirements are not met, the further evidence will be required. Two points need paying attention to: (1) the indicator weight problem: different types of indicators have different degrees of importance in security. (2) the indicator assessing result: if bivalent logic is applied to assess the result in security indicators evaluating, it means that the security evaluation is either "pass" or "failure". But in fact, there are few indicators in full compliance with standards or simply do not meet the standards. Even if all judged to be "passed" indicators, the tested also have differences in the safety performance, but the assessment results of bivalent logic can not reflect those differences.

To solve the problems of indicator weight differences and assessment process control, we propose a more comprehensive solution. The included method—picking the value in a continuous range in cloud computing security assessment—is a fuzzy evaluation method more objective than bivalent logic assessment.

3.1 Principles of Building of Indicator System

The design principles about cloud security indicator system include: (1) Scientificity: the selection of indicators is based on cloud computing security research, in line with the relevant laws and regulations. (2) Hierarchy: cloud computing security indicator system should be divided into different levels in accordance with different attributes. (3) Independence: security indicators can separately reflect the security situation of cloud computing. (4) Operability: cloud computing security indicator system should be objective and practical and meet the need of real security evaluation. (5) Systematic ness: the need to consider various factors of platforms, and to reflect the overall system and the relationship between the internal.

3.2 Architecture of the Indicator System

The constructing process of cloud computing security indicator system includes: (1) The research table is to be designed about cloud computing security evaluation indicator system according to domestic and foreign experts' opinions, combined with the actual situation. Then the tables are used to gather cloud computing platform safety indicators proposed by experts. (2) The feedback from the research table can tell you cloud computing security indicators recognized by experts. (3) Repeat the two previous steps until the majority of experts draw the security indicator system in line with the principles.

Cloud computing security indicator system includes: technical indicator system and management indicator system. Technical security indicator system includes: physical security, network security, host system security, application security, data security, backup and recovery and other indicators. Management security indicator system includes: security management system, security administration, security personnel management, construction management and system operation, maintenance manage-ment and other indicators. These indicator systems cover the needs of cloud computing security assessment.

4 Quantitative Assessment of Cloud Security

Quantitative assessment of cloud computing security is very subjective and there is no absolute line between "meet" and "does not meet". The fuzzy methods are usually adopted. Fuzzy evaluation helps state the security issues. We can break the assembly down into small problems based on the actual situations so that the assessors can make a subjective evaluation. That the assessor makes such a fuzzy judgment as the percentage can more accurately reflect the cloud security. Fuzzy evaluation method is the application of fuzzy mathematical theory to the probability of cloud security quantifying [8, 9]. The probability can be treated as a fuzzy number, through the establishment and quantitative analysis of cloud security event tree with triangular fuzzy tree, LR fuzzy numbers, etc. However, the evaluation method acquires the assessors' subjective selection of evaluation grade and weight. Therefore, the scientific and objectivity of the results need to be verified.

In order to ensure the objective evaluation, Josang's subjective logic evaluation method also provides an effective way for description of subjective behavior, but this method is still too dependent on subjective judgments and correctness deserve doubt. To solve the above problems, we decide to use multi-attribute decision making to quantify the evaluation of cloud platform security considering the three characteristics of quantitative analysis of cloud platform safety assessment–no unified dimensionless indicators, wide coverage and mutual exclusivity. There are several ways of multiple-attribute decision making about the quantitative evaluation of cloud platform security: optimistic type, pessimistic type, optimistic-pessimistic union type, the simple weighted average, compromise. Among them, the compromise decision tends to be as close as to the ideal solution, or as far away from the negative ideal solution, and look for a relatively satisfactory answer between the ideal solution and negative ideal solution. The key is how to choose a benchmark and how to measure the distance between the feasible solution and the benchmark to meet the requirements of security quantitative evaluation.

4.1 Multi-attribute Decision Making Indicator System

Cloud computing platform is a complicated system composed of interacting subsystems. Thus the security assessment of a cloud platform will require multiple interrelated evaluation indicators. According to the hierarchies these indicators are combined to a whole body with the function of specific evaluation. The indicator system includes: economic indicators, technical indicators, indicators of resources, infrastructure indicators and so on.

4.2 Normalization of Decision-Making Index

Ascertain cost-benefit value of index. For instance, with the increasing data sharing rate of cloud computing platform's security index, resource utilization rate improves and cost reduces, however, that brings security reduction as well. Consequently, data sharing rate has to be restricted to a appropriate area.

Non-dimension of index. The biggest problem of cloud computing platform's security evaluation lies in the incommensurability between index, in other words, each column value of attribute value list has different dimension, once adopt different measurement unit for the same attribute, the value of list become diverse as a result.

Thought of normalization. Magnitude of different index's attribute value varies a lot in original attribute value list. In order to compare these values using multi-objective evaluation method, it has to normalize attribute value list's value. That's to shift values to interval [0, 1]. Meanwhile, use nonlinear transformation method to solve incomplete compensatory when preprocess data.

Normalization method of index: (1) Linear scaling transformation. Benefit-oriented attribute: after transformation, the worst value attribute is 0, and optimal is 1. Benefit-oriented attribute: after transformation, worst value attribute is 1, and the optimal is 0. (2) Standard transformation of 0–1 For each attribute, the optimal value is 1, the worst is 0, and difference after transformation is linear. (3) The optimal value is the transformation between interval. The given concrete attribute interval for judging conveniently. (4) Normalization of vector. After normalization, the same attribute value's quadratic sum of each scheme is "1", no matter cost-oriented or benefit-oriented type, the magnitude of attribute value can't be distinguished. (5) Quantitative method of qualitative index. Some index is qualitative type, so they can only be described qualitatively. For instance, reliability of cloud platform's security index. Quantify qualitative index, divide these index into several level and assign different value to them.

4.3   Multi-attribute Decision-Making

1. Preparation for Multi-attribute Decision-Making

(1) Decision Matrix
Assume: set alternative scheme assemble as: $X = \{X_1, X_2, \cdots, X_m\}$
Attribute assemble of scheme is: $Y = \{y_1, y_2, \cdots, y_n\}$

(2) Defination of Decision Matrix is:
$$\begin{bmatrix} y_{11} & \cdots & y_{1j} & \cdots & y_{1n} \\ & \cdots & & \cdots & \\ y_{i1} & \cdots & y_{ij} & \cdots & y_{in} \\ & \cdots & & \cdots & \\ y_{m1} & \cdots & y_{mj} & \cdots & y_{mn} \end{bmatrix}$$

2. Preprocess of data.

(1) Linear transformation
Original decision matrix is $Y = \{y_{ij}\}$, after transformation it becomes $Z = \{z_{ij}\}$, $i = 1,\ldots,m$, $j = 1,\ldots,n$. Suppose yjmax is the max of matrix's j row If j is benefit-oriented attribute, then

$$z_{ij} = y_{ij}/y_j^{max} \tag{1}$$

When preprocess data, the worst value attribute is not necessarily 0 after transformation, but the optimal is 1.

If j is cost-oriented attribute, it can be set

$$z_{ij} = 1 - y_{ij}/y_j^{max} \qquad (2)$$

After (2) transformation, the optimal attribute value is not necessarily 1, the worst is 0. Cost-oriented attribute can be transformated using the following formula:

$$z_{ij} = y_j^{min}/y_{ij} \qquad (3)$$

After using (3) formula to transformate, the worst value is not necessarily 0, the optimal is 1 and is non-linear transformation.

(2) Standard transformation of 0–1.

For linear transformation, after liner transformation, if the optimal value of j is 1, then the worst value is not usually 0; if the worst value is 0, the optimal value is not usually 1. After shift, when the optimal value of attribute is 1 and the worst is 0, can carry out standard 0–1 transformation. For benefit-oriented attribute j, set

$$z_{ij} = \frac{y_{ij} - y_j^{min}}{y_j^{max} - y_j^{min}} \qquad (4)$$

When j is cost – oriented attribute, set

$$z_{ij} = \frac{y_j^{max} - y_{ij}}{y_j^{max} - y_j^{min}} \qquad (5)$$

(3) Shift of the optimal value's given interval.

The article set the optimal attribute interval [yj0, yj*], yj' as intolerance lower limit, yj'' as intolerance upper limit, then

$$z_{ij} = \begin{cases} 1 - (y_j^0 - y_{ij})/(y_j^0 - y_j') & \text{if } y_j' < y_{ij} < y_j^0 \\ 1 & \text{if } y_j^0 \leq y_{ij} \leq y_j^* \\ 1 - (y_{ij} - y_j^*)/(y_j'' - y_j^*) & \text{if } y_j'' > y_{ij} > y_j^* \\ 0 & \text{others} \end{cases} \qquad (6)$$

Function's graph between attribute value zij and original yij is trapezoid.

(4) Normalization of vector.

Whether the cost-oriented or benefit-oriented attribute of this method, either one can adopt the following formula to transform:

$$z_{ij} = y_{ij} / \sqrt{\sum_{i=1}^{m} y_{ij}^2} \qquad (7)$$

The transformation is linear, so the transformed attribute value's magnitude cannot be differentiated. After normalization, the quadratic sum of the same attribute value in all scheme is 1, which is often used to calculate the Euclidean distance between all scheme and some virtual scheme.

(5) Original data statistical processing method.

For original data, its pre-processing is conducted by statistical averaging method. Set up M as the centesimal mean. Set M as the attribute mean of schemes set X, and then transform it with the following formula:

$$z_{ij} = \frac{y_{ij} - \bar{y}_j}{y_j^{max} - \bar{y}_j} (1.00 - M) + M \qquad (8)$$

In the formula, $\bar{y}_j = \frac{1}{m} \sum_{i=1}^{m} y_{ij}$ is the mean of attribute j of all schemes, m is the number of schemes, value of M is between 0.5 and 0.75.

(6) Pre-processing of expert scoring data.

Since performance index is hard to be measured by statistical data, often experts are invited to score the evaluation objects, and then serve the score mean as the attribute of related index, which can determine the condition of objects.

Given that experts' opinions may differ, their opinions is also key to evaluation. In this text, all experts' scores are standardized within the same interval [M0, M*]. Different M0 and M* will not affect results, as long as the scores are in the above interval. The specific algorithm is as follows:

$$z_{ij} = M^0 + (M^* - M^0) \frac{y_{ij} - y_j^{min}}{y_j^{max} - y_j^{min}} \qquad (9)$$

When M0 = 0, M* = 1, the above algorithm is the same with benefit-oriented attribute 0-1, transformation formula (4).

3. The multiple attribute decision making method of maximizing deviations.

For the problem of multiple attribute decision making, if the weight information is unknown and decision matrix is $A = (a_{ij})_{n \times m}$, when A is standardized processed, standardized matrix can be get as $R = (r_{ij})_{n \times m}$

Suppose the attribute's weight vector is $w = (w_1, w_2, \cdots, w_m)$, $w_j \geq 0, j \in M$ and satisfy constraint condition:

$$\sum_{j=1}^{m} w_j^2 = 1 \qquad (10)$$

Then each scheme's attribute value can be defined as:

$$z_i(w) = \sum_{j=1}^{m} r_{ij}w_j \tag{11}$$

Multi-attribute decision-making is the comparison between the ranking of all schemes' attribute values. The smaller difference between schemes' uj is, the weaker the attribute's function to scheme's decision and ranking. Conversely, the bigger difference between schemes' uj is, the stronger the attribute's function to scheme's decision and ranking.

From the respect of ranking all schemes, we can conclude in this text that the bigger the scheme's attribute value deviation is, the greater is the given weight. If there is no difference in all schemes' attributes, attribute uj will have no effect on scheme ranking and the weight is 0.

5 Example of Quantitative Analysis

5.1 Security Evaluation Module

This evaluation module contains multi-attribute decision-making obtaining cloud platform's attribute weight, scheme preference and decision-making weight. Among them, multi-attribute decision-making obtaining cloud platform's security attribute weight is on the basis of MADM's attribute feature, classify cloud platform's security attribute in two respects. First of all, cloud platform' security attribute is divided in quantitative and quantitative type. Second, it can be divided into benefit-oriented and cost-oriented type. Among that, the bigger value of benefit-oriented attribute is, the better. It has positive influence to the evaluation result, but the smaller value of cost-oriented attribute, the better. It has negative influence to the evaluation result. Evaluation attribute that the article put forward belongs to benefit-oriented attribute and quantitative attribute. Preference for scheme is to measure decision maker's preference for scheme and attribute, attribute importance, decision maker's authority(authoritative coefficient) related to the scheme. Usually use interval number to indicate the decision-making weight. You can define the desired value of interval number. Minimize the difference between scheme's evaluation value and expected value and ensure objectification of weight vector's selection.

5.2 Quantization Evaluation

The step of cloud security quantization's evaluation algorithm include: (1) Carry out fuzzy process for attribute of cloud platform' s quantization evaluation, it's practical to use G. A. Miller theory to build form of interval value. In the end, shape the decision-making matrix. (2) Take advantage of formula to normalize decision matrix of cloud platform' security quantization evaluation. (3) Ascertain expected value of attribute in accordance with expert's preference level and experience for cloud platform' security quantization evaluation. (4) Obtain attribute weight of cloud platform' security quantization. (5) Finally, calculate each evaluation scheme's attribute value in

Table 1. Quantitative attribute features of cloud computing security's quantization evaluation

Evaluation method	Physical security	Host security	Application security	Data security	Management
X1	Not bad	Bad	Good	Good	Good
X2	Excellent	Excellent	Very bad	Not bad	Not bad
X3	Not bad	Not bad	Excellent	Good	Good
X4	Excellent	Excellent	Bad	Not bad	Not bad
X5	Very bad	poor	Not bad	Good	Good

accordance with weight, then carry out appropriate sorting. (6) To verify the availability of model, we can conduct related questionnaire survey for expert, and after aggregation get scheme for cloud computing quantization evaluation (Table 1).

(1) Attribute quantization and normative approach.

Normative approach of quantitative attribute value for the above table, results are displayed as Table 2.

Table 2. Normative approach of cloud computing security quantization's evaluation index

Evaluation method	Physical security	Host security	Application security	Data security	Management
X1	[0.322 0.412]	[0.174 0.203]	[0.542 0.633]	[0.393 0.481]	[0.595 0.774]
X2	[0.522 0.656]	[0.561 0.618]	[0.129 0.181]	[0.2680.330]	[0.174 0.207]
X3	[0.511 0.574]	[0.381 0.511]	[0.595 0.707]	[0.395 0.454]	[0.414 0.449]
X4	[0.548 0.631]	[0.522 0.588]	[0.127 0.169]	[0.327 0.357]	[0.214 0.263]
X5	[0.158 0.222]	[0.071 0.093]	[0.412 0.462]	[0.580 0.692]	[0.478 0.571]

The article provide a normalization for cost-oriented and benefit-oriented attribute, thus obtain the decision matrix of standard specification like following:

$$R = \begin{bmatrix} [0\ 31,\ 0\ 41] & [0\ 17,\ 0\ 20] & [0\ 51,\ 0\ 63] & [0\ 39,\ 0\ 48] & [0\ 60,\ 0\ 77] \\ [0\ 55,\ 0\ 66] & [0\ 72,\ 0\ 74] & [0\ 13,\ 0\ 18] & [0\ 27,\ 0\ 33] & [0\ 17,\ 0\ 21] \\ [0\ 51,\ 0\ 57] & [0\ 38,\ 0\ 40] & [0\ 60,\ 0\ 71] & [0\ 40,\ 0\ 45] & [0\ 41,\ 0\ 45] \\ [0\ 55,\ 0\ 63] & [0\ 55,\ 0\ 59] & [0\ 13,\ 0\ 17] & [0\ 33,\ 0\ 36] & [0\ 21,\ 0\ 26] \\ [0\ 16,\ 0\ 22] & [0\ 07,\ 0\ 09] & [0\ 41,\ 0\ 46] & [0\ 58,\ 0\ 69] & [0\ 48,\ 0\ 57] \end{bmatrix}$$

(2) Ascertain expert's subjective judgment and preference for each cloud security's quantization evaluation scheme.

For instance, some expert participate the judgement of cloud platform's security, authority is $b'p = (0.83, 0.74, 0.80, 0.94)$, and attribute importance is $Wj = (0.25, 0.28,$

0.15, 0.21, 0.11). The expert's preference for different cloud security's quantization evaluation scheme can be obtained by this article in accordance with formula.

$$d_i = \begin{bmatrix} [0\ 293\ 0\ 363] & [0\ 359\ 0\ 407] & [0\ 375\ 0\ 418] \\ [0\ 334\ 0\ 375] & [0\ 246\ 0\ 295] \end{bmatrix}$$

(3) Select comprehensive evaluation and potimal weight value of objective attribute

This article allocate Wj in accordance with different parameter, then compare cloud platform' security level in reference with attribute optimal weight of different parameter (Table 3).

Table 3. Result of cloud computing security's quantization evaluation

Model parameter a, b	Attribute optimization weight W_j	Comprehensive value of plan attribute Z_j
a = 1.0, b = 0 (Model P1)	(0.41, 0.13, 0.14, 0.21, 0.11)	(0.4205, 0.4430, 0.5004, 0.4312, 0.3403)
a = 0.5, b = 0.5 (Model P1&P2)	(0.37, 0.15, 0.12, 0.22, 0.14)	(0.4344, 0.4398, 0.4906, 0.4269, 0.3477)
a = 0, b = 1 (Model P2)	(0.34, 0.19, 0.13, 0.18, 0.16)	(0.4215, 0.4438, 0.5060, 0.4247, 0.3347)

Allocation of weight duffers when select different parameter. The reason is subjective judgment information of expert amplify increasingly in the position of model, with the increasing weight, the influence on the cloud platform' quantization result is the biggest. However, the other attributes allocation come out some changes because of the model's transformation.

6 Summary

Above all, this article can adopt multi-attribute decision-making method to evaluate security of cloud computing, which not only establish the weight of attribute, but also give consideration to both factors of expert's preference for evaluation scheme and objective optimal sorting. It's optimization and improvement of fuzzy evaluation method and subjective logic evaluation method, which ensure attribute's weight can reflect cloud platform' security actually and provide an efficient and practical means for cloud computing's quantization evaluation.

References

1. Chen, C., Yu, J.: Security of Cloud System. Science Press, Tokyo (2014)
2. Feng, D.G., Zhang, M., Zhang, Y., et al.: Study on cloud computing security. J. Softw. **22**(1), 71–83 (2011)
3. Lin, C., Su, W., Meng, K., Liu, Q., Liu, W.: Cloud computing security: architecture, mechanism and modeling. Chin. J. Comput. **9**, 1765–1784 (2013)

4. Chen, X., Yu, J., Chen, C., Ren, W.: Cloud computing security framework based on classified protection. China Digital Med. **11**, 44–47 (2014)
5. Chen, X., Chen, C., Tao, Y., Hu, J.: Cloud security assessment system based on classifying and grading. IEEE Cloud Comput. **2**(2), 58–67 (2015)
6. Chen, C., Zhu, X., Shen, P., Hu, J.: A hierarchical clustering method for big data oriented ciphertext search. In: INFOCOM 2014 Workshop on Security and Privacy in Big Data, pp. 559–564 (2014)
7. Jiang, Z., Zhao, W., Liu, Y., Liu, B.: Model for cloud computing security assessment based on classified protection. Comput. Sci. **8**, 151–156 (2013)
8. Yan, Q., Chen, Z., Duan, Y., Wang, L.: Information system security metrics and evaluation model. Acta Electronica Sinica **9**, 1351–1355 (2003)
9. Chen, C., Feng, D., Xu, Z.: A research on quantitative evaluation on the assurance of information security products. Acta Electronica Sinica **10**, 1886–1891 (2007)

A Large-Scale Distributed Sorting Algorithm Based on Cloud Computing

Na Pang$^{(\boxtimes)}$, Dali Zhu, Zheming Fan, Wenjing Rong,
and Weimiao Feng

Institute of Information Engineering,
Chinese Academy of Sciences, Beijing 100093, China
{pangna, zhudali, fanzheming, rongwenjing,
fengweimiao}@iie.ac.cn

Abstract. Large amounts of data processing bring parallel computing into sharp focus. In order to solve the sorting problem of large-scale data in the era of internet, a large-scale distributed sorting algorithm based on cloud computing is proposed. The algorithm uses the ideas of quick-sort and merge-sort to sort and integrate the data on each cloud, which making best of clouds' computing and storage resources. Taking advantage of the idea of parallel computing, we can reduce the computing time and improve the efficiency of sorting. By evaluating algorithm's time complexity and organizing a simulation test, the effectiveness was verified.

Keywords: Cloud computing · Parallel algorithm · Quick sort · Merge sort · Distributed computing

1 Introduction

The increasingly development of Internet business makes total quantity of data which is to be processed grow exponentially. Massive data processing has become a pressing issue, especially for large-scale data sorting. Although there are many mature data sorting methods such as quick-sort, insertion-sort, merge-sort and shell-sort, these technologies can quickly achieve the sorting in case that the amount of data is small. The efficiency of these sorting algorithms would be greatly discounted when faced with large amount of data. The time performing the sorting is intolerable.

Some recent work has been proposed to improve existing algorithms to meet specific requirements. Big data process makes parallel computing get a lot of attention [1–3, 5]. Davidson et al. [4] design a high-performance parallel merge sort for highly parallel system to use more register communication. Minsoo and Dongseung [6] use multiple processors in parallel computing to perform merge-sort. The maximum speedup can reach in which P is the number of processors. Nanjesh et al. [7] aim to form a common single node model for both MPI and PVM which demonstrates the performance dependency of parallel merge sort on RAM of the nodes (desktop PCs) used in parallel computing. Christof et al. [8] propose adaptations of two especially classic sequential sorting algorithms such as bubble sort and insertion sort to parallel

© Springer-Verlag Berlin Heidelberg 2015
W. Niu et al. (Eds.): ATIS 2015, CCIS 557, pp. 226–237, 2015.
DOI: 10.1007/978-3-662-48683-2_20

execution in spatially constrained networks of devices. To reduce the number of comparators required, the method of modified merge sort is proposed in [10].

Wei et al. [13] employs the Expectation Maximization algorithm to iteratively approximate the optimal data partitioning. A novel periodic multi-round data distribution model is presented and a parallel sorting algorithm for Multisets is proposed by using the characteristics of multi-threading technology and multi-level caches on multi-core architectures [14]. Shirahata et al. [15] propose a MapReduce-based out-of-core GPU memory management technique for processing large-scale graph applications on heterogeneous GPU-based supercomputers. Ye and Huang [16] aims to model transient stability as an objective function rather than an inequality constraint and consider classic transient stability constrained OPF (TSCOPF) as a tradeoff procedure using Pareto ideology.

Cloud computing is a model for enabling ubiquitous network access to a shared pool of configurable computing resources [17]. It is the development of distributed processing, parallel processing and grid computing. It relies on sharing of resources to achieve coherence and economies of scale, similar to the utility over a network. It is a novel approach to share infrastructure faced with ultra-large-scale distributed environment. The core is to provide data storage and network services.

With the rapid development of the amount of data in cloud computing environment, it is particular important to study how to analyze and process these data fast and effectively [9, 11, 12]. How to sort large-scale data efficiently in cloud computing becomes a significant research [18–27]. Whether the used sorting algorithm can achieve high performance and how much time and resource in cloud computing it consumes is concerned widely.

A Large-scale sorting algorithm based on cloud computing makes use of parallel processing characteristics to put the vast amounts of data across distributed computer separately. Combined with the traditional sorting algorithm, it can address the sorting problems more efficiently. It not only excludes the inefficiencies of massive data sorting, but also makes better use of computer resources through parallel processing.

2 Construction of Large-Scale Distributed Sorting Platform

One big advantage of cloud computing is the ability to quickly and efficiently process massive amounts of data. A cloud computing platform can be assembled from a set of distributed machines in different locations, connected to a single network or hub service. This model not only gets rid of the limitations of hardware devices, while extending better to respond quickly to changes in user demand.

Large-scale distributed sorting platform is a system prototype, which aims to providing a range of sorting solutions for cloud computing. The main function of this platform concludes sorting of massive data in cloud, completing the sorting process intelligently, gathering the sorting results. The system operating environment is shown in Fig. 1. Each host counts the number of working machine via a specific port and distributes corresponding data to each one. Each working machine is controlled by host to sort data and order the summary data and request host the next scheduling. Host sends "data request" command to the working machine which has completed the sorting and

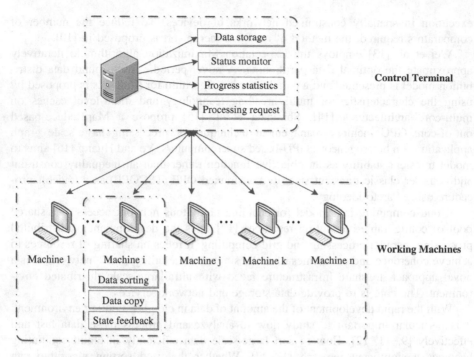

Fig. 1. System operating environment of large-scale distributed sorting platform

enters the status **Done**. It completes the request then the next round until that the final host confirms that $N - 1$ machines, N is the total number of machines, have entered the status Termination. When received a request **Done**, all sorting has been completed.

2.1 Business Logic Design

2.1.1 Business Logic Design of Host

Business logic design of host mainly includes these four aspects:

- Data storage: Host of the platform is mainly based on the cloud server. The stored data is the initial mass of data to be sorted and the final sorted data. Host will achieve even distribution and release of data based on the total number of working machine. It achieves hierarchical storage according to business logic in order to reduce the burden of data transfer.
- Status monitor: The host sets up a state parameter for each working machine to monitor complete schedule. The status parameter consists of two values: **Done** means working machine has completed data sorting and requests new data. **Termination** shows that the work machine enters the status **Termination**, at the same

time, the host will increase the number of working machine which is in the ter-minate status.

- Progress statistics: The host sets a number in order to determine the completion of the entire sorting process based on the state feedback of working machine feedback.
- Processing request: The host analyzes the feedback information sent by working machines and makes the next issue work orders. When the host gets the feedback *Done*, it continues to monitor other working machine. When the working machine B also sends the feedback *Done*, the host will send the number of B to A. Then A will request data to B.

2.1.2 Business Logic Design of Working Machine

Business logic design of working machine mainly includes these three aspects:

- Data sorting: First, plenty of data inside of the working machine use fast sorting algorithm so that data presents ordering. Second, when two or more work machines complete their own data sorting, a working machine will request data from another working machine and merge the two parts of the data and sort them.
- Data copy: When the working machine *A* which is in waiting state requests data from another machine *B* which has completed the sorting, B sends the data through a specific port to *A*. The working machine enters status *Termination*.
- State feedback: A working machine will send data to the host after completion of its sorting and enters the feedback *Done*. The working machine will send *Termination* to host when it has completed the data sending. Host will record the number of working machine which is in status *Termination*.

3   Large-Scale Distributed Sorting Algorithm Design

3.1   Large-Scale Distributed Sorting Algorithm Design of Host

3.1.1   Data Distribution Based on Constraint of the Number of Working Machine

The amount of data distributed to each working machine is the key step. If the dis-tribution is any amount of data, the sorting time of each working machine will be different obviously. Some of them may enter status *Done* to wait while others may still be sorting, which will lead to a waste of time to balance the working machines.

In our large-scale sorting algorithm, by designing the average distribution mech-anism, it can ensure that each data distributed by host is average. The sorting com-pletion time of each working machine is basically the same in order to avoid wasting of resources due to unnecessary waiting. The design ideas are like this:

N represents the number of working machines collected by host through a specific port. The amount of data in the host is M, and *data[n]* ($n = 1, 2, L, N$) represents the data sent to working machine from hosts. The data distribution algorithm based on constraint of working machine is shown in Algorithm 1.

Algorithm 1. Data Distribution Algorithm based on constraint of working machine

Input : N for number of working machines, M for amount of data in the host
Return: data[] for the data send to working machines

Begin:

```
if(M%N == 0)
{
        for (i=0;i<N;i++)
                data[i+1] = M/N;
        endfor
}
else
{
        for(i=0;i<M/N;i++)
                data[i+1] = M/N+1;
        endfor
        for(i=M%N;i<N;i++)
                data[i+1] = M/N;
        endfor
}
endif
```

3.1.2   Task Distribution Based on Constraint of Free Time

Host analyzes the feedback sent by working machines and makes the next issue work orders. Host sets a status parameter *FlagInHost*, in which the attribute has the following states:

None: No machine is in the waiting state.

Termination: The sort is over.

Wait: Waiting for the rest of the work to complete.

There is a set of numbers *waitNum* of the working machine in waiting status. It is used to monitor the progress of sorting in the work machine. The host also sets a statistical attribute *FinishCount* to record the number of status *Termination*.

The host accepts the status request from each working machine. When the working machine A is sending the feedback information *Done* to the host, A will be waiting status. If another working machine B is sending the feedback information "*Done*" to the host, the host will send the port number of B to the waiting working machine A. If the request is *Termination*, the number of the terminated working machine *FinishCount* pluses 1, until the *FinishCount* is $N - 1$. At this point all sort work has been completed. The data distribution algorithm based on constraint of free time is shown in Algorithm 2.

Algorithm 2. Data Distribution Algorithm based on constraint of free time

---

Input: inputNum for the number of requesting working machine

```
Listen(int inputNum, Flag inputFlag)
{
    if ( inputFlag == Termination )
    {
        if( FinishCount == N-1 )
{
    copyFromDataNum(inputNum)
    finish();
}
        else
                FinishCount++;
        endif
    }
    elseif ( inputFlag == Done)
    {
        if( FlagInHost == NONE )
        {
            FlagInHost = Wait;
            waitNum = inputNum;
        }
        else
        {
            postByPortTo(inputNum,waitNum);
            FlagInHost = None;
        }
        endif
    }
    endif
}
```

3.2   Large-Scale Distributed Sorting Algorithm Design of Working Machine

The first time receiving the data host distributing, it will sort their own data quickly. The working machine requests the status *Done* to host after completing the sorting. The waiting mechanism is shown in Algorithm 3.

```
selfSort( Elem A[] )
{
    Qsort(A,i,j);
    postByPortTo(HOST,caculatorNum,Done);
    wait();
}
```

Algorithm 3. *Waiting Algorithm*

Input: cpyNum for the data distribution target
Wait()

```
{
        int cpyNum = getFromHost();
        Elem B[];
        B = requestDataFrom(selfNum,cpyNum);
        int length = A.length + B.length;
        Elem mergeElem[length];
        for(int i = 0 ,left = 0,right = 0; i<length; i++ )
        {
                if(left>=length)
                        mergeElem[i] = B[right++];
                elseif (right>=length)
                        mergeElem[i] = B[left++];
                elseif(Comp::lt(A[left],B[right]))
                        mergeElem[i]=B[left++];
                else
                        mergeElem[i] = B[right++];
                endif
        }
endfor
}
```

When the working machine A enters waiting status, it requests data to working machine B which just completes sorting. Working machine B will send the sorting data to A and send host the status ***Termination***. A will merge the two groups data and send status ***Done*** to host. It re-enters the wait status and repeats the previous step. Running Mechanism is shown in Fig. 2.

4   Implementation and Validation of Algorithm

4.1   Time Complexity

If the amount of data to be sorted is M, and there is N machine for sorting. Then each working machine initial data n is

$$n = M/N \tag{1}$$

Merge sort average time efficiency is

$$t_1 = n \log n \tag{2}$$

When each working machine completes its own data sorting, it needs to request the sorted data in other working machine. And then sort the two parts of the sorted data.

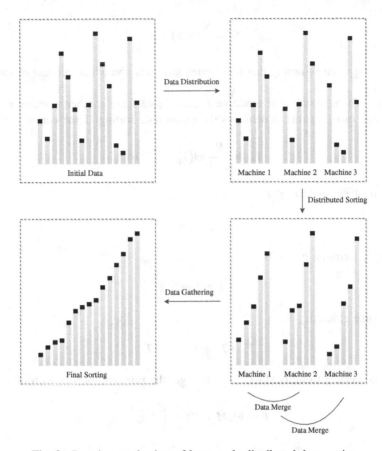

Fig. 2. Running mechanism of large-scale distributed data sorting

Because these two parts of the data have a good order, the two part of the orderly data integration of the time efficiency is

$$t_2 = \Theta(n) \qquad (3)$$

Assuming that the time of the host distribution data is constant and the data transferring time is constant too. And it is $\Theta(1)$.

First Step: Host distributes data to the working machines. The work machine achieves the sort of internal data. We set the time consumed for

$$T_1 = \Theta(1) + n \log n \qquad (4)$$

Second Step: After the each working machine sort completing, half of the working machines will request data. And then execute merge sort. Its time consume is

$$T_2 = \frac{N}{2}\Theta(1) + n \tag{5}$$

By analogy, we assuming that it executes k rounds, the whole process of sorting is completed.

K Step: There is only one machine requests data from another working machine. And through merging sort, it achieves the entire data sorting. Time consumption is

$$T_k = \frac{N}{2^{k-1}}\Theta(1) + 2^{k-2}n \tag{6}$$

After analysis, we can get

$$2^k = N$$

Simplify formula, it will be

$$k = \log N \tag{7}$$

Total time efficiency is

$$T = T_1 + T_2 + \cdots T_k$$

Thus combined formula (1)–(7), we can get the time complexity as follows.

$$T = \Theta(M+N) + \frac{M}{N}\log\frac{M}{N}$$

4.2 Feasibility and Efficiency

Here, we present the experimental result of our large-scale distributed sorting algorithm based on cloud computing. Our evaluation is divided into two parts feasibility and efficiency. In the process of this algorithm experiment, there is no way through real cloud computing environment to implement the algorithm. So we evaluate the algorithm by some computers. The proposed distributed sorting algorithm is deployed into 11 computers. The computer configuration is roughly equivalent. One of these computers is selected to be host. The rest computers are working machines. The experimental environment is shown in Table 1.

Firstly, we implement a Generator in C++ to generate a specified number of random numbers and store them on the storage of host. We use the Generator to produce a set of random numbers with 100 000, 1 000 000, 100 000 000 as data set. The data set are randomly generated, with no distribution.

We implement Quick Sort, Merge Sort and Distributed Sort in these computers. We evaluate the efficiency by the time consumption. The time consumption is record when the algorithm is starting instead of the testing program is starting. The time will be record until the algorithm completes.

Table 1. Experiment environment

Hardware		
Computer configuration	OS	Win 7
	CPU	Inter(R) Core(TM) i5-3470S(2.9 GHz*2)
	RAM	4 GB
Software		
Port	IP arrange	192.168.1.105-192.168.1.115
configuration	Port	8990
	Transfer protocol	TCP
Data	Generator	Function rand() in C++
configuration	Compiler tool	Visual Studio2010

After that, the program will write the result into a file which is used to compare with other algorithms. We can use the result to evaluate the feasibility and correctness. Repeating the environment above 10 times, and the result is shown in Table 2.

Table 2. Time consumption comparison of algorithms

The amount of data set	Quick-sort	Merge-sort	Large-scale distributed sorting
100 000	0.205000 s	0.367000 s	0.092000 s
1 000 000	12.303000 s	21.223000 s	3.120300 s
100 000 000	1162.017000 s	1011.310300 s	147.230000 s

By comparison, we find that the efficiency of large-scale distributed sorting algorithm based on cloud computing algorithm is significantly higher than common data sorting algorithms when processing on large-scale data set. According to optimize the data request and transmission and the memory resource usage, the time to sort large-scale data decreases about 60 %. When the amount of data is larger, the efficiency gap is more obvious.

5 Conclusion

In this paper, we proposes a large-scale distributed sorting algorithm based on the idea of parallel processing of cloud computing. Through experiments, we found out that the algorithm can be implemented to complete a massive data sorting. And the most effective quick-sort and merge-sort are used in the process of the partial preliminarily sorting of data. It aims to ensure the high efficiency of the algorithm running, the cooperative cooperation of multiple working machines and better use of computer resources. The experiment verified the feasibility and efficiency of the proposed algorithm. In the future, our research mainly includes the following aspects: 1. Optimization of the data request and transmission algorithm. 2. Optimization of memory resource usage.

Acknowledgment. This project is supported by Chinese Academy of Sciences under the project Pilot Special Key Technologies on Information Security, No. Y2W0012306.

References

1. Itani, W., Kayssi, A., Chehab, A.: Privacy as a service: privacy-aware data storage and processing in cloud computing architectures. In: Eighth IEEE International Conference on Dependable, Autonomic and Secure Computing. DASC 2009, pp. 711–716. IEEE (2009)
2. Zhang, S., Zhang, S., Chen, X., Huo, X.: The comparison between cloud computing and grid computing. In: ICCASM 2010 - 2010 International Conference on Computer Application and System Modeling, vol. 11, pp. 1172–1175 (2010)
3. Xia, T., Li, Z., Yu, N.: Research on cloud computing based on deep analysis to typical platforms. In: Jaatun, M.G., Zhao, G., Rong, C. (eds.) Cloud Computing. LNCS, vol. 5931, pp. 601–608. Springer, Heidelberg (2009)
4. Davidson, A., Tarjan, D., Garland, M., et al.: Efficient parallel merge sort for fixed and variable length keys. In: Innovative Parallel Computing (InPar), pp. 1–9. IEEE (2012)
5. Jeon, M., Kim, D.: Parallelizing merge sort onto distributed memory parallel computers. In: Zima, H.P., Joe, K., Sato, M., Seo, Y., Shimasaki, M. (eds.) ISHPC 2002. LNCS, vol. 2327, pp. 25–34. Springer, Heidelberg (2002)
6. Minsoo, J., Dongseung, K.: Parallel merge sort with load balancing. Int. J. Parallel Prog. **31**, 21–33 (2003)
7. Nanjesh, B.R., Tejonidhi, M.R., Rajesh, T.H., et al.: Parallel merge sort based performance evaluation and comparison of MPI and PVM. In: 2013 IEEE Conference on Information and Communication Technologies (ICT), pp. 530–534. IEEE (2013)
8. Max, O.H., Christof, T.: Spatial sorting algorithms for parallel computing in networks. In: Proceedings - 2011 5th IEEE Conference on Self-adaptive and Self-organizing Systems Workshops, pp. 73–78 (2011)
9. Manouchehr Zadahmad, J., Parisa Yousefzadeh, F.: Heuristic and pattern based merge sort. Procedia Comput. Sci. **3**, 322–324 (2011)
10. Chang, R.C.H., Wei, M.F., Chen, H.L., et al.: Implementation of a high-throughput modified merge sort in MIMO detection systems. IEEE Trans. Circ. Syst. I: Regular Papers **61**(9), 2730–2737 (2014)
11. Cérin, C., Koskas, M., Fkaier, H., Jemni, M.: Sequential in-core sorting performance for a SQL data service and for parallel sorting on heterogeneous clusters. Future Gener. Comput. Syst. **22**, 776–783 (2006)
12. Lin, H., Li, C., Wang, Q., Zhao, Y., Pan, N., Zhuang, X., Shao, L.: Automated tuning in parallel sorting on multi-core architectures. In: D'Ambra, P., Guarracino, M., Talia, D. (eds.) Euro-Par 2010, Part I. LNCS, vol. 6271, pp. 14–25. Springer, Heidelberg (2010)
13. Wei, J., Yu, H., Chen, J.H., et al.: Parallel clustering for visualizing large scientific line data. In: 2011 IEEE Symposium on Large Data Analysis and Visualization (LDAV), pp. 47–55. IEEE (2011)
14. Zhong, C., Qu, Z., Yang, F., et al.: Parallel multisets sorting using aperiodic multi-round distribution strategy on heterogeneous multi-core clusters. In: 2010 Third International Symposium on Parallel Architectures, Algorithms and Programming (PAAP), pp. 247–254. IEEE (2010)
15. Shirahata, K., Sato, H., Matsuoka, S.: Out-of-core GPU memory management for MapReduce-based large-scale graph processing. In: 2014 IEEE International Conference on Cluster Computing (CLUSTER), pp. 221–229. IEEE (2014)

16. Ye, C.J., Huang, M.X.: Multi-objective optimal power flow considering transient stability based on parallel NSGA-II. IEEE Trans. Power Syst. **30**(2), 857–866 (2015)
17. Xiao, Z., Xiao, Y.: Security and privacy in cloud computing. IEEE Commun. Surv. Tutorials **15**(2), 843–859 (2013)
18. Olman, V., Mao, F., Wu, H., et al.: Parallel clustering algorithm for large data sets with applications in bioinformatics. IEEE/ACM Trans. Comput. Biol. Bioinform. (TCBB) **6**(2), 344–352 (2009)
19. Scaling up Machine Learning: Parallel and Distributed Approaches. Cambridge University Press (2011)
20. Mehlhorn, K.: Data Structures and Algorithms 1: Sorting and Searching. Springer, Heidelberg (2013)
21. Brin, S., Page, L.: Reprint of: The anatomy of a large-scale hypertextual web search engine. Comput. Netw. **56**(18), 3825–3833 (2012)
22. Rao, S., Ramakrishnan, R., Silberstein, A., et al.: Sailfish: a framework for large scale data processing. In: Proceedings of the Third ACM Symposium on Cloud Computing, p. 4. ACM (2012)
23. Di Martino, A., Yan, C.G., Li, Q., et al.: The autism brain imaging data exchange: towards a large-scale evaluation of the intrinsic brain architecture in autism. Mol. Psychiatry **19**(6), 659–667 (2014)
24. Rasmussen, A., Porter, G., Conley, M., et al.: TritonSort: a balanced large-scale sorting system. In: NSDI (2011)
25. Sakr, S., Liu, A., Batista, D.M., et al.: A survey of large scale data management approaches in cloud environments. IEEE Commun. Surv. Tutorials **13**(3), 311–336 (2011)
26. Cuzzocrea, A., Song, I.Y., Davis, K.C.: Analytics over large-scale multidimensional data: the big data revolution. In: Proceedings of the ACM 14th International Workshop on Data Warehousing and OLAP, pp. 101–104. ACM (2011)
27. Vora, M.N.: Hadoop-HBase for large-scale data. In: 2011 International Conference on Computer Science and Network Technology (ICCSNT), vol. 1, pp. 601–605. IEEE (2011)

Analysis and Exploit of Directory Traversal Vulnerability on VMware

Yuanyuan Bai[✉] and Zhi Chen

School of Computer and Information Technology,
Beijing Jiaotong University, Beijing 100044, China
{yuanyuanbai, chenzhi}@bjtu.edu.cn

Abstract. VMware provides cloud and virtualization software and services. This paper focuses on directory traversal vulnerability on VMware. The principle, triggering conditions and the exploit process of this vulnerability is discussed. Furthermore, we design and establish the experimental environment to demonstrate the attack method. Experimental configurations and results discussion are given in detail. Finally, we offer generalized recommendations that can be applied to achieve secure virtualized implementations.

Keywords: VMware · Directory traversal · Vulnerability analysis · Exploit

1 Introduction

Virtualization introduces virtual machine manager (VMM), also called hypervisor. It is an abstraction layer between the hardware and the guest OS and applications [1]. Hypervisors are classified two types: native or bare-mental hypervisors running directly on the physical hardware and hosted hypervisors running as an application [2]. VM Virtualization allows for the concurrent execution of multiple operating systems and applications on the same physical server. However, along with the performance improvements offered by adopting virtualization technologies, there are many vulnerabilities [1]. Therefore, the vulnerabilities in virtualization environments, including VMware, XEN, KVM, and Hyper-V, must be addressed or understood. So far, China National Information Security Vulnerability Database (CNNVD) shows 241 vulnerabilities on VMware, 61 vulnerabilities on XEN and 28 vulnerabilities on KVM [3]. In this paper, we mainly discuss directory traversal vulnerability on VMware.

Directory traversal (or path traversal) is a relatively typical vulnerability on VMware. CVE is a dictionary of publicly known information security vulnerabilities and exposures [4]. CVE-2009-3733, as a representative of directory traversal vulnerabilities, allows remote attackers to read arbitrary files via unspecified vectors. Flick and Morehouse [5] released the exploit of this vulnerability in 2010 and exploit was released as a Perl script [6]. They demonstrated the attack on the vulnerable version of VMware Server. But they did not give the detailed experiment configurations and steps.

The main challenges are as follows: (1) The vulnerability only exists in lower versions of VMware servers and most of these servers are not available or have already been patched; (2) The servers have special hardware configuration requirements [7].

© Springer-Verlag Berlin Heidelberg 2015
W. Niu et al. (Eds.): ATIS 2015, CCIS 557, pp. 238–244, 2015.
DOI: 10.1007/978-3-662-48683-2_21

In this paper, we first analyze the principle and triggering conditions of VMware's directory traversal vulnerability. Then we design and establish the experimental environment to demonstrate the attack method [5]. Experimental configurations and results discussion are given in detail. Finally, we discuss mitigation measures.

The rest of this paper is organized as follows. Section 2 describes the related work. In Sect. 3, we discuss the analysis and exploit of the vulnerability. Section 4 introduces the experiments results and mitigation. Finally, Sect. 5 concludes this paper.

2   Related Work

There are 74194 plugins, covering 30399 unique CVE IDs and 22595 unique Bugtraq IDs in Nessus Vulnerability Scanner. There is a plugin named VMware ESX Local Security Checks [8]. In this paper, we use Nessus 5.2.4 to scan the VMware ESXi5.0.0.

Scan results show that there are seven types of high risk vulnerabilities and three types of medium risk vulnerabilities in ESXi5.0.0.

There is a module of VMware Server Directory Traversal Vulnerability in Metasploit Penetration Testing Framework [9]. However, it only allow remote attackers to read arbitrary files. If we want to download the entire VM, we must check out the guest stealer tool [5].

3   Vulnerability Analysis and Exploit

Vulnerability analysis is a process of analyzing the principle and triggering conditions of the vulnerability. Vulnerability exploit is based on vulnerability analysis, constructing the corresponding attack to trigger the vulnerability.

Up to now, China National Information Security Vulnerability Database (CNNVD) shows up to 241 vulnerabilities on VMware, in which there are 11 directory traversal vulnerabilities, including CVE-2013-3658, CVE-2012-6324, CVE-2012-5978, CVE-2011-4404, CVE-2009-3733, CVE-2008-4281 and other vulnerabilities [4].

In this paper, we mainly discuss the analysis and exploit of CVE-2009-3733.

3.1   Vulnerability Analysis

Directory traversal (or path traversal) consists in exploiting insufficient security validation/sanitization of user-supplied input file names, so that characters representing "traverse to parent directory" are passed through to the file APIs, resulting in unauthorized access to the directory, which is the goal of directory traversal. The attackers exploit some system security flaws, rather than coding errors. Directory traversal is also known as directory climbing and backtracking [10]. CVE-2009-3733 is a representative of directory traversal vulnerabilities that allows remote attackers to read arbitrary files via unspecified vectors [4]. In fact, we can download the relevant documents to restore the entire virtual machine locally.

CVE-2009-3733 is a vulnerability in the VMware management interface. To trigger the vulnerability, an open port check tool is used to detect open ports on your connection. Then, custom data is sent to get feedback. We can add a bunch of "../" sequences to the URL to traverse directory to grab any file on the files system. Therefore, the key is the custom data. The vulnerability, once successfully exploited, the integrity of the system may be destroyed completely. The exploit of the vulnerability have no access restrictions.

3.2 Vulnerability Exploit

In VMware Server and VMware ESX/ESXi, there is a file proxy.xml that shows inventory and location information of virtual machines. It is stored in the path "/etc./vmware/hostd/" in default. As shown in Table 1, we need append "/sdk" to our URL request on VMware ESX/ESXi so that we can get complete access to the host file system [5].

Table 1. The correspondence between servers and paths

Path	Servers type	Port
/sdk	VMware ESX/ESXi	80, 443
/ui	VMware Server	8222, 8333

The traversal methods are as follows: we add a bunch of "../" characters to the URL, across directories of multiple layers, to find the file vmInventory.xml. The file vmInventory.xml is stored in the path "/sdk/../../../../../../etc./vmware/hostd/" [5]. So we send the URL request to get feedback.

Experiment shows that the "vmInventory.xml" consists of configuration entities named "ConfigEntry" which refers to different virtual machines. Each configuration entity has its own "objID" standing for entity number and "vmxCfgPath" standing for the storage path of virtual machines. As described in Fig. 1, there is an Ubuntu virtual machine on the vulnerable host and the "ubuntu.vmx" shows the virtual machine configuration and file location information.

```
1  <ConfigRoot>
2    <ConfigEntry id="0000">
3      <objID>16</objID>
4      <vmxCfgPath>/vmfs/volumes/54fc5c51-
5      f7d8ea17-f744-000c29ae8662/ubuntu/
6      ubuntu.vmx</vmxCfgPath>
7    </ConfigEntry>
8  </ConfigRoot>
```

Fig. 1. vmInventory.xml file

Virtual machines have the following documents: (1) ".vmx": the virtual machine configuration and file location information; (2) ".vmdk": the file points to other ".vmdk" image; (3) ".nvram": the VMware virtual machine BIOS; (4) ".vmsd": the VMware virtual machine snapshot metadata; (5) ".vmxf": the VMware team members [5]. We sum up the exploit process according to the Guest Stealer [6], as shown in Fig. 3.

Figure 2 shows vulnerability exploit process and url represents the following paths:

- url1: https://ip:port; url2: http://ip:port
- url3:   url1/url2+"/sdk/%2E%2E/%2E%2E/%2E%2E/%2E%2E/%2E%2E/%2E% 2E/etc./vmware/hostd/vmInventory.xml" "%2E%2E" is the Unicode characters
- url4: url1/url2+"/sdk/../../../../../..vmware/hostd/vmInventory.xml"

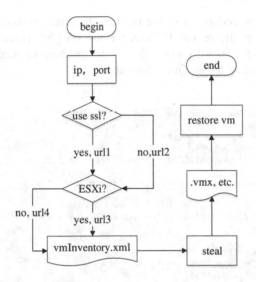

Fig. 2. Vulnerability exploit process

If ssl is used, the attack path is based on url1, otherwise, the attack path is based on url2. In summary, the exploit process is as follows:

- Nmap can be used to detect the open port. If the port is open, then the connection to the vulnerable server can be established. This process requires a valid ip and port.
- Use ssl (Secure Sockets Layer) or not. If used, the attack path is url1, otherwise, the attack path isurl2.
- Determine the type of VMware servers. If ESX or ESXi, the attach path is url3, otherwise, the attack path is url4.
- Read the "vmInventory.xml" to get the storage path of ".vmx".
- Using the same methods to get other relevant documents to restore the entire virtual machine locally and read the sensitive information.

4 Experiments Results and Analysis

4.1 Experimental Environment

In this paper, we demonstrate the attack on VMware ESXi 3.5 Update 3 (Build 123629) that is connected to a remote client, downloaded from the web server. Connection is established between the client and the ESXi to create an ubuntu12.04 on the server. ESXi 3.5.0 requires special hardware configurations and is mounted directly on the bare metal. Experimental prerequisite: vulnerable host's IP and port which can be obtained by using Nmap or other vulnerability scanning tools.

4.2 Experimental Results

Figure 3 shows test procedure. First, we perform the attack VMstealer.pl [6]. IP, port and the type of server are required. Here, we use port 80. Having read the virtual machine configuration file, we choose the virtual machine to steal. We sum up the exploit process according to the Guest Stealer [6].

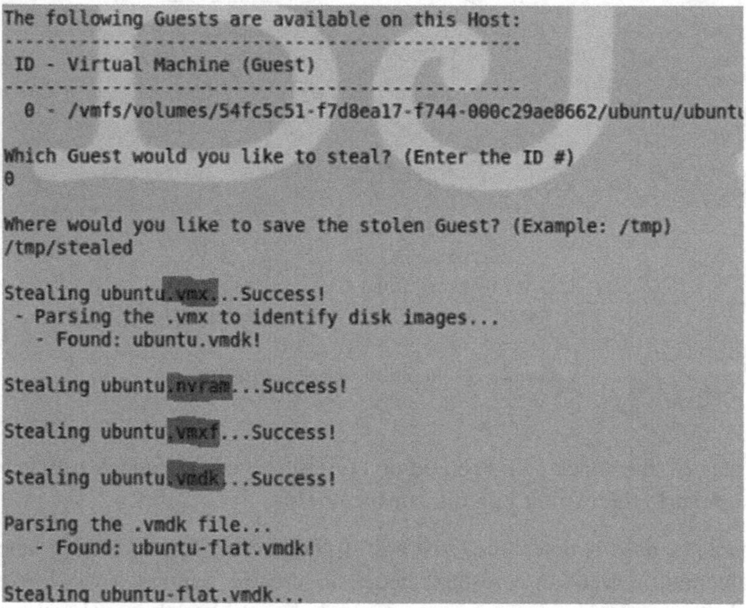

```
The following Guests are available on this Host:
------------------------------------------------
 ID - Virtual Machine (Guest)
------------------------------------------------
  0 - /vmfs/volumes/54fc5c51-f7d8ea17-f744-000c29ae8662/ubuntu/ubuntu

Which Guest would you like to steal? (Enter the ID #)
0

Where would you like to save the stolen Guest? (Example: /tmp)
/tmp/stealed

Stealing ubuntu.vmx...Success!
 - Parsing the .vmx to identify disk images...
    - Found: ubuntu.vmdk!

Stealing ubuntu.nvram...Success!

Stealing ubuntu.vmxf...Success!

Stealing ubuntu.vmdk...Success!

Parsing the .vmdk file...
    - Found: ubuntu-flat.vmdk!

Stealing ubuntu-flat.vmdk...
```

Fig. 3. Test procedure

Finally, we get the ".vmx", ".vmdk", ".vmdk", ".nvram", ".vmsd". We can use all these files to restore the entire virtual machine in VMware Workstation or VMware Player.

4.3   Mitigation Measures

Mitigation is a process of taking defense mechanism so that the vulnerability will not be triggered. Having discovered vulnerabilities in virtualization products, we are bound to patch to mitigate vulnerabilities. However, the related vulnerability information bulletin just gives the corresponding patch information. So the most important thing is to prevent the vulnerability by analyzing related vulnerabilities. Do not let anybody have access to the VMware management interface (the web server). It should be on a separate network. That makes the attack more difficult to perform [11].

For directory traversal vulnerability, we can restrict access to the directory, encrypt parameters, URL encode the parameters and filter the file extension [12]. In this paper, we can encrypt the vmInventory.xml to hide the storage path of the virtual machine configuration file. For example, we can encrypt the vmInventory.xml to hide the storage path of the virtual machine configuration file. Specific encryption function is as follows:

```
public static bool EncryptXmlFile(
String filePath, //vmInvertory.xml
String elementName, //objID and vmxCfgPath
bool bContent, //whether to encrypt element content
object key, //keys
String keyName); //keys name
```

By default, the elements of "vmInventory.xml" is encrypted. Even if the attacker gets the file, it is difficult for him to parse the file to get the location information of the virtual machine. However, when the legitimate user using the server, the system will automatically call the corresponding function to decrypt. In short, this mechanism can effectively prevent attackers to steal the virtual machines.

Above all, privilege user access should be restricted and local and remote hypervisor management interfaces should be secured. Unnecessary hardware and unneeded network and local admin interfaces should be removed [13].

5   Conclusions

Vulnerability analysis is a process of analyzing the principle and triggering conditions of the vulnerability. Vulnerability exploit is based on vulnerability analysis, constructing the corresponding attack to trigger the vulnerability.

In this paper, we first discuss the principle, triggering conditions and the exploit of VMware's directory traversal vulnerability. Then we design and establish the experimental environment to demonstrate the attack method. Experimental configurations and results discussion are given in detail. Finally, we discuss the mitigation measures. It is expected that by further analyzing, it is promising to establish our own penetration testing framework in a virtual environment.

References

1. Brooks, T.T., Caicedo, C., Park, J.S.: Security vulnerability analysis in virtualized computing environments. Int. J. Intell. Comput. Res. **3**(1/2), 277–291 (2012)
2. Borisaniya, B., Patel, D.: Evasion resistant intrusion detection framework at hypervisor layer in cloud. In: International Conference on Advances in Communication, Network, and Computing, pp. 748–756 (2014)
3. China National Information Security Vulnerability Database (CNNVD). http://www.cnnvd.org.cn/
4. CVE. https://cve.mitre.org/cgi-bin/cvename.cgi?name=CVE-2009-3733
5. Morehouse, Flick: Stealing guests the VMWARE Way (2010)
6. Morehouse, Flick: VMstealer.pl. http://security.goldsby.com/2010/02/19/vmware-guest-stealer/
7. ESX3.5. https://www.vmware.com/support/vi3/doc/vi3_esx3i_i_35u3_rel_notes.html
8. Nessus plugins. https://www.tenable.com/plugins/index.php?view=all
9. Kennedy, D., O'Gorman, J., Kearns, D., et al.: Metasploit: The Penetration Tester's Guide
10. Directory traversal attack. https://en.wikipedia.org/wiki/Directory_traversal_attack
11. Nmap script. https://blog.skullsecurity.org/2010/how-to-install-an-nmap-script
12. Khan, S., Saxena, A.: Detecting input validation attacks in web application. Int. J. Comput. Appl. **109**(6), 1–4 (2015)
13. Zeadally, P.M.: Virtualization: issues, security threats, and solutions. ACM Comput. Surv. **45**(2), 94–111 (2013)

OpenStack Vulnerability Detection and Analysis

Li Lu$^{(\boxtimes)}$, Zhen Han, and Zhi Chen

School of Computer and Information Technology, Beijing Jiaotong University,
Beijing 100044, China
{luliluli,zhan,chenzhi}@bjtu.edu.cn

Abstract. OpenStack is a popular cloud management software. Because it is open-source many companies and organizations opt for OpenStack as their solution for cloud computing. This paper focuses on OpenStack vulnerabilities. A variety of vulnerability scanning tools are used to detect vulnerabilities on OpenStack. The process of attack exploiting specific vulnerabilities is presented. Besides, this paper puts forward recommendations on eliminating vulnerabilities and building a more secure OpenStack platform.

Keywords: Vulnerability analysis · Vulnerability detection · Scanning tools

1 Introduction

Cloud computing has become a fast growing IT industry. Its essential characteristics including resource pooling, on-demand self-service, broad network access, measured service, and rapid elasticity help enterprises reduce their resources overhead [1]. Cloud management software such as CloudStack or OpenStack is needed to manage resources provided by cloud [2]. Security is usually the main reason that enterprises are reluctant to use public cloud infrastructures. Researchers and manufacturers are keep trying to provide a more secure cloud environment. We could propose relative valuable improvement suggestions if we know what the vulnerabilities of cloud are. There are more methods to evaluate security of cloud computing environment today and improve performance of cloud. Vulnerability scanning tools usually provide abundant plugins to test different vulnerabilities and fuzzing tools are mainly used for programs that have kinds of inputs. Besides, lots of attack tools could help discover vulnerabilities. Choosing appropriate tools from these various tools to test vulnerabilities of cloud management software together is a method to evaluate security of cloud and will help improve security of cloud. This paper chooses OpenStack as the research object for its outstanding influence and high active level. Ristov et al. [3] use Nessus to detect vulnerabilities on OpenStack and LaBarge et al. [4] focus on penetration tests. In order to discover vulnerabilities on OpenStack more widely and deeply, scanning tool, packet capture tool and cookie analysis tool are used together in this paper. More than that, this paper puts forward some suggestions on eliminating vulnerabilities and new point of view on building a more secure OpenStack platform.

The rest of this paper is as follows. We first present OpenStack architecture in Sect. 2. Then, vulnerability Scanning tools, vulnerability detection, and result analysis are described in Sects. 3–5, respectively. Section 6 concludes the paper.

© Springer-Verlag Berlin Heidelberg 2015
W. Niu et al. (Eds.): ATIS 2015, CCIS 557, pp. 245–251, 2015.
DOI: 10.1007/978-3-662-48683-2_22

2 OpenStack Architecture

OpenStack contains multiple components, in which required components include (1) Nova - computing service (2) Glance – Image service (3) Keystone – identity authentication service [5]. In order to facilitate the management of the virtual machines on OpenStack, Horizon - UI Dashboard service should be also installed. Nova provides virtual machines and manages virtual machine network. Glance manages images that are used to create virtual machines. Keystone provides identity authorization and authentication service for all systems on OpenStack [6]. Dashboard is a scalable Web app which provides administrators and users a graphical interface to access to cloud computing resources. Users can login Dashboard and control their own computing, storage and network resources that are previously registered by using user names and passwords. Cloud administrators login Dashboard and check the state of cloud, create users and projects as well as set user permissions. OpenStack architecture is shown in Fig. 1.

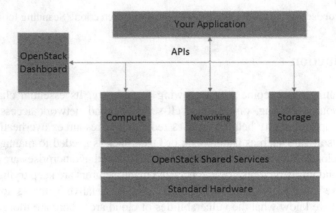

Fig. 1. OpenStack architecture [7]

3 Introduction of Vulnerability Scanning Tools

Today, there are many open-source or free vulnerability scanning tools on Internet for security scanning, such as Nessus [3], Wireshark, Ferret, Hamster [4], OpenVAS [8] and so on.

Nessus is the most popular vulnerability scanner and analysis software [9]. It has a rich vulnerability database, offering a variety of scanning strategies. And Nessus is powerful and easy to operate. As a network packet capture and analysis software, Wireshark can display the most detailed data in network packet. Ferret is also a packet capture tool. It is open-source and specializes in crawling cookie data. Hamster is often in cooperation with Ferret tool. It is developed by Robert Graham and used to analyze captured cookie, from which we can obtain sensitive information [4]. OpenVAS is an open vulnerability assessment system, whose core component is a server, including a set of network vulnerability testing programs which can detect remote systems and application security problems. In this paper, we use above tools to detect vulnerabilities on Open-Stack platform and put forward suggestions to address the vulnerabilities.

4 Vulnerability Detection

4.1 OpenStack Deployment

OpenStack can be deployed on Ubuntu, Red Hat, CentOS, Fedora, openSUSE and SUSE Linux operating system. It can be deployed as a single node or multi-node.

- Single-node deployment. Required components are installed on a single server, and all virtual hosts are also running on this server. Other services can be added according to actual situation.
- Multi-node Deployment. To improve efficiency of services, different services can also be deployed on different servers and multiple Nova nodes can be deployed on different servers, thus virtual hosts can follow specific policy to run on different Nova nodes [3].

In this paper, single-node deployment is adopted. The main services of OpenStack, namely Nova, Keystone, Glance and Dashboard are deployed on Ubuntu Server 12.04 64-bit operating system server.

4.2 Experiment Deployment

In addition to OpenStack server, a computer B with Ubuntu 12.04 64-bit is required to install scanning tools and another computer A with Ferret and Hamster is an attack machine to attack computer B. Wireshark is installed on computer A. Table 1 shows the experiment deployment.

Table 1. Experiment deployment

Physical machine	operating system	Tools/components
OpenStack server	Ubuntu server 12.04 64-bit	Nova, keystone, glance and dashboard
Computer A	Win 7	Wireshark, Ferret and Hamster
Computer B	Ubuntu 12.04 64-bit	OpenVAS, Nessus

4.3 Vulnerability Detection Plan

Nessus and OpenVAS are used to detect vulnerabilities on OpenStack (Essex) in cooperation. Ferret and Hamster are utilized to achieve session hijacking attack on Open-Stack. Wireshark is used to validate some detected vulnerabilities.

- Nessus Scan. Nessus is deployed on computer B. Scanning policies of External Network Scan Policy and Web application test policy are used, which means that Nessus will scan all TCP (Transmission Control Protocol) and UDP (User Datagram Protocol) ports and finds vulnerabilities which are running on open service ports. Besides, Nessus will scan security vulnerabilities which are related to Web application in OpenStack cloud [3]. Nessus 5 is deployed on the same network segment with OpenStack server, on which two virtual machines with Ubuntu 12.04 operating system are running.
- OpenVAS Scan. OpenVAS is deployed on computer B. Full and fast policy is used to scan vulnerabilities regarding the public network IP address of OpenStack as target.
- Session Hijacking Attack with Ferret and Hamster. OpenStack server, computer A and computer B are all required to achieve a successful attack. Ferret on computer A monitors the network connection between OpenStack server and computer B and captures cookie information after authorized user on computer B login OpenStack. Hamster retrieves the stolen session cookie and URL information and enable attacker to login unauthorized Dashboard page if vulnerabilities exist in these processes [4].

4.4   Results of Vulnerability Detection

Comprehensive scan result of Nessus and OpenVAS indicates that there is no high-risk vulnerabilities on OpenStack (level of vulnerabilities is distinguished in accordance with the scanning tools' own classification rules). The result contains a total of four medium-risk vulnerabilities and four low-risk vulnerabilities. Besides, Hamster and Ferret succeed in attacking session attack on OpenStack.

(1) Low-risk Vulnerabilities: Web Server Uses Basic Authentication without HTTPS vulnerability and Web Server Uses Plain Text Authentication Forms vulnerability are detected, which indicates that data transmission on OpenStack uses basic HTTP protocol instead of HTTPS protocol. SSH server CBC ciphers mode is enabled on OpenStack server. The problem increases risk on data transmission, but manual setup can solve this problem. HPLIP vulnerability (USN-1981-1) is discovered on Ubuntu. A local attacker could possibly use this issue to overwrite arbitrary files [10].

(2) Medium-risk Vulnerabilities: Web Server Generic Cookie injection vulnerability and Web Server Generic XSS vulnerability are discovered. An attacker can easily exploit these two vulnerabilities to carry out cookie injection attack and cross-site scripting attack on OpenStack. Another discovered vulnerability is called NTP Amplification Attacks Using (CVE-2013-5211). This vulnerability is in ntpd (Network Time Protocol daemon) which is an operating system daemon. An attacker is able to cause Denial of service attack exploiting the vulnerability. Besides, that OpenStack server implements RFC1323 (TCP Extensions for High Performance) is regarded as a vulnerability by OpenVAS and the reason may be there are some flaws in implementation of RFC 1323.

(3) Result of Session Hijacking Attack: In Fig. 2, Hamster reads session cookie and allows a non-authorized user to login Dashboard Instance &Volumes page with hijacked user's user name and password. The result illustrates that the security vulnerability existing on OpenStack allows attackers to use packet capture and analysis tools to steal legitimate users' session cookie and login unauthorized control interface.

Fig. 2. AttackerLogins dashboard

4.5 Vulnerability Validation

Making use of Wireshark, Web Server Uses Basic Authentication without HTTPS and Web Server Uses Plain Text Authentication Forms vulnerabilities are easy to validate. Figure 3 shows that Wireshark captures some data packets transmitted between the server and computer B and data in packet is transmitted in unencrypted text other than Fig. 4 in which the data has been encrypted.

```
0090  3a 20 41 63 63 65 70 74  2d 4c 61 6e 67 75 61 67   : Accept -Languag
00a0  65 2c 43 6f 6f 6b 69 65  2c 41 63 63 65 70 74 2d   e,Cookie ,Accept-
00b0  45 6e 63 6f 64 69 6e 67  0d 0a 43 6f 6e 74 65 6e   Encoding ..Conten
00c0  74 2d 4c 61 6e 67 75 61  67 65 3a 20 7a 68 2d 63   t-Langua ge: zh-c
00d0  6e 0d 0a 53 65 74 2d 43  6f 6f 6b 69 65 3a 20 20   n..Set-C ookie:
00e0  63 73 72 66 74 6f 6b 65  6e 3d 36 39 34 34 63 61   csrftoke n=6944ca
00f0  36 64 35 38 65 31 64 37  35 35 30 62 64 65 31 33   6d58e1d7 550bde13
0100  30 63 61 34 32 63 30 66  66 32 3b 20 65 78 70 69   0ca42c0f f2; expi
0110  72 65 73 3d 54 75 65 2c  20 30 36 2d 4a 61 6e 2d   res=Tue, 06-Jan-
0120  32 30 31 35 20 31 31 3a  32 34 3a 35 36 20 47 4d   2015 11: 24:56 GM
0130  54 3b 20 4d 61 78 2d 41  67 65 3d 33 31 34 34 39   T; Max-A ge=31449
0140  36 30 30 3b 20 50 61 74  68 3d 2f 0d 0a 43 6f 6e   600; Pat h=/..Con
0150  74 65 6e 74 2d 45 6e 63  6f 64 69 6e 67 3a 20 67   tent-Enc oding: g
0160  7a 69 70 0d 0a 4b 65 65  70 2d 41 6c 69 76 65 3a   zip..Kee p-Alive:
```

Fig. 3. Wireshark packet capture

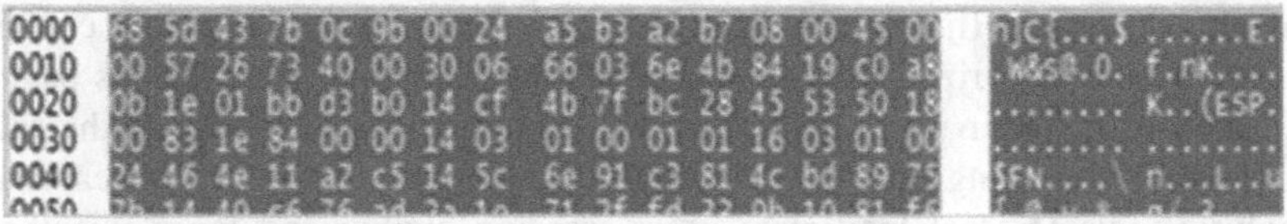

0000	68 5d 43 7b 0c 9b 00 24	a5 b3 a2 b7 08 00 45 00	h]C{...$ .....E.
0010	00 57 26 73 40 00 30 06	66 03 6e 4b 84 19 c0 a8	.W&s@.0. f.nK....
0020	0b 1e 01 bb d3 b0 14 cf	4b 7f bc 28 45 53 50 18	.... K..(ESP.
0030	00 83 1e 84 00 00 14 03	01 00 01 01 16 03 01 00	....
0040	24 46 4e 11 a2 c5 14 5c	6e 91 c3 81 4c bd 89 75	$FN....\ n...L..u

Fig. 4. Encrypted data in packets

5   Analysis

In addition to detected vulnerabilities above, some other vulnerabilities on OpenStack have been exposed, for instance, OpenStack Dashboard allows users to set weak password and Keystone, the authentication component, provides no method to prevent users from logging after their repeated login failures [11]. These vulnerabilities on OpenStack can't be overlooked.

OpenStack is a complete whole, with operating systems on virtual machines or OpenStack components and other elements. In this case, vulnerabilities can be divided into two categories: vulnerabilities on OpenStack components and vulnerabilities on operating system or tools on OpenStack. To build a relative riskless cloud computing environment based on OpenStack, vulnerabilities of these two categories both should be focused on. Vulnerabilities can be handled from these two aspects.

Vulnerabilities such as Web Server Uses Basic Authentication without HTTPS and Web Server Uses Plain Text Authentication Forms as well as session hijacking are on OpenStack components and these vulnerabilities can be eliminated by adopting secure communication protocols for instance HTTPS protocol protecting data from eavesdroppers with SSL protocol.

To reduce vulnerabilities on operating system or tools on OpenStack, OpenStack server could install relative secure operating system and choose high security tool in the same kind of tools. Installing vulnerability patches in time is also required.

6   Summary and Conclusions

This paper uses a variety of vulnerability scanning tools to detect vulnerabilities on OpenStack as well as method of attack. The experimental result indicates that vulnerabilities exist in user login and data transmission on OpenStack. More than that, vulnerabilities exist on operating system on OpenStack too.

OpenStack is a complicated system consisting of a lot of components and parts. Vulnerability may exist in any part of OpenStack. Using kinds of tools to detect vulnerabilities together are efficient and effective. Under the circumstances, advantages of these tools are used fully to discover vulnerabilities deeply and widely. Classifying vulnerabilities will be helpful when handle security problems on OpenStack.

References

1. Dahbur, K., Mohammad, B., Tarakji, A.B.: A survey of risks, threats and vulnerabilities in cloud computing. In: Proceedings of the 2011 International Conference on Intelligent Semantic Web-Services and Applications. ACM (2011)
2. Ristov, S., Gusev, M.: Security evaluation of open source clouds. In: EUROCON, 2013 IEEE, pp. 73–80. IEEE (2013)
3. Ristov, S., Gusev, M., Donevski, A.: Openstack cloud security vulnerabilities from inside and outside. In: CLOUD COMPUTING, pp. 101–107 (2013)
4. LaBarge, R., McGuire, T.: Cloud penetration testing (2013). arXiv preprint, arXiv:1301.1912
5. Ma, Y.L., Chen, S.P.: Research on OpenStack virtual machines security policies. Inf. Technol. **38**(1), 35–38 (2014)
6. Xiong, W., et al.: Research on OpenStack authentication security. Design Technol. Posts Telecommun. **7**, 21–25 (2014)
7. OpenStack homepage. http://www.openstack.org/
8. OpenVAS homepage. http://www.OpenVAS.org/
9. Li, H.C., Liang, P.H., Yang, J.M., Chen, S.J.: Analysis on cloud-based security vulnerability assessment. In: 2010 IEEE 7th International Conference on e-Business Engineering (ICEBE), pp. 490–494. IEEE (2010)
10. Ubuntu homepage. http://www.ubuntu.com/usn/usn-1981-1/
11. Wei, X.W.: Security Analysis and improvement on OpenStack object storage identity and access control. Software **2**, 008 (2015)

Tools and Methodologies

RICS-DFA: Reduced Input Character Set DFA for Memory-Efficient Regular Expression Matching

Qiu Tang, Lei Jiang$^{(\boxtimes)}$, Qiong Dai, Majing Su, and Hongtao Xie

Institute of Information Engineering,
Chinese Academy of Sciences, Beijing 100093, China
{tangqiu,jianglei,daiqiong,sumajing,xiehongtao}@iie.ac.cn

Abstract. Regular expression matching as a core component of deep packet inspection (DPI) is widely used in various kinds of modern network intrusion detection system (NIDS), traffic classification system and network monitoring system, etc. In these systems, regular expressions are typically converted to deterministic finite automaton (DFA), and the DFA is used to scan and check each byte of incoming packet's payload against regular expression rule sets to judge whether current packet is matched by any rule sets. If matched, it means the packet contains specific attacks, viruses, and so on. However, the DFA generally consumes a large amount of memory. Many recent improvement work mainly focus on how to reduce the amount of memory requirement. Like the previous work, in this paper we propose a compact, time-efficient and novel DFA structure to significantly decrease the DFA's space, the new DFA called Reduced Input Character Set DFA (RICS-DFA). A character escaping and replacing scheme is first introduced to decrease DFA's character set size and then to reduce DFA's space requirement with a series of optimization techniques based on RICS-DFA. A RICS-DFA is constructed by transition rewriting. Experimental results on real-life rule-sets reveal that compared to the original DFA, the RICS-DFA reduces the memory consumption by 68 %–92 % while sacrificing trivial matching speed.

Keywords: Regular expression matching · Deep packet inspection (DPI) · Transition rewriting · Reduced input character set

1 Introduction

Due to regular expressions' powerful and flexible signatures descriptive ability, they are widely used to represent attack, virus or other signatures in various network security or management systems. For example, there are used regular expressions to stand for attack or virus features in these famous open source Snort NIDS[1] and network security monitor system Bro[2]. In addition, in Linux application protocol classifier L7-filter[3], all of the 114 protocols are described

---

[1] https://www.snort.org/.
[2] https://www.bro.org/.
[3] http://l7-filter.sourceforge.net/.

© Springer-Verlag Berlin Heidelberg 2015
W. Niu et al. (Eds.): ATIS 2015, CCIS 557, pp. 255–268, 2015.
DOI: 10.1007/978-3-662-48683-2_23

in regular expressions. In these systems, multiple regular expression rules are usually converted into a deterministic finite automaton(DFA) since it can check the incoming packets against rules in a constant time which only constantly relies on the size of packet.

However, new viruses and worms of late years emerge endlessly (include traditional and new platforms, such as smart phone [1,2]) and become more intelligent such as variant lengths of attack signature to escape detection. As a result, the scale of signatures increases sharply and the regular expressions' syntax becomes more complex. When all rule sets are converted to a single DFA, the number of the single DFA's states is exponential (i.e. state explosion [3]) based on the size of rules, which leads to an exponential memory requirement because the DFA space is the size of its transition matrix that is the product of the number of states and the number of transitions per state. According to [4], the L7-filter rule set contains 109 regular expression rules and consumes more than 16 GB memory space when compiled to a composite DFA. The huge memory demand limits relative network security systems' application. Therefore, DFA's space reducing becomes one of the most challenging problems in network security research field.

In recent years, lots of approaches have been proposed to mitigate the state explosion problem. Among these proposed solutions, transition matrix compression is one of the most direct and effective methods to reduce the DFA's prohibitive memory demand, such as the most well-known D^2FA [5] algorithms. Although these solutions decrease a large amount of memory requirement, they suffer from degraded performance. It is because the DFA's transition matrix becomes a sparse matrix instead of a regular one, that results in multiple memory access for each state transition. Thus, compressed DFAs by these solutions are no longer adequate to network security systems in need of line speed traffic matching. In fact, it remains an open and challenging problem to design a compact DFA with high compression ratio and highly effective random access per state transition, because there is an inherent contradiction between the high compress ratio and the fast random access of the compressed DFA.

In this paper, we propose Reduced Input Character Set DFA (RICS-DFA), a novel automaton representation, for regular expression matching. The main idea of RICS-DFA is to use multi-characters to escape and replace one character in DFA's alphabet. For example, two high-frequency characters are used to replace one low-frequency character. As a result, the size of DFA alphabet becomes smaller than that of original DFA and the DFA's transition matrix becomes more compact than original DFA's, which creates opportunities for further compression optimization. Experimental results reveal that compared to the original DFA, the RICS-DFA reduces the memory consumption by 68 %–92 % while keeping a nearly same matching speed. Our main contributions in this paper are summarized below.

1. We propose a novel DFA structure called RICS-DFA which reduces DFA's alphabet to a small size and eliminates the redundant transitions in the DFA.
2. We propose a very efficient RICS-DFA constructing algorithm based on transition rewriting.

3. The RICS-DFA is a novel structure and memory efficient solution. The experimental results show that RICS-DFA saves about 68 %–92 % memory requirement comparing with the original DFA.

The rest of the paper is organized as follows. Section 2 presents the related work. Section 3 presents the principle and implementation of RICS-DFA, which is further optimized in Sect. 4. Section 5 evaluates the performance of RICS-DFA and compares with some state-of-the-art algorithms. Section 6 concludes the paper.

2   Related Work

Most previous work in regular expression matching focus on decreasing the memory requirement of DFA by eliminating the redundant transition. In order to avoid the state explosion, Yu et al. [3] proposes a solution to split a large or complex rule-set into multiple groups and each group is converted to a DFA. This solution reduces the memory usage of DFA by rewriting rules. However, their rule rewriting depends on the rule sets and multiple DFAs slow the matching speed.

Kumar et al. [5] proposes a new algorithm called D^2FA to compress the transition matrix (T) by introducing a default transition to eliminate these same transition between two states. However, D^2FA engine may look up memory multiple times per input character, leading to a higher memory band. Becchi et al. improves the idea of D^2FA and develops a DFA compression algorithm called A-DFA in 2013 [6]. By introducing the notion of "state depth" to quantify a state's distance from the initial state, A-DFA constructs nearly optimal default paths. Compared with D^2FA, A-DFA results in at most 2L state traversals when processing an input string of length L, and yields a tenfold improvement in compression ratio.

Based on the observation that most adjacent states share a large number of identical transitions, Ficara et al. [7] proposes a new representation for DFA, called δFA, which records the transition set of current state into a local memory, and only store the differences between current state and next hop state. In this way, δFA gains a perfect compression result. In addition, this algorithm requires only a state transition per character, and this allows a fast string matching speed. Najam et al. [8] presents a speculative parallel pattern matching technique for processing multiple stride DFA and a transition compression table technique is used to reduce 65 % transitions of stride DFA compared to original DFA. However, Patel et al. [9] has found another drawback of automata construction algorithm where multiple NAFs are joined into a large DFA and then minimize it. That leads to an expensive NFA to DFA subset construction for large NFAs and maybe a small final minimized DFA cannot be generated due to the failure of subset construction. Their change the order construction of DFA, i.e. minimize then join, this change results in the D^2FAs construction reaches on average 155 times faster and uses 1500 times less memory than previous algorithms.

In conclusion, most of the previous methods utilize the space-time tradeoff: reducing space requirement at the cost of increasing matching speed. In this paper, we propose a new space- and time-efficient DFA structure called RICS-DFA, which reduces 68 %–92 % DFA's memory usage and looks up transition matrix twice at most when it matches an input character.

3   RICS-DFA Algorithm

RICS-DFA algorithm is based on this observation: each character appears with different frequency in a rule set. Some characters occur high frequent while the rest appear very rarely, with almost the same frequency. Figure 1 shows this observation from real rule sets. In the figure, frequencies of some most common characters, such as English letters, digital or whitespace characters, are higher than others'; and more than half of the characters appear nearly the same low frequency. However, all of the characters are handled in equal ways in DFA engine. It is not fair for the high-frequency or low-frequency characters. Based on this observation, we propose a new DFA compression algorithm: RICS-DFA. Like the classical idea of RISC CPU design, the RICS-DFA reduces its character-set size by using high-frequency characters to escape and replace low-frequency ones. More specifically, the key idea of these algorithms is to eliminate some characters in the alphabet, in which each eliminated character is represented as an escape character with a reserved character. By this way, the size of RICS-DFA's alphabet is decreased and most of the redundant transitions can be eliminated.

3.1   Principle of RICS-DFA

In RICS-DFA, some original characters are eliminated and replaced by other retained characters. Therefore, we design a character map table (CMT) to map

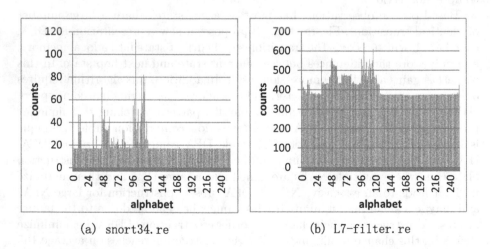

(a) snort34.re   (b) L7-filter.re

Fig. 1. Character frequencies for real regular expression rule set

an original alphabet (orig-alphabet) to a reduced alphabet (RICS-alphabet). The CMT is illustrated in Table 1. In the table, the first column is the orig-alphabet and the last two columns are the RICS-alphabet. Characters 'C' with 'D' are treated as escape characters, 'E' with 'F' are treated as eliminated characters, and 'A' with 'B' are reserved characters. Every escape character or eliminated character is represented by one escape character with one reserved character, while each reserved character is the same in RICS-alphabet as in orig-alphabet. For instance, the eliminated character 'E' in RICS-DFA is composed of one escape character 'D' and one reserved character 'A'. From the table, we conclude that the final RICS-DFA's alphabet consists of reserved characters and escape characters. As a result, the size of the alphabet in the example is reduced from six to four.

Table 1. Character map table for RICS-DFA

orig-alphabet	RICS-alphabet	
	escape-char	reserved-char
A		A
B		B
C	C	A
D	C	B
E	D	A
F	D	B

We formally define CMT as follows.

Let *orig-alphabet* be $\{a_0, a_1, \cdots, a_{|\Sigma|-1}\}$;
Let *Reserved Character Set (RCS)* be $\{r_0, r_1, \cdots, r_{n-1}\}$;
Let *Eliminated Character Set (ECS)* be $\{e_0, e_1, \cdots, e_{m-1}\}$;
Let *esCape Character Set (CCS)* be $\{c_0, c_1, \cdots, c_{l-1}\}$.

In the definition above, $RCS \bigcup ECS \bigcup CCS$ is equal to the *orig-alphabet*, and $RCS \bigcap ECS = RCS \bigcap CCS = ECS \bigcap CCS = \varnothing$. The size of the three character set satisfy $n \times l \geqslant m + l$, $m + l + n = |\Sigma|$. Given a n, we select a maximum m under the constraint conditions.

Therefore, a formal definition of a specific replacement scheme for each character is presented in Eq. 1. Each character $d_t \in ECS \bigcup CCS$ is treated as an element of a 2-dimensional matrix (i.e., the left-side matrix in Eq. 1) and is placed in the ith row and the jth column of the 2-dimensional matrix ($0 \leq t \leq m+l-1$, $i = \lfloor t/n \rfloor$, $j = t \bmod n$). The right-side matrix in Eq. 1 is the replacement matrix with the size of $n \times l$, where the element $c_i r_j$ consists of an escape character c_i and a reserved character r_j and the $c_i r_j$ is used to substitute the character d_t in RICS-DFA. Note that in the Eq. 1, $u = (m + l - 1) \bmod n$ means the number of elements in the last row of the two matrices may be less than n.

$$
\begin{bmatrix}
d_0 & d_1 & \cdots & d_{n-1} \\
d_n & d_{n+1} & \cdots & d_{2n-1} \\
d_{2n} & d_{2n+1} & \cdots & d_{3n-1} \\
\vdots & \vdots & \cdots & \vdots \\
d_{ln-n} & d_{ln-n+1} & \cdots & d_{m+l-1}
\end{bmatrix}
=
\begin{bmatrix}
c_0 r_0 & c_0 r_1 & \cdots & c_0 r_{n-1} \\
c_1 r_0 & c_1 r_1 & \cdots & c_1 r_{n-1} \\
c_2 r_0 & c_2 r_1 & \cdots & c_2 r_{n-1} \\
\vdots & \vdots & \cdots & \vdots \\
c_{(l-1)} r_0 & c_{(l-1)} r_1 & \cdots & c_{(l-1)} r_u
\end{bmatrix}
\tag{1}
$$

3.2   Implementation of RICS-DFA

Basic Idea. The principle of the RICS-DFA algorithm based on transition rewriting is that each transition labeled by an eliminated character in orig-DFA is replaced by two transitions (one for an escape character and the other for reserved character) and an intermediate state in RICS-DFA. There are two transitions labeled by r_0 and e_0 from state S_i to S_j respectively in orig-DFA, as in the example shown in Fig. 2. Suppose that e_0 is an eliminated character and the $c_0 r_0$ is used to substitute the e_0 on the basis of the RICS-DFA's CMT. The transition e_0 in the orig-DFA is equal to two transitions in which state S_i transfers to an intermediate state S_{inter} by c_0 and then transfers to state S_j by r_0 in RICS-DFA.

RICS-DFA Construction. The RICS-DFA algorithm based on transition rewriting is described in Algorithm 1. This algorithm rewrites each transition in order from state 0 to state N. A graphic illustration for this algorithm is shown in Fig. 3. The transition matrix $(T_{N \times |\Sigma|})$ of an orig-DFA is shown in Fig. 3(a) and it has an alphabet $\{r_0, \cdots, r_{n-1}, d_0, \cdots, d_{m+l-1}\}$, where $r_i \in RCS, d_j \in ECS \bigcup CCS, 0 \leqslant i < n, 0 \leqslant j < m+l-1$; the transition matrix $(T'_{N' \times (n+l)},\ N' = N \times (\lceil (m+l)/n \rceil))$ of its corresponding RICS-DFA is shown in Fig. 3(b). In the figure, the $^i a$ stands for the next state of state S_i meeting an input character a. In orig-DFA, transitions labeled by a group characters d_{gk} in ECS or CCS are marked as $group_k$, $0 \leqslant g_0 < n \leqslant \cdots kn \leqslant g_k < (k+1)n \cdots ln \leqslant g_{(l-1)} < (m+l-1)$. Similarly, transitions labeled by characters in RCS are marked as $group_{-1}$. Accordingly, in RICS-DFA, we call $group_{-1}$ as matrix R. Transitions labeled by CCR are referred to as matrix C and transitions of new added states are referred to as matrix E. To keep transition table as a matrix,

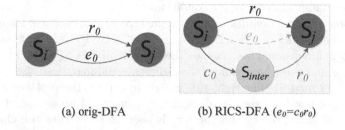

(a) orig-DFA   (b) RICS-DFA ($e_0 = c_0 r_0$)

Fig. 2. Principle of RICS-DFA algorithm based on transition rewriting

---

Algorithm 1. Constructing RICS-DFA's transition matrix T' from orig-DFA's transition matrix T by transition rewriting based on CMT, RCS, ECS, CCS.

Procedure RewriteTransitionMatrix()
1: $interStateID \leftarrow N$;
2: **for** $s \leftarrow 0$ to N **do**
3:   **for** $a \leftarrow 0$ to $|\Sigma| - 1$ **do**
4:     **if** $a \in RCS$ **then** $T'[s, CMT[a]] = T[s, a]$;
5:     **else**
6:       $\{c, r\} \leftarrow CMT[a]$; /*a=cr*/
7:       $T'[s, c] \leftarrow interStateID$;
8:       $T'[interStateID, r] \leftarrow T[s, a]$;
9:       $interStateID \leftarrow interStateID + 1$;
10:     **end if**
11:   **end for**
12: **end for**
13: **return** T'
End Procedure

---

there is a NULL matrix N in the RICS-DFA. The matrix C is an index matrix that indicates which intermediate state should jumps when a current state meets an escape character.

In Fig. 3, these transitions labeled by characters in RCS are the same between T and T'. However, every transition labeled by characters in ECS or CCS needs to be rewritten by introducing a new intermediate state with one escape transition and one reserved transition. That is, $T[S_i, d_t] = {}^i d_t$ is equal to twice of the transitions that $T'[S_i, c_x] = {}^i c_x$ at first and $T'[{}^i c_x, r_y] = {}^i d_t$ in RICS-DFA, where $CMT[d_t] = c_x r_y$ ($x = \lfloor t/n \rfloor$, $y = t \bmod n$), $0 \leqslant i < N$, $0 \leqslant t < m + l$. In fact, the character d_t is equal to an element of the left-side matrix in Eq. 1 and the c_x and r_y is equal to the xth row and y^{th} column element of right-side matrix in Eq. 1.

4   RICS-DFA Algorithm Optimization

Transitions for each state in orig-DFA are split to $l + 1$ groups and each group is placed to $l + 1$ state respectively in RICS-DFA (based on transition rewriting). And the transition matrix becomes narrower. In this section, we use a series of optimization techniques to reduce the memory requirements of RICS-DFA.

4.1   Eliminating Matrix C

The character d_t in ECS or CCS is replaced by $c_x r_y$ in RICS-DFA. That is, for a state S_i, there is the same state S_i in matrix C, in which state S_i is filled with a continuous addresses of newly increased intermediate states in turn, such as ${}^i c_0, {}^i c_1, \cdots, {}^i c_{l-1}$ in Fig. 3(b). Furthermore, all elements in C will be a strictly monotonic increasing sequence, in other words, a current element and 1 is equal

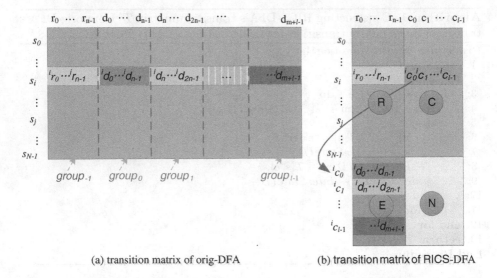

(a) transition matrix of orig-DFA   (b) transition matrix of RICS-DFA

Fig. 3. Transition matrix from orig-DFA to RICS-DFA

to its next element if transitions are rewritten in the order of starting from S_0 to S_N. Consequently, the index matrix C can be eliminated, and each element in C is figured out by the formula: $T'[S_i, c_j] = N + i * l + j$. Therefore, the RICS-DFA is only composed of matrix R and E while N as a NULL matrix is deleted directly. As a result, the RICS-DFA's alphabet is just the RCS, no longer including the CCS.

4.2 Compressing Matrices R and E

Through the analysis of the transition matrix, we find that there are a lot of *same states* among RICS-DFA. *Same state* means all transitions are identical in two states. Even though two states are not identical in orig-DFA, a lot of transitions are the same between two states. Those identical transitions can be eliminated in RICS-DFA, since these transitions are split into $l + 1$ states in RICS-DFA and then these identical transitions may become the same states. Therefore, in order to compress the matrix R and E, all the same states in RICS-DFA are found out and then only one state is retained while the other same states are deleted. At the same time, the address of the retained same state is recorded in an index table for each deleted state. Figure 4 describes a transition matrix of an orig-DFA, in which each state's transitions split into 3 groups as 3 states in the corresponding RICS-DFA according to the CMT described in Table 1. Take Fig. 4 for example, only few transitions in $group_1$ are different between orig-DFA states S_0 and S_1. Thus, in RICS-DFA, for S_1 only one group ($group_1$) is retained and each of other groups is deleted and records index of corresponding identical group in S_0.

States \ Alph.	A	B	C	D	E	F
S0	1	0	2	0	0	0
S1	1	0	3	4	0	0
S2	1	5	2	0	0	0
S3	6	5	2	0	0	0
S4	6	0	2	0	0	0
S5	7	0	2	0	0	0
S6	1	8	3	4	0	0
S7	1	0	3	4	9	9
S8	1	8	2	0	0	0
S9	1	0	2	0	9	9

$$group_{-1} \quad group_0 \quad group_1$$

Fig. 4. Transition matrix of orig-DFA for rules "$A+(C|D)AB+$" and "$CBA(E|F)*$"

By experiment on real-life rule-sets, we find that almost all the same states belong to the same group of orig-DFA. That is, one state in $group_i$ may have many same states in $group_i$ and hardly has the same states in other groups. Similarly, there are scarcely the same states between matrices R and E. Hence, during the process of construction RICS-DFA, the order of rewriting transitions in one state is changed as the group order, states in one group are placed into a successive range (of state ID) and the range of the same states is restricted in a group. For example, the transition matrix described in Fig. 4 is converted into RICS-DFA by transition rewriting as the group order and the matrix C is deleted, as shown in Fig. 5(a). At last, one of same states in a group is retained and the remainder states are deleted, each state records its same state to the index array $idx[\ ]$. The corresponding compressed RICS-DFA is shown in Fig. 5(b).

4.3   Compressing Auxiliary Space

By deleting matrix C and compressing matrices R and E, a large number of redundant transitions are eliminated in RICS-DFA, except an auxiliary array idx. However, the auxiliary array may surpass the size of compressed RICS-DFA in case that input character set (i.e. RCS) is reduced to a very small size and the number of state in orig-DFA (N) is quite large, for example, the size of the idx is 30 items while the size of its transition matrix is just 20 in Fig. 5(b). The auxiliary array also has the grouping feature whose size is $N \times n$. For example, different color regions in Fig. 5(b) belong to different groups which correspond to the $group_i$ in orig-DFA. In order to further utilize redundancy among the index array, each element in a group is subtracted from the group's base index, namely, the first index in a group. In Fig. 5(b), the addresses of base index for each group are 0,10 and 20. By this way, we get a new index array, as shown in Fig. 5(c). In the figure, a lot of elements are identical now, especially, the zero-elements. There are many methods to compress such a long and redundant array, such as run length encoding (RLE) and directly storing sparse elements. But they are not efficient in terms of memory access. We propose an efficient method by using

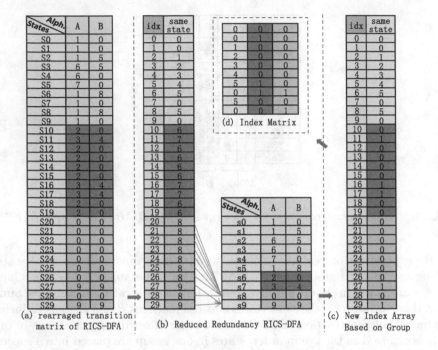

Fig. 5. Example of RICS-DFA

Double-Array Structure [10] to compress the redundant index array *idx*. In order to use the *Double-Array* technique, we rearrange the index array into an index matrix ($N \times (l+1)$) by taking each group as a column of the matrix in order of the group ID. For example, the new index matrix (Fig. 5(c)) is converted into an index matrix (Fig. 5(d)). The index matrix represented by *Double-Array* only retains non-zero elements which occupy three memory spaces, namely, two in *base* array and one in *check* array. By experiments on real rule-sets, we further find that most of the elements in a row of the new index matrix are the same. Before compressing the new index matrix by *Double-Array* technique, we use two methods to increase the number of zero-elements in the index matrix. One method (marked as *DA1*) is to select the first column as a base column and the other columns are subtracted from the base column. The second method (marked as *DA2*) is like the *DA1*, but the base column are composed of these elements who appear most frequently in a row.

5 Performance Evaluation

To evaluate the efficiency of RICS-DFA, we carry out experiments on several real-life regular expression rule-sets. We compare our approach with the original DFA as well as other famous DFA compression methods. The experimental rule-set obtain from several open source system, including Bro, Snort and L7-filter.

Because the rule is too complex to generate a composite DFA, it requires more than 16 GB memory space [4], the L7-filter rule set is divided into 8 rule subsets from l7-1 to l7-8 by using the open source regex-tool [11].

5.1 Compression Ratio

We give four kinds of compression ratio to evaluate the improvement of RICS-DFA in terms of memory consumption: compression ratio without the size of auxiliary array (called non_aux_sz), one with the size of auxiliary array (called add_aux_sz), and two compression ratios of RICS-DFA(called $DA1$ and $DA2$) which use two types of $Double$-$Array$ methods to compress its index matrix respectively, as described in Sect. 4.3. The compression ratio of non_aux_sz is defined as $r = (N' \times n)/(N \times |\Sigma|)$ while add_aux_sz defined as $r = (N' \times n + N')/(N \times |\Sigma|)$. The compression ratios of $DA1$ and $DA2$ are defined as $r = (N' \times n + nz)/(N \times |\Sigma|)$, where nz is the size of the nonzero-elements represented by the $Double$-$Array$ in the index matrix.

Table 2 gives the compression ratio of RICS-DFA with alphabet size 8 on different rule-sets. In the table, the column of non_aux_sz shows the power of RICS-DFA who nearly eliminates more than 90 % of the redundant transitions. The add_aux_sz column shows the size of the index matrix is large in case of small alphabet size. And the last two columns show the effectiveness of using $Double$-$Array$ compressing the index matrix, which further reduces the rest space of RICS-DFA.

5.2 Size of Reserved Alphabet

This subsection primary analyzes the influence of the size of reserved alphabet on the compression ratio. Figure 6 shows the compression ratio of RICS-DFA

Table 2. Compression ratio on different rule-sets ($n = 8$)

Rule set	# of rules	# of states	non_aux_sz	add_aux_sz	DA1	DA2
bro217	217	6475	0.035	0.160	0.078	0.086
snort24	24	8335	0.034	0.159	0.072	0.080
snort31	31	4864	0.038	0.163	0.094	0.077
snort34	34	9754	0.035	0.160	0.057	0.065
l7-1	67	3703	0.213	0.338	0.318	0.289
l7-2	7	1702	0.106	0.231	0.289	0.204
l7-3	12	2863	0.029	0.154	0.132	0.139
l7-4	5	3322	0.122	0.247	0.214	0.214
l7-5	6	3040	0.066	0.191	0.103	0.108
l7-6	5	8704	0.075	0.200	0.149	0.133
l7-7	5	5720	0.077	0.202	0.175	0.108
l7-8	1	308	0.058	0.183	0.088	0.083

with different alphabet size for several real-life rule-sets. We find from the figure that (1) the column of *non_aux_sz* shows the charm of RICS-DFA, especially for the small size alphabet, such as 4 or 8; (2) the column of *add_aux_sz* shows that when the alphabet's size is very small, the space of the auxiliary array cannot be ignored and it occupies most of the storage space; when the alphabet's size is large, such as $n = 32$, the compression ratio of the *add_aux_sz* is nearly equal to the *non_aux_sz*'s. Thus, it is reasonable that the auxiliary array (*idx*) is not compressed any more in case of a large alphabet. (3) On the contrary, the columns of *DA1,DA2* show the effectiveness of using the *Double-Array* compressed the auxiliary array in case of small alphabet; (4) the compression ratio of the *DA2* method only in the *l7_6* rule is more effective than *DA1*'s, it illustrates that the effectiveness of different compressing methods closely depends on the rule-set; (5) in sum, the best compression ratio of RICS-DFA is obtained in case of retaining the alphabet's size as 4 or 8.

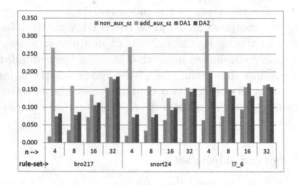

Fig. 6. Compression ratio of RICS-DFA

5.3   Comparison with Previous Work

In this part, we compare our method with two famous DFA compression algorithms: D^2FA [5] and δFA [7], in which the compression ratio of D^2FA is defined as the ratio of the size of labeled transitions and default transitions to the original DFA size. We test D^2FA with the diameter $d = 1$ and $d = 2$, that means each transfer need to look up transition matrix one or $d + 1$ times while RICS-DFA looks up transition matrix once or twice (once for character replacement). Thus, in the same matching speed, it is reasonable to compare RICS-DFA with D^2FA with $d = 1$ and $d = 2$. The compression ratios of the three algorithms are shown in Table 3, where the RICS-DFA is reduced alphabet size to 8 and compressed its index matrix by $DA1$. In the table, numbers in italic mean its results are better than RICS-DFA. From the table, we find that (1) in most of rule-sets, our RICS-DFA is better than other two methods, especially for the complex L7-filter rule set. While the other two methods are a little bit better in the rule-sets of bro217 and snort; (2) for the same DFA matching speed, our RICS-DFA significantly outperforms the D^2FA ($d = 1$).

Table 3. Compression ratio in comparison with previous algorithms

Rule set	RICS-DFA ($n = 8$)	δFA	D^2FA ($d = 1$)	D^2FA ($d = 2$)
bro217	0.078	*0.062*	0.514	0.248
snort24	0.072	*0.037*	0.516	0.098
snort31	0.094	*0.061*	0.519	0.192
snort34	0.057	*0.030*	0.516	0.113
l7-1	0.318	0.552	0.894	0.623
l7-2	0.289	0.842	1.180	0.990
l7-3	0.132	*0.112*	0.519	*0.118*
l7-4	0.214	0.960	1.063	0.702
l7-5	0.103	0.688	1.208	0.808
l7-6	0.149	0.471	0.647	0.294
l7-7	0.175	0.661	0.866	0.492
l7-8	0.088	*0.071*	0.635	0.299

6 Conclusion

In this paper, we propose a novel and compact DFA structure, called RICS-DFA, which is able to reduce the new DFA's alphabet to small size. An efficient construction algorithm for the RICS-DFA is proposed in this paper based on transition rewriting. The RICS-DFA method has obvious advantage of lower matching delay and higher compression ratio than other similar DFA compressing algorithms. And the RICS-DFA has another special feature that it has reserved all features of a common DFA except for a narrower alphabet. In other words, the transition matrix is a normal matrix, rather than sparse one. This feature is very important for the practicality of an optimized DFA. A normal transition matrix makes regular expression matching much more simple and efficient, as the normal matrix does not need to compress and decompress the non-sparse elements like it is usually done with sparse matrix which will lead to additional complexity and increase the processing delay. Experimental results show that on real-life rule-sets, the RICS-DFA reduces a large number of redundant transitions while sacrificing trivial matching speed. In most rule-sets, especially for the complex rule-set L7-filter, the RICS-DFA gets a better compression ratio than other methods.

Acknowledgments. This work is supported by National Natural Science Foundation of China (Nos. 61402475 and 61303171).

References

1. La Polla, M., Martinelli, F., Sgandurra, D.: A survey on security for mobile devices. IEEE Commun. Surv. Tutor. **15**(1), 446–471 (2013)

2. Oh, J.-S., Park, M.-W., Chung, T.-M.: Enhancing security of the android platform via multi-level security model. In: Batten, L., Li, G., Niu, W., Warren, M. (eds.) ATIS 2014. CCIS, vol. 490, pp. 13–24. Springer, Heidelberg (2014)

3. Yu, F., Chen, Z., Diao, Y., Lakshman, T.V., Katz, R.H.: Fast and memory-efficient regular expression matching for deep packet inspection. In: ACM/IEEE Symposium on Architecture for Networking and Communications Systems, ANCS 2006, pp. 93–102. IEEE (2006)

4. Liu, T., Yang, Y., Liu, Y., Sun, Y., Guo, L.: An efficient regular expressions compression algorithm from a new perspective. In: INFOCOM, 2011 Proceedings IEEE, pp. 2129–2137. IEEE (2011)

5. Kumar, S., Dharmapurikar, S., Fang, Y., Crowley, P., Turner, J.: Algorithms to accelerate multiple regular expressions matching for deep packet inspection. ACM SIGCOMM Comput. Commun. Rev. $36(4)$, 339–350 (2006)

6. Becchi, M., Crowley, P.: A-DFA: a time- and space-efficient DFA compression algorithm for fast regular expression evaluation. ACM Trans. Archit. Code Optim. $10(1)$, 4:1–4:26 (2013)

7. Ficara, D., Giordano, S., Procissi, G., Vitucci, F., Antichi, G., Di Pietro, A.: An improved DFA for fast regular expression matching. ACM SIGCOMM Comput. Commun. Rev. $38(5)$, 29–40 (2008)

8. Najam, M., Younis, U., Rasool, R.U.: Speculative parallel pattern matching using stride-k DFA for deep packet inspection. J. Netw. Comput. Appl. 54, 78–87 (2015)

9. Patel, J., Liu, A.X., Torng, E.: Bypassing space explosion in high-speed regular expression matching. IEEE/ACM Trans. Netw. (TON) $22(6)$, 1701–1714 (2014)

10. Aoe, J.: An efficient digital search algorithm by using a double-array structure. IEEE Trans. Softw. Eng. $15(9)$, 1066–1077 (1989)

11. Becchi, M.: Regex tool. http://regex.wustl.edu/

A Clustering Approach for Detecting Auto-generated Botnet Domains

Yang Pu, Xiaojun Chen[✉], Yiguo Pu, and JinQiao Shi

Institute of Information Engineering, Chinese Academy of Sciences, Beijing,
People's Republic of China
clarissayp@163.com, {chenxiaojun,puyiguo,
shijinqiao}@iie.ac.cn

Abstract. Domain fluxing is a general method for botnet operators to control the victims and escape detection. Botnets based on domain fluxing, such as Conficker, Torpig, Kraken, generate a unique list of domain names based on a predefined domain generation algorithm (DGA). If the algorithm is known in advance, it is easy to identify and block botnet traffic. Unfortunately, exploiting details about the algorithm requires reverse-engineering technology and that is not always feasible.

In this paper, we propose a methodology to detect auto-generated domains by measuring the disparity between auto-generated domains and normal domains. The idea is based on the observation that the normal domain names differ from auto-generated domain names in readability, randomness etc., because botnet don't use well-formed words which is highly likely registered. Clustering algorithm is used to group auto-generated domains into several separated clusters and normal domains into other clusters. As shown in the validation and experiment phase, we prove this method can detect DGA domains with high performance.

Keywords: Clustering · Domain fluxing · Botnet domains · Network attack

1 Introduction

Domain fluxing is a useful and general method for botnet operators to control the victims and escape detection simultaneously. In domain fluxing process, bots periodically generate a large number of domain names using a domain generation algorithm (DGA) with a special seed. And then the bots query each of generated domains list until one of them is resolved to a command and control (C&C) server.

Domain fluxing botnets, such as Conficker, Torpig, Kraken, generate a unique list of domain names based on a predefined DGA. Different botnet based on different DGA generates domain names in a different way. For example, Conficker-A [1] bots use the current date and time at UTC (in seconds) as the seed, which is acquired by sending empty HTTP GET queries to a few legitimate sites such as baidu.com or google.com etc. In this way, all bots would generate exactly the same domain names at the same time every day. Torpig [2, 3] bots employ a special way where the seed for the random

© Springer-Verlag Berlin Heidelberg 2015
W. Niu et al. (Eds.): ATIS 2015, CCIS 557, pp. 269–279, 2015.
DOI: 10.1007/978-3-662-48683-2_24

string generator comes from one of the most popular trending topics in Twitter. Kraken generates specific word which is similar to English language with properly matched vowels and consonants, and then combines each of them with a randomly chosen suffix, such as -able, -dom, -ment, -ship, or -ly.

Security vendors deal with this kind of attacks depending on domain names blacklist and reverse-engineering. They updated the domain names blacklist after running a process of domain discovery and then detected malicious DNS requests using technique similar to signature matching. But botnets employed DGA can dynamically produce a large number of random domain names and select a part of them to use for communication. Security vendors have to understanding the details of DGA relying on reverse-engineering technology and update the blacklist dynamically. This way is time-consuming and resource-intensive, and more is not available always.

So we want to know whether are there efficient method to auto detect the malicious domain names generated algorithmically by botnets?

In this papers, a clustering-based detection approach is proposed to decide if domain names are auto-generated domain names. This approach is based on the following two observations [4, 5]: The first one is that domain names generated by the same algorithm can be similar. Different DGAs use different algorithms and dictionaries to generate domain names, and the others generate domain names in a completely random way. The second one is that normal domain names can be expected to vastly differ from malicious domain names, because botnet don't use well-formed words which is highly likely registered, but non-malicious domain names composed with well-formed words usually because the web-owner wish the web domain is easy to remember.

We extract three kinds of features for the key clustering process. That include readability, entropy and structure features wherein readability describes the difference between the non-malicious domains and malicious domains in 2-gram frequency and one-gram frequency; entropy evaluate the randomness and structure features describe length and compositions of the domain name.

On the validation and experiment phase, three datasets are used that are Non-malicious dataset (non-m-ds), malicious dataset (m-ds) and online-traffic dataset (online-ds). Non-malicious data set is composed of normal domain names and collected from alexa [6]. Malicious data set is the auto-generated domain names collection, and we collected them from conficker (A, B, C) [7] and kraken [8] bonnets etc. Online-traffic dataset is the set of domains collected from real-time DNS traffic in our library network environment during one month. Non-malicious dataset and malicious dataset are used for validate the accuracy of the clustering approach. If the clusters after clustering process consists of elements from non-m-ds or consist of elements from m-ds mainly, that means most domain names with same labels (non-malicious or malicious) are grouped into the same cluster. Online-traffic dataset is used to test the clustering approach on real-time dns traffic. Actually, we can't know the labels of real-time domain names clusters. So two methods can be used to label the real-time domain names clusters. One is using Kullback–Leibler (K–L) divergence to judge every domain cluster whether malicious or non-malicious. K–L divergence computes the "distance" between real-time domain cluster and non-malicious dataset or malicious dataset, if the distance to non-malicious dataset is small, the real-time cluster is judged non-malicious and otherwise. Another method is checking every domain name in one real-time cluster manually. McAfee Site Advisor [9] and Web of Trust [10] can be used to query against domain reputation.

The rest of this paper is organized as follows. In Sect. 2, we compare our work against related literature. In Sect. 3, feature selection process is described which shows difference between malicious domain names and non-malicious ones and then introduce the cluster algorithms. Next, in Sect. 4, validation and experiment results applied to different data sets are demonstrated and discussed. Finally, in Sect. 5 we conclude.

2 Related Work

Detection method of domain-flux have been analyzed by Li and Chen [11]. They observed the differences between malicious domain name and non-malicious domain name. Our work build on this earlier work for detection algorithmically generated domain names used in domain-flux. Zhang et al. [12] specifically introduced domain generated algorithm and proved that domain names generated by same algorithm are similar in the measure of character features. In our work, we know that this similarity can be used to separate malicious domain and non-malicious ones. If we group the domain names which is similar to each other on the measure of character features, we have enough reason to believe that most domain names in this group probably have the same label, malicious or non-commercial.

Choosing features is very vital in our work. If the feature couldn't distinguish malicious domain names and legitimate ones, it won't have good result. Li [13] selected four characteristic of three types to detect Fast-Flux domain name, the proxy distribution, the structure characteristics of domain name and features of service quality. All the features in this paper, instead, are structure characteristics. Features from different type is hard to normalized and determine weight for small different in weight can draw big distinction in result.

Jiang et al. [14] introduce domain generated algorithm technique and domain fluxing. A large number of malicious software by means of the specific domain generation algorithm (DGA: Domain Generation Algorithms), generate a large number of domain names for improving their own controlling of organization, enhancing their ability to survive and prolonging the lifetime of the system. It says that different malicious software, since utilizing different algorithm, generated domain names will show different characteristics. In our work, we expect to find the different characteristics between malicious domain names and good ones instead of finding differences between different algorithm generated domain names.

3 Method of Detection

3.1 Framework

In this section, we present our detection method. First we select features which show differences between algorithmically generated domain names and legitimate ones. Then we use clustering algorithm to group domain names into clusters. Finally, we evaluate the group with KL-Divergence. The framework of this paper shows in Fig. 1.

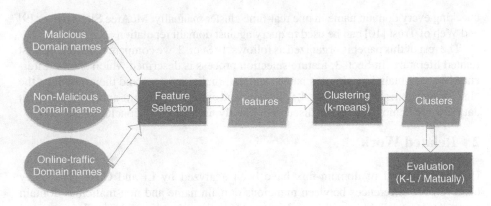

Fig. 1. Framework of detection process

3.2 Features Extraction

In this paper, we proposed a botnet detection approach. The detection approach that is based on the observation about similarity of the generated domain in terms of alphanumeric characters.

We chose features based on three observations obtaining from knowledge above:

- Domain-fluxing domain names is a set which frequency of all characters is almost uniform distribution. This factor reflects the specialization of such domain names generated by the algorithm.
- The frequency of different character in normal domain has huge different between each other. But it has a similar statistics frequency of each character in the English text. This reflects that domain name of legitimate domain usually follows the principle of readability.
- In order to ensure the domain name has not been registered, the generated domain name required makes a difference to non-malicious domain name.

So present three kinds of features are picked to represent and describe the characteristic similarity between domain names: readability, entropy and structure features wherein readability describes the difference between the non-malicious domains and malicious domains in bigram frequency and one-gram frequency; entropy features evaluate the randomness and structure features describe other difference from non-malicious domains. To use these three kinds features to the actual Domain-flux botnet detection method, this section will discuss two questions: (a) can we make a distinction between malicious domains and legitimate ones through these three kinds features? And (b) how to get these features?

Readability. As the DGA domains are not generated by human and don't need to be easy remember, they are always clumsy to read with lower readability than legitimate domains. So readability is a good indicator to distinguish malicious domains and non-malicious ones. The lower the readability is, the greater the difference between unknown domain and domain from Alexa. Therefore, this unknown domain is most likely a malicious domain.

As the top domains in Alexa is popular domains where we can get the information about which kind of character combination can make high readable domains. We calculate every n-gram frequency then use this information to evaluate new domains. Firstly the domain is prefixed and suffixed with a '$', then the frequency and probability of every n-gram in the domain of top 1 million in Alexa are computed For a new domain, we get its readability by summing the probabilities of its n-grams as Eq. (1).

$$\text{Score} = \frac{\sum_{levels} \sum_j freq(gram_j)}{\sum_{levels}(len + n - 1)} \tag{1}$$

where $gram_j$ means the j-th gram and $freq(gram_j)$ representing frequency of $gram_j$ in top 10000000 domain in Alexa. levels means the level of domain. n is the number of character in the gram. In this paper, we use one gram and two gram to evaluate the readability.

Information Entropy. While readability describes the differences in frequency distribution of n-gram, entropy describes randomness in subdomain. When calculate entropy, the firs level and second-level domain is removed, which belong to the country domain suffix or the general domain suffix. For example, if a domain is google.com.cn, the subdomain here is Google.

Firstly, get the frequency of every character in the subdomain. The final aim is to measure the differences in randomness of characters between non-malicioudains and malicious domains. The higher the entropy is, the greater the difference between unknown domain and legitimate domain. Therefore, this unknown domain is most likely a malicious domain. The entropy is evaluated by Eqs. (2) and (3):

$$E = -\sum_{i=1,..,|z|} p_i log p_i \tag{2}$$

$$p_i = \frac{count_i}{length} \tag{3}$$

where p_i is the frequency of the i character in subdomain, length is the length of subdomain. $count_i$ is the number that i character shows in subdomain. $|Z|$ is the total number of character which can appear in domain names. In this paper, $|Z|$ is defined as 256.

Structure Features.
Length rate len_rate. As malicious domains are always longer than legitimate domains, we capture the difference by follow equation:

$$\text{LenRate} = \sum_{i=1,...,levels} \frac{len_i}{i} \tag{4}$$

where len_i is the length of the i-the level domain; levels is the number of level in the domain.

TLD rate TtlRate. We know .com is popular domain because it is always authoritative and difficult or expensive to apply. DGA domains, on the other hand, are inclined to choose domains that are low cost and easy to register, such as .info, .cc and so on. So we can statistics the probability of top level domain as one feature. The TLD probability is computed from the top domains in Alexa.

The number of different charactors NumDiffChar. DGA could choose its characters from a self-defined dictionary, which may be different from the dictionary that human use. This feature is calculated as following:

$$\text{NumDiffChar} = \frac{\sum_{i=1,...,levels} \text{NumDiffChar}(domain_i)}{levels} \tag{5}$$

where *NumDiffChar(domain_i)* is the number of different characters in the i-th level domain.

The maximum length of continuous consonants, vowels and numbers: MaxConCon, MaxConVow, MaxConNum. As malicious domains do not care whether the domain name is easy to remember or not, they may have longer length of continuous consonants, vowels and numbers. We also choose these features to differentiate legitimate domains and malicious ones.

The frequency numbers and vowels: NumRate and VowRate. Legitimate domains always contain enough vowel characters and few number characters to make it simple and comply with English words. Malicious domains do not need obey these rules.

The level of domain Level. The domains generated by same DGA may have same level. We use these feature to cluster similar domains.

3.3 Clustering Algorithm

We use two different clustering algorithm, K-means and MBK-means. The biggest feature of K-means clustering is required to specify the value of k in advance (i.e., the number of clustering). K-means must determine the size of K, and K often cannot be determined by data set in advance.

K-means clustering approach comprises the following two steps:

Step 1: Given an original centroid set of m which is specified randomly

Step 2: Assign each object to the group that has the closest centroid, according to the distance between test point and centroid

Step 3: After all objects have been assigned, recalculate the positions of the k centroids. Stop until the result doesn't change after running step 2 and step 3 again

In order to compare the result after different clustering algorithms, we implement our data on MBK-means clustering too.

MBK-means clustering approach comprises the following two steps:

Step 1:   it generates k new training sets $D_i(i = 1..k)$ from the given standard training set D

Step 2:   Using D_i to run K-means. After obtaining every centroids in every training sets, we combine all centroids and update

3.4   Metric for Labeling Group of Domain Names

This Metric only used for labeling domain names extracted from DNS queries. In this paper we use KL-Divergence with bigrams distribution.

The K–L divergence metric is a non-symmetric measure of divergence between two probability distributions. There are two probability distribution here, P and Q. P represents the test distribution, and Q represents the base distribution from which the metric is computed. The following equation describes the divergence between two distributions P and Q, where i the number of possible values for a discrete random variable [14]

$$D_{kl}(P||Q) = \sum_{i-1}^{n} P(i) log \frac{P(i)}{Q(i)} \tag{6}$$

For a given a test distribution q computed for the domain to be tested, non-malicious probability distribution g and malicious distribution q, respectively, we judge the distribution as malicious or not via the following formula:

$$\text{If} \quad D_{sym}(b||q) - D_{sym}(g||q) > 0 \tag{7}$$

Then, distribution q is a non-malicious distribution.

$$\text{If} \quad D_{sym}(b||q) - D_{sym}(g||q) < 0 \tag{8}$$

Then, distribution q is a malicious distribution.

4   Validation and Experiments

4.1   Data Set

In this part, we describe the datasets and the way we obtain them. Three datasets are used on the validation and experiment phases. First is non-malicious data set. This set is composed of the most popular domain names collected from alexa [6]. Second is malicious data set which collected them from Conficker (A, B, C) and kraken bonnets etc. The last one is Online-traffic data set is the set of domains collected from real-time DNS traffic in our library network environment during one month. If we know the domain is malicious or non-malicious before detection, then we can regard this kind of domain names as domain name with labels

This set of domain names with labels obtained from good domain names from Alexa and malicious domain names generated from domain generated algorithms, while the set of domain names without labels of domain is Online-traffic data set.

4.2   Features Evaluation

To test the efficiency of the four feature above, we selected 50 domain names both in Alexa and malicious domain names set. Then we extract features. Choosing three characteristics every time, we painted three-dimensional map. Black points represent a domain from the collection of malicious domains, red from Alexa. In Fig. 2, each axis represent one feature. We can conclude from the following four figure in Fig. 2 draw by Origin 8.0 that feature selection is successful.

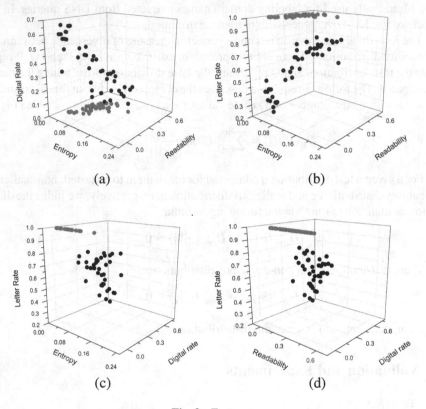

(a)   (b)

(c)   (d)

Fig. 2. Features

4.3   Clustering

After preparing the data of features, we implement K-means and MBK-means by means of Python.

Domain Names with Labels. The dataset is 10,000 domain names from Alexa, 15,000 from conficker and 1,000 from kraken. For K-means, MBK-means need to define group number k first, we define k as 2, 5, 10, 20, 40, 50. We expect that the consistent rate goes up as the group number increase. The result prove our prediction Table 1

Table 1. Result of clustering

K	Groups	Total	Alexa	Con-ficker	Kra-ken	Consistance Rate
2	1	123974	97767	26178	29	78.86%
	2	77033	2233	73822	978	97.10%
5	1	42010	332	40902	776	99.21%
	2	47316	39564	7751	1	83.62%
	3	50212	3635	46350	227	92.76%
	4	57518	52518	4997	3	91.31%
	5	3951	3951	0	0	100.00%

The table show part result of k-means clustering. K means the total group number.

Domain Names Without Labels. The dataset include 103118 domain names collected from real-time DNS traffic.

In the result, some domain names which looks similar in the same group like: as.city8.com, as.com, as.ebz.io, as.eqxiu.com.

4.4 Validation and Evaluation

Domain Names with Labels. For analyzing average of consistence rate in group of different number, we can find out in Table 2 that the consistence rate increase as the group number goes up. Plus, the consistence rate of this method is relatively high. We can conclude that this method is efficient.

Table 2. Average value of consistence rate

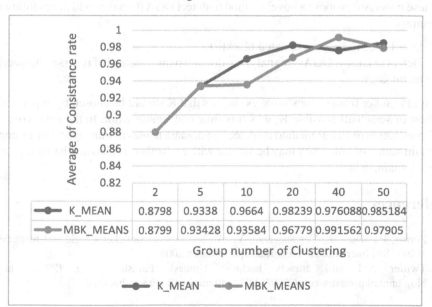

	2	5	10	20	40	50
K_MEAN	0.8798	0.9338	0.9664	0.98239	0.976088	0.985184
MBK_MEANS	0.8799	0.93428	0.93584	0.96779	0.991562	0.97905

Group number of Clustering

Domain Names Without Labels. In this paper, we use KL-Divergence or Internet site to label the group. We cluster 20 groups. Then we use JAVA to calculate K–L divergence. The only point we consider is that if the number is positive or negative. We can see in Table 3, group 11 may be malicious group.

Table 3. KL-Divergence

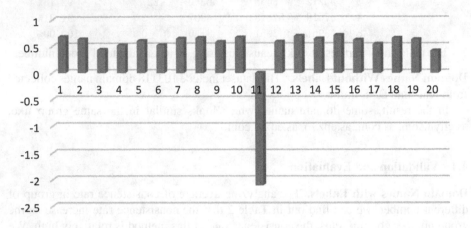

5   Conclusion

In these paper, we propose a novel method to detect DGA domains, which has following advantages:

(1) Don't need to keep an updated blacklist.
(2) Detect unknown DGAs by analyzing domain names instead of reverse-engineering technology.

It also suffer from some shortages such as that K should be chosen by expert information or search all possible K, which is time consuming work. In the next work, we will consider expand our method on detecting domain names in same type. For example. Domain names of university may be similar with each other, for having the same second level domain, .edu.

References

1. Porras, P., Saidi, H., Yegneswaran, V.: An analysis of conficker's logic and rendezvous points. SRI International Technical report, March 2009
2. Twitter API still attracts hackers. Unmask Parasites blog (2009). http://blog.unmaskparasites.com/2009/12/09/twitterapi-still-attracts-hackers/

3. Stone-Gross, B., Cova, M., Cavallaro, L., Gilbert, B., Szydlowski, M., Kemmerer, R., Kruegel, C., Vigna, G.: Your botnet is my botnet: analysis of a botnet takeover. In: Proceedings of ACM CCS, pp. 635–647, November 2009

4. Antonakakis, M., Perdisci, R., Nadji, Y., Vasiloglou, N., Abu-Nimeh, S., Lee, W., Dagon, D.: From throw-away traffic to bots: detecting the rise of DGA-based malware. In: The 21st USENIX Security Symposium, Bellevue, WA, 8–10 August 2012

5. Yadav, S., Reddy, A.K.K., Reddy, A.L.N., Ranjan, S.: Detecting algorithmically generated domain-flux attacks with DNS traffic analysis. IEEE/ACM Trans. Netw. **20**, 1663–1977 (2012)

6. Alexa: http://www.alexa.com/

7. Universität Bonn. http://net.cs.uni-bonn.de/wg/cs/applications/containing-conficker/

8. Kraken. https://www.damballa.com/downloads/r_pubs/KrakenWhitepaper.pdf

9. McAfee site advisor. http://www.siteadvisor.com

10. Web of trust. http://mywot.com

11. Li, Q., Chen, Z.: Detection of domain-flux Botnet domain names. Comput. Eng. Des. **33**(8), 2915–2919 (2012)

12. Zhang, X., Xu, X., Li, Q.: A real time detect method of malicious domains. Mod. Sci. Technol. Telecommun. **7**(7), 3–8 (2013)

13. Li, X.: The Research on Botnet detection. PLA Information Engineering University, P.R. China, April 2013

14. Jiang, J., Zhuge, J.-W., Duan, H.-X., Wu, J.-P.: Research on Botnet mechanisms and defenses. J. Softw. **23**(1), 82–96 (2012)

Modeling of Mobile Communication Systems by Electromagnetic Theory in the Direct and Single Reflected Propagation Scenario

Guo Sheng[1], Shuping Dang[2(✉)], Nadim Hossain[3], and Xu Zhang[4]

[1] Zhejiang Post and Telecommunication College,
Shaoxing 312016, People's Republic of China
sg@zptc.cn

[2] Department of Engineering Science, University of Oxford, Oxford OX1 3PJ, UK
shuping.dang@eng.ox.ac.uk

[3] School of Electrical and Electronic Engineering,
The University of Manchester, Manchester M13 9PL, UK
nadim5700@gmail.com

[4] Department of Mechanical Engineering and Materials Science,
Duke University, Durham, NC 27708-0287, USA
xz70@duke.edu

Abstract. In this paper, we employ electromagnetic theory to analyze the phenomenon of signal propagation and thereby model mobile communication systems. Using electromagnetic theory is different from conventional modeling techniques applied in communication engineering, the advantage being that a more in-depth and accurate model can be provided. This is because the electromagnetism-based model exactly measures the electromagnetic behavior of a signal and hence, more details of the ambient environment are involved in the modeling procedure. However, it should not be tendentiously ignored that the disadvantage is also obvious. Because superabundant details should be involved, this model is sometimes inefficient and even impractical. To investigate this innovative modeling technique in more detail, we provide a simplified propagation scenario through only considering direct and single reflected paths between the transmitter and the receiver. By means of this special case study, the pros and cons of electromagnetism-based modeling can be revealed extensively. A series of familiar concepts and jargons frequently referred to in wireless mobile communication are also interpreted in view of the electromagnetism-based modeling technique. More importantly, in this paper, the nature of signal transmission and reception in free space can be analyzed in depth by virtue of this modeling technique.

Keywords: Mobile communication system · Modeling · Electromagnetic theory · Signal propagation

1 Introduction

The modeling of mobile communication systems is a frequent topic of study since the last century [1,2]. However, it is from the perspective of signals and

© Springer-Verlag Berlin Heidelberg 2015
W. Niu et al. (Eds.): ATIS 2015, CCIS 557, pp. 280–290, 2015.
DOI: 10.1007/978-3-662-48683-2_25

systems that these conventional modeling techniques of mobile communication systems are normally derived from [3]. As a result, these conventional modeling techniques selectively ignore the details of signal propagation and the ambient environment, especially when the networking topology becomes complex [4–7]. This ambiguity is always efficient in practice, since the electromagnetic nature of signals are too complicated to study and involves Maxwell's equations [8]. Also, it is rather difficult, when modeling, to measure the ambient environment precisely and take all potential ambient factors into consideration [9]. Admittedly, it is wise to employ conventional modeling techniques when the details can be ignored and when we only need to focus on the signal input/output relation. However, resorting to these modeling techniques *de facto* degrade modeling precision and shadow the nature of a realistic mobile communication system. Moreover, when the propagation process is required to be analyzed in near field and the velocity of a mobile system is discussed in the order of speed of light levels, these traditional modeling techniques are all stranded and useless [10]. For these special cases, we should view mobile communication systems in terms of electromagnetic theory and build a series of analytical methodologies, especially in certain oversimplified cases where the electromagnetism-based modeling technique can be precise without loss of efficiency. In order to delve into the details of an electromagnetism-based modeling technique of mobile communication systems, we present a case study in this paper which only takes into consideration the direct and single reflected paths between the transmitter and the receiver. By means of this case study, the pros and cons of electromagnetism-based modeling can be revealed and a number of familiar concepts can be reinterpreted through electromagnetic theory. In addition, the nature of signal transmission and reception in free space can be analyzed in depth.

The rest of this paper is organized as follows. In Sect. 2, we present first the fundamentals of signal radiation and propagation which serve as a foundation for further modeling and analysis. Then, the detailed modeling procedure and analysis are provided in Sect. 3. Based on these constructed models, a number of relevant simulations are contacted subsequently and the simulation results are illustrated and discussed in Sect. 4. Finally we conclude this paper in Sect. 5.

2   Fundamentals of Signal Radiation and Propagation

Consider the nature of a wireless radio signal, it is essentially a high-frequency electromagnetic wave and the information contained in the signal is carried by the transmitted electromagnetic field. Three characteristic parameters, i.e. amplitude A, frequency f and phase angle Θ, specialize the carried information. Without loss of generality, we might choose a cosine waveform to express the transmitted electromagnetic field and devise its generic form by [11]:

$$E(t) = A\cos(2\pi ft + \Theta) \tag{1}$$

Assume such an electromagnetic field is transmitted from an isotropic antenna with power P_t as shown in Fig. 1, in which the transmit antenna and the

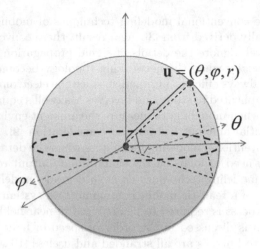

Fig. 1. Free space signal radiation model.

measured point are marked as red and blue points respectively. In the polar coordinate system, each point in free space can be characterized by a vector $\mathbf{u} = (\theta, \varphi, r)$. Assume further that the isotropic antenna is located in the origin and an arbitrary measured point is denoted by $\mathbf{u} = (\theta, \varphi, r)$. Because of the implementation of an isotropic antenna, a set of points over a spherical surface with radius r are mutually equivalent in terms of the field strength. Therefore in this case, the field strength and the received power only depend on the separation distance r between the measured point and the transmitter isotropic antenna. That is, the far field strength is uniformly distributed in free space. Consequently, the three-dimensional space of signal propagation can be reduced to a two-dimensional space. As a result, when the separation distance r is larger than the Fraunhofer distance, the far field power flux density at the measured point can be determined by [12]:

$$\Phi(r) = \frac{P_t}{4\pi r^2} \tag{2}$$

It can be proved that the captured effective area of an isotropic received antenna is [12]:

$$A_{iso} = \frac{\lambda^2}{4\pi} = \frac{1}{4\pi}\left(\frac{c}{f}\right)^2 \tag{3}$$

where λ is the wavelength of the received electromagnetic wave, i.e. the signal; c is the speed of light.

Therefore, if an isotropic antenna is employed at the measured point to receive the electromagnetic wave, the received power is:

$$P_r(r) = \Phi(r)A_{iso} = P_t\left(\frac{c}{4\pi fr}\right)^2 \tag{4}$$

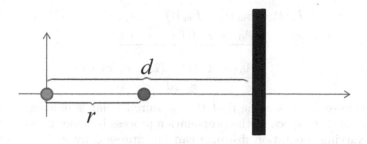

Fig. 2. Direct path and single reflected propagation model. (Color figure online)

From (4), it is clear that the power of the electromagnetic wave decreases as r^{-2}. According to (1) and the relation between the wave amplitude and the power, it is obvious that the wave amplitude decreases as r^{-1}. Therefore, we can determine the received electromagnetic field from the direct propagation path by:

$$E_{dr}(t) = A(r)\cos[2\pi f(t - r/c) + \Theta]$$
$$= \frac{A_0 \cos[2\pi f(t - r/c) + \Theta]}{r} \tag{5}$$

where A_0 is termed critical amplitude, which is the amplitude at the Fraunhofer distance r_0; r_0 is the demarcation between near field and far field regions and normally we have $r_0 \gg \lambda$ [13]. In particular, we should note that the phase shift term $-2\pi f r/c$ presented in this expression is caused by the propagation delay of the electromagnetic field.

3   Modeling Procedure and Analysis

Having constructed the fundamental models of the signal radiation and propagation at the far field region of free space, let us now look into a more complicated scenario. Assume an infinitely long, hard and non-transparent plane exists as shown in Fig. 2 and that the distance between the transmit isotropic antenna and the plane is d $(d > r)$. From the model constructed in Sect. 2, it is easy to derive the reflected wave detected at the measured point:

$$E_{rr}(t) = -\frac{A_0 \cos[2\pi f(t - (2d - r)/c) + \Theta]}{2d - r} \tag{6}$$

According to the linearity of the electromagnetic field at the far field region, the superposition of the field strengths from the direct propagation path and the reflected path can be calculated by:

$$E_r(t) = E_{dr}(t) + E_{rr}(t)$$
$$= \frac{A_0 \cos[2\pi f(t - r/c) + \Theta]}{r}$$
$$- \frac{A_0 \cos[2\pi f(t - (2d - r)/c) + \Theta]}{2d - r} \tag{7}$$

Furthermore, if we assume that the measured point is moving towards the plane at a constant speed v, the propagation process becomes time-varying and the time-varying separation distance can be expressed by $r = r_1 + vt$, where r_1 is the initial separation distance and satisfies the condition $r_1 > r_0$. As a consequence, (7) can be rewritten as:

$$E_r(t) = \frac{A_0 \cos[2\pi f(t - (r_1 + vt)/c) + \Theta]}{r_1 + vt}$$
$$- \frac{A_0 \cos[2\pi f(t - (2d - r_1 - vt)/c) + \Theta]}{2d - r_1 - vt} \tag{8}$$

From (8), because c is a constant as a basic axiom of the special theory of relativity (STR), it thereby cannot be varied by human factors [14]. Therefore, the received resultant field strength of this two-path scenario is determined by r_1, A_0, f, v, t and Θ. More generally and precisely, we might replace $E_r(t)$ by $E_r(r_1, A_0, f, v, t, \Theta)$. However, since A_0 is mainly determined by the transmitter power and only serves as a linear scaler of $E_r(r_1, A_0, f, v, t, \Theta)$, for brevity, we might suppose it to 1 (normalized). Also, because the phase angle is relative and quite arbitrary, without loss of generality, we may specify it as 0. Analogously, r_1 can also be viewed as a constant for the purpose of simplification.

These three clarified conditions result in an elucidation of the analysis and now the received resultant field strength is only associated with f, v and t. Consequently, the general form of the received resultant field strength $E_r(f, v, t)$ can be expressed by:

$$E_r(f, v, t) = \frac{\cos[2\pi f(t - (r_1 + vt)/c)]}{r_1 + vt}$$
$$- \frac{\cos[2\pi f(t - (2d - r_1 - vt)/c)]}{2d - r_1 - vt} \tag{9}$$

By variable control, it is easy to investigate into the effects of these three variables on the received resultant field strength $E_r(f, v, t)$.

4   Simulation and Discussion

To simulate the time-varying property of the mobile communication system constructed above, we first set $f = 9.6$ GHz and $v = 1$ m/s. Further assume the diameter of the transmit isotropic antenna $D = 0.5$ m. Therefore, in this case, the Fraunhofer distance can be determined by [15]:

$$r_0 = \frac{2D^2}{\lambda} = \frac{2D^2 f}{c} = 16 \text{ m} \tag{10}$$

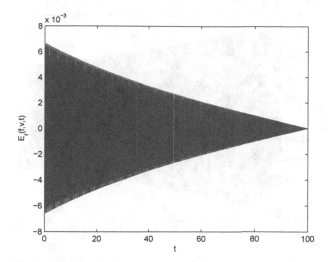

Fig. 3. Simulation of large-scale time variation, providing $f = 9.6$ GHz, $v = 1$ m/s, $r_1 = 100$ m and $d = 200$ m.

From (10), it is reasonable to set $r_1 = 100$ m and $d = 200$ m. Having done so, we can simulate the relation between the received resultant field strength $E_r(f, v, t)$ and the only variable t. The large-scale time variation results are plotted in Fig. 3. From this figure, it is clear that as the moving measured point approaches the reflection plane, these two electromagnetic waves completely cancel each other out and the received resultant field strength $E_r(f, v, t)$ equalts to $o[E_r(f, v, 0)]$. However, one might argue that the decay of the field strength is caused by the enlarged separation distance $r = r_1 + vt$ over time. This argument is correct to some extent, but it should be noted that only the counteraction of two identical electromagnetic waves caused by ideal reflection can yield $E_r(f, v, t) = o[E_r(f, v, 0)]$. To verify this conjecture, let us remove the reflection plane and re-simulate under the same conditions. The simulation results are illustrated in Fig. 4. From this figure, our conjecture has been validated, and the attenuation as r^{-1} is trivial in comparison with $o[E_r(f, v, 0)]$.

To investigate the time-varying property in more detail, we carry out a further small-scale time variation simulation and plot the results in Fig. 5. In this particular case, the impact of the separation attenuation r^{-1} on $E_r(f, v, t)$ is supposed to be negligible. In fact, the high-frequency vibration of $E_r(f, v, t)$ is caused by the displacement of the measured point over time. Once $t = \arg \left\{ \frac{\cos[2\pi f(t - (r_1 + vt)/c)]}{r_1 + vt} = \frac{\cos[2\pi f(t - (2d - r_1 - vt)/c)]}{2d - r_1 - vt} \right\}$, the direct and reflected electromagnetic waves will add destructively and cancel each other out. At this instant in time, the received field strength equals to $o[E_r(f, v, 0)]$ and the received signal is too weak to be precisely detected. Intuitively, the communication reliability will be significantly hindered. On the other hand, the direct wave and the reflected wave can also add constructively causing the received field strength to

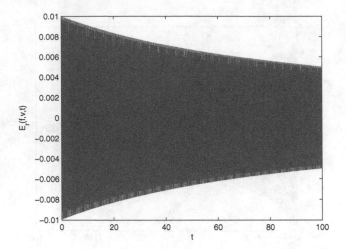

Fig. 4. Simulation of large-scale time variation, providing $f = 9.6$ GHz, $v = 1$ m/s, $r_1 = 100$ m and $d = \infty$.

reach a peak for which the received signal can then be detected with more ease. This vibration phenomenon of $E_r(f, v, t)$ reflects the nature of multipath fading and the distance from a valley to a peak is defined as the coherence distance [3]:

$$\Delta r_c = \frac{\lambda}{4} = \frac{c}{4f} \tag{11}$$

From (11), normally Δr_c is relatively small compared to the antenna coverage [3]. Hence, multipath fading is also termed small-scale fading, since the amplitude of the received signal varies tempestuously within several meters. On the contrary, the envelope attenuation as r^{-1} illustrated in Fig. 4 is termed large scale fading, since it will only become significant when the displacement of the measured point is notably larger then the coherence distance Δr_c. Similarly, we can also understand the nomenclature and classification of slow and fast fading.

Akin to the variable control strategy as we have used above, we now fix t to 0 and vary carrier frequency f within the region $[8.5, 9.6]$ GHz, The simulation results are presented in Fig. 6. As shown in this figure, the drastic fluctuation shuttling $o[E_r(f, v, t)]$ back and forth is expected, since the compensation mechanism of two waves can still be activated by the variation of carrier frequency even though the measured point remains motionless. Similarly, the frequency difference between the valley and the peak of $E_r(f, v, t)$ is fixed and termed coherence bandwidth [3]:

$$\Delta f_c = \frac{1}{2} \left(\frac{2d - r_1}{c} - \frac{r_1}{c} \right)^2 \tag{12}$$

Finally, we set f back to 9.6 GHz again and allow the speed of the measured point v to vary within $[0, 100]$. Furthermore, in order to prevent the collision

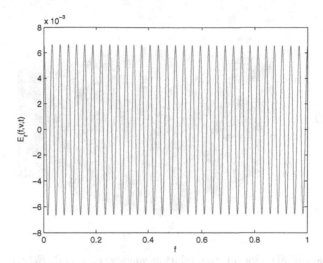

Fig. 5. Simulation of small-scale time variation, providing $f = 9.6$ GHz, $v = 1$ m/s, $r_1 = 100$ m and $d = 200$ m.

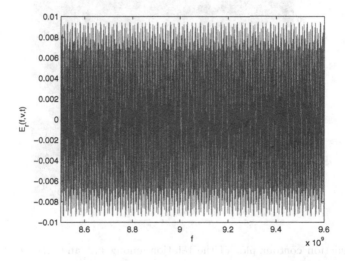

Fig. 6. Simulation of frequency variation, providing $t = 0$, $v = 1$ m/s, $r_1 = 100$ m and $d = 200$ m.

between the measured point and the reflection plane, we reset $d = 2000$. The simulation in this case is conducted and the results are illustrated by a 3D plot and a contour in Figs. 7 and 8 respectively. From these figures, several important points can be summarized. Firstly, the effects of speed v and time t are symmetrical and this can be interpreted by the equivalent coherence distance mechanism activated by the variations of v and t. In addition, the impact of the variation of v has a negligible influence on the small-scale fading but an evident

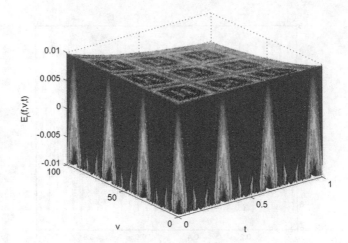

Fig. 7. Simulation 3D plot of the relation among v, t and $E_r(f,v,t)$, providing $f = 9.6$ GHz.

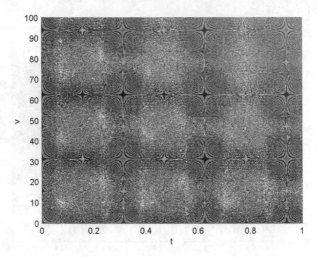

Fig. 8. Simulation contour plot of the relation among v, t and $E_r(f,v,t)$, providing $f = 9.6$ GHz.

impact on the large-scale fading. This is because the small-scale fading mainly depends on the frequency property of the resultant electromagnetic wave, while the Doppler shift (frequency deviation caused by the movement) at the low speed condition ($v \ll c$) is trivial compared to the carrier frequency f adopted in this example. The impact of the Doppler shift caused by movement at the speed v can be qualified by Doppler spread [3]:

$$D_s(f,v) = |\Delta f_{dd}(f,v) - \Delta f_{rd}(f,v)| = \frac{2fv}{c} \tag{13}$$

where $\Delta f_{dd}(f, v)$ is the Doppler shift of the direct wave and $\Delta f_{rd}(f, v)$ is the Doppler shift of the reflected wave.

In this simulation example, $D_s(f, v) \in [0, 6400]$ Hz $\ll f = 9 \times 10^9$ Hz. This result quantitatively explains the reason why Doppler shift can always be ignored in practice when analyzing small-scale fading [12].

5 Conclusion

In conclusion, we have constructed a simplified model of mobile communication systems through the application of electromagnetic theory. Although we have illustrated this model in an oversimplified case where only two-path electromagnetic waves are considered, this paper can still serve as a firm reference for more complicated scenarios. Furthermore, compared to conventional signal system models, the electromagnetic nature of signals and a series of phenomena can be explained and analyzed more extensively by this electromagnetism-based model. However, we can also notice that even for this oversimplified scenario, the electromagnetism-based model is complicated and thus might not be applicable when the ambient environment is complex.

References

1. Proakis, J., Salehi, M.: Digital Communications. McGraw-Hill Education, New York (2007)
2. Lv, Z., Feng, L., Feng, S., Li, H.: Extending touch-less interaction on vision based wearable device. In: IEEE Virtual Reality Conference, France (2015)
3. Tse, D., Viswanath, P.: Fundamentals of Wireless Communication. Cambridge University Press, New York (2005)
4. Ma, Z.X., Zhang, M., Shaham, S., Dang, S.P., Hart, J.: Literature review of the communication technology and signal processing methodology based on the smart grid. Appl. Mech. Mater. **719**, 436–442 (2015)
5. Guo, P., Bai, Y., Ma, Z., Wu, S., Dang, S.: Relay technology for multi-carrier systems: A research overview. In: 2015 Third International Conference on Computer, Communication, Control and Information Technology (C3IT), pp. 1–5. IEEE (2015)
6. Dang, S., Coon, J.P., Simmons, D.: Combined bulk and Per-Tone relay selection in super dense wireless networks. In: IEEE ICC 2015, London, United Kingdom (2015)
7. Ma, Z., Gholamzadeh, A., Tang, B., Dang, S., Yang, S.: Matlab based simulation of the efficiency of the complex OFDM on power line communication technology. In: 2014 Fourth International Conference on Instrumentation and Measurement, Computer, Communication and Control (IMCCC), pp. 374–378. IEEE (2014)
8. Johler, J.: Propagation of the low-frequency radio signal. Proc. IRE **50**, 404–427 (1962)
9. Hashemi, H.: The indoor radio propagation channel. Proc. IEEE **81**, 943–968 (1993)
10. Sobot, R.: Wireless Communication Electronics: Introduction to RF Circuits and Design Techniques. Springer, New York (2012)

11. Clemmow, P.: An Introduction to Electromagnetic Theory. Cambridge University Press, Cambridge (1973)
12. Rappaport, T.: Wireless Communications: Principles and Practice, 2nd edn. Prentice Hall PTR, Upper Saddle River (2001)
13. Balanis, C.: Antenna Theory: Analysis and Design. Wiley, New York (2012)
14. Banerjee, B., Banerjee, A.: The Special Theory of Relativity. Prentice Hall India Pvt., Limited, Upper Saddle River (2004)
15. Cheng, D.: On the simulation of Fraunhofer radiation patterns in the Fresnel region. IRE Trans. Antennas Propag. **5**, 399–402 (1957)

Bayesian Reliability Assessment Method for Single NC Machine Tool Under Zero Failures

Hongzhou Li[1,2], Fei Chen[1(✉)], Zhaojun Yang[1], Yingnan Kan[1], and Liding Wang[1]

[1] College of Mechanical Science and Engineering, Jilin University, Changchun 130025, China
{287505156,2358584773,306219157}@qq.com,
{jluchenfei,yinshun_9999}@163.com
[2] College of Mechanical Engineering, Beihua University, Jilin 132011, China

Abstract. Reliability modeling and assessment for a single numerical control (NC) machine tool with zero-failure is a new problem that cannot be solved using classic statistical methods. Thus a Bayesian method is proposed aiming at this problem. In combination with the two-parameter Weibull distribution, the Bayes model of zero-failure problem for a single NC machine tool is built. The method of building the Weibull parameters' prior distributions is presented. The theoretical formula for the parameter vector's posterior distribution is derived. In software WinBUGS, the Markov chain Monte Carlo (MCMC) simulation is developed to simulate each parameter's posterior distribution, solving calculation difficulties in high-dimensional integration and parameter estimation. The proposed method is applied to real data, obtaining the parameter estimators and meant time between failures (MTBF). The result is in consistent with the engineering reality. Given the fact that the actual MTBF cannot be achieved by any means, the proposed method achieves the fusion of the expert experience, multi-source prior information and data. The proposed method is advocated to be a standard solution to the zero-failure reliability assessment for NC machine tools.

Keywords: Reliability · Zero failures · NC machine tools · WinBUGS

1 Introduction

1.1 Zero-Failure Problem for a Single Machine Tool

Traditionally, a reliability test on NC machine tools relies on many machines and a long time to collect sufficient data required by classic statistical methods. For, example, Keller et al. [1], collected field data on 35 NC machine tools over three years, and Yang et al. [2], collected field data on 12 NC machine tools over five years. Nowadays, some high-end NC machine tools are of high cost and few copies. Thus the reliability test on a single machine tool has come to reality, and sometimes, zero failures occur. The zero-failure result is an event that the time between failures (TBF) is larger than the

© Springer-Verlag Berlin Heidelberg 2015
W. Niu et al. (Eds.): ATIS 2015, CCIS 557, pp. 291–302, 2015.
DOI: 10.1007/978-3-662-48683-2_26

total test time. This event is equivalent to a censored datum. Under zero-failure case, the reliability modeling and assessment is named the zero-failure problem, and classic statistical methods cannot solve this problem since they require sufficient failure data. To solve this new problem, literatures on other products' zero-failure cases are firstly reviewed, and then the solution to the zero-failure problem of single machine tool is developed.

1.2   Zero-Failure Cases of Other Products

In reliability demonstration tests, the zero-failure cases are common. Martz and Waller [3] presented a Bayesian reliability demonstration testing plan, which expects zero failures to demonstrate the pre-specified reliability target and determine the test time and the number of products to be tested, and the failure time of the tested products is assumed to follow an exponential distribution. To demonstrate a level of reliability of a technical system under zero failures, such as an alarm system, Coolen et al. [4] analyzed optimal test numbers for a type of task using Bayesian method, and tasks arrive as a Poisson process. Fan et al. [5] employed an accelerated experiment on electro-explosive devices of which the lifetime follows an exponential distribution, and the minimum sample size and testing length were designed under the assumption that zero failures occur. Obviously, in reliability demonstration test, the zero-failure is expected by researchers.

However, in reliability modeling and assessment, a zero-failure result is not expected by people, since it causes difficulties in reliability modeling and assessment. Some scholars have proposed methods to implement reliability modeling and assessment under zero failures. For example, Miller et al. [6] estimated the failure probability of software products under zero failures using Bayesian theory. Guo et al. [7] designed a Bayesian method to estimate the reliability of one-shot systems such as missiles and rockets when there are few or no failures. Aiming at zero-failure data, Mao et al. [8] estimated the reliability of engines, of which the failure time follows a Weibull distribution, and the method is based on Bayesian theory and expert experience.

After reviewing literatures, it is found that nearly all the above methods dealing with zero-failure problems fall into the framework of Bayes statistics. So far, no reports have been found aiming at the zero-failure problem of a single NC machine tool. Therefore, a Bayesian reliability modeling and assessment method is proposed aiming at the zero-failure result for a single NC machine tool.

1.3   Bayesian Method of the Zero-Failure Problem

In Sect. 2, the two-parameter Weibull distribution is firstly used to model the Bayesian zero-failure problem for a single machine tool. In Sect. 3, the method of obtaining the Weibull parameters' prior distributions is proposed; Sect. 4 derives the formula of calculating parameter vector's posterior distribution and parameters' estimators. Section 5 applies the proposed method to real zero-failure data and develops an MCMC algorithm in software WinBUGS, obtaining the MTBF of the tested product.

2 Bayesian Model of Zero-Failure Problem for Single NC Machine Tools

In machine tools industry, the two-parameter Weibull distribution is usually adopted to describe the time between failures (TBF) by many scholars, such as Keller [1] and Jia [9]. In this study, random variable T denotes the TBF of a single machine tool; t denotes an observation of T. The cumulative distribution function (CDF) and reliability function of the two-parameter Weibull distribution are given as follows.

$$F(t|\alpha, \beta) = F(t|\theta) = 1 - \exp\left[-\left(\frac{t}{\alpha}\right)^{\beta}\right], t > 0 \tag{1}$$

$$R(t|\alpha, \beta) = R(t|\theta) = \exp\left[-\left(\frac{t}{\alpha}\right)^{\beta}\right] \tag{2}$$

Where $\alpha > 0$ and $\beta > 0$ are the scale and shape parameters, respectively. The parameter vector is denoted by $\theta = (\alpha, \beta)$.

The prior distributions of the Weibull parameters are denoted by two probability density functions (PDF): $\pi(\alpha)$ and $\pi(\beta)$, respectively; the prior distribution of the parameter vector is denoted by $\pi(\theta)$. The two parameters are assumed to be mutually independent and thus $\pi(\theta)$ is obtained as follows:

$$\pi(\theta) = \pi(\alpha, \beta) = \pi(\alpha) \times \pi(\beta) \tag{3}$$

Suppose the total test time on a single NC machine tool is t_c (c for censored), and zero failures occur after the test. This event is denoted as: $T > t_c$, which is a censored datum. The likelihood function of data given parameter vector is given by Eq. (4).

$$\Pr(T > t_c|\theta) = R(t_c|\theta) = \exp\left[-\left(\frac{t_c}{\alpha}\right)^{\beta}\right] \tag{4}$$

The marginal probability distribution of data is given by Eq. (5)

$$\Pr(T > t_c) = \int \pi(\theta) \Pr(T > t_c|\theta) d\theta \tag{5}$$

Let $\pi(\theta|T > t_c)$ denote the posterior distribution of the parameter vector, which is obtained by the Bayes theorem given by Eq. (6).

$$\pi(\theta|T > t_c) = \frac{\pi(\theta) \Pr(T > t_c|\theta)}{\Pr(T > t_c)} \tag{6}$$

A detailed theoretical formula for the posterior distribution can be obtained by substituting Eqs. (3)–(5) into (6).

$$\pi(\boldsymbol{\theta}|T > t_c) = \pi(\alpha, \beta|T > t_c) = \frac{\pi(\boldsymbol{\theta})R(t_c|\boldsymbol{\theta})}{R(t_c)}$$

$$= \frac{\pi(\alpha)\pi(\beta)\exp\left[-\left(\frac{t_c}{\alpha}\right)^{\beta}\right]}{\int \pi(\alpha)\pi(\beta)\exp\left[-\left(\frac{t_c}{\alpha}\right)^{\beta}\right]d\alpha d\beta} \tag{7}$$

The posterior distributions of α and β are denoted by $\pi(\alpha|T > t_c)$ and $\pi(\beta|T > t_c)$, which are obtained from Eq. (7). The posterior means are usually adopted as the Bayesian parameter estimators. When the two parameters are both random variables, the double integral in (7) has no closed form, which is called the high-dimensional integration according to the study of Soland [10]. Thus, to get the estimators analytically based on formula (7) is impossible, and some numerical method is needed to calculate the estimators. Therefore, a Markov chain Monte Carlo algorithm is developed in software WinBUGS to simulate the parameters' posterior distributions, calculate the parameter estimators and estimate MTBF.

3   Building Weibull Parameters' Prior Distributions

In Bayesian methods, parameters are treated as random variables which have prior distributions. Parameters' prior distributions are generally obtained by historical data, engineering experience and expert judgment [11]. However, experts with abundant engineering experience in machine tools industry are generally not familiar with probability or reliability knowledge. To ask experts to directly give the prior distributions of the Weibull parameters is not feasible. Hence, to assist the experts, an indirect method of building the Weibull parameters' prior distributions are as follows.

The type of NC machine tool to be tested is denoted by A. The expert panel should identify two similar types of NC machine tools, $A-$ and $A+$, with large samples of history data. If RL denotes reliability level of a product, then the following relations should be satisfied, that is, $RL(A-) < RL(A) < RL(A+)$. Considering the multi-source prior information such as machine's type, structure, functions, cost, and manufacturer's technology level, the expert panel is responsible to identify $A-$ and $A+$ satisfying the above requirements qualitatively based on their expertise.

Based on the large sample of history data, the Weibull parameter estimators for $A-$ can be obtained by classic method such as least squares estimation (LSE) and denoted by α_{A-} and β_{A-}. Similarly, the Weibull parameter estimators for $A+$ can be obtained and denoted by α_{A+}, β_{A+}. Let $\alpha_L = \min(\alpha_{A+}, \alpha_{A-})$ and $\alpha_U = \max(\alpha_{A+}, \alpha_{A-})$, then the prior distribution interval for the Weibull scale parameter α for A is (α_L, α_U). Let $\beta_L = \min(\beta_{A-}, \beta_{A+})$ and $\beta_U = \min(\beta_{A-}, \beta_{A+})$ then the prior distribution interval for the Weibull shape parameter β for A is (β_L, β_U).

The two parameters are assumed to be uniformly, independently distributed on their own ranges of value, respectively. Thus the prior distributions are given by PDFs as follows:

$$\pi(\alpha) = \frac{1}{\alpha_U - \alpha_L}, \alpha_L < \alpha < \alpha_U \tag{8}$$

$$\pi(\beta) = \frac{1}{\beta_L - \beta_U}, \beta_L < \beta < \beta_U \tag{9}$$

4 Posterior Distribution and Parameter Estimation

Based on discussion in Sect. 2, there are no analytic solutions to the posterior distributions. Since the double integral in Eq. (7) is a constant which represents the unconditional probability of the event $T > t_c$, Eq. (7) is rewritten in a proportionality form. See Eq. (10).

$$\pi(\theta|T > t_c) \propto \pi(\alpha)\pi(\beta) \exp\left[-\left(\frac{t_c}{\alpha}\right)^\beta\right] \tag{10}$$

Given Eq. (10), the high-dimensional integration can be avoided and an MCMC algorithm can be developed. The developed MCMC algorithm can generate a large number of random values of parameters denoted as $\{\alpha_i, \beta_i\}$, $i = 1, 2, \ldots, N$. Two Markov chains are formed which are denoted as $\{\alpha_i\}$ and $\{\beta_i\}$, $i = 1, 2, \ldots, N$. If the first B values of $\{\alpha_i\}$ and $\{\beta_i\}$ are discarded as the burn-in period, the remaining values $\{\alpha_{B+1}, \alpha_{B+2}, \cdots, \alpha_N\}$ and $\{\beta_{B+1}, \beta_{B+2}, \cdots, \beta_N\}$ are assumed to be generated from the posterior distributions $\pi(\alpha|t)$ and $\pi(\beta|t)$, and this is how the MCMC algorithm simulate the posterior distributions [11].

MCMC algorithm or simulation is a name of a family of specific algorithms. The famous MCMC algorithms include the Metropolis algorithm, Metropolis-Hastings algorithm, Gibbs sampling [11] and Slice sampling [12]. The free software product WinBUGS can develop and run various algorithms. The MCMC algorithm for the zero-failure problem in this study is developed in WinBUGS.

The arithmetic averages of values of two sets $ALPHA = \{\alpha_{B+1}, \alpha_{B+2}, \cdots, \alpha_N\}$ and $BETA = \{\beta_{B+1}, \beta_{B+2}, \cdots, \beta_N\}$ are usually adopted as the point estimator of the parameters.

$$\hat{\alpha} = \frac{1}{N-B} \sum_{i=B+1}^{N} \alpha_i \tag{11}$$

$$\hat{\beta} = \frac{1}{N-B} \sum_{i=B+1}^{N} \beta_i \tag{12}$$

The elements of the two sets are sorted in an ascending order respectively, to obtain $ALPHA^* = \{\alpha(1), \alpha(2), \ldots, \alpha(N-B)\}$ and $BETA^* = \{\beta(1), \beta(2), \cdots, \beta(N-B)\}$. Let $m1 = \lfloor 0.025 \times (N-B) \rfloor$ and $m2 = \lfloor 0.975 \times (N-B) \rfloor$; thus $[\alpha(m1), \alpha(m2)]$ and

[$\beta(m1)$, $\beta(m2)$] are the 95 % credible intervals for α and β, respectively. WinBUGS calculates these statistics automatically after running algorithms.

Based on the theoretical formula of the expectation of the two-parameter Weibull distribution, the MTBF is given by Eq. (13).

$$MTBF = \hat{\alpha} \times \Gamma\left(1 + 1\big/\hat{\beta}\right) \tag{13}$$

5 Case Study

5.1 Zero-Failure Data

A reliability test was implemented on a single NC machine tool. Zero failures were observed. The type of this machine is denoted by A. the total test time is 415 h. See Table 1.

Table 1. The zero-failure data of test on a single machine tool

Index	Type	Number of machines	Test time (h)	Number of failures
1	A	1	415	0

5.2 Building Prior Distributions

Two types of NC machine tools $A-$ and $A+$ were identified by the expert panel according to the multi-source prior information on structure, type, functions, cost and the technology levels of manufacturers. $A-$ and $A+$ have large samples of history data, and based on LSE [13], the Weibull parameters for these two types are $\alpha_{A-} = 803.15$, $\beta_{A-} = 0.9377$, $\alpha_{A+} = 1298.33$, $\beta_{A+} = 1.5554$. Thus the prior distributions are $\pi(\alpha) = 1/1$ $(1298.33 - 803.15)$, $\alpha \in (803.15, 1298.33)$, $\pi(\beta) = 1/1(1.5554 - 0.9377)$, $\beta \in (0.9377, 1.5554)$.

5.3 BUGS Model for the Zero-Failure Problem

Substituting $t_c = 415$ (h), $\pi(\alpha)$ and $\pi(\beta)$ into Eq. (10) obtains the basis for developing an BUGS model in WinBUGS, and WinBUGS develops a suitable MCMC algorithm according to the BUGS model. A BUGS model consists of 3 parts: (1) describing prior distributions; (2) describing the likelihood function; and (3) describing the data.

Firstly, the prior distributions of α and β is described using BUGS language as follows

```
alpha~dunif(803.15, 1298.33)
beta ~ dunif(0.9377, 1.5554)
```

Where alpha and beta denote α and β, respectively; and "dunif" represents the uniform distribution.

Secondly, the likelihood function given by reliability function $R(t_c|\theta)$ in Eq. (4) needs to be described. In WinBUGS, any likelihood function is treated as a probability distribution function, but the reliability function given by (4) is a non-standard distribution function. Non-standard distributions are common in Bayesian methods and programming skills are needed to represent them. The "zeros-trick" is utilized to describe the likelihood function. That is, Poisson distribution is utilized to represent R $(t_c|\theta)$ equivalently. The principle of "zeros-trick" is introduced in literature [14], and the BUGS code for the case in this study is given as follows:

```
L <- exp(-pow(tc/alpha,beta))
lambda<- -log(L)
z <- 0
z ~ dpois(lambda)
```

Where "L" denotes the likelihood function; "dpois" denotes the Poisson distribution; "lambda" is the parameter of the Poisson distribution; and "z" is a random variable following Poisson distribution.

Thirdly, since tc = 415 h, the data is described as follows

```
list(tc = 415)
```

The complete BUGS model is obtained by (1) creating a new blank document in WinBUGS; (2) typing the above three parts of BUGS code in the document; (3) enclosing the code of prior distributions and liklihood with a pair of curly braces; and (4) adding a keyword "model" at the front. The BUGS model for the zero-failure Bayesian problem is as follow.

```
model;
{
    alpha ~ dunif(803.15,1298.33) #Prior distribution
    beta ~ dunif( 0.9377, 1.5554) #Prior distribution
            z<- 0                 #Likelihood
                z ~ dpois(lambda)     #Likelihood

            lambda <- -log(L)      #Likelihood
            L <- exp(-pow((tc)/alpha,beta))   #Likelihood
}
list(tc=415)
```

After checking model, loading data, compiling code, generating initial values, setting nodes (monitoring alpha and beta) and specifying length of Markov chain (N = 10,000 in this application), WinBUGS is ready to select a suitable MCMC algorithm and run it. Clicking on "update" starts the simulation. See Fig. 1.

The dymanic trace of iterations in the simulation process are shown in Figs. 2 and 3. The complete trace of iterations of the MCMC simulation is shown in Figs. 4 and 5.

The various posterior statistics are obtained by specifying the burn-in period B = 2000 and using the remaining 8000 generated values. See Fig. 6 and Table 2.

Based on Table 2, the posterior statistics are listed in Table 3.

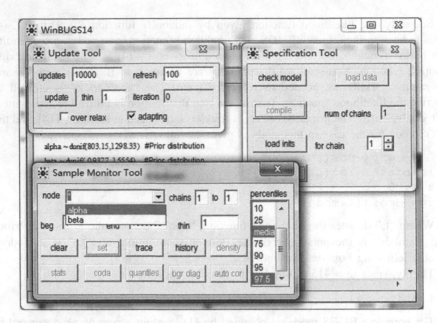

Fig. 1. The settings of WinBUGS given BUGS model

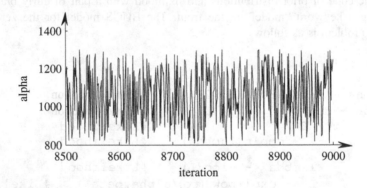

Fig. 2. Dynamic trace of iterations of MCMC simulation for α

The approximated posterior PDF curves for alpha and beta after simulation are displayed in Figs. 7 and 8.

Based on the simulation result, the posterior means are adopted as the parameter estimators, where $\hat{\alpha} = 1058.0$ and $\hat{\beta} = 1.257$. Substituting the corresponding values into Eq. (13) obtains the MTBF = 984.1609 h for the single NC machine tool A.

According to the parameters for $A-$ and $A+$, the MTBFs are 827.1905 (h) and 1167.3 (h) repectively. It is concluded that MTBF(A$-$) < MTBF(A) < MTBF (A+). This conclusion is consistent with the expert judgment.

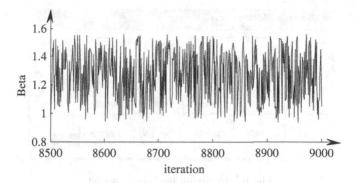

Fig. 3. Dynamic trace of iterations of MCMC simulation for β

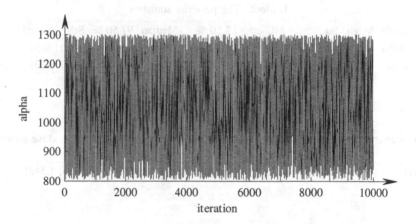

Fig. 4. Complete trace of iterations of the MCMC simulation for α

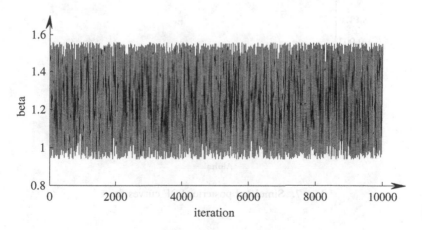

Fig. 5. Complete trace of iterations of the MCMC simulation for β

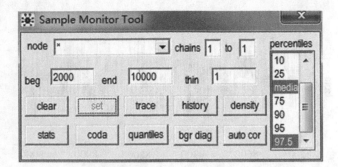

Fig. 6. Specifying the burn-in period

Table 2. The posterior statistics

Node	Mean	Sd	MC error	2.50 %	Median	97.50 %	Start	Sample
alpha	1058	143.3	1.645	817.5	1061	1288	2000	8001
beta	1.257	0.1801	0.001935	0.9563	1.263	1.542	2000	8001

Table 3. Posterior statistics after the MCMC simulation

Point estimator of α	Point estimator of β	95 % credible interval of α	90 % credible interval of β
1058.0	1.257	[817.5, 1288.0]	[0.9563, 1.542]

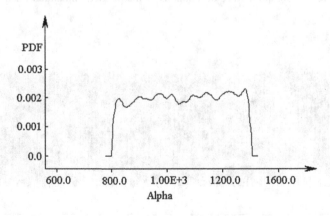

Fig. 7. Simulated posterior PDF curves for α

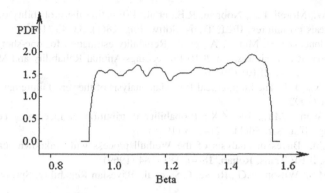

Fig. 8. Simulated posterior PDF curves for β

6 Conclusion

(1) Compared with the expert judgment which only gives the qualitative conclusions, the proposed method achieves the combination of the subjective experience and the data and gives the quantitative results.
(2) Given the zero-failure case, the actual value of MTBF cannot be obtained by any means, and the MTBF estimated by the proposed method cannot be compared with the actual MTBF mathematically.
(3) However, since the proposed method utilizes the multi-source prior information in combination with the data, the results of the proposed method is believed to reflect the engineering realities and the expert experience accurately. The proposed method can serve as a new method of reliability assessment for a single NC machine tool under zero-failure case currently.

Acknowledgments. The work is supported by The Science and Technology Development Program of Jilin Province(20130302009GX) and Project of Priority Funding for Basic Scientific Research Business of Jilin University(450060521026).

References

1. Keller, A.Z., Kamath, A.R.R., Perera, U.D.: Reliability analysis of CNC machine tools. Reliab. Eng. **3**(6), 449–473 (1982)
2. Yang, Z.J., Chen, C.H., Chen, F., et al.: Reliability analysis of machining center based on the field data. Eksploatacja i Niezawodność **15**(2), 147–155 (2013)
3. Martz, H.F., Waller, R.A.: A Bayesian zero-failure reliability demonstration testing procedure. J. Qual. Technol. **11**, 128–138 (1979)
4. Coolen, F.P.A., Coolen-Schrijner, P., Rahrouh, M.: Bayesian reliability demonstration for failure-free periods. Reliab. Eng. Syst. Saf. **88**(1), 81–91 (2005)
5. Fan, T.H., Chang, C.C.: A Bayesian Zero-failure reliability demonstration test of high quality electro-explosive devices. Qual. Reliab. Eng. Int. **25**(8), 913–920 (2009)

6. Miller, K.W., Morell, L.J., Noonan, R.E., et al.: Estimating the probability of failure when testing reveals no failures. IEEE Trans. Softw. Eng. **18**(1), 33–43 (1992)
7. Guo, H., Honecker, S., Mettas, A., et al.: Reliability estimation for one-shot systems with zero component test failures. In: 2010 Proceedings-Annual Reliability and Maintainability Symposium, pp. 1–7. IEEE (2010)
8. Mao, S.S., Xia, J.F.: The hierarchical Bayesian analysis of the zero-failure data. Appl. Math. **7**, 411–421 (1992)
9. Jia, Y.Z., Wang, M.L., Jia, Z.X.: Probability distribution of machining center failures. Reliab. Eng. Syst. Saf. **50**(1), 121–125 (1995)
10. Soland, R.M.: Bayesian analysis of the Weibull process with unknown scale and shape parameters. IEEE Trans. Reliab. **18**(4), 181–184 (1969)
11. Hamada, M.S., Wilson, A.G., Reese, C.S., et al.: Bayesian Reliability. Springer, New York (2008)
12. Neal, R.M.: Slice sampling. Ann. Stat. **31**(3), 705–767 (2003)
13. Zhang, L.F., Xie, M., Tang, L.C.: A study of two estimation approaches for parameters of Weibull distribution based on WPP. Reliab. Eng. Syst. Saf. **92**(3), 360–368 (2007)
14. Lunn, D., Jackson, C., Best, N., et al.: The BUGS Book: A Practical Introduction to Bayesian Analysis. CRC Press, Boca Raton (2012)

MIRD: Trigram-Based Malicious URL Detection Implanted with Random Domain Name Recognition

Cuiwen Xiong[1,3], Pengxiao Li[4], Peng Zhang[1,2(✉)], Qingyun Liu[1,2], and Jianlong Tan[1,2]

[1] Institute of Information Engineering,
Chinese Academy of Sciences, Beijing, China
{xiongcuiwen,pengzhang,liuqingyun,
tanjianlong}@iie.ac.cn
[2] National Engineering Laboratory for Information
Security Technologies, Beijing, China
[3] University of Chinese Academy of Sciences, Beijing, China
[4] National Computer Network Emergency Response Technical Team,
Beijing, China
lpx@cert.org.cn

Abstract. This paper proposed an approach of malicious URL detection using trigrams-based common pattern of URL, which implanted with random domain recognition, named MIRD. In MIRD the common patterns were composed of three segments common patterns of URL, namely domain segment, path name segment and file name segment. An inverted index based on trigrams was used to improve common pattern extraction of each segment. MIRD used the common patterns based on inverted index to match with the detected URL. Moreover, MIRD implanted with Random Domain Name Recognition Module, named RDM. The RDM identified the length of the domain name and resolved the domain name in iteration to recognize the domain name unresolved, reducing the cumulative error rate of malicious URL detection. Extensive experiments showed that the MIRD is efficient and scalable.

Keywords: Malicious URL detection · Common pattern · Trigram · Inverted index · Radom domain name

1 Introduction

With the development of internet technology, the means of cybercrime is varying, and the form of network threat which promotes cybercrime also becomes more diversity. As a result, the new technology of network threat detecting need to be proposed to cope with the change. The report of Ponemon Institute showed that the occurrence of cyber-attacks on the enterprises or organizations was about 122 every week in 2013 and the financial loss has increased by nearly 78 % in 2013 than the past four years and the State cost more than one million on average to fix up with cyber-attacks [1]. The cybercrime group improved their technology to attack the strengthened intrusion

© Springer-Verlag Berlin Heidelberg 2015
W. Niu et al. (Eds.): ATIS 2015, CCIS 557, pp. 303–314, 2015.
DOI: 10.1007/978-3-662-48683-2_27

prevention system (IPS), so proposing an efficient technology to detect network threat is necessary. A key feature of network threat is using other protocols and components to access internet while all of the protocols and components use HTTP or HTTPS protocol to transport their pages [2], which makes detecting network threats based on URLs feasible. The research of Le et al. also supported detecting network threats based on URLs is feasible [3]. Otherwise, the attackers hide themselves by some means. For example, Porras et al. randomly generated range from 250 to 50,000 domains using current time and date as seeds [4, 5]. It is more difficult to detect the malicious URLs with random domain. On the other hand, the similarities between malicious URLs and benign URLs mislead users. Users may stray the malicious web site with "login" changed to "log1n" or "index" changed to "1ndex" leading to leak personal information. To prevent privacy disclosure, the malicious URLs must be detected when users click them. A qualified malicious URL detection should meet the followings.

1. Effectiveness, an approach must detect malicious URLs as accurate as possible. The amount of malicious URLs is far less than the benign URLs on the internet. Some malicious URLs are different with benign URLs only in some letter. The two things make it difficult to detect malicious URL accurately.
2. Efficiency, an approach must detect malicious URLs as soon as possible. If a client clicked one URL, the browser sends a request to the server and the server responses the content the client wants. The approach must alert the user that the URL is malicious before the corresponding server responses.
3. Scalability, an approach must detect new malicious URLs as many as possible. The attackers use Domain Generation Algorithm to generate numerous URLs such that avoid be detected. The approach should detect new and uncommon malicious URL.

The paper proposed an approach of trigrams-based malicious URL detection implanted with random domain name recognition, MIRD. MIRD is only based on lexical feature of URL, saving time on extracting extra features, such as WHOIS and geographical location information of each URL. MIRD extracted common patterns of URLs. According to the URL Reference [6], one URL consists of alphanumeric and specific characters such as "?", "=", "-", "_". MIRD created dynamical inverted index with the trigrams of URLs as terms to quickly search URLs which the common pattern can extract from. The inverted index was conducive to avoid the length of common pattern too short. MIRD detected the URL matching up with the malicious common patterns as malicious one. MIRD implanted with random domain name recognition to recognize the random domain name, improving the accuracy of the approach. The paper is organized as follows: Sect. 2 introduces some related works and the contributions. Section 3 introduces the principle of MIRD in details. Section 4 illustrates experiments and analysis. Section 5 makes a conclusion of the research.

2   Related Works

The malicious URL detection can be divided into three categories according to the object been detected, namely the blacklist based approaches, the content based approaches and the URL based approaches.

The blacklist based approaches are simple and accurate in maintaining blacklist, such as Google Safe Browser [7], Netcraft Tool Bar and eBay Tool Bar. Zhang et al. introduced the principle of blacklist in [8]. If the detected URL exists in blacklist, the URL is malicious. That makes it suitable for existed network threats but impossible to detect the new malicious URL.

The content based approaches extract features from the web page. Provos et al. [9], Liu et al. [10] judged the JavaScript exists and whether iFrames is out of range or not to detect malicious URL. Zhang et al. analyzed the TF-IDF of every term in page and then used lexical labels to detect that the website is malicious or not [11]. The approach is appropriate for offline analyze for analyzing content of page inducing significant delay not suit for the high-speed online detection.

The URL based approaches classify URL based on features such as the length of URL and geolocation of URL etc. Garera et al. analyzed the structure of URL of phishing, chose 18 features, classified URL using Logistic regression filter [12]. Ma et al. analyzed lexical feature and host property of suspicious URL, obtained thousands of features using bag of words and proposed the classical algorithm CW [13–15]. These proposed approaches are delay for obtaining features from remote host and cannot process the malicious URL with random domain name.

The MIRD is based on URL, only considers the lexical feature of URL, uses common pattern extracted from URL as lexical feature matching up with detected URL and determines whether the detected URL is malicious or not. The MIRD has the following two contributions. On one hand, using dynamical inverted index accelerates the process and avoids redundancy computation searching common patterns which may match with the detected URL. On the other hand, introducing the random domain name recognition improves the accurate of detection detecting malicious URL with random domain name which cannot be resolved.

3 The Principle of MIRD

3.1 Concepts and Definitions

This section introduces the concepts involved in MIRD. According to the URL Reference [6], URL contains three irrelevant segments with different meanings—domain name, path name, file name. MIRD takes the three segments separately into consideration when computing common patterns. MIRD defines a normal characters set containing the alphanumeric and specific characters such as "?", " = ", "-", "_", "&", and the elements of the normal set is regarded as normal characters except the "/" as segments connector or delimiter of path name and "." as delimiter of domain name and file name. The all three segments are constituted by the characters from the normal set, so MIRD extract separately common patterns of the three segments with same rule. The common pattern of domain name, path name and file name was denoted by s_d, s_p, s_f separately.

Definition 1 (Segment common pattern). A segment common pattern is a string constituted by normal characters, denoted by $s = c_1 \cdots c_1$, where 1 is the length of segment common pattern, and c_i is a normal character or wildcard meta-symbol "*", which can match with a string of random length of normal characters except the special character "/" or ".". For any $i(1 \leq i < l)$, if $c_i = $ "*", $c_i \neq$ "*".

Rule 1 (Segment matching up with segment common pattern). For a segment common pattern $s = c_1 \cdots c_l$ and segment $u = c'_1 \cdots c'_m$, if there is a function $f : [1, m] \to [1, l]$ such that: 1, $1 \leq m, 2$, for any $j(1 \leq j < m)$, $f(j) \leq f(j+1), 3$, for any $i(1 \leq i < l)$, if c_i $_{+1} \neq$ "*", there are only one $j(1 \leq j < m)$, such that $f(j) = i$ and $c'_j = c_i$. The segment u matches up with the common pattern s.

Just as URL common pattern is based on the three segment common patterns, URL matching up with URL common pattern is based on the three segment common patterns.

Definition 2 (URL common pattern). URL common pattern, shorted as common pattern, is consisted of the three segment patterns with the same URL ID, denoted by $p = s_d/s_p/s_f$.

Rule 2 (URL matching up with common pattern). If the three segments of URL match up with the corresponding segment of common pattern respectively, MIRD considers the URL matching up with the common pattern.

3.2 The Procedure of MIRD

The URL data set used by the paper was crawled at specific time by the open source software Larbin [16] from the specified website. The whole procedure of MIRD from obtaining data set to detecting malicious URL is showed in Fig. 1. The MIRD consists of three modules—Data Set Preprocessing, Common Pattern Extraction and URL Determination, implanted with Random Domain Name Recognition. The Data Set Preprocessing segregates URL into three segments—domain name, path name and file name. The Common Pattern Extraction splits segment into trigrams, creates inverted index of segments, extracts common pattern of each segments and connects common patterns to obtain URL common pattern. The URL Determination matches detected URL with common pattern to determinate the URL is malicious or not. Finally, the Random Domain Name Recognition improves the accuracy of detection.

After MIRD obtained URL data set, MIRD invokes the Data Set Preprocessing to segregate the URL into three segments. Then, the Common Pattern Extraction processes each segment in the same step. Taking domain name for example, the Common Pattern Extraction splits domain into trigrams, creates dynamically inverted index with trigrams as term. The reason of choosing trigram as term is that the probabilities of two arbitrary URL shared same bigram and 4-gram are 95.7 % and 33.6 %, while shared same trigram is 75.8 % [17]. To avoid the common pattern too short or computed too frequently, common pattern can be extracted from two segments shared at least one trigram. The Common Pattern Extraction extracts domain segment common pattern based on the domain inverted index, and domain segment common pattern meets the Definition 1 described in Sect. 3.1. The Common Pattern Extraction extracts the common patterns of path name and file name in the same step, then connects segment common patterns sharing same URLIDs to generate common pattern. Finally, the URL

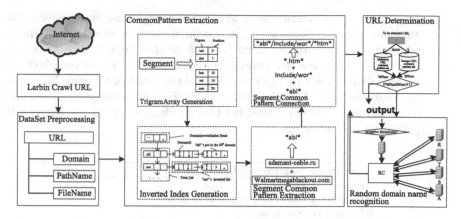

Fig. 1. The principle of the MIRD.

Determination matches the detected URL up with common pattern using the rule 1 and 2, then determines the detected URL and outputs the result. The Random Domain Name Recognition further detects the malicious URL containing with random domain name which cannot be detected by the above step, introduced in detail in Sect. 3.3. The following introduces the three modules in detail.

1. Data Set Preprocessing

   The MIRD invokes open source software Larbin [16] at specific time to crawl URLs from specified website to obtain two kinds of data set with malicious URLs and benign URLs, then process two kinds of data set separately. Considering all processed URLs using http or https protocol, the module delete the "protocol://" from the URL strings. Then, the module segregates the URL into domain name, path name and file name. For example, URL_0 "walmartmegablackout.com/include/wordpress/login.htm" is segregated into $Domain_0$ "walmartmegablackout.com", $Path_0$ "include/wordpress" and $FileName_0$ "login.htm". URL_1 "adamant-cable.ru/include/world/index.html" is segregated into $Domain_1$ "adamant-cable.ru", $Path_1$ "include/world" and $FileName_1$ "index.html". After processed by this module, MIRD gets two kinds of segment sets, one from malicious URL set and another from benign URL set. Malicious segment sets contain domain set MDomain, path set MPath and file name set MFile. Benign segment sets contain domain set BDomain, path set BPath and file name set BFile.

2. Common Pattern Extraction

   The Common Pattern Extraction of MIRD contains the following four steps:

   (1) **Trigram Array Generation:** The Common Pattern Extraction module processes the segment set one by one in the same way, taking domain segment for example. To avoid the common pattern too short and extracted too frequently, this module splits domain segment into trigrams, then creates dynamically inverted index with trigrams as term. This module splits domain into several trigrams using Algorithm 1, where Count is used to store the number of trigrams and its value is not greater than the length of domain minus 2, the

TrigramArray is a structure array to store the trigrams and their position. The algorithm uses the character "." as a delimiter split domain into substrings, which ensures each trigram come from one level of domain, then splits each substring into trigrams and saves into trigram array. The time complexity of the algorithm is linear for just traversing one segment twice. Figure 2(a) shows the TrigramArray of $Domain_0$. This module splits file name segment and path name segment in the same way, but uses the character "/" as a delimiter split path name into substrings.

Algorithm 1. SplitDomainIntoTrigrams

```
01: Input: Domain, Count
02: Output: an array of trigrams of Domain
03: initial TrigramArray← ø
04: CurrentPos = 0
05: Split Domain into SubStrings
06:   while SubString != ø
07:     if strlen(SubString) ≥ 3
08:       Split SubString into successive Trigrams
09:       TrigramArray←Trigram and Position
10:     else
11:       SubString regard as Trigram
12:       TrigramArray←Trigram and Position
13:     end if
14:     Count++
15:   end while
16: return TrigramArray and write back Count
```

---

(2) **Inverted Index Generation:** When one trigram array was generated, the module adds the domain and its trigrams into inverted index of domain DomainInvertedIndex, whose structure showed in Fig. 2(b). The node of index term contains a Trigram, a pointer to the next node of the term list and a pointer to the inverted list of this term. The node of inverted list contains DomainId,

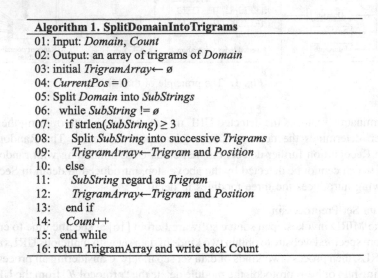
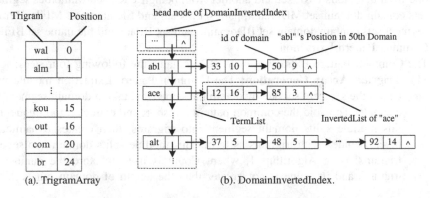

(a). TrigramArray   (b). DomainInvertedIndex.

Fig. 2. The primary data structure of MIRD.

Position of the trigram in domain and a pointer to the next node of the inverted list. The inverted list is sorted by ascending order of DomainId. The module also generates dynamically inverted index of path name PathInvertedIndex and inverted index of file name FileInvertedIndex.

Algorithm 2. ExtractDomainCommonPattern

01: Input: $DomainId_1$, $DomainId_2$
02: Output: the common patter of $Domain_1$ and $Domain_2$
03: initial $CommonString \leftarrow \emptyset$
04: Traverse TrigramArrays of $Domain_1$ and $Domain_2$
05: if $TrigramArray_1[i].Trigram == TrigramArray_2[j].Trigram$
06:    if $CommonString == \emptyset$
07:      Judge($Position_{1i}$, $Position_{2j}$)
08:        $CommonString = Trigram \,|\, ".*" + Trigram \,|\, "*" + Trigram$
09:    else
10:      Judge($Position_{1i}$, $Position_{2j}$)
11:        Append($CommonString$, the last letter of $Trigram \,|\, "*." + Trigram \,|\, "*" + Trigram$
            $\,|\, Trigram$)
12:    end if
13:    $Position_1 = Position_{1i}$; $Position_2 = Position_{2j}$;
14: end if
15: if any position is not the last Trigram of two Domain
16:   $CommonString$ append "*"
17: end if
18: return $CommonString$

---

(3) **Segment Common pattern Extraction:** This module traverses the Domain-InvertedIndex to search the domains where domain segment common pattern can be extracted from. Segment common pattern can be extracted from segments in the same inverted list for these domains share one trigram at least. Running algorithm 2, this module scans two trigram arrays of two domains to extract segment common pattern. According to the experimental statistic, the probability of more than one segment common pattern between two domains is not exceeding 2 % [17]. So, extracting one segment common pattern from two domains is feasible. The extraction of segment common pattern is computed by the position of trigrams in the two segments. According to the positions, this module appends the trigram or character of trigram or wildcard to the common string. The time complexity of the algorithm is polynomial without beyond the product of the length of two arrays. For example, domain common pattern of $Domain_0$ and $Domain_1$ is "*abl*". At last, all domain segment common patterns are deposited into DomainPatternSet. Using Algorithm 2 process path name and file name obtains path name common pattern set PathPatternSet and file name common pattern set FilePatternSet. Path name common pattern of $Path_0$ and $Path_1$ is "include/wor*", and file name common pattern of $File_0$ and $File_1$ is "*.htm*".

(4) **Segment Common Pattern Connection:** This module connects segment common patterns shared the same URLID using segment connector "/". For example, the common pattern of URL_0 and URL_1 is "*abl*/include/wor*/*.htm*". All common patterns of malicious URLs and benign URLs input into the URL Determination module.

3. URL Determination

The URL Determination module matches the detected URL up with two kinds of common patterns following the rule 1 and 2 described in Sect. 3.1. The ratio of training set of malicious URL and benign URL is 0.5. The number of the detected URL matching up with malicious common patterns is denoted as MNum, and the number of the detected URL matching up with benign common pattern is denoted as BNum. According to the experimental statistic, the size of the intersection between malicious common pattern set and benign set is less than 1 %. This module uses linear classifier to determinate the detected URL is malicious or not. If $2 * MNum/BNum \geq 1$, the detected URL is malicious. To improve the accuracy, if $2 * MNum/BNum < 1$, this module outputs the detected URL into the Random Domain Name Recognition Module.

3.3   Random Domain Name Recognition

The cyber-attackers use domain name generation algorithm (DGA) generating a large number of URLs with random domain periodically, which share one server. The random domain is not predefined binary string and its length is often longer than the normal length of domain described in reference [18]. On the other hand, the domain user registers a domain for a period of time, and the time to live of random domain is short. If the time limit was exceeded, it is difficult to re-access the domain name, and the DNS cannot resolve the domain name. Most importantly, the attackers deliberately hide the related information of the domain name.

For the sake of the above three features of random domain name, the Random Domain Name Recognition module (RDM) processes the URL which was considered as benign URL by the URL Determination module as the Fig. 3. After received the URL, RDM checks the length of the domain name. If the length of the domain name is longer than 26, which is the threshold of domain name stipulated in reference [18], RDM outputs the detected URL is malicious. Otherwise, RDM resolves the domain name as iterative, and checks out the benign URL step by step, avoiding redundant resolving and enhancing the whole speed. RDM runs a thread of resolving controller to control the progress of domain name resolving. And the progress of domain name resolving is as follows.

(1) Checking the local domain name server (local DNS). The local DNS cached related information, such as the IP address of the host, after a URL was visited. If the local DNS check out the information about the domain, responds that the corresponding URL is benign. Otherwise, RDM sends the domain name to the Resolving Controller.

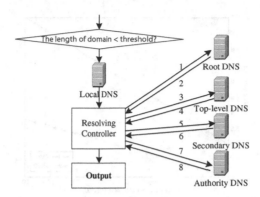

Fig. 3. The progress of domain name resolving.

(2) Checking the root domain name server (root DNS). The Resolving Controller sends a command to the root DNS. The root DNS responds the controller the address information about the top level domain name server.

(3) Checking the top level domain name server (top-level DNS). The Resolving Controller sends the domain name to the top-level DNS. The top-level DNS checks its cache. If the domain name in the cache, responds that the corresponding URL is benign. Otherwise, the top-level DNS responds the address information of the secondary domain name server to the controller.

(4) Checking the secondary domain name server (secondary DNS). The Resolving Controller sends the domain name to the secondary DNS. The secondary DNS checks its cache. If the domain name in the cache, responds that the corresponding URL is benign. Otherwise, the secondary DNS responds the address information of the authority domain name server to the controller.

(5) Checking the authority domain name server (authority DNS). The Resolving Controller sends the domain name to the authority DNS. The authority DNS checks its cache. If the domain name in the cache, responds RDM that the corresponding URL is benign. Otherwise, the authority DNS responds RDM that the corresponding URL is malicious.

4   Experiments and Analysis

There were two kinds of URL data set, namely malicious URL data set and benign URL data set crawled from specific websites by open source software Larbin [16] on October 13th, 2014. The malicious URL data set contained 4,000,000 URLs crawled from Phish Tank [19] and Malware Patrol [20]. The benign URL data set contained 8,000,000 URLs crawled from Google and DMOZ. The source of testing sets was the same with training sets, which contained 800,000 malicious URLs and 1,200,000 benign URLs. For each experiment, MIRD randomly chose malicious and benign URLs in proportion of 1 to 2 in training sets and 2 to 3 in testing set. The experimental

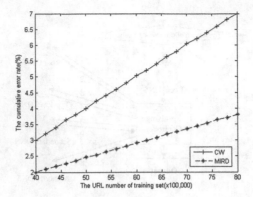

Fig. 4. Comparison of cumulative error rate between MIRD and CW.

training set and testing set was in proportion 5 to 1. The experiments were carried out on computer with 8 cores and 128 GB memory.

To verify the effectiveness of MIRD, the experiments compared the MIRD with the classical URL based approach—CW algorithm proposed by Ma et al. [13–15] in the same environment using the same data sets. The Fig. 4 showed the comparison of cumulative error number of MIRD and CW, and the cumulative error number consisted of the number of malicious URLs mis-detected as benign URL and the number of benign URLs mis-detected as malicious URL. The horizontal axis of Fig. 4 is the URL number of training set in each experiment, hundred thousand, and the vertical axis of Fig. 4 is the cumulative error number, %. The cumulative error number of MIRD was less than CW in each experiment, which showed that MIRD was more effective in detecting malicious URL than CW. The reason is the MIRD implanted with random domain name recognition, which can recognize the URL with random domain name improving the accuracy of detecting malicious URL.

To verify the efficiency of MIRD detecting malicious, Fig. 5 compared the runtime of MIRD with CW in the same environment detecting same number of malicious URLs

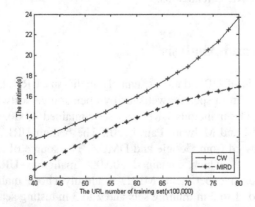

Fig. 5. Comparison of runtime between MIRD and CW.

with the same data sets. In Fig. 5, the horizontal axis is the URL number of training set in each experiment, hundred thousand. The vertical axis is the time of detecting same number of malicious URL, second. The figure showed that the MIRD needs less time than the CW in same data sets and the ratio of increasing is lower than CW. On one hand, the inverted index avoids redundant computation of common patterns and redundant matching. On the other hand, the time complexity of MIRD is linear, for the overhead time of each step in MIRD is only relative to the number of URLs. So the MIRD is more efficiency than CW.

To verify the scalability of MIRD, Fig. 6 compared the number of patterns of MIRD with blacklist of Google Safe Browser [7] to detect same number of malicious URLs. The horizontal axis is the number of detected malicious URLs in each experiment, thousand. The vertical axis is the necessary patterns of detecting same number of malicious URL, thousand. The paper regarded the URL in the blacklist as patterns for convenience. The number of patterns of MIRD is in logarithmic growth, while the number of patterns of blacklist is in linear growth. One common pattern of MIRD may match up with several URLs, so MIRD can detect some unknown malicious URLs. On the other hand, the random domain name recognition module can recognize the random domain which cannot be resolved by domain name servers. So the scalability of MIRD is good.

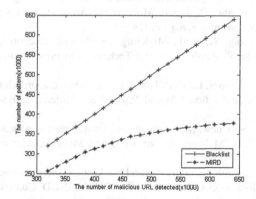

Fig. 6. Comparison of number of pattern between MIRD and blacklist.

5   Conclusion

The paper proposed an approach of malicious URL detection using trigrams-based common pattern of URL, which implanted with random domain recognition, named MIRD. MIRD used common patterns extracted from URLs based on inverted index with trigram as term to match with the detected URL. To fix up the random domain name, MIRD implanted with random domain name recognition module RDM, which identify the length of the domain name and resolve the domain name of the preliminary determined URL to recognize the unresolved domain name. The experimental result proof the MIRD is effectiveness, efficiency and scalability.

Acknowledgments. The research work is supported by Supported by the Strategic Leading Science and Technology Projects of Chinese Academy of Sciences (No. XDA06030200); the National Natural Science Foundation under Grant (No. 61402464).

References

1. [EB/OL] 2015. http://www.hpenterprisesecurity.com/ponemon-2013-cost-of-cyber-crime-study-reports
2. [EB/OL] 2015. http://en.wikipedia.org/wiki/Web_threat
3. Le, A., Markopoulou, A., Faloutsos, M.: Phishdef: url names say it all. In: The 30th IEEE International Conference on Computer Communication, Shanghai, China (2011)
4. Porras, P., Saidi, H., Yegneswaran, V., Conficker, C.: P2P protocol and implementation. SRI International Technical Report (2009)
5. Porras, P., Saidi, H., Yegneswaran, V.: An Analysis of Conficker's Logic and Rendezvous Points (2009)
6. [EB/OL] 2015. https://url.spec.whatwg.org/
7. Likarish, P., Jung, E.: Leveraging google safebrowsing to characterize web-based attacks. Association for Computing Machinery, Chicago, IL, USA (2009)
8. Zhang, J., Porras, P., Ullrich, J.: Highly Predictive Blacklisting. In: Proceedings of the 17th Conference on Security symposium, San Jose, CA (2008)
9. Provos, N., Mavrommatic, P., Rajab, M.A., et al.: All your Iframes point to us. In: 17th Usenix Security Symposium, San Jose, CA (2008)
10. Liu, H., Ma, X., Wang, T., et al.: Modeling the effect of infection time on active worm propagations. In: The 5th Applications and Techniques in Information Security, Melbourne Australia (2014)
11. Zhang, Y., Hong, J., Cranor, L.: CANTINA: a content-based approach to detecting phishing web sites. In: 16th International World Wide Web Conference, Banff, Alberta, Canada (2007)
12. Garera, S., Provos, N., Chew, M.: A framework for detection and measurement of phishing attacks. In: The 5th ACM Workshop on Recurring Malcode, Alexandria, Virginia, USA (2007)
13. Ma, J., Saul, L.K., Savage, S., et al.: Beyond blacklists: learning to detection malicious web sites from suspicious URLs. In: The 15th ACM SIGKDD Conference on Knowledge Discovery and Data Mining, Paris, France (2009)
14. Ma, J., Saul, L.K., Savage, S., et al.: Identifying suspicious URLs: an application of large-scale online learning. In: Proceedings of the 26th International Conference on Machine Learning, Montreal, Canada (2009)
15. Thomas, K., Grier, C., Ma, J., et al.: Design and evaluation of a real-time url spam filtering service. In: Proceedings of the 2011 IEEE Symposium on Security and Privacy, San Francisco, CA (2011)
16. [EB/OL] 2014. http://larbin.sourceforge.net/index-eng.html
17. Huang, D., Xu, K., Pei, J.: Malicious URL detection by dynamically mining patterns without pre-defined elements. In: The 22nd World Wide Web Conference, Rio de Janeiro, Brazil (2013)
18. [EB/OL] 2014. http://tools.ietf.org/html/rfc2181
19. [EB/OL] 2014. http://en.wikipedia.org/wiki/Phishtank
20. [EB/OL] 2014. http://www.malware.com.br/

A Novel NB-SVM-Based Sentiment Analysis Algorithm in Cross-Cultural Communication

Yuemei Xu[1]([✉]), Zihou Wang[2], and Yuji Chen[1]

[1] Department of Computer Science, Beijing Foreign Studies University,
Beijing, China
[2] National Computer Network Emergency Response Technical Team, Coordination
Center of China, Beijing, China
xuyuemei@bfsu.edu.cn

Abstract. Mining opinions and sentiment from cross-cultural communication Web sites can deepen mutual understanding among people between countries and provides an important channel for researching China's cross-cultural communication. The sentiment analysis in the context of cross-cultural communication faces the challenges of *culture-dependent, fine-grained sentiment understanding*, and *topic-centralization*. Traditional approaches use machine learning methods, such as Naive Bayes, maximum entropy and support vector machine. In this paper, we exploit the machine learning methods in the context of cross-cultural communication, take the advantages of Naive Bayes and support vector machine methods and propose a novel NB-SVM based sentiment analysis algorithm. Extensive experiments show that the proposed approach performs well and can achieve 0.3 % error rate of sentiment classification with appropriate parameter settings.

Keywords: Sentiment analysis · Naive Bayes · Support Vector
Machine · Cross-cultural communication

1 Introduction

Nowadays, culture globalization has been a trend which means a great deal to a country. How to keep and enhance cultural influence has been a tough question for most countries. Meanwhile, the rapid development of the Internet makes the online social networks (OSNs) an important channel for cross-cultural communication, such as Web forum, microblog and etc.

China has initially formed eight central key news Web sites as the backbone of the outreach system, such as http://english.peopledaily.com.cn/, http://www.news.cn/english/ and http://www.china.org.cn/index.htm. These news Web

This work is supported by the Fundamental Research Funds for the Central Universities (No. 023600-500110002), the major program of National Social Science Funds of China (No. 14@ZH036), the National Natural Science Foundation of China (No. 61502038).

W. Niu et al. (Eds.): ATIS 2015, CCIS 557, pp. 315–325, 2015.
DOI: 10.1007/978-3-662-48683-2_28

sites, including their massive users' data forum, provide a great deal of empirical data for the study of China's cross-cultural exchange to. A crucial characteristic of these massive on-line forum data is their *sentiment*, or overall opinion towards the subject matter. For example, whether foreigners' attitude to the topic "Child traffickers should be put to death?" is positive or negative. Labeling these topics and data on cross-cultural communication forum with sentiment would provide succinct summaries to the researches of China's cross-cultural communication.

The sentiment analysis is a hot topic in the Nature Language Process (NLP) research community, involved with linguistic heuristics, cognitive linguistics and knowledge learning. However, sentiment analysis based on cross-cultural communication raises a series of problems and challenges. First, sentiment expression in cross-cultural communication relates to culture background and culture context, which is also called *culture-dependent*, therefore the sentiment analysis should be taken in a subtle manner. Second, in comparison with the traditional sentiment analysis, threads and data from cross-cultural communication Web sites and forums are more diverse and have more perspectives. Therefore, sentiment analysis based on cross-cultural communication requires less *fine-grained sentiment understanding* than the traditional sentiment analysis. For example, how to identify the meaning of emerging words in the culture background. Third, The topics of high frequency in the context of cross-cultural communication are about "Credit", "Country", "School", "World" and "Government". Therefore, the sentiment analysis should target at these topics and use these high frequency key word to improve the accuracy of sentiment classification.

In this paper, we exploit the sentiment analysis in the context of cross-cultural communication and try to solve the three challenges discussed above. The sentiment analysis often uses machine learning methods, such as Naive Bayes (NB), maximum entropy and support vector machine (SVM). Studies show that NB works better than SVM for short snippet sentiment tasks, while for longer documents the opposite result holds [1]. In this paper, we take the forums of China central key news web sites (e.g., http://english.peopledaily.com.cn/) as the raw data, where the threads and data might be short or long sentences. Therefore, in order to study sentiment in the intercultural communication process, we novelly propose to combine the advantages of NB and SVM, and propose a NB-SVM combination sentiment analysis algorithm. First, we perform data preprocess on the raw data, dividing the raw data into subjective and objective, and carrying out document segmentation, word cleaning and feature abstraction on the subjective data. Naive Bayes is then used to calculate the probability of sentiment polarity for each document. Based on the probability values, documents can be considered as nodes in a 2-dimensional domain. Finally, SVM method is adopted to map the nonlinear nodes in the 2-dimensional domain to linear examples in higher dimensional domain, and then classify documents into positive and negative clusters by a separating hyperplane. The major contributions of this paper are summarized as follows:

- We propose a NB-SVM combination sentiment analysis algorithm to analyze the sentiment of Internet users in the field of intercultural communication.

- Through data preprocess and probability calculation of sentiment polarity, documents are mapped as nodes in a 2-dimensional domain. Then the sentiment classification problem is formulated as an optimization problem.
- Extensive simulation results show that the proposed NB-SVM performs well and achieves 0.3 % error rate of sentiment classification with appropriate parameter settings.

The rest of this paper is organized as follows. Section 2 presents a survey of the related work. Section 3 describes the details of data process procedure. Section 4 presents the NB-SVM based sentiment analysis algorithm. Section 5 is the experiment evaluation and conclusions are summarized in Sect. 6.

2   Related Work

Sentiment analysis is the field of study that analyzes people's opinions, sentiments and attitudes and has been handled as a NLP task at many levels of granularity, such as document level [2], sentence level [3] and the phrase level [4]. The study of sentiment analysis in cross-cultural communication belongs to the research line of document level classification task.

Document-level sentiment classification is essentially a text classification problem. Existing literature mainly uses supervised learning method, e.g., Naive Bayes [5] classification and SVM [6]. Pang *et al.* [7] was the first one to analyze the sentiment of movie reviews and compared effectiveness of Naive Bayes, maximum entropy and SVM. Experiments in [7] showed that these three machine learning methods are better than the human-based classifiers.

Instead of using a standard machine learning method, researchers have also proposed several custom techniques specifically for document-level sentiment classification. Martineau *et al.* proposed a weight word score called Delta TFIDF, which assigned words scores using the difference of their TFIDF scores in the positive and negative training corpora [8]. Wang et al. proposed a graph-based hashtag approach [9] and Nakagawa *et al.* proposed a dependency tree-based classification method, which used conditional random fields with hidden variables to improve the accuracy of sentiment classification [10].

This paper exploits the efficiency of machine learning methods in the context of cross-cultural communication. Pang et al. tested that SVM method using bag of words feature sets reached accuracy of 82.7 % in sentiment classification [7] and further improved its accuracy up to 90 % by using minimum cuts [2]. In this paper, we try to further improve the efficiency of SVM by taking the advantages of Naive Bayes and SVM and proposes a NB-SVM combination sentiment analysis algorithm.

3   Data Preprocess

The crawled raw data are threads and articles from cross-cultural communication web sites. Let d_i, $i \in [1, N]$, represents thread or article i. N is the total number of

318   Y. Xu et al.

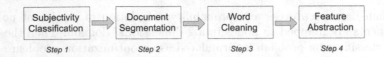

Fig. 1. Four steps of data preprocess.

threads and articles. Figure 1 shows the data preprocess, consisting of four steps: subjectivity classification, document segmentation, word cleaning and feature abstraction.

Subjectivity Classification. It is the first step to decide if d_i is subjective or objective. The objective documents which are assumed to express or imply no opinion are removed from the data set.

Document Segmentation. Each document is segmented into words by regular expressions. A simple rule-based model is also built to correct simple spelling errors and variations into normal form, such as "gooood" to "good" and "luve" to "love".

Word Cleaning. (a) The words whose length are shorter than 3 are considered meaningless and then they are removed from the word dataset. (b) Strings of uppercase and words that are capitalized are converted into all lowercase. (c) All the words are filtered by a stop word dictionary. The words frequently used by irrelative with emotion are removed, such as "is, this, the". (d) Word Stemming is performed by a word stem mapping algorithm. (e) Finally, word lemmatization is carried out to acquire the prototype of words, such as "left" to "leave" and "amazing" to "amaze".

Feature Abstraction. The presence or absence of a word is considered as a feature of sentiment expression. A bag-of-words model is used to convert each document into a vector. If a word appears more than once in a document, that might convey some sort of information about the document over just the word occurring in the document or not. Let W be a predefined set of n features that can appear in a document. $W = \{w_1, w_2, ..., w_k, ...w_n\}$, where w_k represents a feature indicated by a word and n is the number of all the unique features. Then each document d_i, $i \in [1, N]$, can be represented by the document vector d_i:

$$d_i = (t_1(d_i), t_2(d_i), ..., t_k(d_i), ...t_n(d_i)) \tag{1}$$

where $t_k(d_i)$ indicates how many times the word w_k appears in the document d_i.

4   NB-SVM Combination Sentiment Analysis

In this section, we describe the proposed NB-SVM combination sentiment analysis in details. First, Naive Bayes is used to calculate the probability of sentiment polarity of each document vector. Then, based on the probability calculation results of sentiment polarity, a NB-SVM combination sentiment classification algorithm is proposed.

4.1 Probability Calculation of Sentiment Polarity

As the first step of data preprocess, the raw data set has been classified into subjective and objective. Here, we mainly analyze the sentiment polarity of the subjective documents and explore a two classification task: classifying sentiment into positive and negative classes. Let c_1 and c_2 represent the sentiment category of positive and negative, respectively.

Naive Bayes is a simple and effective method to perform text classification. Here, we use it to calculate the probability of sentiment polarity. Based on Bayes' rule, given the document vector d_i, $i \in [1, N]$, its probability of belonging to the category c_m, $m \in [1, 2]$, is calculated as:

$$P(c_m|d_i) = \frac{P(c_m)P(d_i|c_m)}{P(d_i)} \tag{2}$$

where $P(d_i)$ plays no role in selecting sentiment category of d_i, therefore it can be ignored in the calculation; $P(c_m)$ is the probability of given a document that belongs to the category c_m, which can be calculated as: $P(c_m) = \frac{N_m}{\sum_{m=1}^{2} N_m}$. N_m is the number of documents that belongs to the category c_m in the total document set. To estimate the term $P(d_i|c_m)$, Naive Bayes decomposes it by assuming feature w_k, $k \in [1, n]$, is conditionally independent with each other in a given the d_i document. Therefore, $P(d_i|c_m)$ can be estimated as:

$$P(d_i|c_m) = P(w_1|c_m)^{(d_i)} P(w_2|c_m)^{(d_i)}...P(w_k|c_m)^{(d_i)}...P(w_n|c_m)^{(d_i)} \tag{3}$$

where $P(w_k|c_m)^{(d_i)}$ is the probability of feature w_k belonging to document d_i in the given category c_m.

Based on the conditional independent assumption, the probability of document vector d_i belonging to sentiment polarity c_m is:

$$P(c_m|d_i) = \frac{P(c_m)P(w_1|c_m)^{(d_i)}...P(w_k|c_m)^{(d_i)}...P(w_n|c_m)^{(d_i)}}{P(d_i)} \tag{4}$$

4.2 NB-SVM Based Sentiment Classification Algorithm

Traditionally, Naive Bayes can classify documents into positive and negative clusters on the basis of their probability values of sentiment polarity. For a given document d_i, if $P(c_1|d_i) > P(c_2|d_i)$, the class of d_i is positive, and vice versa. However, Naive Bayes also has its shortcomings. First, Naive Bayes is a probability-based classification algorithm. Therefore, when the probability values of sentiment polarity are close to each other, the classification result might be erroneous. Second, its conditional independence assumption might affect the classification result in certain problems with highly dependent features.

This paper, based on the probability calculation results of sentiment polarity, tries to overcome the disadvantages of Naive Bayes, novelly embeds Naive Bayes into SVM method, and then proposes a NB-SVM combination sentiment classification algorithm.

SVM is highly effective to perform sentiment classification. Its basic idea is to find a hyperplane represented by a vector v that separates the document vectors in one class from those in the other. After analyzing the probability calculation results by Naive Bayes, each document d_i can be considered as a node X_i in a 2-dimensional domain and expressed as:

$$X_i = \{P(c_1|d_i), P(c_2|d_i)\}, X_i \in R^2 \tag{5}$$

Then our task aims to find a vector v to classify the documents into *positive* and *negative* clusters. Let $label = \{+1, -1\}$ represents the *positive* and *negative* clusters, respectively. Let the separating hyperplane between *positive* and *negative* clusters be $w^T x + b$. We need to find the w and b values that maximize the distance between the separating hyperplane and the points closest to separating hyperplane. This can be written as:

$$arg \max_{w,b} \{\min_n (label \cdot (w^T x + b) \cdot \frac{1}{\|w\|})\} \tag{6}$$

In order to solve the optimization problem of Eq. (6), Lagrange Multipliers method can be used, which transfers the optimization problem to be:

$$\max_\alpha [\sum_{i=1} \alpha - \frac{1}{2} \sum_{i,j=1} label^{(i)} \cdot label^{(j)} \cdot a_i \cdot a_j < x^{(i)}, x^{(j)} >]$$

$$\text{subject to: } \sum_{i-1} \alpha_i \cdot label^{(i)} = 0 \tag{7}$$

$$C \geq \alpha \geq 0$$

where constant C is an argument that can be tuned for getting different results. In Eq. (7), the separating hyperplane is written in terms of the paraments of α. There are many methods to solve Eq. (7) and find α values. Here, we adopt a popular method called Sequential Minimal Optimization (SMO) [11]. SMO algorithm chooses two α to optimize on each cycle. Once a suitable pair of α is found, one is increased and the other is decreased. Until a suitable set of α is found, the parameter w and separating hyperplane can be calculated.

Algorithm 1 is the procedure of NB-SVM based sentiment classification algorithm. The input of Algorithm 1 is the probability values of sentiment polarity for each document, termed as $P(c_m|d_i)$, which is computed by Naive Bayes. Then the output of Algorithm 1 are the results of sentiment classification. Besides, the error rate of sentiment classification, termed as $ErRate$, is computed.

5   Performance Evaluation

Our experiments are conducted on a data set crawled by a software called PORTIA [12]. The collection contains 32,000 threads from seven famous cross-cultural communication Web forums, such as http://bbs.chinadaily.com.cn/home.php?. We randomly select one subset as our experiment set, which contains

Algorithm 1. NB-SVM based Sentiment Classification Algorithm

INPUT: $P(c_1|d_i)$, $P(c_2|d_i)$, $i \in [1, N]$.
OUTPUT: Sentiment Classification Results, $ErRate$.
1. Transfer each document d_i to a node X_i in the 2-dimensional domain.
2. Create an α and initial it to be 0.
3. While the number of iterations is less than the defined maximum values:
    (1) For each node X_i:
    (2)   If X_i can be optimized:
    (3)   Randomly select another node X_j, $j \neq i$;
    (4)   Optimize X_i and X_j together;
    (5)   If X_i and X_j can not be optimized
    (6)   Break;
    (7)   End if
    (8)   End if
    (9) End for
    (10) If no nodes were optimized:
    (11)   Increment the iteration count;
    (12) End if
4. Calculate parameter w and the separating hyperplane $w^T x + b$.
5. Perform Sentiment classification and Calculate error rate.
    (1) Initialize $ErRate$=0.
    (2) For each document d_i
    (3)   If $w^* X_i + b > 0$ Then Label(X_i)=1;
    (4)   Else Label(X_i)=-1;
    (5)   End If
    (6)   If Label(X_i) is not equal to its original label
    (7) $ErRate$++;
    (8)   End If
    (9) End for

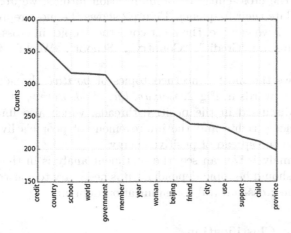

Fig. 2. The most concerned topics in cross-cultural communication forums.

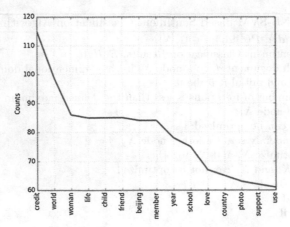

Fig. 3. The most concerned topics of positive threads in cross-cultural communication forums.

600 threads and is manually labeled with sentiment. The threads with praise, happiness, joy sentiment are labeled to be *positive*, while the threads with criticism, blame, complain sentiment are labeled to be *negative*. We randomly select 500 threads out of 600 ones as the training set and the rest 100 threads are taken as the testing set.

5.1 Topic Discussion

Firstly, we analyze the experimental threads. In order to obtain the most concerned topic in the cross-cultural communication forums, we abstract the key words and calculate their frequency. Figure 2 shows the most representative key words. From Fig. 2 we can see, the most concerned topics in cross-cultural communication forums are "Credit", "Country", "School", "World", "Government" and etc.

Figure 3 shows the most concerned topics of *positive* threads. Besides the most frequent key words in Fig. 2, *woman, life, child, Beijing* are also the most popular topics discussed in the positive threads, which also implies that the progress of women's rights and the improvement of people's living standards play a key role in the spread of positive energy.

From these analysis we can see, the sentiment analysis in the cross-cultural communication should be topic-dependent, it is necessary to construct sentiment dictionary for the cross-cultural communication domain.

5.2 Sentiment Classification

We compare the proposed NB-SVM based sentiment classification algorithm, termed as NB-SVM, with the traditional Naive Bayes method. The traditional Naive Bayes is a probability based sentiment classification method. For a given

Table 1. Experimental results with different settings of $k1$ and C.

Kernel Function, k1,C	Error Rate	Number of Support Vector
Linear, 1.3, 0.3	0.35	280
RBF, 20, 200	0.1025	280
RBF, 20, 10	0.09	236
RBF, 20, 0.0001	0.3425	92
RBF, 20, 0.1	0.2925	126
RBF, 20, 5	0.05	287
RBF, 20, 7	0.0175	282
RBF, 20, 8	0.035	283
RBF, 1.3, 0.3	0.003	360

document d_i, if $P(c_1|d_i) > P(c_2|d_i)$, d_i is classified as positive, otherwise negative.

Error Rate of Sentiment Classification. Figure 4 shows the error rate comparison of sentiment classification between Naive Bayes and NB-SVM. In the experiments, *hold-out cross validation* is used, which randomly selects 80 % of data set for the training set and 20 % of data set for the test set. In order to get a good estimate of the sentiment classification, we do such a data set selection for 10 times and the error rate of sentiment classification for both Naive Bayes and NB-SVM are shown in Fig. 4. We can see that the proposed NB-SVM algorithm is much better than Naive Bayes method with kernel functions when parameters $k1 = 0.3$ and $C = 1$. $k1$ is a user parameter and C controls weighting between functional margin of nodes in the 2-dimensional domain. We will discuss their effectiveness later. Averagely, the error rates of sentiment classification in the traditional Naive Bayes and NB-SVM are 0.32 and 0.24, respectively. NB-SVM greatly improves the accuracy of sentiment classification.

Discussion of Parameters $k1$ and C in NB-SVM. Here we discuss the impact of parameters $k1$ and C on the proposed NB-SVM methods. Table 1 shows the experimental results with different settings of kernel function, $k1$ and C.

The kernel function can be *linear* or *radial bias function* (RBF). The difference between linear and RBF lies in whether the nodes are mapped from low dimension domain to high dimension or not. If *linear* kernel function is used, there is no dimension mapping and the sentiment classification problem equals to a linear classification problem. RBF is usually used when the nodes are not linearly separated, which can make the nodes from a lower-dimensional feature space to a higher-dimensional space. Then we can solve the problem linearly in high-dimensional space. From the results in Table 1 we can see, RBF is more suitable for the sentiment classification problem than *linear* kernel function.

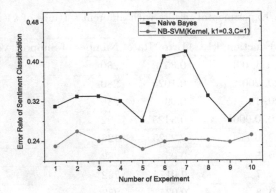

Fig. 4. Error rate comparison of sentiment classification between Naive Bayes and NB-SVM.

Constant C greatly affects the sentiment classification results. C controls the balance between making sure all of the nodes have a margin of at least 1.0 and making the margin as wide as possible. If C is large, the classifier will try to make all of the nodes in the 2-dimensional domain properly classified by the separating hyperplane.

The error rate of sentiment classification decreases with the increment of number of support vectors. There is an optimum number of support vectors. If the number of support vectors is too small, the error rate of sentiment classification will increase. For example, when the number of support vectors are 92 and 126, the error rate are 0.3425 and 0.2925, respectively. If we have too many support vectors, we are using the whole data set every time for classification.

6 Conclusion

This paper analyzes the challenges of sentiment analysis in the context of cross-cultural communication, which can be summarized as *culture-dependent, fine-grained sentiment understanding*, and *topic-centralization*. In order to solve these challenges, this paper exploits the supervised machine learning methods, novelly takes the advantages of Naive Bayes and SVM, and proposes a NB-SVM combination sentiment analysis method.

Experiments show that topics in cross-cultural communication focus on "Credit", "Country", "School", "World", "Government" and etc. Besides, positive threads focus on topics of *woman, life, child, Beijing*, which also implies that the progress of women's rights and the improvement of people's living standards play a key role to spread positive energy in the cross-cultural communication. Furthermore, the proposed approach performs well in sentiment classification.

References

1. Wang, S., Manning, C.D.: Baselines and bigrams: simple, good sentiment and topic classification. In: Proceedings of the 50th Annual Meeting of the Association for Computational Linguistics: Short Papers, vol. 2, pp. 90–94. Association for Computational Linguistics (2012)
2. Pang, B., Lee, L.: A sentimental education: sentiment analysis using subjectivity summarization based on minimum cuts. In: Proceedings of the 42nd annual meeting on Association for Computational Linguistics, p. 271. Association for Computational Linguistics (2004)
3. Hu, M., Liu, B.: Mining and summarizing customer reviews. In: Proceedings of the tenth ACM SIGKDD international conference on Knowledge discovery and data mining, pp. 168–177. ACM (2004)
4. Agarwal, A., Biadsy, F., Mckeown, K.R.: Contextual phrase-level polarity analysis using lexical affect scoring and syntactic n-grams. In: Proceedings of the 12th Conference of the European Chapter of the Association for Computational Linguistics, pp. 24–32. Association for Computational Linguistics (2009)
5. McCann, S., Lowe, D.G.: Local naive bayes nearest neighbor for image classification. In: CVPR2012, pp. 3650–3656. IEEE (2012)
6. Eshghi, K.: Support vector machine. Google Patents. US Patent App. 13/873,587, April 2013
7. Pang, B., Lee, L., Vaithyanathan, S.: Thumbs up?: sentiment classification using machine learning techniques. In: Proceedings of the ACL-02 Conference on Empirical Methods in Natural Language Processing, vol. 10, pp. 79–86. Association for Computational Linguistics (2002)
8. Martineau, J., Finin, T.: Delta tfidf: an improved feature space for sentiment analysis. In: ICWSM (2009)
9. Wang, G., Xie, S., Liu, B., Yu, P.S.: Identify online store review spammers via social review graph. ACM Trans. Intell. Syst. Technol. (TIST) 3(4), 61 (2012)
10. Nakagawa, T., Inui, K., Kurohashi, S.: Dependency tree-based sentiment classification using crfs with hidden variables. In: Human Language Technologies: The 2010 Annual Conference of the North American Chapter of the Association for Computational Linguistics, pp. 786–794. Association for Computational Linguistics (2010)
11. Huang, X., Shi, L., Suykens, J.A.K.: Sequential minimal optimization for svm with pinball loss. Neurocomputing 149, 1596–1603 (2015)
12. Accentax, Adai0808, adewinter, et al.: Portia: Visual scraping for scrapy (2015)

Time-Varying Impulsive Anticontrol
of Discrete-Time System

Qian Wang[1(✉)], Wei Xiong[2], and Ya Shuang Deng[1]

[1] School of Information and Safety Engineering, Zhongnan University
of Economics and Law, Wuhan, Hubei, People's Republic of China
{icedlitchi, dys0377}@163.com
[2] College of Computer Science, South Central University for Nationalities,
Wuhan, Hubei, People's Republic of China
ccnuxw@sina.com

Abstract. This brief proposes a chaotification algorithm for a kind of nonlinear discrete-time systems. A time-varying impulsive approach to generating chaos in n-dimensional discrete system is described in detail, which can lead to uniformly bounded state vectors of the controlled system with positive Lyapunov exponents, thereby yielding chaotic dynamics. Numerical simulations are presented to show the effectiveness of the theoretical results.

Keywords: Chaotification · Time-varying · Impulsive control · Lyapunov exponent

1 Introduction

In recent years, "Anti-control or chaotification", has attracted some growing interests due to its great potential in nontraditional applications such as liquid mixing [1], human brain [2], secure communications [3] and so on.

In the pursuit of chaotifying discrete dynamical systems, Chen and Lai proposed a simple yet effective scheme [4], which yields chaos in the sense of Devaney [5] for linear systems, or Wiggins [6] for nonlinear systems. All the Lyapunov exponents of controlled system become strictly positive by a linear interior state feedback controller thereby the system orbits diverging from each other and all system orbits are confined to a bounded region in the phase space by a mod operation. Li and Chen show this work is universal subsequently [7]. Further studies show that the mod operation in this scheme can be replaced by other nonlinear functions such as sine function [8], sawtooth function [9], and more general functions [10]. In a word, the basic idea for chaotification is "expanding" and "folding", the combination of which can produce chaos in the given system, so it is approved that a bounded system with positive Lyapunov exponent is chaotic.

More and more traditional control methods are used to realize the chaotification of systems. In many cases, impulse control is more effective than the continuous one, and sometimes only the pulse method can achieve the purpose of control. Impulsive control method has attracted increasing interests due to its small amount of information and robustness against the disturbances. Periodical impulsive inputs were applied to make the

© Springer-Verlag Berlin Heidelberg 2015
W. Niu et al. (Eds.): ATIS 2015, CCIS 557, pp. 326–336, 2015.
DOI: 10.1007/978-3-662-48683-2_29

poincare map of the controlled continuous system identical with a redesigned discrete chaotic map, thereby making an originally well-behaved continuous system chaotic [11], which is effective for continuous system but not for discrete system. Impulsive control method was applied to make the poincare map of the continuous-time fuzzy hyperbolic model track a certain chaotic system, thereby realizing the chaotification of the given FHM system [12], which can also be extended to the discrete nonlinear systems. However, it is one kind of synchronization control essentially thereby being unsuitable for some situations. An impulsive control method is applied to generate chaos for a class of linear discrete system [13] or linear time-delayed system [14] by configurating the Lyapunov exponents of controlled system. Generally speaking, it is still an open problem on how to chaotity general nonlinear discrete systems via impulsive control.

In this paper, a class of stable nonlinear discrete-time system has been studied. An impulsive approach is proposed to make the given system become a bounded system with positive Lyapunov exponent. In this scheme, the impulsive interval changes with the evolution of the system state, which greatly reduces the control energy for anticontrol of chaos and is crucial for certain circumstances.

The rest of paper is organized as follows: A time-varying impulsive chaotier is proposed in Sect. 2. Some examples are presented in order to verify the effectiveness of the theoretical results in Sect. 3. Finally, conclusions are drawn in Sect. 4.

2   Problem Statement and Design of the Chaotier

Consider a discrete dynamical system, which is locally asymptotic stable in origin.

$$\begin{cases} x_{n+1} = f(x_n) = Ax_n + \varphi(x_n) \\ x_0 \text{ - given} \end{cases} \tag{1}$$

where $x_n \in R^m$, $A \in R^{n \times n}$, and φ is assumed to be continuously differentiable, at least locally in the region of interest.

The objective is to design an impulsive control input sequence $\{u_n\}_{n=1}^{\infty}$, such that the controlled system

$$\begin{cases} x_{n+1} = f(x_n) & n \neq n_k \\ \Delta x_{n+1} = u_{n+1} & n = n_k \\ x_0 \text{ - given} \end{cases} \tag{2}$$

are bounded with one or more positive Lyapunov exponents.

Since the system is locally asymptotic stable in origin, the absolute value of all the eigenvalues of matrix $f'(0)$ is smaller than 1, where $f'(0)$ denotes the Jacobian matrix of system (1), and there exist a moment n and a positive value M, such that $\|x_n\| \leq M$. We define M by the boundary of impulsive control.

An impulsive control rule is designed as follow:

If and only if the orbit reaches the boundary M, a diffused impulse will be active at next moment.

For simplicity, the controller can be designed in the form of

$$u_n = C_n f(x_n) \tag{3}$$

where $C_n(n = 1, 2, \cdots)$ is the strength of impulse. Then the impulsive controlled system is

$$\begin{cases} x_{n+1} = f(x_n) & n \neq n_k \\ x_{n+1} = C_n f(x_n) & n = n_k \\ x_0 \text{ - given} \end{cases} \tag{4}$$

Suppose the moments of impulse satisfy $n_1 < n_2 < \cdots < n_k < \cdots$, and $\lim\limits_{k \to \infty} n_k = \infty$, $\Delta_k = n_k - n_{k-1} < \infty$ is the impulsive interval.

Obviously, impulse intervals are relevant to the state of system and impulsive control boundary M, which are time-varying.

First, the jacobian matrix of controlled system (4) is

$$J(x_n) = \begin{cases} A + \varphi'(x_n) & n \neq n_k \\ C_{n_k}(A + \varphi'(x_n)) & n = n_k \end{cases} \tag{5}$$

Let $T_n = T_n(x_0 x_1 \cdots x_n) = J_n(x_n) \cdots J_1(x_1) J_0(x_0)$, μ_i denotes the ith eigenvalue of $T_n^T T_n(x_0)$, and $\mu_1 \leq \cdots \leq \mu_i \leq \cdots \leq \mu_n$.

When $n \in [n_k, n_{k+1})$

Suppose $C_{n_i} = c_{n_i} I_m (i = 1, 2 \cdots k - 1)$, then for system (2),

$$T_n = J_n(x_n) \cdots C_{n_k} J_{n_k}(x_{n_k}) J_{n_k-1}(x_{n_k-1}) \cdots J_{n_{k-1}+1}(x_{n_{k-1}+1}) \cdot$$
$$C_{n_{k-1}} J_{n_{k-1}}(x_{n_{k-1}}) \cdots C_{n_1} J_{n_1}(x_{n_1}) J_{n_1-1}(x_{n_1-1}) \cdots J_0(x_0)$$
$$= J_n(x_n) \cdots J_1(x_1) J_0(x_0) \prod_{i=1}^{k} c_{n_k}$$

$$T_n^T T_n(x_0) = \left(J_n(x_n) \cdots J_1(x_1) J_0(x_0) \prod_{i=1}^{k} c_{n_k} \right)^T$$
$$\cdot \left(J_n(x_n) \cdots J_1(x_1) J_0(x_0) \prod_{i=1}^{k} c_{n_k} \right)$$
$$= J_0(x_0)^T J_1(x_1)^T \cdots J_n(x_n)^T J_n(x_n) \cdots J_1(x_1) J_0(x_0) \prod_{i=1}^{k} c_{n_k}^2$$

where

$$J_n(x_n)^T J_n(x_n) = (A + \varphi'(x_n))^T (A + \varphi'(x_n))$$
$$= A^T A + \varphi'(x_n)^T \varphi'(x_n) + A^T \varphi'(x_n) + \varphi'(x_n)^T A$$

So the ith Lyapunov exponent of the orbit of controlled system (4) starting from x_0, can be indicated by

$$l_i(x_0) = \lim_{n\to\infty} \frac{1}{2n} \ln(\mu_i(T_n^T T_n(x_0)))$$

Suppose

$$\lim_{n\to\infty} \frac{\|\varphi(x_n)\|}{\|x_n\|} = 0 \tag{6}$$

thus, there exists a moment N and a fully small positive number η, such that

$$\|\varphi'(x_n)\| \leq \eta$$

Suppose all the eigenvalues of $A^T A$, $J_n(x_n)^T J_n(x_n)$ are listed in order

$$0 < \lambda_1 \leq \lambda_2 \leq \cdots \leq \lambda_m$$
and
$$0 < \mu_1(x_n) \leq \mu_2(x_n) \leq \cdots \leq \mu_m(x_n)$$

First, let's review and introduce a basic result in the eigenvalue of matrix.

Lemma 1. [15] Suppose that A and its perturbation Q are real symmetric matrixes. Suppose also the eigenvalues of A and A + Q are listed in order,

$$\lambda_1 \leq \lambda_2 \leq \cdots \leq \lambda_m \text{ and } \mu_1 \leq \mu_2 \leq \cdots \leq \mu_m$$
then
$$\|\lambda_i - \mu_i\| \leq \|Q\|, \ i = 1, 2, \cdots m$$

It immediately follows that:

Theorem 1. If the following conditions are satisfied,

$$c > 1 \tag{7}$$

$$\frac{\ln(\sqrt{\lambda_1} - \eta) - \ln \hat{c}}{\ln(\sqrt{\lambda_m} + \eta)} > 0 \tag{8}$$

$$2 \ln c + \ln(\lambda_i - \eta^2 - 2\eta\sqrt{\lambda_m}) > 0, i = 1, 2, \cdots, m \tag{9}$$

where $\eta < \min\{1 - \sqrt{\lambda_m}, \sqrt{\lambda_m} + \lambda_1 - \sqrt{\lambda_m}\}$, $\hat{c} = \max_i\{|c_i|\}$, $c = \min_i\{|c_i|\}$.   then the controlled system

$$\begin{cases} x_{n+1} = f(x_n) & n \neq n_k \\ x_{n+1} = c_{n_k} f(x_n) & n = n_k \\ x_0 \text{ - given} \end{cases} \tag{10}$$

is chaotic.

Proof. Without of generality, suppose $f(0) = 0$.

Since the system is locally asymptotic stable in origin, we have $\lambda_i < 1 (i = 1, \cdots, n)$. From the impulsive control rule, we can get

$$\|x_{n+1}\| = \|c_n f(x_n)\| \leq \hat{c}(\sqrt{\lambda_m} + \eta) M$$

and all the orbits are limited in the region $\Omega = \{x \in R^m | \|x\| \leq M'\}$, where $M' = \max\{\|x_0\|, \hat{c}(\sqrt{\lambda_m} + \eta) M\}$.

Applying **Lemma** 1, one has

$$\begin{aligned} \mu_i(x_n) &\geq \lambda_i - \|\varphi'(x_n)^T \varphi'(x_n) + A^T \varphi'(x_n) + \varphi'(x_n)^T A\| \\ &\geq \lambda_i - \eta^2 - 2\eta\sqrt{\lambda_m} \end{aligned}$$

It immediately follows that

$$T_n^T T_n(x_0) \geq c^{2k} (\lambda_i - \eta^2 - 2\eta\sqrt{\lambda_m})^k$$

So, the ith Lyapunov exponent of the orbit of controlled system (4) starting from x_0 can be indicated by

$$\begin{aligned} l_i(x_0) &= \lim_{n \to \infty} \frac{1}{2n} \ln(\mu_i(T_n^T T_n(x_0))) \\ &\geq \lim_{n \to \infty} \frac{1}{2n} \ln(c^{2k} (\lambda_i - \eta^2 - 2\eta\sqrt{\lambda_m})^k) \\ &= \lim_{n \to \infty} \frac{k}{2n} \ln(c^2 (\lambda_i - \eta^2 - 2\eta\sqrt{\lambda_m})) \end{aligned} \tag{11}$$

When $n \in [n_1, n_2)$, for system (4) we can obtain that

$$\begin{aligned} x_{n_1+1} &= c_{n_1} f(x_{n_1}) \\ x_{n_1+2} &= f(x_{n_1+1}) \\ &\vdots \\ x_{n_2} &= f(x_{n_2-1}) \\ x_{n_2} &= c_{n_1} f^{n_2-n_1}(x_{n_1}) \end{aligned}$$

$$\|x_{n_2}\| \leq \|c_{n_1} f^{n_2-n_1}(x_{n_1})\| \leq \hat{c}(\sqrt{\lambda_m} + \eta)^{n_2-n_1} M.$$

On the other hand,

$$||x_{n_2}|| = ||f(x_{n_2-1})|| = ||Ax_{n_2-1} + \varphi(x_{n_2-1})|| \geq (\sqrt{\lambda_1} - \eta)M.$$

It follows that

$$(\sqrt{\lambda_1} - \eta)M \leq \hat{c}(\sqrt{\lambda_m} + \eta)^{n_2-n_1} M$$

$$n_2 - n_1 \leq \frac{\ln(\sqrt{\lambda_1} - \eta) - \ln \hat{c}}{\ln(\sqrt{\lambda_m} + \eta)}$$

Thereupon,

$$n_k - n_{k-1} \leq \frac{\ln(\sqrt{\lambda_1} - \eta) - \ln \hat{c}}{\ln(\sqrt{\lambda_m} + \eta)}$$

$$n \leq (k+1) \frac{\ln(\sqrt{\lambda_1} - \eta) - \ln \hat{c}}{\ln(\sqrt{\lambda_m} + \eta)}, \text{ where } n \in [n_k, n_{k+1})$$

Then the ith Lyapunov exponent of controlled system (4) is

$$l_i(x_0) \geq \lim_{n\to\infty} \frac{k}{2n} \ln(c^2(\lambda_i - \eta^2 - 2\eta\sqrt{\lambda_m}))$$
$$\geq \lim_{n\to\infty} \frac{k}{2(k+1)\frac{\ln(\sqrt{\lambda_1}-\eta)-\ln\hat{c}}{\ln(\sqrt{\lambda_m}+\eta)}} \ln(c^2(\lambda_i - \eta^2 - 2\eta\sqrt{\lambda_m}))$$
$$\geq \frac{\ln(\sqrt{\lambda_m}+\eta)\ln(c^2(\lambda_i-\eta^2-2\eta\sqrt{\lambda_m}))}{2\ln(\sqrt{\lambda_1}-\eta)-\ln\hat{c}} > 0$$

From above, there is at least one strictly positive Lyapunov exponent of the controlled system so that the orbits are expanding in some directions. In addition to, all the orbits are limited in a bounded region, so the orbits have to fold within the region, thereby leading to the appearance of complex chaotic dynamics.

3   Some Illustrative Examples

Example 1. Consider the well-known Logistic map [16],

$$\begin{cases} x_{n+1} = rx_n - rx_n^2 \\ x_0 \text{ - given} \end{cases}, x_n \in [0,1], n = 1, 2, \ldots, N, \ldots \quad (12)$$

where r = 0.25 and initial value is chosen at random.

It is obvious the origin is an equilibrium point of the system (12). Since the system orbit is asymptotic stable in origin (see Fig. 1).

It is distinct that the convergence rate of orbit is so fast that the orbit has converged to the origin before the iteration time reaches 10.

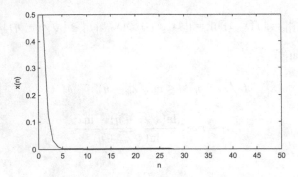

Fig. 1. Phase portrait of the system (12)

We use the impulsive approach previously stated to realize the chaotification of system (12).

Obviously, the assumption (6′) is satisfied. Choose $\eta = 0.01$, then the conditions in **Theorem** 1 can be satisfied when $c \geq 2.1$, that is

$$\frac{\ln\left(\sqrt{\lambda_1} - \eta\right) - \ln \hat{c}}{\ln\left(\sqrt{\lambda_m} + \eta\right)} > 0$$
and
$$2 \ln c + \ln\left(\lambda_i - \eta^2 - 2\eta\sqrt{\lambda_m}\right) > 0.$$

Without loss of generality, let $c_i = (-1)^{i+1} \times \max(30 \times rand(1), 3)$, and then the simulation results are presented in Fig. 2.

Obviously, Fig. 2 is more non-regular and complicated that Fig. 1.

Meanwhile, it is very important to choose a proper M. Only we select a proper M, the effect of chaotification of system can be well. M is neither too big nor too small. If it's too big, the effect of chaotification will not be good; otherwise, the moment of impulsive control may be dense, which means the impulsive interval is very small, which is not expected.

Example 2. Consider a two-dimensional discrete map,

$$\begin{cases} x_{n+1} = ax_n^2 + \frac{1}{2}y_n \\ y_{n+1} = bx_n \end{cases} \tag{13}$$

where a = 1.4, b = 0.3.

Obviously, the origin is an equilibrium point of system (13).

The Jacobian matrix of system (13) in origin is

$$\begin{pmatrix} 0 & 0.5 \\ 0.3 & 0 \end{pmatrix}$$

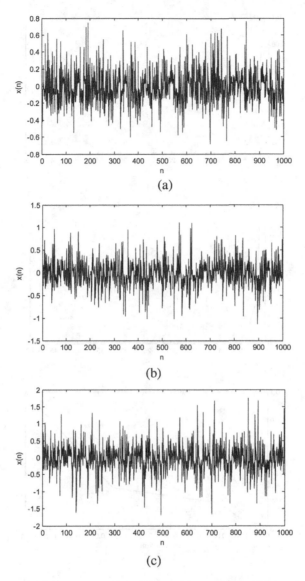

Fig. 2. Phase portrait of the system (12) with impulsive control: (a) M = 0.1. (b) M = 0.15. (c) M = 0.2

and its eigenvalues is as follow

$$\lambda_1 = 0.3 < 1, \ \lambda_2 = 0.5 < 1.$$

So all the orbits of system are locally asymptotic stable in origin (see Fig. 3, where the initial value $(x_0, y_0) = (0.1, 0.1)$).

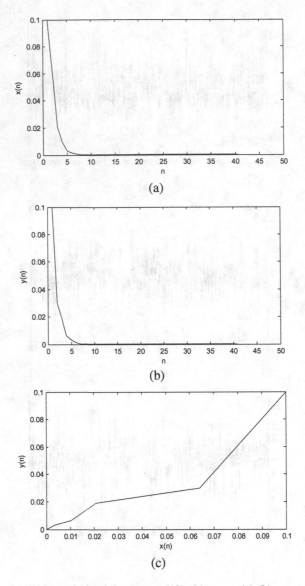

Fig. 3. Phase portrait of the system (13): (a) n − x (n) (b) n − y (n).

We use the impulsive approach previously stated to realize the chaotification of system (13).

Choose M = 0.1, let $c_i = (-1)^{i+1} \times \max(30 \times rand(1), 5)$, then the simulation results are presented in Fig. 4.

Obviously, Fig. 4 is more non-regular and complicated compared to Fig. 3.

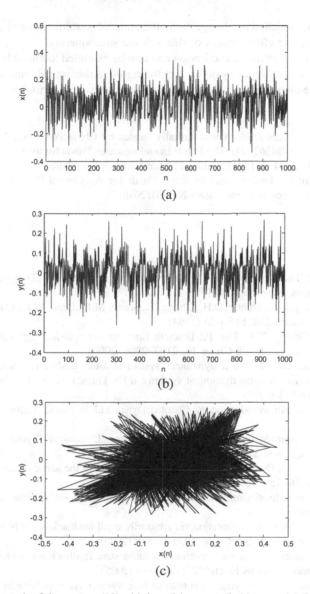

Fig. 4. Phase portrait of the system (13) with impulsive control: (a) n − x (n) (b) n − y (n) (c) x (n) − y (n)

4 Conclusions

A time-varying impulsive control scheme for locally stable nonlinear dynamical systems has been proposed in this paper, which can make the controlled system produce strictly positive Lyapunov exponent, and the system is bounded simultaneously, thereby leading to the chaotic behavior. The impulse control is not necessary at every step of iteration, which will change with the state of system. Several examples are given to illustrate the effectiveness of this scheme subsequently.

Moreover, this chaotification criterion can also be extended to unstable discrete-time systems and even continuous systems, but the rigorous theoretical analysis for continuous systems are also an open problem in the future research due to the complex of the systems.

Acknowledgments. This research was partially funded by China Postdoctoral Science Foundation (Grant No. 2014M562026); The Fundamental Research Funds for the Central Universities projects (Grant No. 31541511301); National Natural Science Foundation of Hubei, China (Grant No. 2013CFC090); the Fundamental Research Funds for the Central Universities, Zhongnan University of Economics and Law (Grant No. 2012096).

References

1. Ottino, J.M.: The Kinematics of Mixing: Stretching, Chaos, and Transport. Cambridge University Press, New York (1989)
2. Schiff, S.J., Jerger, K., Duong, D.H., Chang, T., Spano, M.L., Ditto, W.L.: Controlling chaos in the brain. Nature **370**, 615–620 (1994)
3. Lian, K.Y., Chiang, T.S., Liu, P.: Discrete time chaotic systems: applications in secure communications. Int. J. Bif. Chaos **10**, 2193–2206 (2000)
4. Chen, G., Lai, D.: Making a dynamical system chaotic: feedback control of lyapunov exponents for discrete-time dynamical systems. IEEE Trans. Circ. Syst. I: Fundam. Theory Appl. **44**, 250–253 (1997)
5. Devaney, R.L.: An introduction to Chaotic Dynamical Systems. Addison-Wesley, New York (1987)
6. Wiggins, S.: Introduction to Applied Nonlinear Dynamical Systems and Chaos. Springer-Verlag, New York (1990)
7. Li, C.P., Chen, G.: On a universal chaotification scheme in the sense of Li–Yorke. J. Syst. Sci. Complex **16**, 159–164 (2003)
8. Li, C.: On super-chaotifying discrete dynamical systems. Chaos, Solitons & Fractals. **21**, 855–861 (2004)
9. Wang, X.F., Chen, G.: Chaotification via arbitrarily small feedback controls: theory, method, and applications. Int. J. Bif. Chaos **10**, 549–570 (2000)
10. Lu, J.G.: Generating chaos via decentralized linear state feedback and a class of nonlinear functions. Chaos, Solitons Fractals **25**, 403–413 (2005)
11. Yang, L., Liu, Z.: Chaotifying a continuous-time system via impulsive input. Int. J. Bif. Chaos **12**, 1121–1128 (2002)
12. Zhang, H., Wang, Z.L.: Chaotifying fuzzy hyperbolic model using impulsive and nonlinear feedback control approaches. Int. J. Bif. Chaos **15**, 2603–2610 (2005)
13. Liu, N., Guan, Z.H.: Chaotification of discrete dynamical systems via impulsive control. Phys. Lett. A **373**, 2131–2136 (2009)
14. Guan, Z.H., Liu, N.: Generating chaos for discrete time-delayed systems via impulsive control. Chaos **20**, 013135.1–013135.6 (2010)
15. Cheng, Y.P.: Matrix theory. Northwestern Polytechnical University Press, Xi'an (2001)
16. May, R.M.: Simple mathematical models with very complicated dynamics. Nature **161**, 459–467 (1976)

Leakage Prevention Method for Unstructured Data Based on Classification

Hao Li[1], Zewu Peng[1], Xinyao Feng[1], and Hongxia Ma[2($\boxtimes$)]

[1] Information Center, Guangdong Power Grid Corporation, Guangzhou, China
lihao2046@163.com, {pengzewu,fengxinyao}@gdxx.csg.cn
[2] SKLOIS, Institute of Information Engineering, CAS, Beijing, China
mahongxia@iie.ac.cn

Abstract. There is often a lot of sensitive information in the unstructured data of enterprise information network, if not controlled, the sensitive data will flow from the Intranet to the Extranet, which can easily lead to disclosure of corporate information assets, causing serious damage to enterprises. This paper combines the methods of keyword filtering and data label to protect the unstructured data in the corporate data assets based on grading and classification. It is an effective solution to the problem of data leakage, and can greatly reduce false positives in the information protection process, finally improve the accuracy of unstructured data protection. It uses the ElGamal signature algorithm to generate a digital label. Only those people with sensitivity level of keys can make tags with a sensitivity level of document, others cannot replace digital label. At the same time, the network protection server only needs to use the corresponding public key to verify the signature without knowing the private key, thereby effectively ensuring the security of the system.

Keywords: Keyword filtering · Data labels · Signature algorithm

1 Introduction

The enterprise network architecture is generally divided into three parts, that is, the internal network (Intranet), the production Extranet (Extranet) and Internet (Internet). The unstructured data (such as various documents, pictures, etc.) in the enterprise information network is sent from the company's internal network to the Internet or the production Extranet, mainly through a variety of terminal transmission software (such as QQ, Baidu Cloud, mail systems, etc.). Yet there is often a lot of sensitive information in these unstructured data, if such information is not controlled, the sensitive data will flow from the Intranet outside to the Extranet, which can easily lead to disclosure of corporate information assets, resulting in heavy losses to the enterprise [1].

This paper presents the unstructured data assets leakage prevention method based on grading and classification, which combines the methods of keyword filtering and data label to protect the unstructured data in the corporate data assets based on grading and classification. Thereby it is an effective solution to the problem of data leakage, and can greatly reduce false positives in the information protection process, finally improve

© Springer-Verlag Berlin Heidelberg 2015
W. Niu et al. (Eds.): ATIS 2015, CCIS 557, pp. 337–343, 2015.
DOI: 10.1007/978-3-662-48683-2_30

the accuracy of unstructured data protection. In addition, it uses the ElGamal signature algorithm to generate a digital label. Only those people with sensitivity level of keys (that is, secret-related people) can make tags with a sensitivity level of document, others cannot replace digital label. At the same time, the network protection server only needs to use the corresponding public key to verify the signature without knowing the private key, thereby effectively ensuring the security of the system.

2   Related Work

Sensitive information is contained in the enterprise unstructured data, including documents, images, audio and video materials, so in addition to leakage prevention for structured data, leakage prevention for unstructured data is also an important means of corporate data assets disclosure [2]. Gartner notes that among the five major steps of protecting corporate data assets from loss and information from leaking, the first step is to monitor and filter the content of export network traffic [3, 4]. And its premise is identifying the unstructured data containing sensitive information [5, 6]. However, it is not accurate to use labels with sensitivity level to identify unstructured data containing sensitive information, or to use content filtering method to prevent unstructured data with sensitivity level from leaking, both of which tend to have some false positives. It is clear that today with the network and the big data technology growing, it is not enough to solely rely on the traditional content filtering method to prevent disclosure of unstructured data assets [7]. S.W. Ahmad *et al.* has proposed that currently it is a new research direction of leakage prevention for sensitive data with the cryptographic algorithm method [8]. For unstructured data leakage prevention, Michael Hart *et al.* proposed a text classification method for data loss prevention [9]. Recently, X. Chen *et al.* proposed a cloud security assessment system based on classifying and grading [10].

3   Leakage Prevention Method for Unstructured Data Based on Classification

3.1   Automatic Verification Methods Based on Data Label

In general, he who generates sensitive information is the personnel who matches with the secret level or with a higher level. So from the time when sensitive information is generated, it is added a digital label with secret levels by the secret-related personnel who has produced it, that is, its producer uses a pre-assigned private key adapted to the secret level to sign the document. When the document arrives at the Intranet and Extranet exits, in addition to using keywords filtering method to detect the sensitivity level of the document, the network protection server also needs to use the public key with the secret level to verify the signature. If both are validated, it will indicate that the document is sensitive information, whose request should be blocked immediately.

Specifically, the system first should be three public-private key pairs (sk1, pk1), (sk2, pk2), (sk3, pk3) of high sensitivity level, of sensitivity level and with internal data pre-assigned respectively. For example, when a high sensitive document is produced, the producer needs to use highly-sensitive private sk1 to have an ElGamal signature on the document and add the signature to the end of the document. When the document reaches the exit of the Intranet, the network protection server will firstly use the keyword filtering method to determine the sensitivity level of the document, and then use the appropriately highly-sensitive public pk1 to verify the signature. If it is verified, the network request will be blocked.

Among them, the digital signature for unstructured data using ElGamal signature algorithm and the verification of it include the steps as follows:

1. Initialization

   Select a large prime number p and a generator Z_p in the controlled terminal, and publish p and g;

   Then select a random number $sk \in Z_{p-1}$, and calculate $pk = g^{sk}(\mathrm{mod}p)$, and disclosure pk as a public key and make sk as a secret key;

2. Sign the document 'm'

   Choose a random number $k \in Z_{p-1}^*$, to calculate $r = g^k(\mathrm{mod}p)$;

   Solve the equation $m \equiv skr + ks(\mathrm{mod}p - 1)$, then get s. In the equation, m is the document needed encrypting; and (r, s) generated after encryption is the signature of the document m, which is attached to the end of the document m;

3. Verification

   Verify the equation $g^m \equiv pk^r r^s(\mathrm{mod}p)$ is right or not, if right then it can be verified.

3.2 Protection Policy of Network Protection Server

Policy = <data type> <sensitivity level of data> <match type> <filter range> <request type> <source IP> <purpose IP> <if the signature is verified> <response action> <severity level>

   <Data type> = {. doc, .docx, .txt, .xls, .xlsx, .rar, .wps, .ppt, .pptx, .vsd}
   < Sensitivity level of data > = {highly sensitive, sensitive, internal, public}
   <Match type> = {case sensitive, case insensitive}
   <Filter range> = {cover, subject, body, attachments}
   <Request type> = {HTTP, HTTPS, FTP, SMTP}
   <Source IP> indicates a device IP sending this information
   <Purpose IP> indicates the device IP receiving this information
   <Whether the signature is verified> = {Yes, No}
   <Response action> = {block, record}
   <Severity level> = {high, medium, low, none}

Leakage Prevention Strategy of Highly Sensitive Data. Strategy 1 = <data type = all> <sensitivity level of data = high sensitivity> <match type = case-insensitive> <filter range = all> <request type = any> <source IP = Intranet IP> <destination IP = Extranet IP> <if the signature is verified = yes> <response action = block> <severity rating = high>

Strategy 1 is that it filters the keywords of all data types with case-insensitive, and checks their cover, subject, body and attachments, if it finds the keywords of highly-sensitive, the source IP being the Intranet IP, the destination IP being the Extranet IP, and the use of highly-sensitive public keys to sign the document and get the validation, then it will immediately block any form of the request in HTTP/HTTPS/FTP/SMTP. The event severity rating is high.

Leakage Prevention Strategy of Sensitive Data. Strategy 2 = <data type = all> <data sensitivity level = sensitive> <match type = case-insensitive> <filter range = all> <request type = any> <source IP = Intranet IP> <purpose IP = Extranet IP> <if the signature is verified = yes> <response action = block> <severity rating = high>

Strategy 2 is that it filters the keywords of all data types with case-insensitive, and checks their cover, subject, body and attachments, if it finds the keywords of sensitive, the source IP being the Intranet IP, the destination IP being the Extranet IP, and the use of sensitive public keys to sign the document and get the validation, then it will immediately block any form of the request in HTTP/HTTPS/FTP/SMTP. The event severity rating is medium.

Leakage Prevention Strategy of Internal Data. Strategy 3 = <data type = all> <data sensitivity level = internal> <match type = case-insensitive> <filter range = all> <request type = any> <source IP = Intranet IP> <purpose IP = Extranet IP> <if the signature is verified = yes> <response action = block> < rating = low>

Strategy 3 is that it filters the keywords of all data types with case-insensitive, and checks their cover, subject, body and attachments, if it finds the keywords of internal, the source IP being the Intranet IP, the destination IP being the Extranet IP, and the use of internal public keys to sign the document and get the validation, then it will immediately block any form of the request in HTTP /HTTPS/FTP/SMTP. The event severity rating is low.

Leakage Prevention Strategy of Public Data. Strategy 4 = <data type = all> <data sensitivity level = public> <match type = case-insensitive> <filter range = all> <request type = any> <source IP = Intranet IP> <purpose IP = Extranet IP> <response action = register> <severity rating = none>

Strategy 4 is that it filters the keywords of all data types with case-insensitive, and checks their cover, subject, body and attachments, if it finds the keywords of public, the source IP being the Intranet IP, and the destination IP being the Extranet IP, then it will record any form of the request in HTTP/HTTPS/FTP/SMTP.

3.3   The Implementation of Unstructured Data Assets Leakage Prevention Method Based on Classification

It comprises the following steps as in Fig. 1:

1. The controlled terminal makes classification and grading of unstructured data assets, and makes digital signatures of the unstructured data based on sensitivity levels according to corresponding types, including the following steps: The controlled

terminal makes classification and grading of unstructured data assets, and divides them into data of highly-sensitive level, sensitive level, internal level and public level. Then it pre-assigns public and private key pairs to data of highly-sensitive level, sensitive level and internal level respectively, and uses each data to the corresponding private key to make ElGamal signature. The specific steps of using ElGamal signature algorithm to make digital signatures for highly sensitive, sensitive and internal levels of unstructured data, and verifying the signatures, please refer to Sect. 3.1.

2. When the controlled terminal requests to send unstructured data to the Internet or Extranet, the network protection server will filter the data with mirror traffic and sensitive keywords. It includes such details as follows: When the controlled terminal issues the requests of HTTP, HTTPS, FTP or SMTP to send unstructured data to the Internet or the Extranet, the network protection server will judge - if the source IP is the Intranet IP, and the destination IP is the Extranet IP, then it will filter the cover, subject, body and attachments of the unstructured data with mirror traffic and sensitive keywords, to determine if it contains sensitive keywords.

3. If the unstructured data contains sensitive keywords, then use the public key of the corresponding sensitivity level to verify the signature of the unstructured data;

4. If it is verified, then it will block the request of the controlled terminal to send data to the Internet or to the Extranet.

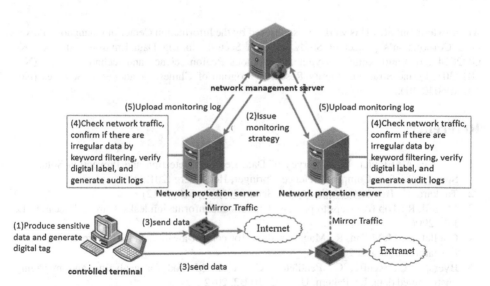

Fig. 1. Hardware connection structure and work principle sketch map in the information leakage protection system

4 Conclusion

There is often a lot of sensitive information in the unstructured data of enterprise information network, if not controlled, the sensitive data will flow from the Intranet to the Extranet, which can easily lead to disclosure of corporate information assets, causing serious damage to enterprises. This paper combines the methods of keyword filtering and data label to protect the unstructured data in the corporate data assets based on grading and classification. It effectively solves the problem of data leakage, and greatly reduces false positives in the information protection process (such as taking the non-sensitive information sensitive information), finally improve the accuracy of unstructured data protection.

In addition, if you use the Hash algorithm in the existing technology to generate a digital label, as long as you know the Hash algorithm, anyone can generate and verify the Hash value, and for the same document, the Hash value generated is the same, then it cannot guarantee that the documents with sensitive level- can only be produced by a person with the corresponding secret level, and anyone can modify the document to re-generate Hash value, therefore it is not conducive to the system safety. Only those people with sensitivity level of keys (that is, secret-related people) can make tags with a sensitivity level of document, others cannot replace digital label. At the same time, the network protection server only needs to use the corresponding public key to verify the signature without knowing the private key, thereby effectively ensuring the security of the system.

Acknowledgement. This work was sponsored by the Information Center of Guangdong Power Grid Corporation's project of Study on Data Security in Big Data Environments (No. K-GD2014-1019) and Xinjiang Uygur Autonomous Region science and technology plan (No. 201230121), the Strategic Priority Research Program of Chinese Academy of Sciences (No. XDA06040601).

References

1. Shabtai, A., Elovici, Y.: A Survey of Data Leakage Detection and Prevention Solutions. SpringerBriefs in Computer Science. Springer, Heidelberg (2012)
2. Tankard, C.: Big data security. Netw. Secur. **2012**(7), 5–8 (2012)
3. Mogull, R.: Top five steps to prevent data loss and information leaks. Gartner Research, 12 July 2006
4. Ouellet, E., McMillan, R.: Magic quadrant for content-aware data loss prevention. Gartner Research, 10 August 2011
5. Byers, A.C., Renfro, C., Pendleton, C., et al.: Method for analyzing and managing unstructured data. US Pattern. US8122510 B2. 2012.2.21
6. Geethakumari, G., Srivatsava, A.: Big data analysis for implementation of enterprise data security. Int. J. Comput. Sci. Inf. Technol. Secur. **2**(4), 742–746 (2012)
7. Besser, S.: Stopping information leaks: Why traditional content filtering is no longer enough. White paper of Port Authority Technologies (2005)
8. Ahmad, S.W., Bamnote, G.R.: Data leakage detection and data prevention using algorithm. Int. J. Comput. Appl. **6**(2), 394–399 (2013)

9. Chen, X., Chen, C., Tao, Y., Hu, J.: Cloud security assessment system based on classifying and grading. IEEE Cloud Comput. Mag. **2**(2), 58–67 (2015)
10. Hart, M., Manadhata, P., Johnson, R.: Text classification for data loss prevention. In: Fischer-Hübner, S., Hopper, N. (eds.) PETS 2011. LNCS, vol. 6794, pp. 18–37. Springer, Heidelberg (2011)

System Design and Implementations

Decryption and Forensic System for Encrypted iPhone Backup Files Based on Parallel Random Search

Liang Ge[✉] and Lianhai Wang

Shandong Provincial Key Laboratory of Computer Networks,
Shandong Computer Science Center (National Supercomputer Center in Jinan),
Jinan, Shandong, China
{gel,wanglh}@sdas.org

Abstract. The forensics for the iPhone backup files is an important problem in digital forensics. Since the backup files are often encrypted and the key chain data is always encrypted even if the data is not completely encrypted, it is difficult to deal with this problem by the traditional methods such as sequence brute force. In this paper, we give a new method based on parallel random search on CPU+GPU platform to solve this problem. The main principle of this method is to parallel random search the passwords in the given dictionary based on the CPU+GPU platform in order to crack the password of the encrypted iPhone backup files. An analysis of decryption and reduction method as well as the file structure is also shown in this paper. Finally the experiment result shows that the method given in this paper can greatly improve the efficiency of forensics for the encrypted iPhone backup files.

Keywords: iPhone forensics · Encrypted backup files · Parallel random search · GPU

1 Introduction

With the development and popularity of mobile devices and smart operating system, smart mobiles are increasingly involved in our daily life and work. Among them, iPhone has occupied a large market share of mobile device [1]. Especially in china, it is more and more common that personal and business users communicate and handle business through iPhone. The way of criminals through the iPhone is increasingly sophisticated, while the frequency of iPhone appearing in the criminal cases is also increasing. So in order to effectively combat crime and safeguard the lives and property of the people, all countries have gradually paid more attention to the forensics technology for iPhone.

There are efforts from both commercial and individual forensic experts on iPhone forensics. Commercial products include Aceso by Radio Tactics [2], UFED from Cellebrite [3], Device Seizure by Paraben [4], .XRY by Micro Systemation [5] and CellDEK by LogiCube [6]. Also some researchers have put their attention on the iPhone forensics, such as [7–9]. Overall, there are three ways to acquire evidence from iPhone: (1) logically acquire data after Jailbreaking the iPhone; (2) physically acquire data by disassembling the iPhone; (3) acquire data from the backup files.

© Springer-Verlag Berlin Heidelberg 2015
W. Niu et al. (Eds.): ATIS 2015, CCIS 557, pp. 347–358, 2015.
DOI: 10.1007/978-3-662-48683-2_31

The first method was developed in order to overcome the access restriction set up by Apple so that only application approved by them can be installed and executed, which makes it extremely difficult to acquire any type of meaningful forensics data. Jail-breaking the iPhone is the process that provides a root access to the device in order to install third-party applications that aren't available through official channels. This method was proposed by Zdziarski [10] which could get a bit-to-bit copy logical image of the iPhone. However jailbreaking the iPhone would firstly change the IOS system of the device, which will make the integrity of the gathered evidence questionable. So the evidence given by this method in most cases may not be accepted by the law.

The second method is the physical acquiration which needs to disassemble the iPhone [11]. In order to do that, the investigators need to unsolder the flash ROM chips from the iPhone and extract the data with a NAND dump. But this method may damage or destroy the iPhone, which will make all data lost. So it is not also accepted by some cases.

The third method is a relatively easy method, which only needs to view the backup files of iPhone in the computer [9]. When the iPhone connect to a computer which has iTunes, it would make a logical copy of the data to the computer. So the investigators could analyze the backup data to obtain the evidence. Several tools have been designed to accomplish this task such as mdhelper [12] which could acquire and display the data of iPhone backup files. However there is also some shortcoming of this method. An important problem is that many backup files are encrypted. And even the whole folder is not encrypted, the key data such as the key of the iPhone is still encrypted.

At present, there are mainly four methods for password recovery in the field of computer forensics, such as guess [13], dictionary attack [14], brute force cracking [15–18] and rainbow table crack [19]. For the encrypted iPhone backup files, there are also some works, such as Belenko [20] give a password recovery method for IOS 4. But most of these works based on brute force need to take a long time to crack the password.

In [21], the authors give a password recovery method for RAR based on parallel random search. This method has the feature of fast operation and high hit rate which has synthesized the advantage of parallel computing and random search. In this paper, we will provide a method that is designed to acquire evidence from the encrypted iPhone backup files. This method is based on parallel random password recovery method on CPU+GPU platform. After the password has been cracked, the encrypted files and the key chain would be restored by an algorithm given in this paper. Finally an experiment is given to verify the effectiveness of our method for the encrypted backup files.

The rest of this paper is organized as follows. Section 2 presents some related works for the structure of iPhone backup files, the decryption and reduction of the encrypted iPhone backup file, and the knowledge of GPU with CUDA. Section 3 presents our forensics system based on parallel random search. In Sect. 4, we show the contrast of our method and brute force by an experiment. Finally in Sect. 5, we show our conclusions.

2   Related Work

In this section we will introduce the structure of iPhone backup files, the decryption and reduction of the encrypted iPhone backup file, and the knowledge of GPU with CUDA.

2.1 Backup File Structure of iPhone

iTunes is used to backup the iphone to a computer. iTunes is the free software application used by Apple to synchronize content on iPhone, iPad or iPod Touch with a coupled computer. When the iPhone is synched with the computer, the device's configuration, address book, calendar, images, SMS database, email accounts, web history, network configuration information and other sorts of personal data is saved on the computer in backup files in a single directory. By default, the iTunes application creates a backup of the IOS devices' data during the sync process. Different operating system has different storage location when iPhone backups data by using iTunes, the detail information is shown in Table 1. When iTunes syncs the iPhone with the computer, it copies data from the IOS device to the PC and vice versa to ensure that content is same on both.

Table 1. Backup file's storage location of using iTunes

Operation system	Location
Windows XP	C:\documents and setting\[user name]\Application Data\Apple Computer\MobileSync\Backup\[UDID]
Windows Vista/Windows 7	C:\Users\[user name]\AppData\Roaming\Apple Computer\MobileSync\Backup\[UDID]
Mac OS X	~/Library/Application Support/MobileSync/Backup/ (~ represents user's home directory)

It is possible to have an arbitrary number of backups, as each backup is stored in a subdirectory of the previously described path. The name of the backed-up folder is a string of 40 hexadecimal digits, and represents a unique identifier for the device from where the backup was obtained. Example file name is:

8ca4ea8fbc3591e5facbf8de6dcb3bb1eeb6a817

The backup folder contains a list of files which are not in a readable format, and it consists of uniquely name files with a 40 digit alphanumeric hex value without any file extension. Among them, .mbdb file and .plist files contain some information about the backup. The file Status.plist store information about the status of the backup itself, such as whether the backup is complete or not. The file Manifest.plist describes the contents of the backup. In this file we could find the applications installed on the backup device (each with its version number), along with the date the backup was made, whether the backup is encrypted or not. The file Manifest.mbdb are binary files which store the information about all other files in the backup along with the file sizes and file system structure data. Other files that do not have an extension are the real backup files. This 40 digit hex file name is the SHA1 hash value of the file path appended to the respective domain name with a '-' symbol. If these files are encrypted after backup, we need to decrypt them.

2.2   Decryption and Reduction of iPhone Encrypted Backup Files

The backup encryption system is a big obstacle for the investigators in the forensic analysis of the iPhone backup data. If they want to acquire the data of mobile, they must firstly obtain the password of backup files. We next discuss the technology for decryption and reduction of iPhone encrypted backup files, such as password recovery, file decryption and reduction, and the extraction of keychain data.

Password Recovery. Through the analysis of the iPhone backup files, we find that there is a few data relevant with decryption saved in manifest.plist and PBKDF2 algorithm, AES algorithm, SHA-1 algorithm are used in the process of iPhone backup file decryption. The password recovery of iPhone backup file is as following:

(1) Generate a password with the generation scheme;
(2) find the salt value in manifest.plist;
(3) put the password and salt into the PBKDF2 algorithm, and obtain the Passcode key after 10000 SHA-1 computation;
(4) get the cipertext of class key in manifest.plist;
(5) use the AES Unwrap algorithm and Passcode key to decrypt the cipertext of class key, and use some parameters in manifest.plist to check for the completeness. If successful, then output the password; else go to (1) to generate a new password.

Reduction of Backup Files. The password of the encrypted backup file has been obtained in the above subsection. But this is just the first step for the reduction of backup files. If we want to obtain the original backup files, we need to further analyze.

Usually there are two features of the encrypted iPhone backup files: one is that the filename is changed into serial number; other is that the information of files is encrypted. So the reduction of encrypted backup files is divided into three steps to achieve. The process is shown in Fig. 1.

(1) Decryption of filename: Since the filenames of backup file are stored in manifes.mbdb, we could compute the SHA-1 value of the original filename to obtain a new filename and then compare with the real filename. If the comparison is successful, we could establish the one to one corresponding relationship between the original filenames and the encrypted filename. Then we could decrypt the filename.
(2) Decryption of backup file: Firstly use the password and PBKDF2 algorithm to obtain the Passcode key; then use the Passcode key and the AES Unwrap algorithm to obtain class key; and then use the class key and AES Unwrap algorithm to decrypt the ciphertext of AES key in manifest.mbdb to obtain the plaintext of the AES key; finally use the AES key and AES algorithm to decrypt the encrypted backup files.
(3) Merge the results of the first two steps, and we could complete the reduction of documents.

Extraction of Keychain Data. Keychain is the password management system of iPhone. It contains a lot of key information of iPhone, such as account password, serial number, credentials, and so on. It is very important for the investigators. There are a few key chain files contained in the backup files. But they are always encrypted even if the

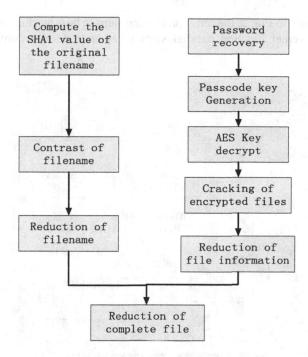

Fig. 1. Reduction of the encrypted backup files

backup files have been decrypted. In order to obtain the private message of keychain database, we need to analyze the encrypted keychain files.

The reduction process of keychain file is similar to the reduction of encrypted backup files. Firstly use the password and PBKDF2 algorithm to obtain the Passcode key; then use the Passcode key and the AES Unwrap algorithm to obtain class key; and then use the class key and AES Unwrap algorithm to decrypt the ciphertext of AES key in keychain-backup.plist to obtain the plaintext of the AES key; finally use the AES key and AES-CBC algorithm to decrypt the encrypted keychain-backup.plist and obtain the information of keychain.

2.3   Related Knowledge of GPU with CUDA

The programming model of CUDA is the currency most commonly used for programming on GPU. It usually uses the model of slave/master, which takes the CPU as the host and takes the GPU as the co-processor [22]. In this heterogeneous model, the GPU must be team working with CPU. The CPU usually is used to execute the strong logic transaction and the serial arithmetic, and GPU is usually used to perform highly threaded parallel processing tasks. If the parallel part is computation-intensive, we can use the GPU to achieve these computational tasks. Kernal function is a CUDA parallel computing function running in the GPU. A separate kernel function is not a complete procedure. It is just one step that can be executed concurrently in the whole CUDA program. As shown in Fig. 2, the serial processing steps in host machine and a series of equipment end kernel function parallel steps together to form a complete CUDA program.

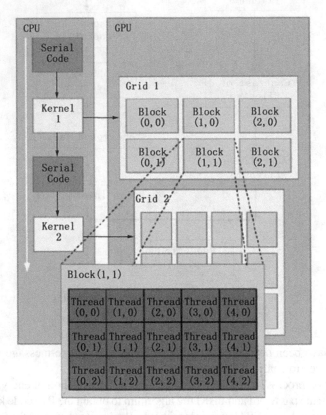

Fig. 2. CUDA programming model

3   Decryption and Forensics System Based on Parallel Random Search

From the above section, we could find that the key of forensics for iPhone encrypted backup files is the password recovery. So we will give a decryption and forensics system for encrypted iPhone backup files based on parallel random search in this section. The password recovery based on parallel random search was firstly given in [21], and we will give a new scheme based on the CPU+GPU platform.

From [21], there are two key steps of parallel random password recovery: one is the generation of random number; other is the encryption cracking. Firstly we show the parallel random number generation method. We use the double linear congruence random generation and CPU+GPU hybrid mode to achieve this algorithm. The algorithm is shown as following, where a is the multiplier, M is the remainder, x_0 is the initial value and P is the number of GPU cores.

1. In CPU
    Input: a, x_0, M, P
    Output : A_j, x_j, j=1,2,...,P
    Let A_0=a;
    For j=1; j<=P; j++
        A_j=a×A_{j-1} mod M
        x_j=a×x_{j-1} mod M
2. In GPU
    Input: A_j, x_j, M, n
    Output: P_j^k, k=1,2, ..., n; j=1,2, ...,P
    Let R_j^0=x_j
    For k=1; k<=n; k++
    Loop:
    R_j^k =A_j×R_j^{k-1} mod M
    P_j^k=f(R_j^k);
    C=Encrypt(P_j^k);
    If(C'satisfies the condition of iPhone password verification in Sect. 2.2)
    Break;
    Else
    Goto Loop;

In the above algorithm, the parallel technology is used to the generation of random numbers and the password verification of iPhone backup file. Since the linear congruence parameters of random number generator for each slave node are derived from the same master, random number generated can't repeat. And each core of GPU can deal with the password cracking independently. Comparing with the traditional sequential brute force password recovery, the parallel random password recovery method based on GPU could be more quickly since the probability to hit the proper key of each random search is same meanwhile the probability of each sequential search is 1/N (N is the size of the key space).

Following the reduction method for iPhone backup files given in Sect. 2.2, we can easily give the decryption and forensics system after the correct password has been obtained. The principle of the parallel random password recovery for encrypted iPhone backup files based on CPU+GPU is shown (Fig. 3).

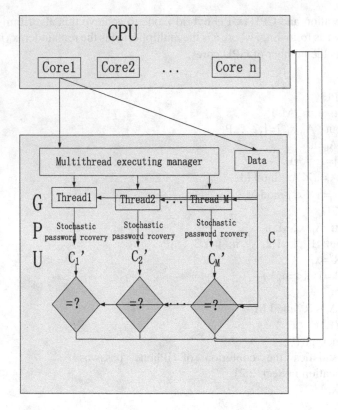

Fig. 3. Parallel random password recovery for encrypted iPhone backup files based on GPU

4   Experiment

In this section we would give a experiment to verify the efficiency of our password recovery method for encrypted iPhone backup files. This section contains two parts: firstly we would show the experiment environment, and then we would give the comparison between our method and the sequential brute force method.

4.1   Test Platform

In order to test the performance of parallel random search for the password recovery of encrypted iPhone backup files, we set up the CPU and GPU platform. Relevant parameters of experiment environment: the GPU is NVIDA Geforce GT420 and the CPU is Intel(R) Core™ i5 CPU 2500 @3.30 GHz, with 4.00 GHz RAMS, and the operation system is 32-bit Windows 7.

4.2   Contrast Between Parallel Random Search on CPU+GPU and Sequential Search on CPU

The contrast is performed in a known dictionary. We divide the dictionary into 7 parts and for each part we repeat 100 tests to obtain a mean result. The average value of search times is used in comparison of the sequential and the parallel random process. In the first, searched word is located in the first 1/4 of the wordlist. In the next test case, the word is located in the first 2/4 of the wordlist, and so on. In the last test case the searched word is located in the last 1/4 of the whole wordlist. Table 2 shows locations of the searched word for all 7 test cases. And all of the chosen one would be as a password to generate the new encrypted iPhone backup files.

Table 2. Ranges of picked words

Test case	Parts of dictionary for selection			
1	1/4	1/4	1/4	1/4
2	1/4	1/4	1/4	1/4
3	1/4	1/4	1/4	1/4
4	1/4	1/4	1/4	1/4
5	1/4	1/4	1/4	1/4
6	1/4	1/4	1/4	1/4
7	1/4	1/4	1/4	1/4

Two sizes of wordlists have been used for the testing purposes, containing 0.5×10^6 words and 1.0×10^6 words. Although the selected word is located in the special part of the wordlist, the search range of the parallel random search and sequential search is all of the wordlist. The result is shown in Fig. 4.

The contrast between the parallel random search on CPU+GPU and sequential search on CPU for the encrypted iPhone backup files password recovery of all the 7 cases for the two wordlists are shown in Fig. 4. On the X axis there are 7 test cases from 1 to 7, and on the Y axis an average time of the parallel random search and sequential search is shown. From Fig. 4, we can see that the average times of the parallel random search is lower than these in the sequential search.

It can be concluded that our parallel random search is much better than the traditional sequential brute force password recovery for the encrypted iPhone backup files. And our decryption and forensics system for the encrypted iPhone backup files is powerful.

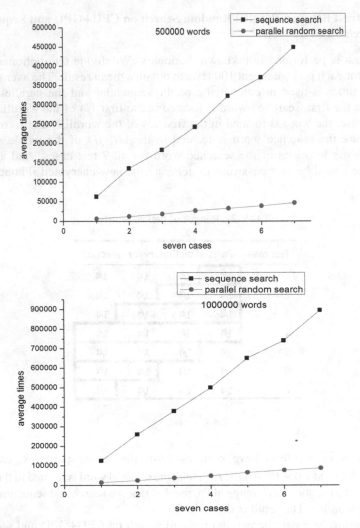

Fig. 4. Contrast between the parallel random search and sequential search

5   Conclusion

At present iPhone forensics is an important problem for fighting against cybercrime. There are three main methods for iPhone forensics, such as logical forensics, physical forensics and forensics on iPhone backup. And these methods also have some short-coming. For the method that acquires evidence from the encrypted iPhone backup files, the encryption is a big obstacle. We give a decryption and forensics system for the encrypted iPhone backup files based on parallel random search on CPU+GPU platform. And the experiment has shown that it could be more efficiency than the traditional brute force method for the forensics of the encrypted iPhone backup files. So this is a good way to solve the problem of iPhone forensics.

Acknowledgments. Special appreciative to reviewers for useful advices and comments. This study is supported by the Shandong Province Outstanding Young Scientists Research Award Fund Project(Grant No. BS2013DX010), by the Natural Science Foundation of Shandong Province, China(Grant No. ZR2014FM003, ZR2013FQ001, ZR2013FM025, ZR2015YL018), and by the Shandong Academy of Sciences Youth Fund Project(Grant No. 2013QN007).

References

1. Milanesi, C., Gupta, A., Vergne, H., et al.: Garner technology business research insight. In: Dataquest insight market share for mobile device, 1Q09. http://www.gartner.com/Display Document?id=984612
2. Radio Tactics Ltd: Aceso-Mobile forensics wrapped up. In: Radio Tactics|Mobile Phone Forensics. http://www.radio-tactics.com/products/aceso/
3. Cellebrite Forensics: Cellebrite mobile data synchronization UFED standard kit. In: cellebrite mobile data synchronization. http://www.cellebrite.com/UFED-Standard-lit.html
4. Paraben Corporation: Cell Phone Forensics. In: Paraben Coropation, Cel Phone Forensics Software. http://www.paraben-forensics.com/cell_models.html
5. Micro Systemation: XRY Physical Software. In: XRY the complete mobile forensic solution. http://www.msab.com/products/xry0/overview/page.php
6. Logicube: Logicube CellDEK Cell Phone Data Extraction. In: Logicube.com, hard drive duplication, copying hard drive and computer forensics. http://www.logicubeforensics.com/products/hd_duplication/celldek.asp
7. Husain, M., Baggili, I., Sridhar, R.: A simple cost-effective framework for iPhone forensic analysis. LNICST **53**, 27–37 (2011)
8. Mcp, B., Cissp, A., Obaidli, H.: A novel method of idevice(iPhone, iPad, iPod) forensics without jailbreaking. In: 2012 International Conference on Innovations in Information Technology, pp. 238–243 (2012)
9. Satish, B.: Forensic analysis of iPhone backups. http://www.exploit-db.com/docs/19767.pdf
10. Zdziarski, J.: iPhone Forensics: Recovering Evidence, Personal Data, and Corporate Assets. O'Reilly, Sebastopol (2008). ISBN 978-0-596-15358-8
11. Kubasiak, R.R., Morrissey, S.: Mac OS X, iPod, and iPhone Forensic Analysis DVD Toolkit, vol. 13. Elsevier Inc., Burlington (2009). ISBN 978-1-59749-297-3
12. Mdhelper. http://ericasadun.com/ftp/Macintosh
13. Ding, Y., Horster, P.: Undetectable on-line password guessing attacks. SIGOPS Operating Syst. Reviex **29**(4), 77–86 (1995)
14. Delaune, S., Jacquemard, F.: A theory of dictionary attacks and its complexity. In: Proceedings of 17th IEEE Computer Security Foundations Workshop, pp. 2–15, Cambridge, UK (2004)
15. Hu, G., Ma, J., Huang, B.: Password recovery for RAR files using CUDA. In: Proceedings of 8th IEEE International Conference on Dependable, Autonomic and Secure Computing, pp. 486–490, Chengdu, China (2009)
16. Apostal, D., Foerster, K., Chatterjee, A., Desell, T.: Password recovery using MPI and CUDA. In: The 19th International Conference on High Performance Computing, pp. 1–9 (2012)

17. Zhan, X.J., Hong, J.X.: Study on GPU-based password recovery for MS Office 2003 document. In: The 7th International Conference on Computer Science and Education, pp. 517–520 (2012)
18. Kim, K.: Distributed password cracking on GPU nodes. In: The 7th International Conference on Computing and Convergence Technology, pp. 647–650 (2012)
19. Narayanan, A., Shmatikov, V.: Fast dictionary attacks on passwords using time-space tradeoff. In: Proceedings of the 12th ACM Conference on Computer and Communications Security, pp. 364–372 (2005)
20. Belenko, A.: Overcoming iOS data protection to re-enable iPhone forensics, Blackhat (2011)
21. Ge, L., Wang, L.: Research of password recovery method for RAR based on parallel random search. In: Batten, L., Li, G., Niu, W., Warren, M. (eds.) ATIS 2014. CCIS, vol. 490, pp. 211–218. Springer, Heidelberg (2014)
22. NVIDIA Corporation CUDA. http://www.nvidia.com/object/cudahomenew.html

The Method and System Implementation of Unstructured Data Tracking and Forensics

Guangyu Gu[1], Shujuan Zhang[1], Xuefei Wang[1], Xiang Cai[1], and Sheng Chen[2(✉)]

[1] Anhui Electric Power Research Institute, Hefei 230601, China
{gugy2051,zhangsj202x}@ah.sgcc.com.cn, shaffey@sina.com,
caixiangcx3@163.com
[2] SKLOIS, Institute of Information Engineering, CAS, Beijing, China
chensheng@iie.ac.cn

Abstract. For the problem that unstructured data is widespread, not under the centralized management of data resource management platform, and currently the safety monitoring of unstructured data is only for a part of data creation, transmission and destruction, lacking a data security management view with a whole life cycle, which is difficult to track data breaches and other security incidents, this paper studies that through log audit records and analysis report, it establishes a safety management view with a whole life cycle of unstructured data to effectively solve the problem of data breaches and other security incidents which cannot be traced. It uses unique file identifiers for the tracking of the whole lifecycle of unstructured data, establishes an evidence chain of the whole life cycle of the creation, transmission, access and destruction of data assets. It aims at providing analytical basis and forensic data support for events occurring at each aspect of data assets, and facilitating the tracking of data breaches and other security incidents, which has improved the accuracy and real-time of data monitoring.

Keywords: Whole life cycle · Security management view · Security policy · Identifiers

1 Introduction

The unstructured data of enterprises includes such things as office documents, texts, pictures, XML, HTML, images, and audio/video information stored in each terminal and system server. Different from structured data, unstructured data is often widespread, dispersedly managed and stored by each department. According to business needs, unstructured data is frequently transferred between each terminal and server in enterprise networks, thereby it is difficult to have a security control over it with a full life cycle [1].

Currently, the safety monitoring of unstructured data is only security audit [2–5] and monitoring [6–10] usually for a portion of data creation, transmission and destruction.

© Springer-Verlag Berlin Heidelberg 2015
W. Niu et al. (Eds.): ATIS 2015, CCIS 557, pp. 359–367, 2015.
DOI: 10.1007/978-3-662-48683-2_32

If security incidents happen, what you can do is just to view the audit logs of devices one by one. When data is transferred frequently between multiple devices, all the data operating information is difficult to master, and it lacks security management view of data life cycle as a whole, thereby it is difficult for the tracking of data breaches and other security incidents.

This paper presents a method of unstructured data tracking and forensics to study that through log audit records and analysis report, it establishes a safety management view with a whole life cycle of unstructured data, thereby effectively solving the problem of data breaches and other security incidents which cannot be traced. In addition, it also uses unique file identifiers for the tracking of the whole lifecycle of big data, establishes an evidence chain of the whole life cycle of the creation, transmission, access and destruction of data assets. It aims at providing analytical basis and forensic data support for events occurring at each aspect of data assets, and facilitating the tracking of data breaches and other security incidents, which has improved the accuracy and real-time of data monitoring.

2   Establishment of Security Management View with a Whole Life Cycle of Unstructured Data

2.1   Establishment of Safety Management View

The main design is conducted from two aspects, that is, data tracking and forensics: First, it records the data operation in such various stages as creation, storage, use, transfer, destruction and recovery of unstructured data file, and store them as log audit records to complete data tracking. Then, it reads the records of unstructured data file in various stages, and analyzes the data operation in violation of security policy to generate analysis reports, thereby completing data forensics. Finally, it establishes a secure management view of unstructured data with whole life cycle (Fig. 1), which shows the information of all stages of the creation of data transfer, operation and destroy, providing analysis evidence and forensic data support the data in each part of the data assets events.

2.2   Establishment of Unstructured Data Evidence Chain

Data tracking and forensics take data object as the core, monitor and manage the entire life cycle of data objects (creation, storage, use, transmission, destruction and recovery), and can provide a detailed record of the data whole life cycle (for example, creator, usage, transferee, and destroyer). When you need forensics, you can query the data object to get its full life cycle record, and which operation of the specific operator (or operators) when and where violates the security policy. You can form a complete chain of evidence for forensics and accountability.

As can be seen from Fig. 2, the evidence chain of unstructured data refers to the detailed record generated by the life cycle of unstructured data, which includes records creation (quantity: 1), use record (quantity: 0-n), transfer record (quantity: 0-m), destruction record (quantity: 0–2), recovery record (quantity: 0–1). Among them, the word use refers to such operations as copying, modification, renaming, moving and printing of the file; transmission means copying by USB flash disk, file transfer through network and other means; destruction includes logical deleting and physical destroying.

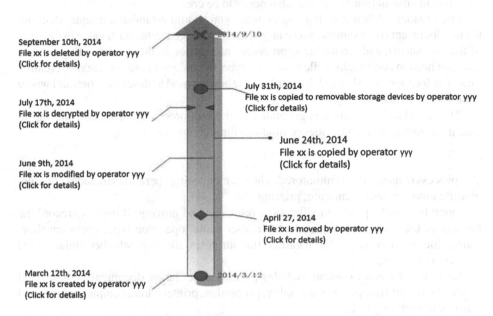

Fig. 1. A schematic diagram of safety management view

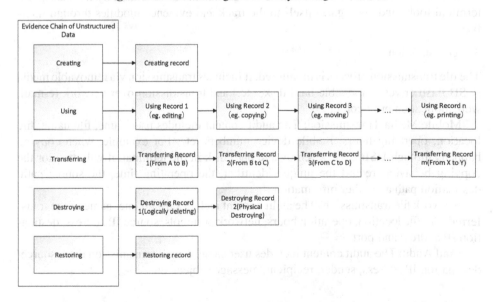

Fig. 2. A specific schematic diagram of the evidence chain of unstructured data

Specifically the process of establishing the evidence chain of unstructured data is as follows:

1. Creation

When a new file is created, the metadata information of the document, that is, the description information of the file, also needs to be created.

File creation: When creating a document, you should establish a unique identifier for the document (for example, you can add a randomly generated hash value in the head of the document), and record the appropriate information in the database; the contents that you need to audit include file name, file type, file unique identifier, creator, creation time, file location, file size and file attributes. They are used to describe when and where what file is created.

The metadata information is generated by the leak-proof terminal tools, and aggregate itself to the track and evidence modules through interfaces.

2. Use

The process of using files is monitored. The file monitoring operations includes copying, modification, renaming, moving, printing, etc.

Operations of Copying, modification, renaming and moving: It needs to record the file name, file type, file unique identifier, user name, operation type, operation time, source file location, target file location, file attributes, file size, whether violating the security policy, etc.

Printing: The audit content includes printing time, target document path, printed pages, document size, paper size, quality, proportion, printer name, computer names and users in the printing task.

The above operating information of the documents is generated by the leak-proof terminal tools, and aggregates itself to the track and evidence modules through interfaces.

3. Transmission

The file transmission process is monitored. It Includes transmission via removable media (USB flash drives, removable hard disk, etc.) and transmission over network (e-mail, web application protocol, etc.).

Mobile Media Transmission: The audit content includes user name, file name, file location, operating hours, mobile device numbers, etc. For example, when copying happens through USB disk or removable hard disk in the terminal, it will monitor the copying behavior, record the unique identifier, the operating time, the source path, destination path and other information.

Network file transmission: The audit content includes user name, name of the transferred file, file location, operation hours, network protocols, source IP address, destination IP address and port.

Mail Audit: The audit content includes user name, e-mail transmission time, source/destination IP address, sender, recipient, message subject, etc.

When a file is sent via network protocol, the device at the outlet of the network will identify the file by the unique file identifier, record such related information of the transferred file as source IP, destination IP, time, unique file identifier, etc.

Removable media transmission is collected by terminal leak-proof, and network file transmission and e-mail auditing are collected by network leak-proof tool, and aggregate themselves to the track and evidence modules through interfaces.

4. Destruction and Recovery

The process of destruction (recovery) of documents is monitored. It includes deleting (recovering) data logically and destroying (recovering) storage medium physically.

Deleting (recovering) file logically: It needs to record the file name, file type, user name, operation type, operating time, file location, file attributes, file size, whether violating the security policies, etc.

Destroying (recovering) document physically: It needs to record the media name, media type, operating time, media size, etc.

The logical deletion (recovery) of files is collected by terminal leak-proof tools, and the physical destruction (restoration) of documents is collected by the data destruction (recovery) equipment, aggregating themselves to the track and evidence modules through interfaces.

3   Implementation of Unstructured Data Tracking and Forensics Systems

As can be seen from Fig. 3, in the analysis of physical category, the bottom line of the entity is on behalf of unstructured data assets in different states in the life cycle, the middle row of the entity is on behalf of different engines which protect data assets in all round way, and the top represents log servers of different engines. From the functional point of view, different protection engines at different locations of lifecycle within data assets form the underlying tracking chains for protecting and marking data assets, and then analyze logging records of different protective engines in a comprehensive and associating way to form a forensic chain of data assets.

It is made according to the classification management and protection strategy of data assets. The sensitive assets with specific security classification level will be incorporated into the scope of monitoring the entire protection system. It will describe the flow shown in Fig. 3 in a detailed way as follows:

1. According to the data security level and security protection policy, the (sensitive) plaintext data with low security level is encrypted by encryption engine to become the ciphertext data. The encryption engine then tags the data in the encrypting process and saves the encrypting operation record to the log server;

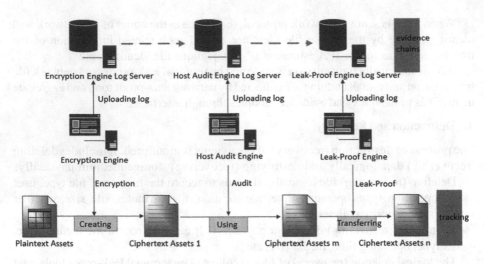

Fig. 3. A schematic diagram of unstructured data tracking and forensics system

2. The host audit engine monitors and records the operation behavior of the ciphertext data used in the controlled terminal (including copying, deletion, modification and reading). The host audit engine reads data tags, and saves the monitoring information as log in the log server;

3. When the ciphertext data is transmitted over the network to another network location, the leak-proof engine will filter and monitor the transmitted data, and the leak-proof engine will read data tags, and save the monitoring and filtering information as log in log server.

Data objects mainly refer to office documents, images, audios, videos and other unstructured data files.

3.1   Document Tracking Process

Creation phase. As shown in Fig. 4, in accordance with the audit log created by the terminal leak-proof tools or encryption and decryption tools, it creates file metadata, and generates metadata database. For such operational behavior as file using, file sent from terminal, file sent through the network, document destruction and recovery, it will conduct such operations as terminal DLP audit, removable storage DLP audit, network DLP audit, destroying and recovering equipment logs, and it will save log audit records centrally in the metabase.

Other stages. When a data file is changed from the creation stage, it will capture the change through safe management and control tools and then produce an audit log, that is, terminal leak-proof tools create audit logs which files and removable storage devices use, network leak-proof tools generate audit logs which files transfer, and data destruction and recovery equipment generate audit logs of data destruction and recovery. It saves the audit logs additionally in the metabase.

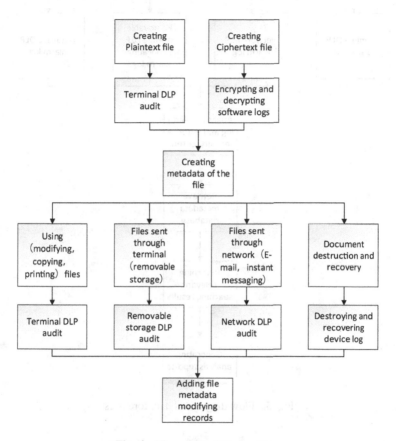

Fig. 4. Flowchart of file tracking

3.2 File Forensics Process

As shown in Fig. 5, it reads and analyzes alarm logs (alarm log records data operation behaviors violating the security policy) in the audit log record. It queries the corresponding data of alarm logs, gets a unique identifier of the corresponding data, and goes into metabase to query according to the unique identifier. And then it returns to the queried metadata information, and generates analysis report.

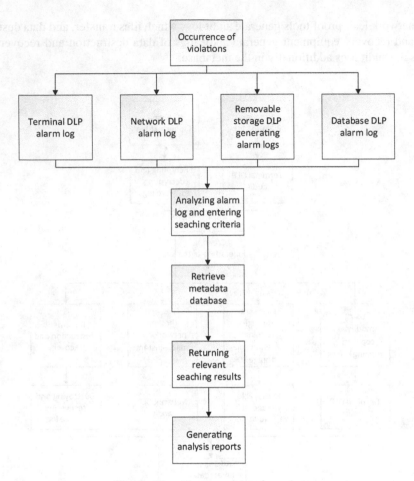

Fig. 5. Flow diagram of data forensics

4   Conclusion

For the problem that unstructured data is widespread, not under the centralized management of data resource management platform, and currently the safety monitoring of unstructured data is only for a part of data creation, transmission and destruction, lacking a data security management view with a whole life cycle, which is difficult to track data breaches and other security incidents, this paper studies that through log audit records and analysis report, it establishes a safety management view with a whole life cycle of unstructured data to effectively solve the problem of data breaches and other security incidents which cannot be traced. This paper takes data object as the core, monitors and manages the entire life cycle of data objects (creation, storage, use, transmission, destruction and recovery), and can provide a detailed record of the data whole life cycle (for example, creator, usage, transferee, and destroyer). When you need forensics, you can query the data object to get its full life cycle record, and which operation of the specific operator (or operators) when and where violates the security policy. You can form a complete chain of evidence for forensics and accountability. It uses unique file identifiers for the tracking of the whole lifecycle of unstructured data, establishes an evidence chain of the whole life cycle of the creation, transmission, access and destruction of data assets. It aims at providing analytical basis and forensic data support for events occurring at each aspect of data assets, and facilitating the tracking of data breaches and other security incidents, which has improved the accuracy and real-time of data monitoring.

Acknowledgement. This work was sponsored by the Information Center of Guangdong Power Grid Corporation's project of Study on Data Security in Big Data Environments (No. K-GD2014-1019) and Xinjiang Uygur Autonomous Region science and technology plan (No. 201230121), the Strategic Priority Research Program of Chinese Academy of Sciences (No. XDA06040601).

References

1. Simms, D.: Big data, unstructured data, and the cloud: perspectives on internal controls. In: Xhafa, F., Barolli, L., Barolli, A., Papajorgji, P. (eds.) Modeling and Processing for Next-Generation Big-Data Technologies. MOST, vol. 4, pp. 319–340. Springer, Heidelberg (2015)
2. Mounji, A., Le Charlier, B., Zampunieris, D.: Distributed audit trail analysis. In: Proceedings of the Symposium on Network and Distributed System Security (NDSS), pp. 102–112 (1995)
3. Becker, R.A., Chambers, J.M.: Auditing of data analyses. SIAM J. Sci. Stat. Comput. 9(4), 747–760 (1988)
4. Dodd, T., Heinrich, N.: Method and system for calculating risk in association with a security audit of a computer network. US Patent, US 20020147803 A1 (2002)
5. Watanabe, A.: Security audit system and method. US Patent, US8505066 B2 (2008)
6. Kumari, P., Sharma, H., Shekhar, A.: Monitoring aspects of cloud over the big data analytics using the hadoop for managing short files. Data Min. Knowl. Eng. 7, 131–139 (2015)
7. Neels, A., Vasan, S., Fishel, S.: Generating Reports from Unstructured Data. United States Patent Application 20150019537
8. Cain, F., Cotichini, C., Nguyen, T.C.: Security monitoring apparatus and method. US Patent, US 8606971 B2 (2013)
9. Li, D.: Poster: toward a theoretical privacy framework for electronic locks in context of home security monitoring system for clouds of things. In: MobiHoc 2015, pp. 393–394 (2015)
10. Alexander, B., Talley, P., Hicks, J.: System and method for providing configurable security monitoring utilizing an integrated information system. US Patent, US 8392552 B2 (2013)

The Design and Implementation of Data Security Management and Control Platform

Hong Zou[1], Yang Qian[1], Yanshuai Zhao[1], and Kun Ding[2](✉)

[1] Information Center, Guangdong Power Grid Corporation, Guangzhou, China
{zouhong,qianyang,zhaoyanshuai}@gdxx.csg.cn
[2] SKLOIS, Institute of Information Engineering, CAS, Beijing, China
dingkun@iie.ac.cn

Abstract. This paper proposes a new data security management and control platform to solve the problem that it lacks differentiated protection for the mass and heterogeneous data assets of enterprises, the data asset protection strategy is at a much coarse-grained level, and the enterprise security products are concerned only with their own protected equipment, lacking a unified security view, and unable to conduct big data tracking and forensics. First, it assigns the confidentiality, integrity and availability of data assets based on three characteristics of data security (confidentiality C, integrity I, usability A), to better reflect the business value of data assets, and it distinguishes the levels of data assets value, to improve the utilization of security protection tools. Then the platform automatically assigns specific data levels according to data classification, making fine-grained access control possible. It also studies the construction method of safety view, so as to effectively solve the problem that it lacks differentiated protection for corporate data assets, the data asset protection strategy is at a much coarse-grained level and lacks a unified security view, and unable to conduct big data tracking and forensics.

Keywords: Data security management and control · Data classification and grading · Access control · Encryption and decryption · Security management view

1 Introduction

As the development of enterprise business and information technology, business data as a kind of corporate assets (data assets), shows the characteristics of large amount, diversity and high-value. Data assets have entered the era of big data. The significance of data security is not limited to data itself, but also directly affects whether data can be promoted to data assets to serve business development and enhance the core competitiveness; In 2014, China puts forward the idea that information security is crucial to national security, it also illustrates that business data security is crucial to corporate security and national security.

At present, the enterprise information system security tools and technology cannot satisfy the large and diverse and massive data security protection requirements in the big data environment. The specific performance can be shown in the following areas:

© Springer-Verlag Berlin Heidelberg 2015
W. Niu et al. (Eds.): ATIS 2015, CCIS 557, pp. 368–378, 2015.
DOI: 10.1007/978-3-662-48683-2_33

(1) It lacks differentiation protection for the massive and heterogeneous data assets of enterprises. The corporate data asset sources is diversified, including traditional business systems, data resource management platforms, platforms built based on big data, as well as terminals used in daily office work. For different structures and different types of data, the value of data itself is not the same. Currently, the data assets protection policy is at a much coarse-grained level, with the unreasonable situation that it lacks data protection, and some of the data protection is too harsh, affecting business use.

(2) The enterprise security products are only concerned with their own protected equipment, lacking a unified security view. For example, firewalls only focus on the network layer protection, and terminal table management security software only focus on the terminal protection. Security products lack interaction, and safety views are dispersed and fragmented, lacking a unified safety management view of all equipment in the whole network, thus it cannot be informed of an overall security situation of all equipment.

(3) In the big data scene, data at all stages of its life cycle is faced with different security risks, and has different security needs, but currently it lacks security protection throughout the life cycle of data, and cannot conduct unified security protection and management of the entire life cycle of data generation, access, transmission, recovery and destruction, nor can it guarantee the security in all aspects of data storage, transmission, use and destruction.

(4) After the security breach event, it is difficult to quickly and accurately locate those responsible.

This paper presents the design and implementation of a kind of data security management and control platform. It automatically assigns specific data levels according to data classification, making fine-grained access control possible. It assigns the confidentiality, integrity and availability of data assets based on three characteristics of data security of ISO27001 system [1] (confidentiality C, completeness I, usability A), to better reflect the business value of data assets, and it distinguishes the levels of data assets value, to improve the utilization of security protection tools. It also studies the construction method of safety view, so as to effectively solve the problem that it lacks differentiated protection for corporate data assets, the data asset protection strategy is at a much coarse-grained level and lacks a unified security view, and unable to conduct big data tracking and forensics.

2 Implementation of the Security Management and Control Platform

The data security management and control platform is divided into four levels, from bottom to top are the controlled object layer, tools layer, function module layer and user interface layer. The data security management and control platform architecture is shown as in Fig. 1:

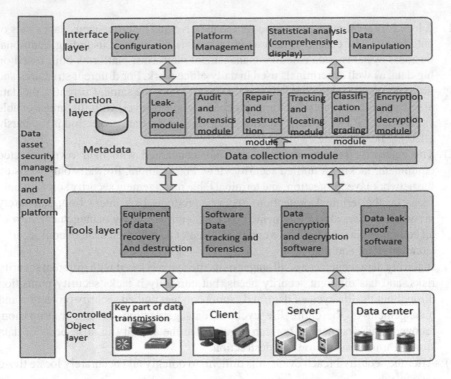

Fig. 1. Chart of platform architecture

The meaning of controlled object layer is as follows: the structured and unstructured data that the data security management and control platform needs to regulate. Wherein the structured data includes, but is not limited to critical business data generated by the business system, and the unstructured data includes documents, images, audios, videos and other data generated by routine office system. These data objects come from clients, the traditional model of file servers and database servers, big data platforms in mainstream, as well as key nodes of data transmission.

Tool layer means as follows: data security management and control tools intended to be integrated by the management and control platform. It includes data tracking and forensic software, data encryption and decryption software and data leakage prevention software. Tools layer is integrated with the existing mature equipment or software.

Function layer is the core layer of the platform, which is the secondary development on top of tools layer. It is responsible for implementing the features of security protection of the data security management and control platform, statistical analysis, and platform management. The specific function of function layer functions includes data assets classification and grading management, policy management, log management and alarm management.

Control platform layer, the uppermost interface layer, is a service window with friendly interfaces provided by the management and control platform, including rich reporting query interfaces, alarm reminder interfaces and entries of data classification and grading management operations, platform management operations and policy configuration. The report query includes the geographical, organizational, alarm and hotspot distribution of data assets provided by the integrated display module. The platform management interface includes such user interface platforms as agency management, role management, user management and log management. The policy configuration interface includes the policy configuration for encryption and decryption tools, leakage prevention tools, tracking and forensics tools, as well as the parameter configuration for the keys of encryption and decryption tools.

As can be seen from Fig. 2, it is mainly divided into such four modules according to applications as platform management, data assets classification and grading management, log management, and policy management. Platform management mainly includes the behavior and role management of users in the platform to ensure that only authorized users can access the system and the conduct legitimate and lawful operation. The asset classification and grading data management primarily maps the offline data assets classification and grading results to the meta-information of data assets in the system, thereby providing basic information which can identify different levels of assets for the following-up protection strategy. Log management is divided into such processes as log collection and log mining analysis, whose fundamental purpose is to conduct statistical analysis of the protection of data assets and track of alarm events, as well as mining and analysis of potential hazards and risks. While policy management is responsible for sending strategies for different protection tools, thereby different protection tools can identify the appropriate level of assets, and can conduct corresponding protection and analysis.

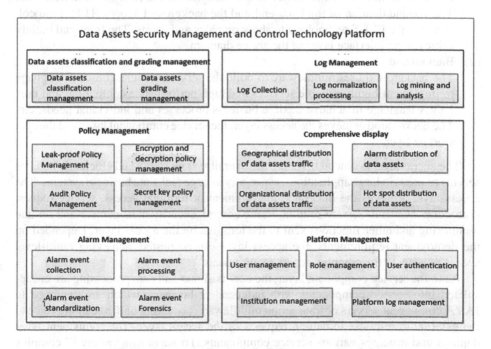

Fig. 2. Schematic diagram of platform system module

From the deployment perspective, the protective equipment are mainly deployed at the border exits of major data assets, and at the operating environment of hosts. The log collection tools are responsible for collecting logs of all the protective equipment log servers into a unified HDFS file system [2] for storage and analysis. The platform management is deployed in the application server for users to access.

In the specific implementation of data security management and control platform, it is based on the SOA multi-tier architecture [3], uses Spring framework [4], adopts the thin client with the B/S mode to show the interface of the front-end, and realizes RIA(Rich Internet Applications) through JSP + AJAX technology [5]. The WEB layer responds to the HTTP request of the front-end through SERVLET [6], and calls service of the background to complete the business logic operation. The application service component layer adopts hybrid model, with no restrictions on the development of language, and uses C or JAVA to develop for different services in order to take full advantage of C and JAVA languages. The data storage layer uses the MySQL database and distributed platforms HDFS to improve the system performance. The service interface layer, based on a unified service framework, gets support services from 4A and data resource management platforms through Web Service, JMS, HTTP and other internet protocols.

(1) Front-end

The front-end uses JSP technology to show itself in the browser, and achieves RIA with AJAX components. The WEB layer uses the SERVLET technology to response to the request of the front-end. The SERVLET converts HTTP(S) data to JAVA data, and then calls service of the background and returns to the front-end. The communication of the front-end and the background adopts HTTP protocol, and uses the FLEX technology to show graphics and charts. The front-end mainly achieves the interface layer of the above diagram.

(2) Background

The background uses middleware to build the service module. It uses C language to implement highly-reliable services and high-performance computing; and uses JAVA language to achieve flexible business processes and individual needs, etc. The background achieves the access layer, the service component layer and the data storage layer.

The access layer is crucial to ensure the overall system stably and efficiently handles service requests in large applications, especially in large real-time business systems. The access layer achieves the integrated management of terminal access, service request protocol conversion, service routing, traffic control, security management and on-line monitoring and other functions sent to the terminal by the access layer. Depended on the deployment requirements, the access layer can be nested, achieving multi-level access to adapt to the complex access requirements.

As to the service component layer, the core business and data processing are encapsulated into service components with independent business, which are deployed to JAVA component servers or transaction middleware, providing unified call interface to the external to response to calling requests of the access layer. The component layer deploys and manages various service components. To adapt to a variety of complex real-time applications and great concurrent service requests, the service component layer can achieve restructuring in server level or the dynamic restructuring within servers according to business classification, concurrency quantity and response rate, based on the actual operating conditions. For the features of high reliability of real-time operational systems, the service component layer supports dynamic online adding servers, or dynamic online changing the service components running within servers, to actually realize the 24 * 7 uninterrupted services.

As to the data storage layer, it is responsible for all business data storage of the entire system, and is a layer with the largest amount of data in the system, the most frequent IO and affecting the system performance most, and through the good services design it can implement the non-data table level association in the service component layer. Using MySQL database to store classification and grading information, policy data and user data of data assets, it can provide good operating performance of structured data. Using HDFS (Hadoop distributed File System) to store a large number of log data collected by data security management and control platform, it can provide massive storage spaces and high concurrent processing properties, to greatly enhance the efficiency of log storage and analysis.

Based on the systems and device types needing to be integrated, the system integration can be divided into internal system integration, external system integration, and equipment integration. The system integration strategy has the following three types:

The internal systems integration (see Fig. 3) integrates the internal application systems through enterprise information platforms. It takes priority of unified integrated interfaces for the outside applications, and uses a personalized integration method for the specific applications.

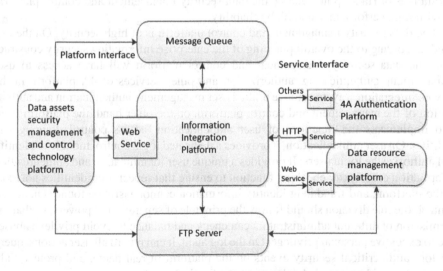

Fig. 3. A schematic view of internal platform integration

For the external system integration, part of the systems use development standard interface to integrate with the external systems, and part of the external application systems use front-end processor to integrate with the external application systems, and the deployment location is determined by the working range.

For the external device integration, it takes priority of the unified protocols and interfaces of hardware device, and considers the personalized development of special equipment.

The data security management and control platform needs to obtain the information of users and organizations from the data resource management platform, and needs to be integrated with the 4A platform to access user authentication, account management, authorization, auditing and other services.

The data security management and control platform collects vast amounts of log data from tools in the lower level, and processes the log information in a normalizing way, and then digs and analyzes the tracking and forensics information of alarm events. If these massive log processing cannot be effectively stored and conducted, it will greatly affect the performance of the entire management and control platform. In order to make the platform even more quickly and efficiently to access and process log data, we use HDFS to store log data at the back-end. Hadoop has the characteristics of high fault tolerance, and can be deployed in low hardware. It provides high throughput to access the data of applications, which is suitable for those applications with large datasets. It relaxes the requirements for POSIX [7] to access data in the file system in the form of streams. It can works in a parallel manner, to speed up data processing speed through parallel processing. In addition, Hadoop assumes the failure of computed elements and storage in design, thus it maintains multiple copies of work data, to ensure the redistributed-processing of the failed nodes, with high reliability. It can be seen that these advantages of Hadoop just enable the data security management and control platform be with high performance and high reliability.

The data security management and control platform is of high security. On the one hand, according to the overall planning of the enterprise information security construction, the data security management and control platform will have access to user management, authentication, authorization and other services of 4A platform in the service integration way, to achieve unified user management, authentication and authorization of the management and control platform, on the other hand, the platform itself also implements the functions of user authentication, access control, logging and auditing. On user authentication, it provides a dedicated login control module to identify and authorize the login users. It provides a unique user identification and authentication information complexity checking function to ensure that repeat user identities not exist in the platform, and fraudulent identity information cannot easily be found. On access control, the role division should follow the principle of separation of powers, so that the permission of different administrators can check and balance to avoid privilege abuses due to excessive personal privilege. On the log audit, it can record all user actions, query the log, audit critical security events on the platform in real name, and protect audit records, to avoid unintended deletions, modifications, and overwritten.

3 Implementation of Three Main Modules

3.1 Data Classification and Grading Module

The data classification and grading module divides data according to its category and dense. The data category can be divided in the following method: According to the relationship of the content, type, department, business activity or business system of the data itself, data is divided into large class of data, subclass of data, small class of data, and data, which are corresponding to data field, business function field, business process field and business activities.

It uses automatic classification and grading technology, namely, natural language processing and text classification algorithm, to implement that according to the semantic features and formats of the data contents, it associates data with one or more predefined categories, and automatically assigns specific categories of data according to the data classification. The data classification method process is as follows:

1. Based on data classification, it identifies the data to determine the business processes, business function fields or data fields corresponding to the data of the specific business activities;
2. After identification, according to the category, the proposal of CIA assignment and CIA weight, it calculates the asset value. The assignment and weight recommended by CIA may be appropriate to be modified if there are sufficient reasons, but it should make sure the value of data assets be reasonably estimated;
3. According to the fair value of data assets, combined with their secret nature, data assets are finally rated. Once the level is determined, it should be protected in accordance with regulations and requirements.

According to the relevant category of the data, it calculates the value of data assets based on CIA assignment and CIA weight, and then combined with the secret nature of the data, it classifies data into different security levels. Then according to security levels, it divides data into highly sensitive data, internal data and public data. The value V of data assets can be calculated in accordance with the formula $V = Round1 \left\{ Log2 \left[(A \times 2Conf + B \times 2Int + C \times 2Ava)/3 \right] \right\}$, where in A represents confidentiality weights; B integrity weights, C availability weights; the function of $Round$ is set digits according to the numerical system and rounds numbers, $Round\ 1$ means reserving a decimal.

3.2 Leakage Prevention Module of Database

The leakage prevention module of database encrypts each column of data in the database containing sensitive information mainly according to data classification and grading, and conducts fine-grained access control for database users through appropriate access policies, thereby realizing sensitive information leakage prevention in the database. The specific process is as follows:

1. The database protection server generates system root keys, column keys, security classification values and encryption keys of highly sensitive data in each column,

sensitive data and internal data, and uses the above encryption keys to encrypt highly sensitive data in each column, sensitive data and internal data;

2. The user client sends a request to the database server to access data columns in the structured data through the application server, the database server sends the median value used to calculate the value of user's security level in the form of access certificate to the user, based on user's security level, and then the user client calculates each value of its visited security level through the dense tree according to the access certificate of the median value;

3. The protection server database analyzes the SQL statements through the traffic of the mirror to determine whether the access request contains access violations: It estimates whether the user secret level matches the sensitivity level of the data that he accesses. Meanwhile, it estimates whether the user's identity and his operation of the data that he accesses are legitimate. If not, then it contains illegal access;

4. If it does not contain violating access and the data columns accessed are public data, then you should return to the access data request. If it does not contain violating access and the data columns accessed are highly sensitive data, or internal data, then the user client sends the corresponding value of secret level of the above data. Based on the value of secret level and the corresponding column key, the database server generates a decryption key of the data column, uses the decryption key to decrypt the appropriate data column in the database server, and returns the data access request.

3.3   Encryption and Decryption Module of Data

The encryption and decryption module of data conducts encrypted storage and protection of data containing sensitive information based on classification and grading. The specific process is as follows:

1. System initialization. According to data classification and grading, the system generates an encryption key for each data class.

2. Data encryption. The secret encryption module adopts the State SM1 algorithm [8] to encrypt highly sensitive data, uses AES-128 encryption algorithm [9] or the State SM4 algorithm [10] to encrypt sensitive data, and uses the lightweight PRESENT-80 algorithm [11] to encrypt internal data, while public data is not encrypted.

3. User registration. The trusted center verifies the user who accesses the data whether meets the conditions of the registration system, if meet, the trusted center will issue a system identity credential to the user as the credential to access the system.

4. Requesting access. The trusted center verifies the identity credential of the user, if validated, it will for issue the access credential containing user security level, roles and data identification information granted to the user.

5. Decryption. The trusted center verifies the access credential of the user, if validated, the user will be able to assess the decryption key, and access by himself, and access the requested data.

3.4 Tracking and Forensics Module

The tracking and forensics module is used to collect the log information generated by security tools, process it in a normalization way, and establish a security view of unstructured data with full life cycle. The specific process is as follows:

1. It records the manipulation behaviors of unstructured data at various stages of file creation, storage, use, transmission, destruction and recovery, and then stores them as log audit records;
2. It reads the log audit records of unstructured data at each stage of file creation, storage, use, transmission, destruction and recovery, and analyzes the data operation behaviors in violation of the security policy to generate analysis reports;
3. Establishing the safety management view of unstructured data with a whole life cycle.

Log information includes alarm information. When security tools generate breaching events or the remaining amount of system resources are below the set threshold, then it will generate alarm information. The normalization process of the alarm information includes classification, grading, consolidation and standardization of alarm events.

Security audit refers to the security controls of recording and supervising normal flow, abnormal state and security events in the running process of information systems to prevent the occurrence of violations of information security policies. It can also be used for the purposes of responsibility confirmation, performance tuning and safety assessment. The carrier and target of security audit are generally logs produced by all kinds of components in the system, meaningful audit information formed by log data with diversified formats going through standardization, cleaning and analysis, and effective recognition of the system operation formed by the assistant superintendent.

4 Conclusion

This paper proposes a new data security management and control platform to solve the problem that it lacks differentiated protection for the mass and heterogeneous data assets of enterprises, the data asset protection strategy is at a much coarse-grained level, and the enterprise security products are concerned only with their own protected equipment, lacking a unified security view, and unable to conduct big data tracking and forensics. First, it assigns the confidentiality, integrity and availability of data assets based on three characteristics of data security (confidentiality C, completeness I, usability A), to better reflect the business value of data assets, and it distinguishes the levels of data assets value, to improve the utilization of security protection tools. Then the platform automatically assigns specific data levels according to data classification, making fine-grained access control possible. It also studies the construction method of safety view, so as to effectively solve the problem that it lacks differentiated protection for corporate data assets, the data asset protection strategy is at a much coarse-grained level and lacks a unified security view, and unable to conduct big data tracking and forensics.

Acknowledgement. This work was sponsored by the Information Center of Guangdong Power Grid Corporation's project of Study on Data Security in Big Data Environments (No. K-GD2014-1019) and Xinjiang Uygur Autonomous Region science and technology plan (No. 201230121), the Strategic Priority Research Program of Chinese Academy of Sciences (No. XDA06040601).

References

1. ISO/IEC 27001 - Information security management
2. Shvachko, K., Kuang, H., Radia, S., et al.: The hadoop distributed file system. In: 2010 IEEE 26th Symposium on Mass Storage Systems and Technologies (MSST), pp. 1–10. IEEE (2010)
3. Wu, L., Alto, P., Barash, G., Bartolini, C.: A service-oriented architecture for business intelligence. In: IEEE International Conference on Service-Oriented Computing and Applications, SOCA 2007, pp. 279–285 (2007)
4. Johnson, R., Hoeller, J., Arendsen, A., Thomas, R.: Professional Java Development with the Spring Framework. Wiley, New Jersey (2009)
5. Zakas, N.C., Fawcett, J.: Professional Ajax. Wiley, New Jersey (2007)
6. Hunter, J., Crawford, J.: Java Servlet Programming. O'Reilly Media Inc, Sebastopol (2001)
7. Butenhof, D.R.: Programming with POSIX Threads. Addison-Wesley Professional, Boston (1997)
8. Yang, Y., Guan, J., Tian, T.: A CPU card solution based on the SM1 cryptographic algorithm for multi-applications. Sci. J. Comput. Sci. 1, 16–26 (2012)
9. Announcing the ADVANCED ENCRYPTION STANDARD. Federal Information Processing Standards Publication 197. United States National Institute of Standards and Technology (NIST), 26 November 2001
10. SM4 Block Cipher, GM/T 0002-2012 (2012)
11. Bogdanov, A., Knudsen, L.R., Leander, G., Paar, C., Poschmann, A., Robshaw, M.J.B., Seurin, Y., Vikkelsoe, C.: PRESENT: an ultra-lightweight block cipher. In: Paillier, P., Verbauwhede, I. (eds.) CHES 2007. LNCS, vol. 4727, pp. 450–466. Springer, Heidelberg (2007)

A Data Recovery Method for NTFS Files System

Zewu Peng[1], Xinyao Feng[1], Liangliang Tang[1], and Meijie Zhai[2]($\boxtimes$)

[1] Information Center, Guangdong Power Grid Corporation,
Guangzhou 510000, China
{pengzewu,fengxinyao,tangliangliang}@gdxx.csg.cn
[2] State Key Laboratory of Information Security, Institute of Information
Engineering, Chinese Academy of Sciences, Beijing 100093, China
zhaimeijie@iie.ac.cn

Abstract. Data recovery technology is a method to recover valuable data from deleted files. When important data are lost, data recovery is able to rescue at least partial data from deleted files, which makes the loss to a minimum. NTFS is a Microsoft developed files system and will replace earlier FAT32 files system gradually. This paper introduces the structure of NTFS files system and describes a method to recover data in NTFS file system.

Keywords: Data recovery · NTFS · Files system

1 Introduction

Data recovery is a method to recover valuable data from broken data carrier or deleted files [1,2]. Although the United States, Japan and Russia and other countries is able to restore and cover data for many times with advantage of the hardware technology, from the Angle of the software, only the data, which are uncovered by the new data, is recoverable. However, this recovery is based on the specific characteristics of the file system: the current mainstream files system includes FAT32 and NTFS.

NTFS (New Technology File System) [3,4] is a good files system with attributes of fault tolerance and high security. It is developed by Microsoft and designed for the data security requirements such as higher business and enterprise applications. For its stability, safety and a series of excellent characteristics, NTFS system is gradually replacing FAT32 files system [5]. Since Microsoft does

This paper is supported by Strategic Priority Research Program of Chinese Academy of Sciences (No. XDA06040601), Xinjiang Uygur Autonomous Region science and technology plan (No. 201230121), National Natural Science Foundation of China (No. 61402468), State Grid Corporation Science and Technology Project (NO. SGAHDK00DYJS1500010), and the Information Center of Guangdong Power Grid Corporations project of Study on Data Security in Big Data Environments (No. K-GD2014-1019).

© Springer-Verlag Berlin Heidelberg 2015
W. Niu et al. (Eds.): ATIS 2015, CCIS 557, pp. 379–386, 2015.
DOI: 10.1007/978-3-662-48683-2_34

not open detailed structures of NTFS files system and NTFS is more complex than FAT32, making the structure of NTFS clear completely is a very difficult task [6–8]. However, some storage structure relevant to data recovery technology can be clearly described.

In NTFS files system, file and directory information are stored in MFT. File data is stored in data area with the unit of clusters. The file system locates these file data according to MFT [9]. Generally speaking, when recovering data, the files system first scans MFT data of NTFS partitions to find deleted data in the hard disk partition, and then tries to recover data as maximum as possible through the file data attributes in the MFT record. The hard disk scan, file recovery, and file content view rely on detailed structure of NTFS files system. Therefore, understanding data structure of NTFS file system is the key to the file data recovery technology.

At present, the Windows operation system occupies a large component in personal desktop computers, NTFS file system is a major files system used in Windows operation system [10,11]. This paper analyzes file deletion and recovery principle of NTFS file system.

2   Storage Structure of NTFS Files System

In NTFS files system, file is stored by means of the cluster. The size of a cluster will be allocated automatically by a formatter according to the size of the volume. NTFS files system is mainly composed of the partition boot sector (PBR), master file table (MFT), and file data storage area. Its overall structure is shown in Fig. 1 [12,13].

Boot sector & NTLDR	MFT metadata file	MFT allocation space	File storage	MFT metadata file backup	File storage

Fig. 1. Structure of NTFS files system

Partition boot sector is used to store information about volume file structure and boot loader. It mainly includes DBR and NTLDR sectors. DBR is the first sector of the partition, and NTLDR area follows it. They take up a total of 16 sectors. NTLDR is part of the boot loader in the DBR. Some important parameters of hard disk partition are stored in the BPB table of DBR. The function of BPB table is to let the operation system locate files, such as $MFTMirr, $MFT, and database files. It is a remarkable fact that some important parameters, such as start cluster of $MFT, sectors per cluster, and bytes per sector, for data recovery are stored in BPB table. The MFT records some very important system data, called Metadata files [14]. It includes the data structure used in file location and restore, bootstrap data, as well as the bitmap information of whole volume. These data are understood and managed as files by NTFS files system. Users are unable to access them. Their file names begin with "$", which indicates the file is hidden. These kinds of files have a total of 24 and these 24 metadata files always occupy the first 24 items of MFT. Files or folders set up by users are store after the 24 metadata files.

Viewing from above function description, metadata file is very important for NTFS files system. In order to prevent data lost, NTFS files system backup them in the middle of the volume. In NTFS files system, all the data stored in the volume are included in files, including the data structures used for locating and get files, bootstrap programs, and the bitmap file to record their own size and usage. It embodies the principle of NTFS: everything in disk partition is file. A benefit to store all data in the file is to make the files system easy to locate and maintenance data. A file confirms its location on the hard disk partition through MFT [15,16]. MFT is composed of a series of file record. Each file in the volume has a file record, and, for large file, there are multiple records at the same time. MFT itself also has its own file record.

Finally, MFT has following characteristics:

1. In fact, the MFT itself is also a file. So, the first record of MFT is itself.
2. The MFT files and other 23 together make up the metafile. The front 16 files (labeled 0–15) the 24 files are fixed and the rest files are reserved.
3. User files or directories are saved after the 24 files.
4. The size of MFT file record is 1 K no matter what the size of the cluster is.
5. Theoretically, MFT occupies 12 % space of the hard disk; the file data storage area occupies other 88 %.

When we browse the NTFS disk, metafiles ahead of MFT record are hidden. However, we can use the command dir/ah to see information of these files at command line mode.

The NTFS files system deal files as attribute or a set of attributes. The file data is the value of unnamed attribute. Other file attributes include the file name, file owner, file timestamp, etc. The Fig. 2 shows the MFT record of file/directory.

File record header	Attribute/attribute value	End flag	idel

Fig. 2. Structure of MFT record

The file record header includes a serial number for integrity test, a pointer to record the first attribute, and a pointer to the records of the first free byte. If the record is not the first one of the file, the header also includes record number of the basic file record in the MFT.

Each file stored in the disk can be simply viewed as two parts [17]. The first part is the data flow of the file. This part is stored in data area. Obviously, this part is the data content of the file. The second part is the attributes of the file and is stored in MFT. The essence is the attribute record of a file. This part contains much information of the file. It is clear that the role of MFT is to quickly find the documents, because an item of the MFT is only 1 K and the operation system is able to find MFT very quickly to obtain information of the file.

Each attribute in MFT record composes of a single flow, namely simple character queues. NTFS, strictly speaking, does not operate file but reads/writes attribute flow. NTFS provides various operations on attribute flow: create, delete, read and write. Usually, read and write operations are for unnamed file attributes. For named file attributes, NTFS is able to operate files with named data stream.

A file usually occupies a file record. However, when a file has a lot of attributes or is very fragmentary, it may take up more than one file record. In this case, the first file record is the basic file records to store the address of the other file records of that file. For example, small files/folders less than 1500 bytes will be stored in MFT records of a file. Folder record includes index information. The small folder record is completely stored in the MFT structure. But big folder record is organized as B+ tree structure with a pointer to an external cluster. That cluster is used to store the folder attributes cannot be stored in MFT.

The volume attributes in NTFS are classified into resident attributes and nonresident attributes. When a file is very small, all its attributes and corresponding attributes values can be stored in the file records of MFT. If an attribute value can be directly stored in MFT, this attribute is a resident attribute. Otherwise, if an attribute of the attribute value is too big to store in a file record, the files system will allocate storage space for that attribute from DATA area. Usually, this storage space is called a running. The attribute whose value stored in a running is nonresident attribute. In the standard attributes, only those attributes whose value is able to increase is nonresident. For a file, increasable attributes include data, attribute list, etc. Normally, standard attribute and file attribute are resident, and the data attribute in most cases are nonresident.

Each attribute begins with a standard header. Information about that attribute is contained in the header and NTFS usually used it to manage the attribute information. Standard header is always resident and records whether the attribute values are resident. For resident attributes, the offset and length of the attribute value are contained in the header. The structure of attribute header depends on two factors: one is whether the attribute header includes the attribute name; another is whether the attribute is the resident attribute. These two factors can be arranged into 4 different situations. If the attribute value can be directly stored in MFT [18,19], the time that NTFS access to it will be shorten greatly. NTFS only needs to access disk for once to get the data. Different from FAT32 files system, it does not need to first look up file in FAT32 table, then read continuous allocation unit, finally find the data file. For NTFS files system, read the MFT file attributes directly is able to get the relevant data file.

Standard information attribute is a resident attribute and its attribute type is 0x10. It includes some basic file attributes, such as read-only, system, archive, time, and how many directories point to the file. Filename attribute is a resident attribute and its attribute type is 0x30. It is used to store the filename and occupies at least 68B and at most 578B, which is able to accommodate most 255 Unicode characters as the filename. NTFS almost does not limit file name. In order to support old applications, NTFS assigns a short DOS filename for each file that is not compatible with DOS filename. Therefore, if the file name is not compatible with DOS, there will be two file names in filename attributes: one is to the record full filename; another is to record DOS short filename. Data recovery needs to get full filename rather than DOS short filename. Filename attribute also contains a file reference number of the parent directory.

Data attribute contains a flag bit to indicate whether the attribute is resident, the starting VCN and the end VCN, the offset of data running, etc. Its attribute type is 0x80.

Flag bit is 0 indicates that data is stored in the file record of MFT. Data can be operated directly in the file record. If flag bit is 1, the data is stored in the data running.

When a file or directory attribute cannot be placed on a file record of MFT, NTFS records its partition or running through the mapping relationship between LCN (Logical Cluster Number) and VCN (Virtual Cluster Number) of MFT. LCN is a sequence to number clusters of the volume from 0 to n in, and VCN is used to number some particular files. NTFS computes physical offsets on the volume by means of the volume factor times LCN to obtain the disk address. VCN number the clusters belonging to particular file from beginning to the end such that the data in that file can be referenced. VCN can be mapped into LCN. LCN does not need to be continuous in physics.

Data area stores actual data. It is at the back of the system file area and occupies most of the hard disk space. When deleting files, the contents in the data area are often not covered by 0. This offers us possibility for data recovery. Although data occupied most of the disk space, the contents in the data zone are useless without other parts introduced before.

3   Data Recovery Method in NTFS Files System

Data recovery in NTFS files system is based on file scanning. In this section, we study the file scanning and data recovery methods.

3.1   Basic Idea

In NTFS files system, file and directory information are stored in MFT. File data is stored in data area by cluster. The files system locates files according to MFT. Generally speaking, when recovering data, the files system first scans MFT data of NTFS partition to find deleted files in maximal extent. Disk scan and file recovery rely on the basic data structure of NTFS.

3.2   File Scan in NTFS Files System

Files system first scans the disk before data recovery. When a user formats an NTFS partition, the formatter resets the data of $Bitmap file to 0 and clear index of the root directory. Although some other files change, MFT data, file data as well as the index data out of the root directory do not change. Since all of the files information, such as file name, file clusters chain information, are stored in the MFT, even the NTFS partition is formatted, we may recover data through analyzing data in MFT as long as the data file is not covered. Thus, we only need to scan MFT to achieve file scan for NTFS partition. We do not need to distinguish rapid scan and depth scan as in FAT32 files system. Generally speaking, NTFS files system first scans from BPB table of the NTFS disk partition and gains $MFT starting logic sector of that partition in offset address 0x30. Then it continues to read 1 KB MFT data. If the data is valid, it analyzes the related MFT attribute flow information, including basic information attribute of the file, filename attribute, data attribute, etc. If the data is invalid, the traversing process to MFT is end. Viewing from above process, the NTFS files system is relatively complex. However, since NTFS files system stores all the file information in MFT, it is very convenient for the data recovery.

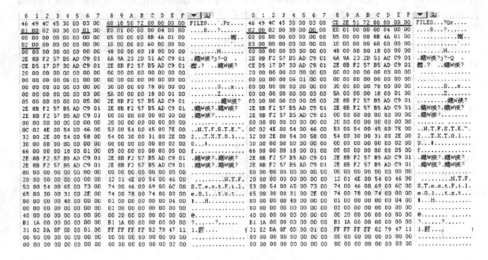

Fig. 3. The change of MFT record after deleting NTFSTestFile01.txt

3.3   Data Recovery Method in NTFS Files System

We study the data recovery method in NTFS files system file through experiment of deleting file. From the data changes, we can grasp the data recovery principle of NTFS files system intuitively. First we create two files, NTFSTestFile01.txt and NTFSTestFile02.txt, in NTFS partition of the hard disk. Both of the two files take up continuous two clusters. We use WinHex software to check data changes after deleting files. Finally, we draw the method to recover deleted files through analysis of data changes. For NTFSTestFile01.txt, we press Shift + Del to delete, relevant data are changed as Fig. 3:

After Shift + Del operation, NTFSTestFile01.txt is deleted. We compare changes in file records of MFT. Viewing from above figure, the changes occurs only in the first part of MFT. The contents of the files data attribute (0x80) do not change. Thus, we as also able to locate the file data in the positions of the hard disk through 0x80 attribute information. In this case, only if the old data is not covered by new data files, we can gain all the clusters of data in the data area through the data attribute of the file and further realize the full recovery of the file data. We right click NTFSTestFile02.txt to delete it and then clear the recycle bin. Data are changed as Fig. 4:

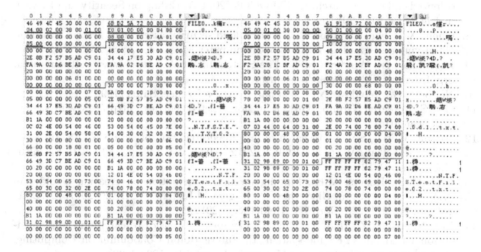

Fig. 4. The change of MFT record after deleting NTFSTestFile02.txt

The contrast before deleting NTFSTestFile02.txt and after can be seen from above figure. Both 0x10 and 0x30 attributes are changed besides the data on MFT head. However, the key contents of 0x80 data attribute also do not change. Although filename attribute (0x30) changes will lead to a situation that filename cannot be recovered, as long as the content of the old file data is not covered by new data, deleted data can be recovered with the same way as the first method. Finally, we can gain all the clusters of data in the data area through the data attribute of the file and further realize the full recovery of the file data.

4 Conclusions

This paper proposed a data recover method for NTFS file system. This method is able to recover deleted file with NTFS format and valuable in data forensics.

References

1. Custer, H.: Inside the Windows NT. Microsoft Press, Redmond (1993)
2. Viscarola Peter, G., Anthony Mason, W.: Windows NT device driver development, Published by OSR Open Systems Resources (1999)
3. Williams, M.: Programming Microsoft windows 2000 unleashed, Published by Sams (1999)
4. Russinovich, M., Solomon, D.A.: Inside Microsoft Windows 2000. Microsoft Press, Redmond (2004)
5. Russon, R., Fledel, Y.: NTFS documentation. http://www.linux-ntfs.org/content/view/104/43/
6. Chi, C., Zhu, X., Shen, P., Hu, J., Guo, S., Tari, Z., Zomaya, A.: An Efficient Privacy-Preserving Ranked Keyword Search Method. IEEE Transactions on Parallel & Distributed Systems, (1)1, PrePrints. doi:10.1109/TPDS.2015.2425407
7. Chi, C., Zhu, X., Shen, P., Hu, J.: A hierarchical clustering method for big data oriented ciphertext search. In: INFOCOM 2014 Workshop on Security and Privacy in Big Data, May 2014
8. Chen, X., Chen, C., Tao, Y., Hu, J.: Cloud security assessment system based on classifying and grading. IEEE Cloud Computer Magazine, April 2015
9. Bezroukov, N.: Windows NTFS File System Internals. http://www.softpanorama.org/Internals/Filesystems/ntfs.shtml
10. Nebbett, G.: Windows NT/2000 native API reference, Sams (1999)
11. NTFS Research Group, Disk scan for deleted entries. http://www.ntfs.com/disk-scan.htm
12. Huang, J., Wu, S.: The research of fast file destruction based on NTFS. In: Mao, E., Xu, L., Tian, W. (eds.) ECICE 2012. AISC, vol. 146, pp. 613–619. Springer, Heidelberg (2012)
13. Cho, G.-S., Rogers, M.K.: Finding forensic information on creating a folder in $LogFile of NTFS. In: Gladyshev, P., Rogers, M.K. (eds.) ICDF2C 2011. LNICST, vol. 88, pp. 211–225. Springer, Heidelberg (2012)
14. Liu, N., Wang, Z., Hao, Y., Qin, K.: Computer forensics research and implementation based on NTFS file system. In: International Colloquium on Computing, Communication, Control, and Management, pp. 519–523 (2008)
15. Fellows, G.: NTFS volume mounts, directory junctions and $Reparse. Digit. Invest. 4(3–4), 116–118 (2007)
16. Huang, J., Wu, S.X.: The research of fast file search engine based on NTFS and its application in fast electronic document destruction. In: Jin, D., Lin, S. (eds.) Advances in CSIE, vol. 2. AISC, vol. 169, pp. 523–528. Springer, Heidelberg (2012)
17. Cho, G.-S.: A computer forensic method for detecting timestamp forgery in NTFS. Comput. Secur. 34, 36–46 (2013)
18. Kai, Z., En, C., Qinquan, G.: Analysis and implementation of NTFS file system based on computer forensics. In: 2nd International Workshop on Education Technology and Computer Science, pp. 325–328 (2010)
19. Ewa, H., Derek, B., Kai, W.C.: Data hiding in the NTFS file system. Digit. Invest. 3(4), 211–226 (2006)

Design and Implementation of Aircraft Pan-Tilt Control System Based on Mobile Terminal

Minghai Shao[1], Yingding Zhao[1(✉)], and Jianlong Tan[2]

[1] College of Computer and Information Engineering, Jiangxi Agricultural University, Nanchang 330045, Jiangxi, China
shaominghai@nelmail.iie.ac.cn, zhaoyingding@163.com
[2] Institute of Information Engineering, Chinese Academy of Sciences, Beijing 100093, China

Abstract. To make it easier to control aircraft pan-tilt, pan-tilt control signal extraction and reconstruction technique were studied. After these, control system based on android mobile terminal was implemented. By extracting the control signal of hand controller mouth of FUTABA T8J, analyzing and decoding the format file of signal, and then to manipulate the data by reading and rewriting. After the waveform file recovery, the precision of the signal control of pan-tilt was improved and the probability of reuse of waveform was reduced by eliminating the noise. In the experiments, using the android software with waveform signal after processing has controlled the direction of the pan-tilt successfully by wireless way.

Keywords: UAV remote controller · PPM decoder · Pan-tilt control system · Waveform processing

1 Introduction

Remote-control aircraft has been widely applied. People on the land can manipulate aircraft with vidicon installed on pan-tilt to realize the functions like taking photos in the air, monitoring ground and so on. However, using in the reality, we find that the remote control volume is too big to carry it conveniently. If the control signal can be extracted from the remote-control, and used on mobile phone or any other mobile terminal with software to control aircraft and pan-tilt, in this way, not only it solve the problem about carrying conveniently but also reduces the cost [1]. Extracting and analyzing wave signal must be done.

Presently, the signals of UAV remote controller mostly are PPM and PCM. PPM approach is to use the time width of a square wave signal to show the size of a proportional channel. The expression also calls the simulation mode. The way of PCM is to use the binary to encode the signals of several channels. The way of encoding in JR, FUTABA Company is classified and two kinds of encoding are incompatible with each other. For this, PPM is chose as the source signal. Compared with other experiment, the process of generating source signal is complex, but this experiment does not

© Springer-Verlag Berlin Heidelberg 2015
W. Niu et al. (Eds.): ATIS 2015, CCIS 557, pp. 387–396, 2015.
DOI: 10.1007/978-3-662-48683-2_35

need Signal generating device. Only need to gather the signal from FUTABA as the source signal. According to this way, the stability of the signal can be guaranteed. In order to control more accurately, PPM signal gathered from controller must be decoded and optimized that purer and precise control signal can be obtained [2].

Most of the existing articles is the study of the generation of signal and the existing signal decoding. The focus of this paper is the existing signal processing, analysis and application. This paper used a new way of signal processing that the signal of coach mouth of remote control signal was processed to be the hexadecimal data, and the hexadecimal data processing recover the original signal into standard rectangular wave signal. This makes waveform more pure and control more accurate. Section 2 described the extraction of control signal, Sect. 3 described the analysis and process, at the end of this section introduced the design of system software which used to play the signal recovered.

2 Control Signal Extraction

The recording tool reading the signal source is Adobe Audition which was called CoolEditPro before that. This recording tool was a powerful, good effect of multi-track recording and audio processing software was researched and developed by American company Adobe Systems. Using software to connect signal from FUTABA T8J remote-controller and then save the file as.wav, this signal was used as signal source with the software we developed to control pan-tilt. CoolEditPro has two recording modes, stereo and mono. When recording in stereo mode, the signal waveforms in left and right track are shown in Fig. 1. In the figure, the abscissa is time, ordinate is SMPL maximum permissible electrical level.

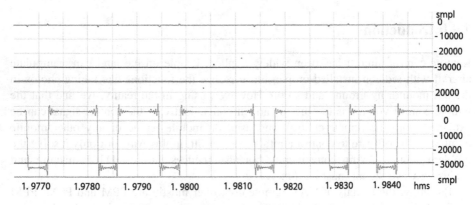

Fig. 1. Signal waveform in stereo mode

Above is the signal waveform of left sound channel and below is the signal of right channel. As the Fig. 1 shown, the signal waveform of left channel is almost a straight line, this suggests that remote-control output signal is mono effective and the only actual control signal is the right channel. For this, when recording, choose the mono recording mode with right channel. The single channel waveform was got and shown in Fig. 2. From the picture, we can see the waveform is the same in stereo and mono mode. But the signal collected only from right channel has less data quantity that can simplify the data analysis later.

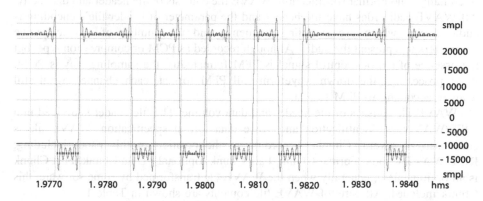

Fig. 2. Signal waveform in mono mode (right channel)

From Fig. 2, you can clearly see that the waveform is not standard rectangular wave, and the size of the high and low level is floating, this is because the audio recording is affected by many factors, such as noise. In order to control pan-tilt better, signal recording and applying again, the waveform need to be processed. Make it become a standard rectangular wave, will not lead to problems such as distortion when using and recording later.

3 Signal Analysis and Reconstruction

In this section, we main discuss signal analysis and reconstruction in below three parts: wave file format analysis, UltraEdite reading and analyzing WAVE file, data processing and waveform reconstruction.

3.1 WAVE File Format Analysis

At present, two kinds of pulse coding way PPM and PCM are most commonly used in the proportional remote control equipment. Remote control of UAV through the signal transmitter transmit signal to image transmission equipment, which processes signal [3]. After mixing signal with carrier, using carrier signal to control pan-tilt and aircraft by radio, then through the receiver receiving aircraft and pan-tilt feedback signals. Transmitter encodes the change data from controller for that user manipulate it, and transmitted by the high frequency circuit to realize the wireless control. In practical application, need to record the signal of each direction, accelerator, elevator, and aileron separately. In this paper, in view of the direction of signal analysis, for example, other channel signal can also be processed by the similar method of processing signal of direction.

WAVE format of the recording is to use the standard WINDOWS file format. The file name extension is ".wav". The Format of the data itself is PCM or compression model and it adopts RIFF File Format structure, conform to the RIFF Resource Interchange File Format specification. WAVE file consists of file header and data body. All WAVE audio files have file header and the parameter of header file's encoding is audio stream which use sampling frequency and the number of channels three parameters to represent the audio. Although recorded as PCM or compression type, but the essence of remote control signal is PPM format. Just the sampling way is PCM. After processing, the drawn waveform still PPM format, each channel signal still analyze according to PPM format.

WAVE file consists of file header and data volume. The file header is divided into RIFF/WAV files, identification and voice data format specification. WAVE file is composed of several Chunk. According to the position in this paper including: RIFF WAVE Chunk, Format Chunk, Fact Chunk (optional), Data Chunk. Fact Chunk is an optional field, generally when the WAVE file transformed by some software, this Chunk included. All parts of WAVE file contents are shown in Table 1.

Table 1. Parts of .Wav file header

Chunk name	Construction	Length	Content
RIFF WAVE Chunk	ID, Size, Type	Each 4 Bytes	ID = RIFF, size = FileLen-8, Type = WAVE
Format Chunk	ID	4 Bytes	
	Size	4 Bytes	Size of structure (except ID, Size)
	Format Tag	2 Bytes	Way of encoding
	Channels	2 Bytes	Channel number
	Samples Per Sec	4 Bytes	Sampling frequency
	Avg Bytes Per Sec	4 Bytes	Amount of data per second
	Block Align	2 Bytes	Block alignment unit
	Bits Per Sample	2 Bytes	Bit per sample
	Additional information	2 Bytes	Additional information
Fact Chunk (optional)	ID, Size, data	Each 4 Bytes	ID = fact, size = 4
Data Chunk	ID	4 Bytes	data
	Size	4 Bytes	Data size
	data	4 Bytes	Data field

WAVE file data blocks containing samples of pulse code modulation format, is composed of multiple samples. In mono WAVE file, channel 0 and 1 are respectively on behalf of the left channel and right channel. In multichannel WAVE audio file, the samples of right and left channels appear alternately. Each sample value of the WAVE file is contained in an integer type i, whose length is the minimum number of bytes needed for containing the specified sample length. Low efficient bits store first, indicating the sample amplitude are placed on high effective bits and 0 on the idle position. Such 8-bit or 16-bit PCM waveform sample data format has been made up. WAVE file is one of the sound file format used in the multimedia.

There are two channel modes: mono and stereo, which have three different sampling frequency: 11025 Hz (11 kHz), 22050 Hz (22 kHz) and 44100 Hz (44 kHz). The value of WAVE file capacity is the product of sampling frequency, BitsPerSample, channel and the result of recording time divided by eight. When sampling with CoolEdit, the default mode is stereo, choose the right channel and sampling frequency of 44.1 kHz.

3.2 WAVE File Reading and Analysis with UltraEdit

Open the recording WAVE audio file of two direction with UltraEdit software. The software show the audio file with hexadecimal numbers. The result is shown in Fig. 3 below.

```
00000000h: 52 49 46 46 A4 FF 07 00 57 41 56 45 66 6D 74 20 ; RIFF?..WAVEfmt
00000010h: 10 00 00 00 01 00 01 00 44 AC 00 00 88 58 01 00 ; ........D?. 本..
00000020h: 02 00 10 00 64 61 74 61 80 FF 07 00 00 00 00 00 ; ....data€ ...
00000030h: 00 00 FF FF 00 00 00 00 00 00 00 00 00 00 00 00 ; ............
00000040h: 00 00 00 00 00 00 00 00 00 00 00 00 49 7F 52 7E ; ............I I
00000050h: 9D 7D 1B 7D C2 7C 87 7C 60 7C 4A 7C 40 7C 3D 7C ; 潁.}聕醠`  J @ =
00000060h: 39 7C 36 7C 31 7C 2F 7C 2B 7C 28 7C 24 7C 21 7C ; 9 6 1 / + ( $
00000070h: 1D 7C 1A 7C 16 7C 12 7C 0F 7C 0C 7C 09 7C 04 7C ; . . . . . . .
```

Fig. 3. Hexadecimal file of up direction

```
00000000h: 52 49 46 46 24 97 06 00 57 41 56 45 66 6D 74 20 ; RIFF$?.WAVEfmt
00000010h: 10 00 00 00 01 00 01 00 44 AC 00 00 88 58 01 00 ; ........D?. 本.
00000020h: 02 00 10 00 64 61 74 61 00 97 06 00 00 00 00 00 ; ....data. ?....
00000030h: 00 00 FF FF 00 00 00 00 00 00 00 00 00 00 00 00 ; ............
00000040h: 00 00 00 00 00 00 00 00 00 00 00 00 49 7F 52 7E ; ............I
00000050h: 9D 7D 1B 7D C2 7C 87 7C 60 7C 4A 7C 40 7C 3D 7C ; 潁.}聕醠 J @
00000060h: 39 7C 36 7C 31 7C 2F 7C 2B 7C 28 7C 24 7C 21 7C ; 9 6 1 / + ( $
00000070h: 1D 7C 1A 7C 16 7C 12 7C 0F 7C 0C 7C 09 7C 04 7C ; . . . . . . .
```

Fig. 4. Hexadecimal file of down direction

Compared with the first line data of Figs. 3 and 4, only 4th to 7th bytes are different, which is to identify the size of WAVE file. Figures 3 and 4 shows hexadecimal data of two different direction of audio file, so this four bytes of data are different. 0H-3H bytes identify the file is "RIFF" standard. The hexadecimal number 52, 49, 46, 46 of these four bytes are the ID content of RIFF WAVE Chunk, respectively ASCII of R, I, F, F. 8H- bH bytes are to identify the audio file format that is "WAVE". The last four bytes are the symbol of "fmt". For the two different WAVE file is only 4th to 7th bytes is not the same. Note here, when recording audio file by UltraEdit, the bytes are read two bytes by two bytes. The low eight bits are read earlier than the high eight bits. Every two bytes of data in the figure and sampling values of CoolEdit waveform are the same. If want to know the content of every chunk, look up how many bytes the chunk take and calculate the begin of the chunk in Table 1, then read the numbers of these bytes from right to left in the figure. For example, sampling frequency take four bytes, begin at 18H and end at 1bH, in the figure, the value of these four bytes is 0000AC44 means the sampling frequency is 44.1 kHz.

The datum in Figs. 3 and 4 of second line are the same. In this line, 10H-13H are the transition bytes (10H byte identifies this audio data format is PCM). 14H-15H bytes indicate format categories. 16H-17H bytes indicate the sound track is mono or double track. When the data in 16H-17H is 00 01 means mono, 00 02 means double track. In sound recording, we chose the right channel, so the datum in two picture are both 00 01. The data of 18H-1bH indicates sampling frequency. In the picture, hexadecimal data of four bytes 18H-1bH is 0000AC44 converted to decimal is 44.1 k, means that the sampling frequency is 44.1 kHz. Transfer rate value of waveform audio data is identified in bytes 1cH-1fH indicates, whose computational formula is that Channels multiply BitsPerSec and the result of SamplesPerSec divided by eight. In the Figs. 3 and 4. This value which the player software used to estimate size of buffer is hexadecimal 00 01 58 88 equal decimal 88200. For recording with the same software, the datum of second line is the same. Data block adjustment number (calculate by byte) is identified in 20H-21H. Its computational formula is that Channels multiply the result of SamplesPerSec divided by eight. In order to use the value of data block adjustment number to adjust size of buffer, player software need to process many bytes data which size is equal to the value. 22H-23H bytes indicate the bits of sampling, which are data bits of each sample in every sound channel. If the sound channel is not mono, for every channel, the size of sample is the same. The content of 24H-27H bytes is "data". 28H-2bH these four bytes identify the length of sound data.

3.3   Data Processing and Waveform Reconstruction

Use C programs in Visual Studio2010 to read WAVE audio file and then write this datum into a TXT file by decimal [4].

Put the datum written into a TXT before in a column of an Excel table and draw a broken line graph with this datum as Fig. 5 shows. Compared the broken line graph with the waveform that the CoolEdit showed at recording, following is the result.

In the picture, below is the waveform shown in CoolEdit (original waveform) and above is broken line graph drawn in Excel (drawing waveform). The two waveforms look the same that means recovering waveform successfully. Mentioned in the control signal extraction section, the waveform is not strict rectangular wave that easily lead to the problem of waveform distortion when recording or any other operations later. With these problems, pan-tilt can be control better. This waveform as the control signals is not best signal. In order to improve the controllability of signal source, following

Fig. 5. Contrast of original and drawing waveform

process the wave to be the standard rectangular wave. The way of processing is setting up the judgment condition, when use C program to read and write WAVE file and do not use the real value while writing data in the TXT. Before writing into TXT, the real value need to be judged whether it is bigger than zero. Writing the average of high electrical level into TXT if real value is bigger. If not bigger, writing the average of low electrical level. A rectangular wave shown in Fig. 6 which has standard, constant high and low electrical level can be got in this way. PPM is the modulation method which use the relative position of pulse to transfer the information. Each periodic signal contain signal of multiple channel that the signal of each channel is at different position of the periodic signal. As can be seen from the picture below, the pulse width of each low level is the same, and the width of each high level is different. It makes low level pulse signals at different positions of the periodic signal. The widths between each two low level are the control signals of the different channels.

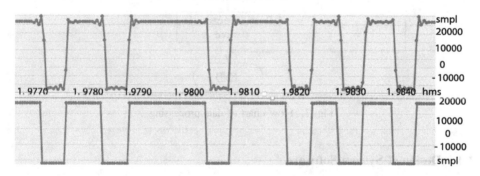

Fig. 6. Standard rectangular waveform and original waveform

Recover the WAVE file with rectangular waveform and use the new file as control signal. When recovering the WAVE file, the header file has 44 bytes. The structure members in C program filled in the number of bytes following Table 1. Recovering the WAVE file like this, can control the size of signal file thus also can control pan-tilt rotation angle. The whole process of data processing is below shown in Fig. 7.

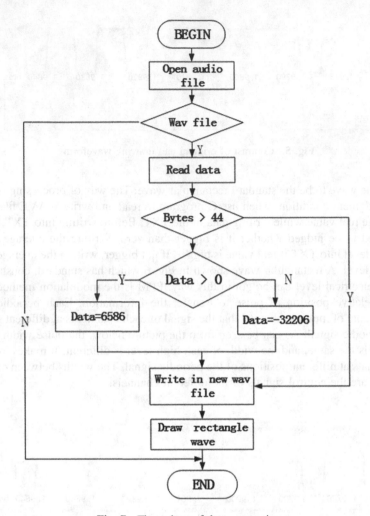

Fig. 7. Flow chart of data processing

3.4   Design of System Software

Design of software is based on Android SDK. Software set four direction (up, down, right, left) which is the two channels of the remote controller as the Fig. 8 shows. There are eight channels of FUTABA T8J, of which direction to take up two channels. Direction up and down take one channel and direction right and left take another channel. Signal of other channels also can be processed with this method that collect the original control signal and process to produce the rectangular wave control signal. Fine-tuning button corresponding fine-tuning signal can control pan-tilt to rotate with small angle. At the time of generating rectangular wave signal, choose the appropriate period count of direction control signal as fine-tuning signal.

When develop the audio software, need to download the Eclipse software which the Android SDK and an Android virtual machine embedded in. Use Java classes given by the existing function to build a framework of 3 * 3 buttons [5], each button corresponding to the different control signal. Use the MediaPlayer in Android for each button to realize monitoring and playing a WAVE file. After debugging and running correctly, one. APK file generate in work space which is the installation package of the software [6]. Before installing the APP on mobile terminal, run it on Android virtual machine first. In order to control pan-tilt to rotate, mobile terminal transmit the audio signal to image transmission equipment. Software play WAVE audio files of different directions, pan-tilt rotates in different directions.

Due to the mobile phone has low voltage, directly through the phone transmit control signal to image transmission equipment can't control the pan-tilt. Between image transmission equipment and mobile phone to add an audio power amplifier, signal level value can be amplified to reach level values needed for the direction control of pan-tilt. This completes the control of general direction of pan-tilt. Fine-tuning of small angle can realize the precise control by changing the number of period and the times to play. Change the low level position to generate a new direction control signal to control different direction of pan-tilt. Change the position of the low level is change the width of high level in the waveform, but keep the length of period unchanged. Figure 8 is the interface of software [7].

Fig. 8. Interface of software

4 Conclusion

This paper analyzes PPM signal of FUTABA T8J. According to recover the Waveform file and compare the real signal and recovery. From this paper, we has understood the rule of PPM encoding. Pan-tilt is controlled successfully by using the software to play signal of recovery. If the method of processing signal of pan-tilt is used to process the signals of any other channels that the aircraft also can be controlled by a mobile terminal. Due to limitation of time and experiment, only design the software of pan-tilt. When processing signal, use the way of keeping other variables constant that means making other signals unchanged and only changing the signal of pan-tilt. So that the signal of each channel needn't be separated. This method reduces the difficulty of signal processing, but the deficiency is that the signal still contain signal of other channels. There are nine low electrical levels that each low level represents a signal of a channel in the standard rectangular. But as long as the signal of other channels have no changes that would do not affect the result of the experiment. For play software, it can be upgraded at many points. Such as programming to add video play function, real-time receive and display real-time image in the same terminal to meet two functions of control and real-time images show [8].

References

1. Senior, A.W., Hampapur, A., Lu, M.: Acquiring multi-scale images by pan-tilt-zoom control and automatic multi-camera calibration. In: Seventh IEEE Workshops on Application of Computer Vision, WACV/MOTIONS 2005, vol.1. IEEE, pp. 433–438 (2005)
2. Shimohara, K.: Remote control signal processing circuit for a microcomputer: U.S. Patent 5,436,853, 25 July 1995
3. Crosbie, J., Acharya, S., Balakrishnan, A, et al.: Use of a remote control with a device having a built-in communication port: U.S. Patent 7,047,326, 16 May 2006
4. C Program. Tsinghua university press, (2000)
5. Lee, S., Jeon, J.W. Evaluating performance of Android platform using native C for embedded systems. In: International Conference on Control Automation and Systems (ICCAS). IEEE, pp. 1160–1163 (2010)
6. Crowther, G.O., Douglas, T. A., Farmer, H.M.: Remote control system capable of transmitting the information with the aid of an infra-red beam using PPM or an ultrasonic beam using PDM: U.S. Patent 4,231,031, 28 October 1980
7. Steele, J., To, N.: The Android developer's cookbook: building applications with the Android SDK. Pearson Education, Upper Saddle River (2010)
8. Wan-xin, S.U.: Design of a large array CMOS image and display system in real-time synchronization. Acta Photonica Sinica 3, 025 (2012)

Author Index

Printed in the United States
By Bookmasters